5,000
Gems of
Wit &
Wisdom

5,000 Gems of Wit & Wisdom

Compiled by

Dr Laurence Peter

TREASURE PRESS

First published in Great Britain in 1978 by
Souvenir Press under the title *Quotations for Our Time*

This edition published in 1991 by Treasure Press
an imprint of Reed Consumer Books Ltd
Michelin House, 81 Fulham Road, London SW3 6RB
and Auckland, Melbourne, Singapore and Toronto

Reprinted 1991, 1992 (twice), 1993

A CIP catalogue record for this book is
available at the British Library

Printed and bound in Great Britain
by William Clowes

CONTENTS

INTRODUCTION

> I quote others only the better to express
> myself.   —Michel de Montaigne

The purpose of this book is quite simple—to bring together in easily accessible form some of the best expressed thoughts, ancient and modern, that are especially illuminating *for our time*.

Frequently, when writing about contemporary subjects, I use humorous or serious quotes to emphasize important points in my manuscripts. In order to have an adequate supply of suitable quotes from which to choose I have collected over the years many gems of brevity, wit, and originality that said something relevant to today's problems.

> Why not spend some time in determining
> what is worthwhile for us, and then go
> after that?   —William Ross

The basis for inclusion of every quote in my collection was the idea it contained and the relationship of that idea to our time. I was not concerned with the literary status or notoriety of the author of the quote, although many famous names did appear. What evolved was a collage of living ideas about the future of our planet earth, ecology, peace, technology, human beliefs, and other subjects related to our present condition. My quote file became uniquely valuable by serving a purpose not fufilled by any of the published collections of quotations. It dealt with contemporary subjects that were not adequately represented by other quotation references. Secondly, it focused on ideas rather than words, that is, a quote in my collection appeared under a subject heading because the central idea of the quote related to the subject heading and not merely because the word of the subject heading occurred in the quote. And thirdly, my collection contained an abundance of unusual or lesser known quotations, many of great wit, that deserved to be enjoyed by a wider audience.

> The two most engaging powers of an author are to make new things familiar, familiar things new.
> —William Makepeace Thackeray

Quotes that passed the criterion of relevance were then subjected to the criterion of brevity. What, for instance, could be more brief than the words of Jean-Paul Sartre: "Childhood decides"? It says as much in two words as Dr. Spock says in twenty: "In my opinion, the close emotional ties of an all-round good family provide the strongest stimulus to mental development." Brevity implies condensed expression, succinct style. The quotes chosen for inclusion in this book were characterized by their pertinence to the subject and by their lack of verbiage.

The only valid rule about the proper length of a statement is that it achieve its purpose effectively. The total message to be communicated often consists of attitudes or feelings beyond those conveyed by the bare minimum of words. When Hamlet said: "The rest is silence," the short-form advocate might have said: "Why say it in four words when you can say it in three—'It is finished!' " The shortest is not the briefest if it fails to achieve its full objective.

> A man's legs must be long enough to reach the ground.   —Abraham Lincoln

A popular form of expression used to encapsulate an idea in a few brief words is the epigram. It was employed somewhat in the manner of our modern day one-liner to one-up an opponent in a contest of wits.

> What is an epigram? A dwarfish whole,
> Its body brevity, and wit its soul.
> —Samuel Taylor Coleridge

The type of quotation favored for this collection is one that is concisely and cleverly worded and makes a pointed observation about our own time. Ideas are modern whether uttered by First Century Rome or Twentieth Century-Fox.

> I write long epigrams, you yourself write
> nothing. Yours are shorter.
> —Martial (A.D. 40–102)

Conscientious effort has been expended in an attempt to ascribe properly the authorship of the quotations, although it is recognized that consistent accuracy is virtually an impossibility. Some quotations have become identified with famous persons though they themselves were not the original source. We have been content to play it as it lies in cases such as: "Let them eat cake."—Marie Antoinette. "I disapprove of what you say, but I will defend to the death your right to say it."—Voltaire. "There is nothing to fear but fear itself."—Franklin Delano Roosevelt. "The iron curtain."—Winston Churchill, and "Ask not what your country can do for you . . ."—John F. Kennedy. In looking up quotations such as the above, most of us are seeking the individual identified with these statements, rather than their originators.

> Everything has been thought of before,
> but the problem is to think of it again.
> —Johann W. von Goethe

A different problem is presented where more than one famous person has been credited with authorship of the same familiar quote. "I can resist everything except temptation" has appeared in the writings of Oscar Wilde, Mark Twain, Mae West and W. C. Fields, but because the statement was first presented to a large public in the play *Lady Windermere's Fan* I have credited the quote to Wilde. This does not necessarily prove that Oscar said it first.

I have seen the quote, "Winning isn't everything. It's the *only* thing," credited alternately to Vince Lombardi and to Bill Veeck. Investigation of newspaper and magazine sources indicates that the quote is a paraphrase of statements made by both men. The earliest of the two quotes to appear in print seems to be Bill Veeck's "I do not think that winning is the most important thing. I think winning is the only thing," while Vince Lombardi's first printed version of his now famous statement appeared as "Winning is not the most important thing; it's everything."

Because the purpose of this book is to present ideas, when quotes express the same ideas in almost identical words I have accepted the earlier source. Therefore, Leo Rosten's "Anybody who hates dogs and babies can't be all bad" was selected over W. C. Fields' "Anybody who hates children and dogs can't be all bad," but I accepted Fields' "Anybody who hates dogs and loves whiskey can't be all bad" as being sufficiently different in meaning to justify inclusion.

Some of the included quotes were derived from oral sources and include lines excerpted from lectures or other live performances, as well as from the utterances of friends and relatives. The only documentation I have for these quotes is my notebook. And sometimes my memory.

Although the decisions I had to make were made on a basis of less than perfect evidence, I did put forth a serious effort to avoid mistakes and avoid becoming a party to the initiation, perpetuation, or proliferation of error.

> A falsehood once received from a famed
> writer becomes traditional to posterity.
> —John Dryden

In preparing the collection for publication, the birth and death dates were provided for authors living up to and including the year 1900. In the process of editing, a balance was sought between quotes that are light in tone and those that are serious in intent, but as a personal selection my background and interest influenced the inclusion of certain categories. For example, I was born and raised a Canadian but as an adult have lived in the United States for more than ten years, and for a short period in England. Thus, as a result of this experience, I have taken a particular interest in quotes about Canada, America, and England. These are the only countries that appear as subject headings.

> Wisdom is meaningless until your own ex-
> perience has given it meaning . . . and
> there is wisdom in the selection of wisdom.
> —Bergen Evans

So here are my favorites, some because I agree with them, some because they arouse my ire, some because they make me laugh, but all because they say something to me about the time in which I live.

HOW TO USE
THIS BOOK

> I suppose every scholar has had the experience of reading something in a book which was significant to him, but which he could never find again. Sure he is that he read it there; but no one else ever read it, nor can he find it again.
> —Ralph Waldo Emerson

To my knowledge, only W. C. Fields, in the movie *The Man on the Flying Trapeze,* maintained the perfect filing system. He kept his accumulation of papers piled in his rolltop desk. When asked to produce a specific paper he would merely run a forefinger down one of the stacks and unhesitatingly withdraw the exact item requested. It was as simple and easy as that! In compiling this collection of quotes it was my goal to produce the world's second-best reference system.

TABLE OF SUBJECTS

If you are seeking quotations that will illustrate or develop a specific idea, you should turn to the Table of Subjects, located in

13

the front of the book, and look for the appropriate subject heading. After reading the quotes under a subject title you may wish to return to the Table and follow up on the recommendations in the cross-references.

> The next best thing to knowing something
> is knowing where to find it.
> —Samuel Johnson

Although standard subject titles are used throughout, you will discover some little detours into seldom-visited avenues of thought and fantasy such as: "Abyss of Self"; "Laws"; "Mod Malaprops"; "Opium for Underachievers"; "Odium Literatim"; "Parallels"; and "X-Rated."

A special feature of this book is that the arrangement of quotes under each subject heading constitutes a collective composition incorporating the sayings of a range of people. This is accomplished by having the quotes on one subject compiled so as to present a *flow* of ideas. For example, under the subject title, CANADA, the quotes are presented so that reading the quotations in sequence adds meaning to the category as a whole. Usually the first quotes to appear are those that are notable for their wit and for their contributions to a definition of the subject:

Canada is a collection of ten provinces with strong governments loosely connected by fear.   —Dave Broadfoot

The beaver is a good national symbol for Canada. He's so busy chewing he can't see what's going on.   —Howard Cable

These are followed by quotes of a generally more serious nature:

There has never been a war of Canadian origin, nor for a Canadian cause.   —William Arthur Deacon

Canadians represent, as it were, the least militant North American minority group. The white, Protestant, heterosexual ghetto of the North.   —Mordecai Richler

For the convenience of the reader looking for parallel ideas, some quotes with similar meanings are grouped in pairs that follow the above described general category:

> When they said Canada, I thought it would
> be up in the mountains somewhere.
> —Marilyn Monroe

> I don't even know what street Canada is
> on!   —Al Capone

*   *

Those interested in locating dissimilar ideas about a particular subject will find pairs of contrasting quotes as the last group:

> I have no desire to bolster the sagging cultural economy of this country.
> —Brendan Behan

> If Canada is underdeveloped, so is Brigitte Bardot.   —H. R. MacMillan

Occasionally I have added an editorial comment (in parenthesis) following a quote:

> Canada's climate is nine months winter and three months late in the fall.
> —Evan Esar. (Man wants but little here below—zero.)

The above arrangement, starting a subject with humorous and defining quotes, moving on to more serious ideas, and closing with pairs of similar and contrasting quotes, is not a rigid system. It is simply a means of presenting quotations in an order based on the ideas contained therein, and of providing a meaningful, if somewhat subjective, arrangement. This helps guide you, the reader, to the specific kind of statement being sought. It also makes each subject category more interesting for the reader whose object is to enjoy the thoughts, experiences, expressions and company of the greatest thinkers and wittiest writers of ancient and modern times.

> In every work of genius we recognize our own rejected thoughts.
> —Ralph Waldo Emerson

INDEX OF NAMES AND AUTHORS

If you recall a name appearing in the body of a quote, or of the author of a quote, or if you wish to pursue all of an individual author's contributions included in this book, turn to the Index of Names and Authors.

> There are three things I always forget. Names, faces—the third I can't remember.   —Italo Svevo

TABLE
OF
SUBJECTS

Completely cross-indexed
by related categories

THE QUOTATIONS

A

ABILITY

It is all one to me if a man comes from Sing Sing or Harvard. We hire a man, not his history.   —Henry Ford

Ability is the art of getting credit for all the home runs somebody else hits.   —Casey Stengel

There is something that is much more scarce, something rarer than ability. It is the ability to recognize ability.   —Robert Half

The Carpenter is not the Best/Who makes More Chips than all the Rest.   —Arthur Guiterman

Do what you can, with what you have, where you are.
          —Theodore Roosevelt

When people find a man of the most distinguished abilities as a writer their inferior while he is with them, it must be highly gratifying to them.   —Samuel Johnson (1709–1784)

People are always ready to admit a man's ability after he gets there.
          —Bob Edwards

It may be those who do most, dream most.   —Stephen Leacock

My green thumb came only as a result of the mistakes I made while learning to see things from the plant's point of view.
          —H. Fred Ale

The thing is to be able to outlast the trends.   —Paul Anka

If they try to rush me, I always say, "I've only got one other speed—and it's slower."   —Glenn Ford

My greatest strength as a consultant is to be ignorant and ask a few questions.   —Peter Drucker

I'm better about things than about people. I'm more interested in people, but I'm better at ideas.   —Peter Drucker

Natural abilities are like natural plants that need pruning by study. —Francis Bacon (1561–1626) (On second thought, I inherited my ability from both parents; my mother's ability for spending money, and my father's ability for not making it.)

Natural ability without education has more often raised a man to glory and virtue than education without natural ability.
                              —Cicero (106–43 B.C.)

Native ability without education is like a tree without fruit.
                              —Aristippus (435?–356? B.C.)

A man may be so much of everything that he is nothing of anything.
                              —Samuel Johnson (1709–1784)

Since we cannot know all that is to be known of everything, we ought to know a little about everything.
                              —Blaise Pascal (1623–1662)

                    *   *

From each according to his abilities, to each according to his needs.
                              —Karl Marx (1818–1883)

Men take only their needs into consideration—never their abilities.
                              —Napoleon Bonaparte (1769–1821)

ABSENCE / SEPARATION

Absence extinguishes small passions and increases great ones, as the wind will blow out a candle, and blow in a fire.
                              —Duc de La Rochefoucauld (1613–1680)

Failing to be there when a man wants her is a woman's greatest sin, except to be there when he doesn't want her.
                              —Helen Rowland

Absence makes the heart grow fonder.
       —Thomas Haynes Bayly (1797–1839) (Of someone else?)

ABYSS OF SELF

Why should we honour those that die upon the field of battle? A man may show as reckless a courage in entering into the abyss of himself.   —William Butler Yeats

How did I get here? Somebody pushed me. Somebody must have set me off in this direction and clusters of other hands must have touched themselves to the controls at various times, for I would not have picked this way for the world.   —Joseph Heller

Rabbi Zusya said that on the Day of Judgment, God would ask him, not why he had not been Moses, but why he had not been Zusya.
—Walter Kaufmann

O wad some power the giftie gie us/To see oursel's as others see us.
—Robert Burns (1759–1796) (Or is it the giftie we'd be *least* likely to choose?)

I think somehow, we learn who we really are and then live with that decision.   —Eleanor Roosevelt

The mass of men lead lives of quiet desperation.
—Henry David Thoreau (1817–1862)

None of us can help the things life has done to us. They're done before you realize it, and once they're done they make you do other things until at last everything comes between you and what you'd like to be, and you have lost your true self forever.
—Eugene O'Neill

In his private heart no man much respects himself.
—Mark Twain

Seeing ourselves as others see us would probably confirm our worst suspicions about them.   —Franklin P. Jones

I know well what I am fleeing from but not what I am in search of.   —Michel de Montaigne (1533–1592)

At the bottom of the modern man there is always a great thirst for self-forgetfulness, self-distraction . . . and therefore he turns away from all those problems and abysses which might recall to him his own nothingness.   —Henri Frédéric Amiel (1821–1881)

*   *

Poor, dismal, ugly, sterile, shabby little man . . . with your scrabble of harsh oaths . . . Joy, glory, and magnificence were here for

you . . . but you scrabbled along . . . rattling a few stale words
. . . and would have none of them.　　—Thomas Clayton Wolfe

And nothing to look backward to with pride,/And nothing to look
forward to with hope.　　—Robert Frost

* *

How vain it is to sit down to write when you have not stood up to
live!　　—Henry David Thoreau (1817–1862)

How many people eat, drink, and get married; buy, sell, and build;
make contracts and attend to their fortune; have friends and
enemies, pleasures and pains, are born, grow up, live and die—but
asleep!　　—Joseph Joubert (1754–1824)

There are many people who have the gift, or failing, of never understanding themselves. I have been unlucky enough, or perhaps fortunate enough to have received the opposite gift.
　　　　　　　　　　—Charles de Talleyrand (1754–1838)

Only the shallow know themselves.
　　　　　　　　　　—Oscar Wilde (1854–1900)

ACTS / ACTION

Act well at the moment, and you have performed a good action to
all eternity.　　—Johann Kaspar Lavater (1741–1801) (And
do it now! There may be a law against it tomorrow.)

In the country of the blind the one-eyed king can still goof up.
—Laurence J. Peter (On second thought, nothing ventured nothing
goofed.)

Leadership is *action*, not position.　　—Donald H. McGannon

Miss Stein was a past master in making nothing happen very slowly.
　　　　　　　　　　—Clifton Fadiman

That action alone is just that does not harm either party to a dispute.
　　　　　　　　　　—Mohandas Gandhi

By annihilating desires you annihilate the mind. Every man without
passions has within him no principle of action, nor motive to act.
—Claude Adrien Helvétius (1715–1771) (The man who believes
he can do it is probably right, and so is the man who believes he
can't.)

As life is action and passion, it is required of man that he should share the passion and action of his time, at peril of being judged not to have lived.   —Oliver Wendell Holmes, Jr.

*   *

Action and faith enslave thought, both of them in order not to be troubled or inconvenienced by reflection, criticism and doubt.
—Henri Frédéric Amiel

For purposes of action nothing is more useful than narrowness of thought combined with energy of will.   —Henri Frédéric Amiel

*   *

And thou wilt give thyself relief, if thou doest every act of thy life as if it were the last.   —Marcus Aurelius (121–180) (On second thought, and if thou doest, it may very well be thy last.)

I shall tell you a great secret, my friend. Do not wait for the last judgment, it takes place every day.   —Albert Camus

---

Think like a man of action, act like a man of thought.
—Henri Bergson

When you see a snake, never mind where he came from.
—W. G. Benham

*   *

[Action] is the last resource of those who know not how to dream.
—Oscar Wilde (1854–1900)

Mistrust first impulses, they are always good.
—Charles de Talleyrand (1754–1838)

*   *

The great end of life is not knowledge but action.
—Thomas Henry Huxley (1825–1895)

To do nothing is in every man's power.   —Samuel Johnson (1709–1784) (On second thought, the young tell you what they are doing, the old what they have done, and everyone else what they are going to do.)

ADVERTISING / PUBLICITY / PUBLIC RELATIONS

Advertising may be described as the science of arresting the human intelligence long enough to get money from it.
—Stephen Leacock

I don't care what is written about me so long as it isn't true.
—Katharine Hepburn

Unmentionables—those articles of ladies' apparel that are never discussed in public, except in full-page, illustrated ads.
—*Changing Times*

The purpose of public relations in its best sense is to inform and to keep minds open; the purpose of propaganda in the bad sense is to misinform and to keep minds closed.   —John W. Hill

Advertising is what you do when you can't go see somebody.
—Fairfax Cone

Advertising, in its spirit and purpose, is germinal fascism. Hitler was the first European politician who saw the significance of the techniques of commercial advertising for politics.
—J. B. Matthews and R. E. Shallcross

Advertising is the rattling of a stick inside a swill bucket.
—George Orwell

Few people at the beginning of the nineteenth century needed an adman to tell them what they wanted.
—John Kenneth Galbraith

Planned public relations is usually a stepchild of conflict.
—Kinsey M. Robinson

Let advertisers spend the same amount of money improving their product that they do on advertising and they wouldn't have to advertise it.   —Will Rogers

If advertising encourages people to live beyond their means, so does matrimony.   —Bruce Barton

The advertising industry is one of our most basic forms of communication and, allegedly, of information. Yet, obviously, much of this ostensible information is not purveyed to inform but to manipulate and to achieve a result—to make somebody think he needs something that very possibly he doesn't need, or to make him think one version of something is better than another version when the grounds for such a belief really don't exist.
—Marvin E. Frankel

Nothing's so apt to undermine your confidence in a product as knowing that the commercial selling it has been approved by the company that makes it.   —Franklin P. Jones

Freedom! to spit in the eye and in the soul of the passerby and the passenger with advertising.   —Alexander I. Solzhenitsyn

The advertising quack who wearies/With tales of countless cures,/
His teeth, I've enacted,/Shall all be extracted/By terrified amateurs.
—W. S. Gilbert

I do not read advertisements—I would spend all my time wanting
things.   —Archbishop of Canterbury

*   *

Invention is the mother of necessity.   —Thorstein Veblen

It used to be that people needed products to survive. Now products
need people to survive.   —Nicholas Johnson

*   *

Advertising has done more to cause the social unrest of the twentieth
century than any other single factor.   —Clare Barnes, Jr.

Advertising is the art of making whole lies out of half truths.
—Edgar A. Shoaff

*   *

. . . the routine hypocrisy in . . . advertising, [and] publicity
. . . It is doubtful whether dishonesty has ever before been so
pervasive, systematic, dynamic, and respectable as it is in America
today.   —Herbert J. Muller

The art of publicity is a black art.   —Judge Learned Hand

Advertising is a valuable economic factor because it is the cheapest
way of selling goods, particularly if the goods are worthless.
—Sinclair Lewis

No one can deny that much of our modern advertising is essentially
dishonest; and it can hardly be maintained that to lie freely and all
the time for private profit is not to abuse the right of free speech,
whether it be a violation of the law or not. But again the practical
question is, how much lying for private profit is to be permitted by
law?   —Carl Becker

Advertisements contain the only truths to be relied on in a newspaper.   —Thomas Jefferson (1743–1826)

Advertising is legalized lying.   —H. G. Wells

*   *

You can tell the ideals of a nation by its advertisements.
—Norman Douglas

The laws of a nation form the most instructive portion of its history.
—Edward Biggon

ADVICE

Never play cards with a man called *Doc*. Never eat in a place called *Mom's*. Never sleep with a woman whose troubles are worse than your own.   —Nelson Algren

Old people love to give good advice; it compensates them for their inability to set a bad example.   —Duc de La Rochefoucauld (1613–1680). (On second thought, we hate to have some people give us advice because we know how badly they need it themselves.)

In those days he was wiser than he is now—he used frequently to take my advice.   —Winston Churchill

If someone gives you so-called good advice, do the opposite; you can be sure it will be the right thing nine out of ten times.
                              —Anselm Feuerbach (1829–1880)

When a man comes to me for advice, I find out the kind of advice he wants, and I give it to him.
          —Josh Billings (Henry Wheeler Shaw) (1818–1885)

I have found the best way to give advice to your children is to find out what they want and then advise them to do it.
                                        —Harry S Truman

*   *

He who can take advice is sometimes superior to him who can give it.   —Karl von Knebel (1744–1834) (On the other hand, if you can tell the difference between good advice and bad advice, you don't need advice.)

AGNOSTICISM / ATHEISM

An atheist is a man who has no invisible means of support.
                              —John Buchan, Lord Tweedsmuir

An atheist is a man who believes himself an accident.
—Francis Thompson (On second thought, maybe the atheist cannot find God for the same reason a thief cannot find a policeman.)

An atheist is a guy who watches a Notre Dame-SMU football game and doesn't care who wins.   —Dwight D. Eisenhower

The agnostic's prayer: "O God, if there is a god, save my soul, if I have a soul."   —Ernest Renan (1823–1890)

I don't know if God exists, but it would be better for His reputation if He didn't.   —Jules Renard

The equal toleration of all religions . . . is the same thing as atheism.   —Pope Leo XIII

The worst moment for the atheist is when he is really thankful and has nobody to thank.   —Dante Gabriel Rossetti (1828–1882) (In other words, an atheist is someone who believes that what you see is all you get.)

I was a freethinker before I knew how to think.
—George Bernard Shaw

Most people have some sort of religion—at least they know what church they're staying away from.   —John Erskine

Fervid atheism is usually a screen for repressed religion.
—Wilhelm Stekel (On second thought, atheism is a fervid belief in disbelief.)

The writers against religion, whilst they oppose every system, are wisely careful never to set up any of their own.
—Edmund Burke (1729–1797)

Agnosticism simply means that a man shall not say he knows or believes that for which he has no grounds for professing to believe.
—Thomas Henry Huxley (1825–1895)

*   *

The mystery of the beginning of all things is insoluble by us; and I for one must be content to remain an agnostic.
—Charles Darwin (1809–1882)

Don't be agnostic—be something.   —Robert Frost

AMERICA / AMERICANISM / AMERICANS

America is the country where you buy a lifetime supply of aspirin for one dollar, and use it up in two weeks.   —John Barrymore

How prophetic L'Enfant was when he laid out Washington as a city that goes around in circles!   —John Mason Brown

America is a country that doesn't know where it is going but is determined to set a speed record getting there.
—Laurence J. Peter

This will never be a civilized country until we spend more money for books than we do for chewing gum.   —Elbert Hubbard

Don't get the idea that I'm one of those goddamn radicals. Don't get the idea that I'm knocking the American system.
—Al Capone

Americans are like a rich father who wishes he knew how to give his sons the hardships that made him rich.   —Robert Frost

America is a land where a citizen will cross the ocean to fight for democracy—and won't cross the street to vote in a national election.
—Bill Vaughan

Americans: People who laugh at . . . African witch doctors and spend 100 million dollars on fake reducing systems.
—Leonard Louis Levinson (How is it that George Washington slept so many places and yet never told a lie?)

Ours is the only country deliberately founded on a good idea.
—John Gunther

America is much more than a geographical fact. It is a political and moral fact—the first community in which men set out in principle to institutionalize freedom, responsible government, and human equality.   —Adlai Stevenson (On second thought, America is a land of taxation that was founded to avoid taxation.)

I tremble for my country when I reflect that God is just.
—Thomas Jefferson (1734–1826)

Who was the first around the moon? An atheist Russian or God-fearing Americans?   —Don Carpenter

You hear about constitutional rights, free speech and the free press. Every time I hear these words I say to myself, "That man is a Red, that man is a Communist!" You never hear a real American talk like that.   —Frank Hague (Including Washington, Jefferson, Lincoln, and Wilson?)

If we let idiots like the Black Panthers survive under our form of government, maybe we'll have to change it.   —Frank Rizzo

I don't feel we did wrong in taking this great country away from them. There were great numbers of people who needed new land, and the Indians were selfishly trying to keep it for themselves.
—John Wayne

We are now at the point where we must decide whether we are to honor the concept of a plural society which gains strength through diversity or whether we are to have bitter fragmentation that will result in perpetual tension and strife.   —Justice Earl Warren

The mission of the United States is one of benevolent assimilation.
—William McKinley

What's right about America is that although we have a mess of problems, we have great capacity—intellect and resources—to do something about them.   —Henry Ford II (On second thought, America is the land of opportunity if you are a businessman in Japan.)

A thousand years hence, perhaps in less, America may be what Europe is now . . . the noblest work of human wisdom, the grand scene of human glory, the fair cause of freedom that rose and fell.
—Thomas Paine (1737–1809)

The American experiment is the most tremendous and far reaching engine of social change which has ever either blessed or cursed mankind.   —Charles Francis Adams (1807–1886)

The tendency everywhere in America to concentrate power and responsibility in one man is unmistakable.   —James Bryce

This is still a very wealthy country. The failure is of spirit and insight.   —Governor Jerry Brown

Double—no triple—our troubles and we'd still be better off than any other people on earth.   —Ronald Reagan

Because systems of mass communication can communicate only officially acceptable levels of reality, no one can know the extent of the secret unconscious life. No one in America can know what will happen. No one is in real control.   —Allen Ginsberg

In America immediately after World War II, anti-Semitism reached peaks never before attained, despite all Nazi contributions to our universal conscience; and the literature of the period will bear me out.
—Robert Ardrey

I don't see much future for the Americans . . . Everything about the behavior of American society reveals that it's half judaized, and the other half negrified. How can one expect a state like that to hold together?   —Adolf Hitler

I confess that I cannot understand how we can plot, lie, cheat and commit murder abroad and remain humane, honorable, trustworthy and trusted at home.   —Archibald Cox

There must have been something so very right about Americanism, for in the days it was practiced it brought us from thirteen undeveloped colonies to the world's greatest-ever nation and brought Americans to new highs in life, liberty and well-being.
—J. Kesner Kahn

What the country needs are a few labor-making inventions.
—Arnold Glasow

The terrible newly-imported American doctrine that everyone ought to do something.   —Sir Osbert Sitwell

We don't know what we want, but we are ready to bite somebody to get it.   —Will Rogers

*   *

Some people want to impeach Earl Warren. Hanging would be more deserved.   —Colonel Mitchell Paige

. . . the day will come when men like Judges Carswell and Haynsworth can and will sit on the high court.   —Richard M. Nixon

---

America is the only nation in history which miraculously has gone directly from barbarism to degeneration without the usual interval of civilization.   —Georges Clemenceau

The old platitude must be repeated once again: the United States is the society with the least history prior to the age of progress.
—George P. Grant

*   *

This country will not be a good place for any of us to live in unless we make it a good place for all of us to live in.
—Theodore Roosevelt

This land of ours cannot be a good place for any of us to live in unless it is a good place for all of us to live in.
—Richard M. Nixon

*   *

At the moment the United States is the most powerful, the most prosperous, and the most dangerous country in the world.
—Robert Maynard Hutchins

The U. S. is the most dangerous and destructive power in the world.
—Anthony Lewis

*   *

Behold a republic gradually but surely becoming the supreme moral factor in disputes.   —William Jennings Bryan

I think we must save America from the missionary idea that you must get the whole world on to the American way of life. This is really a big world danger.   —Gunnar Myrdal

*   *

There is a malaise that exists in your land—what appears to many as the sudden and tragic disappearance of the American dream which, in some ways, has turned to nightmare.   —J. J. Greene

We must stop talking about the American dream and start listening to the dreams of Americans.   —Reubin Askew

*   *

The only foes that threaten America are the enemies at home, and these are ignorance, superstition, and incompetence.

—Elbert Hubbard

True, there is government harassment, but there still is that relative freedom to fight. I can attack my government, try to organize to change it. That's more than I can do in Moscow, Peking, or Havana.

—Saul Alinsky

*   *

America is a mistake, a giant mistake!   —Sigmund Freud

*   *

I feel that I am a citizen of the American dream and that the revolutionary struggle of which I am a part is a struggle against the American nightmare.   —Eldridge Cleaver

*   *

We talk about the American Dream, and want to tell the world about the American Dream, but what is that Dream, in most cases, but the dream of material things? I sometimes think that the United States for this reason is the greatest failure the world has ever seen.

—Eugene O'Neill

We need some great statements about what America is about and what we can do about it.   —Theodore M. Hesburgh

*   *

No foreign policy will stick unless the American people are behind it. And unless Congress understands it. And unless Congress understands it, the American people aren't going to understand it.

—W. Averell Harriman

The American Revolution was a beginning, not a consummation.

—Woodrow Wilson

*   *

I believe that the heaviest blow ever dealt at liberty's head will be dealt by this nation [the United States] in the ultimate failure of its example to the earth.   —Charles Dickens (1812–1870)

[America is] still the best country for the common man—white or black . . . if he can't make it here he won't make it anywhere else.
                                          —Eric Hoffer

*   *

Americanism is a question of principle, of idealism, of character: it is not a matter of birthplace or creed or line of descent.
                                          —Theodore Roosevelt

I don't know much about Americanism, but it's a damned good word with which to carry an election.   —Warren G. Harding

ANCESTRY / ANCESTORS

Gentility is what is left over from rich ancestors after the money is gone.   —John Ciardi

It's kinder funny, but no matter how common our blood is, we hate to lose any of it.   —Will Rogers

Genealogy: Tracing yourself back to people better than you are.
                                          —John Garland Pollard

Whoever serves his country well has no need of ancestors.
          —Voltaire (François Marie Arouet) (1694–1778)

We pay for the mistakes of our ancestors, and it seems only fair that they should leave us the money to pay with.
                                          —Don Marquis

A nation is a society united by a delusion about its ancestry and by common hatred of its neighbours.   —Dean William R. Inge

The best blood will sometimes get into a fool or a mosquito.
                                          —Austin O'Malley

I don't have to look up my family tree, because I know that I'm the sap.   —Fred Allen (On second thought, every man serves a useful purpose: a miser, for example, makes a wonderful ancestor.)

A man's destiny stands not in the future but in the past. That, rightly considered, is the most vital of all vital facts. Every child thus has a right to choose his own ancestors.   —Havelock Ellis

The family you come from isn't as important as the family you're going to have.   —Ring Lardner

*   *

There were human beings aboard the Mayflower, not merely ancestors.   —Stephen Vincent Benét

My folks didn't come over on the Mayflower, but they were there to meet the boat.   —Will Rogers

ANGER

This makes me so sore it gets my dandruff up.
—Samuel Goldwyn (On second thought, it usually takes two people to make one of them angry.)

Never forget what a man says to you when he is angry.
—Henry Ward Beecher (1813–1887) (Speak when you're angry—and you'll make the best speech you'll ever regret.)

ANIMALS

We declare henceforth that all animals shall enjoy these inalienable rights: The right to freedom from fear, pain and suffering—whether in the name of science or sport, fashion or food, exhibition or service. The right, if they are wild, to roam free, unharried by hunters, trappers or slaughterers. If they are domestic, not to be abandoned in the city streets, by a country road, or in a cruel and inhumane pound. And finally the right, at the end, to a decent death—not (whether they are endangered or not) by a club, by a trap, by harpoon, cruel poison or mass extermination chamber. We have only one creed—to speak for those who can't.   —The Fund for Animals, Inc.

I have always thought of a dog lover as a dog that was in love with another dog.   —James Thurber

All animals are equal, but some animals are more equal than others.
—George Orwell

It is in the nature of cats to do certain amounts of unescorted roaming . . . the state of Illinois . . . already has enough to do without trying to control feline delinquency.   —Adlai Stevenson

No matter how much cats fight, there always seem to be plenty of kittens.   —Abraham Lincoln (1809–1865)

We hope that, when the insects take over the world, they will remember with gratitude how we took them along on all our picnics.
—Bill Vaughan

The hen is an egg's way of producing another egg.
—Samuel Butler

The caribou seems to have no idea whatever of personal comfort.
—William Parker Greenough

Behind each beautiful wild fur there is an ugly story. It is a brutal, bloody and barbaric story. The animal is not killed—it is tortured. I don't think a fur coat is worth it.   —Mary Tyler Moore

Heaven goes by favour. If it went by merit, you would stay out and your dog would go in.   —Mark Twain

The greatest pleasure of a dog is that you may make a fool of yourself with him, and not only will he not scold you, but he will make a fool of himself, too.   —Samuel Butler (So it's nice for children to have pets—until the pets start having children.)

Pigs and cows and chickens and people are all competing for grain.
—Margaret Mead

If modern civilized man had to kill the animals he eats, the number of vegetarians would rise astronomically.
—Christian Morgenstern

That's my private ant. You're liable to break its legs.
—Albert Schweitzer, to a ten-year-old boy

I believe all animals were provided by God to help keep man alive.
—Iwao Fujita

Young gorillas are friendly but they soon learn.   —Will Cuppy

Money will buy a pretty good dog but it won't buy the wag of his tail.
—Josh Billings (Henry Wheeler Shaw) (1818–1885)

———————————

They [the animals] do not make me sick discussing their duty to God.
—Walt Whitman (1819–1892)

All animals except man know that the ultimate of life is to enjoy it.
—Samuel Butler

*   *

We Germans, who are the only people in the world who have a decent attitude toward animals, will also assume a decent attitude towards these human animals.   —Heinrich Himmler

. . . when one loves animals and children *too much,* one loves them against human beings.   —Jean-Paul Sartre

*   *

I tend to be suspicious of people whose love of animals is exaggerated; they are often frustrated in their relationships with humans.
—Ylla (Camilla Koffler)

[Being] good to animals . . . the bad man's invariable characteristic.   —Robert W. Chambers (1802–1871) (On second thought, the noblest of all dogs is the hot dog; it feeds the hand that bites it.)

APATHY

The worst sin towards our fellow creatures is not to hate them, but to be indifferent to them; that's the essence of inhumanity.
—George Bernard Shaw (Apathy is worse than antipathy.)

The great secret, the deeply buried mystery of the apparent apathy to crime and to proposals for better controlling crime, lies in the persistent, intrusive wish for vengeance.
—Dr. Karl Menninger

The tyranny of a prince in an oligarchy is not so dangerous to the public welfare as the apathy of a citizen in a democracy.
—Baron de Montesquieu (1689–1755)

Bad officials are elected by good citizens who do not vote.
—George Jean Nathan

The only thing necessary for the triumph of evil is for good men to do nothing.   —Edmund Burke (1729–1797)

*   *

The death of a democracy is not likely to be an assassination by ambush. It will be a slow extinction from apathy, indifference and undernourishment.   —Robert Maynard Hutchins

In Germany they came first for the Communists, and I didn't speak up because I wasn't a Communist. Then they came for the Jews, and I didn't speak up because I wasn't a Jew. Then they came for the trade unionists, and I didn't speak up because I wasn't a trade unionist. Then they came for the Catholics, and I didn't speak up because I was a Protestant. Then they came for me, and by that time no one was left to speak up.   —Martin Niemoeller

*   *

The hottest places in Hell are reserved for those who in time of great moral crises maintain their neutrality.
—Dante Alighieri (1265–1321)

Science may have found a cure for most evils; but it has found no remedy for the worst of them all—the apathy of human beings.

—Helen Keller

ARGUMENT / CONTROVERSY

No matter what side of an argument you're on, you always find some people on your side that you wish were on the other side.
—Jascha Heifetz (On the other hand, there are two sides to every argument, until you take one.)

I dislike arguments of any kind. They are always vulgar, and often convincing.   —Oscar Wilde (1854–1900)

How come nobody wants to argue with me? Is it because I'm always so right?   —Jim Bouton

He always had a chip on his shoulder that he was ready to use to kindle an argument.   —Fred Allen

The finding of arguments for a conclusion given in advance is not philosophy, but special pleading.   —Bertrand Russell

The most savage controversies are those about matters as to which there is no good evidence either way.   —Bertrand Russell

There is no arguing with him, for if his pistol misses fire, he knocks you down with the butt end of it.   —Oliver Goldsmith (1728–1774) (On second thought, the surest sign that you haven't any sense is to argue with one who hasn't.)

It is not necessary to understand things in order to argue about them.   —Pierre Augustin de Beaumarchais (1732–1799) (An argument always leaves each party convinced that the other has a closed mind.)

I never make the mistake of arguing with people for whose opinions I have no respect.   —Edward Gibbon (1737–1794) (There's only one thing worse than the man who will argue over anything, and that's the man who will argue over nothing.)

People are usually more convinced by reasons they discovered themselves than by those found by others.

—Blaise Pascal (1623–1662)

Discussion is an exchange of knowledge; argument an exchange of ignorance.   —Robert Quillen

Change means movement, movement means friction, friction means heat, and heat means controversy. The only place where there is no friction is in outer space or a seminar on political action.

—Saul Alinsky

Silence is one of the hardest things to refute.
—Josh Billings (Henry Wheeler Shaw) (1818–1885)

How many a dispute could have been deflated into a single paragraph if the disputants had dared to define their terms.
—Aristotle (384–322 B.C.)

The man who strikes first admits that his ideas have given out.
—Chinese Proverb

Argument is the worst sort of conversation.
—Jonathan Swift (1667–1745)

*　　*

Protagoras it was who first left facts out of consideration and fastened his arguments on words. He it was who first invented the sort of argument which is called Socratic.
—Diogenes Laertius (c. 150 B.C.)

The Socratic manner is not a game at which two can play.
—Max Beerbohm

*　　*

When you have no basis for an argument, abuse the plaintiff.
—Marcus Tullius Cicero (106–43 B.C.)

If you can't answer a man's argument, all is not lost; you can still call him vile names.　　—Elbert Hubbard

ART

Art is not a thing; it is a way.　　—Elbert Hubbard

Every child is an artist. The problem is how to remain an artist once he grows up.　　—Pablo Picasso

There are three forms of visual art: Painting is art to look at, sculpture is art you can walk around, and architecture is art you can walk through.　　—Dan Rice

Any work of art that can be understood is the product of journalism.
—Tristan Tzara

Abstract Art: A product of the untalented, sold by the unprincipled to the utterly bewildered.　　—Al Capp

If that's art, I'm a Hottentot!　　—Harry S Truman

Life is short, art long, opportunity fleeting, experience treacherous, judgment difficult.　　—Hippocrates (460?–370? B.C.)

All art is a revolt against man's fate.   —André Malraux

Art is like a border of flowers along the course of civilization.
                                        —Lincoln Steffens

Buy Old Masters. They fetch a much better price than old mistresses.
                                        —Lord Beaverbrook

Every time an artist dies, part of the vision of mankind passes with
him.   —Franklin Delano Roosevelt

A painting in a museum hears more ridiculous opinions than anything else in the world.   —Edmond de Goncourt (1822–1896)
(Except, perhaps, a corpse in a coffin.)

Art for art's sake makes no more sense than gin for gin's sake.
                                        —Somerset Maugham

Art, like morality, consists in drawing the line somewhere.
                                        —G. K. Chesterton

He knows all about art, but he doesn't know what he likes.
                                        —James Thurber

My tutor does watercolors; they are like the work of a girl of
fourteen—when she was twelve.   —Ben Nicholson

For every artist with something to say but the inability to say it well,
there are two who could say something well if they had something
to say.   —Paul C. Mills

An artist may visit a museum but only a pedant can live there.
                                        —George Santayana

Bad artists always admire each other's work.
                                        —Oscar Wilde (1854–1900)

A subject that is beautiful in itself gives no suggestion to the artist.
It lacks imperfection.   —Oscar Wilde

It is only an auctioneer who can equally and impartially admire all
schools of Art.   —Oscar Wilde (On the other hand, he may sell
a painting he doesn't like, to another man who doesn't want it, for
twice its value.)

It does not matter how badly you paint so long as you don't paint
badly like other people.   —George Moore

Occasional vulgarity is a by-product of the vitality and passion without which there can be no great art.   —Francis Toye

An artist never really finishes his work; he merely abandons it.
                                        —Paul Valéry

A doctor can bury his mistakes but an architect can only advise his client to plant vines. —Frank Lloyd Wright

Art flourishes where there is a sense of adventure.
—Alfred North Whitehead

Art is the difference between seeing and just identifying.
—Jean Mary Norman

Everything is art if it is chosen by the artist to be art.
—Samuel Adams Green

One reassuring thing about modern art is that things can't be as bad as they are painted.
—M. Walthall Jackson

Modern art is what happens when painters stop looking at girls and persuade themselves they have a better idea. —John Ciardi

For the mystic what is how. For the craftsman how is what. For the artist what and how are one. —William McElcheran

A great artist is always before his time or behind it.
—George Moore

He paints as a bird sings. —Paul Signac, of Monet

Don't talk to me of Gauguin. I'd like to wring the fellow's neck!
—Paul Cézanne

He bores me. He ought to have stuck to his flying machines.
—Auguste Renoir, of Leonardo da Vinci

You are the first in the decadence of your art.
—Charles Baudelaire, to Manet

The connoisseur of art must be able to appreciate what is simply beautiful, but the common run of people are satisfied with ornament.
—Johann W. von Goethe (1749–1832)

The rule in the art world is: you cater to the masses or you kowtow to the elite; you can't have both. —Ben Hecht

There is nothing new in art except talent. —Anton Chekhov

The great artist is the simplifier.
—Henri Frédéric Amiel (1821–1881)

Art happens—no hovel is safe from it, no Prince may depend upon it, the vastest intelligence cannot bring it about.
—James McNeill Whistler

Painting is silent poetry, and poetry is painting that speaks.
—Simonides (6th–5th century, B.C.)

A nation in which a congressman can seriously ask, "Do you think the artist is a special person?" is a nation living in cultural jeopardy.
—James Thurber

They leaned toward the honest and explicit in art, a picture, for instance, that told its own story, with generous assistance from its title.   —H. H. Munro ("Saki")

All day long I add up columns of figures and make everything balance. I come home. I sit down. I look at a Kandinsky and it's wonderful! It doesn't mean a damn thing!
—Solomon Guggenheim

There is no *must* in art because art is free.   —Vasily Kandinsky

Number seven . . . What's it meant to be, dear? . . . A "Study"? . . . It doesn't say what of? . . . Well, that's an easy way out for an artist.   —Ruth Draper

Art is either a revolutionist or a plagiarist.   —Paul Gauguin

[Art is] the reasoned derangement of the senses.
—Kenneth Rexroth

With an apple I will astonish Paris.   —Paul Cézanne

I shut my eyes in order to see.   —Paul Gauguin

It is better to paint from memory, for thus your work will be your own; your sensation, your intelligence, and your soul will triumph over the eye of the amateur . . . Do not finish your work too much.
—Paul Gauguin

[The object of painting is] not to reflect the visible but to make visible.
—Paul Klee

All our knowledge has its origins in our perceptions.
—Leonardo da Vinci (1452–1519)

I am for an art that is political-erotical-mystical, that does something other than sit on its ass in a museum.   —Claes Oldenburg

A primitive artist is an amateur whose work sells.
—Grandma Moses

While I recognize the necessity for a basis of observed reality . . . true art lies in a reality that is felt.   —Odilon Redon

A painter who has the feel of breasts and buttocks is saved.
—Auguste Renoir

For the most part theories serve only to mask the shortcomings of the artist . . . Theories are worked out afterwards.
—Auguste Renoir

Because a work of art does not aim at reproducing natural appearances, it is not, therefore, an escape from life . . . but an expression of the significance of life, a stimulation to greater effort in living.   —Henry Moore

Less is more.   —Mies van der Rohe

We shape our buildings; thereafter they shape us.
—Winston Churchill

Variety of uniformities makes complete beauty.
—Sir Christopher Wren (1632–1723)

All profoundly original art looks ugly at first.
—Clement Greenberg

There is no abstract art. You must always start with something.
—Pablo Picasso

Nothing in the world requires more courage than to applaud the destruction of values which we still cherish. If a work of art or a new style disturbs you, then it is probably good work. If you hate it, it is probably great.   —Leo Steinberg

---

Art is the lie that enables us to realize the truth.

—Pablo Picasso

Art-speech is the only truth. An artist is usually a damned liar, but his art, if it be art, will tell you the truth of his day.
—D. H. Lawrence

*   *

All great art is by its very essence in conflict with the society with which it coexists. It expresses the truth about existence regardless of whether this truth serves or hinders the survival purpose of a given society. All great art is revolutionary because it touches upon the reality of man and questions the reality of the various transitory forms of human society.   —Erich Fromm

The artist is the seismograph of his age.   —Robert W. Corrigan

*   *

Only work which is the product of inner compulsion can have spiritual meaning.   —Walter Gropius

The aim of art is to represent not the outward appearance of things, but their inward significance.   —Aristotle (384–322 B.C.)

*   *

The artist has a special task and duty: the task of reminding men of their humanity and the promise of their creativity.

—Lewis Mumford

I have always believed and still believe that artists who live and work with spiritual values cannot and should not remain indifferent to a conflict in which the highest values of humanity and civilization are at stake.   —Pablo Picasso

*   *

Without art, the crudeness of reality would make the world unbearable.   —George Bernard Shaw

To be deprived of art and left alone with philosophy is to be close to Hell.   —Igor Stravinsky

*   *

Art is much less important than life, but what a poor life without it.

—Robert Motherwell

To have read the greatest works of any great poet, to have beheld or heard the greatest works of any great painter or musician, is a possession added to the best things of life.

—Algernon Charles Swinburne

*   *

All the really good ideas I ever had came to me while I was milking a cow.   —Grant Wood

What has reason to do with the art of painting?

—William Blake (1757–1827)

No art was ever less spontaneous than mine. What I do is the result of reflection and study; of inspiration, spontaneity, temperament, I know nothing.   —Edgar Degas

Art is the most frenzied orgy man is capable of.

—Jean Dubuffet

*   *

A picture is not a window . . . an abstract refers to no reality but its own.   —Jean Cocteau

The artist is a perceptual window.   —Jack Chambers

*   *

Art is idea. It is not enough to draw, paint, and sculpt. An artist should be able to think.   —Gurdon Woods

Art hath an enemy called Ignorance.
—Ben Jonson (1572?–1637)

*   *

When one is painting one does not think.
—Raphael Sanzio (1483–1520)

A man paints with his brains and not with his hands.
—Michelangelo (1475–1564)

*   *

To paint a fine picture is far more important than to sell it.
—Edward Alden Jewell

Once Degas witnessed one of his paintings sold at auction for $100,000. Asked how he felt, he said, "I feel as a horse must feel when the beautiful cup is given to the jockey."

*   *

Anyone who sees and paints a sky green and pastures blue ought to be sterilized.   —Adolf Hitler

Artists can color the sky red because they know it's blue. Those of us who aren't artists must color things the way they really are or people might think we're stupid.   —Jules Feiffer

ATOM

Since I do not foresee that atomic energy is to be a great boon for a long time, I have to say that for the present it is a menace. Perhaps it is well that it should be. It may intimidate the human race into bringing order into its international affairs, which, without the pressure of fear, it would not do.   —Albert Einstein

You're an old-timer if you can remember when setting the world on fire was a figure of speech.   —Franklin P. Jones

If we wish to make a new world we have the material ready. The first one, too, was made out of chaos.   —Robert Quillen

We hold these truths to be self-evident: All men could be cremated equal.   —Vern Partlow

The Atomic Age is here to stay—but are we?   —Bennett Cerf

Babies Satisfactorily Born—U. S. Army code message on the successful test of the atomic bomb at Alamogordo, New Mexico

Aside from being tremendous, it was one of the most aesthetically beautiful things I have ever seen.   —Donald Horning, of the first atomic test

A reciprocal insanity [involving nuclear armaments] is at work in the world.   —Norman Cousins

The release of atomic energy has not created a new problem. It has merely made more urgent the necessity of solving an existing one . . . I do not believe that civilization will be wiped out in a war fought with the atomic bomb. Perhaps two-thirds of the people of the earth will be killed.   —Albert Einstein

Hitherto man had to live with the idea of death as an individual; from now onward mankind will have to live with the idea of its death as a species.   —Arthur Koestler

Some day science may have the existence of mankind in its power, and the human race can commit suicide by blowing up the world.
—Brooks Adams

*   *

The control man has secured over nature has far outrun his control over himself.   —Ernest Jones

Ours is a world of nuclear giants and ethical infants. If we continue to develop our technology without wisdom or prudence, our servant may prove to be our executioner.   —General Omar Bradley

*   *

Gods are born and die, but the atom endures.
—Alexander Chase

History is the short trudge from Adam to atom.
—Leonard Louis Levinson

Outlawing all atomic weapons could be a magnificent gesture. However, it should be remembered that Gettysburg had a local ordinance forbidding the discharge of firearms.   —Homer D. King

There will one day spring from the brain of science a machine or force so fearful in its potentialities, so absolutely terrifying that even man, the fighter, who will dare torture and death in order to inflict torture and death, will be appalled, and so abandon war forever. What man's mind can create, man's character can control.
—Thomas Alva Edison

*   *

I'm not frightened about the world ending. A few nuclear devices may explode and cause immense damage.   —Robert Graves

What the scientists have in their briefcases is terrifying.
—Nikita Khrushchev

AUTOBIOGRAPHY

An autobiography usually reveals nothing bad about its writer except his memory.   —Franklin P. Jones

Autobiography is an unrivaled vehicle for telling the truth about other people.   —Philip Guedalla

Only when one has lost all curiosity about the future has one reached the age to write an autobiography.   —Evelyn Waugh

The lives of great men rarely remind us of anything sublime.
—Lord Vansittart

AUTOMATION

Computers can figure out all kinds of problems, except the things in the world that just don't add up.   —James Magary (The toughest decision a purchasing agent faces is when he is about to buy the machine designed to replace him.)

In a few minutes a computer can make a mistake so great that it would take many men many months to equal it.
—Merle L. Meacham

The computer is a moron.   —Peter Drucker (Computers can solve all kinds of problems except the unemployment problem they create.)

The new electronic independence recreates the world in the image of a global village.   —Marshall McLuhan

It is questionable if all the mechanical inventions yet made have lightened the day's toil of any human being.
—John Stuart Mill (1806–1873)

Civilization advances by extending the number of important operations which we can perform without thinking of them.
—Alfred North Whitehead (But computers will never be perfected until they can compute how much more than the estimate the job will cost.)

The main impact of the computer has been the provision of unlimited jobs for clerks.   —Peter Drucker

---

The danger of the past was that men became slaves. The danger of the future is that man may become robots.   —Erich Fromm
(And further, that to err may become inhuman.)

Lo! Men have become the tools of their tools.
         —Henry David Thoreau (1817–1862)

*   *

Man-machine identity is achieved not by attributing human attributes to the machine, but by attributing mechanical limitations to man.   —Mortimer Taube

The real danger is not that computers will begin to think like men, but that men will begin to think like computers.
         —Sydney J. Harris

B

BEAUTY

In architecture, the beauty is in the line and design. In painting, it is the form and color. In works of fine art, it is the craftsmanship. Possession of these things brings pleasure to some, but the real joy comes from the enjoyment of their beauty.   —William Ross

If Jack's in love, he's no judge of Jill's beauty.
                              —Benjamin Franklin (1706–1790)

Though we travel the world over to find the beautiful, we must carry it with us or we find it not.
                              —Ralph Waldo Emerson (1803–1882)

When the candles are out all women are fair.
                                        —Plutarch (46?–120?)

Every girl should use what Mother Nature gave her before Father Time takes it away.   —Laurence J. Peter

Beauty is only skin deep, and the world is full of thin-skinned people.   —Richard Armour (There are more pretty photographs of women than there are photographs of pretty women.)

Beauty is altogether in the eye of the beholder.   —General Lew Wallace (Like truth and a contact lens.)

Beauty—the adjustment of all parts proportionately so that one cannot add or subtract or change without impairing the harmony of the whole.   —Leon Battista Alberti (1404–1472)

Beauty is the promise of happiness.
                    —Stendhal (Henri Beyle) (1783–1842)

Beauty is eternity gazing at itself in a mirror.   —Kahlil Gibran (Say that again, please?)

Why should beauty be suspect?   —Auguste Renoir

I'm tired of all this nonsense about beauty being only skin-deep. That's deep enough. What do you want—an adorable pancreas?
                    —Jean Kerr

It's a good thing that beauty is only skin deep, or I'd be rotten to the core.   —Phyllis Diller

*   *

Remember always that the least plain sister is the family beauty.
                    —George Bernard Shaw

Not every woman in old slippers can manage to look like Cinderella.
                    —Don Marquis

*   *

Gather ye rose-buds while ye may,/Old Time is still a-flying:/And this same flower that smiles today,/Tomorrow will be dying.
                    —Robert Herrick (1591–1674)

Then of thy beauty do I question make,/That thou among the wastes of time must go.   —William Shakespeare (1564–1616)

When I am working on a problem, I never think about beauty. I think only how to solve the problem. But when I have finished, if the solution is not beautiful, I know it is wrong.
                    —Buckminster Fuller

Beauty and folly are generally companions.
                    —Baltasar Gracián (1601–1658)

BEHAVIOR

Don't jump on a man unless he's down.
                    —Finley Peter Dunne (Mr. Dooley)

I like men to behave like men—strong and childish.
                    —Françoise Sagan

Walk groundly, talk profoundly, drink roundly, sleep soundly.
—William Hazlitt (1778–1830)

Behavior modification is the manipulation of environmental conditions to which an individual is exposed so as to bring about a desired behavioral response.   —Laurence J. Peter

Society attacks early when the individual is helpless.
—B. F. Skinner

Behavioral psychology is the science of pulling habits out of rats.
—Dr. Douglas Busch

Cruelty must be whitewashed by a moral excuse, and pretense of reluctance.   —George Bernard Shaw

Be pleasant until ten o'clock in the morning and the rest of the day will take care of itself.   —Elbert Hubbard

The impossible is often the untried.   —Jim Goodwin

The time to relax is when you don't have time for it.
—Sydney J. Harris

Perhaps it may someday turn out that in the microscopic freedom of the individual rather than in the macroscopic predictability and controllability of the mass resides a releasable force as much more powerful than any which the mechanistic psychology can manipulate.   —Joseph Wood Krutch

My only policy is to profess evil and do good.
—George Bernard Shaw

Obedience is a deeply ingrained behavior tendency, indeed a potent impulse overriding training in ethics, sympathy, and moral conduct . . . For a person to feel responsible for his actions, he must sense that the behavior has flowed from *the self*. It is easy to ignore responsibility when one is only an intermediate link in a chain of action.   —Stanley Milgram

When a judge in a court of law is forced to distinguish between a free and a compelled act, he is not helped by being told by either a psychoanalyst or a behaviorist that all acts are compelled.
—Willard Gaylin

BELIEF

People only think a thing's worth believing in if it's hard to believe.
—Armiger Barclay

I never cease being dumfounded by the unbelievable things people believe.   —Leo Rosten

Man is what he believes.   —Anton Chekhov

A miracle: an event described by those to whom it was told by men who did not see it.   —Elbert Hubbard

Though a good deal is too strange to be believed, nothing is too strange to have happened.   —Thomas Hardy

Sometimes I've believed as many as six impossible things before breakfast.   —Lewis Carroll (Charles Lutwidge Dodgson) (1832–1898)

Seek not to understand that you may believe, but believe that you may understand.   —Saint Augustine (Oh what tangled webs we weave when first we practice to believe!)

Generally the theories we believe we call facts, and the facts we disbelieve we call theories.   —Felix Cohen

We are inclined to believe those we do not know, because they have never deceived us.   —Samuel Johnson (1709–1784)

If we let ourselves believe that man began with divine grace, that he forfeited this by sin, and that he can be redeemed only by divine grace through the crucified Christ then we shall find a peace of mind never granted to philosophers. He who cannot believe is cursed, for he reveals by his unbelief that God has not chosen to give him grace.
        —Blaise Pascal (1623–1662)

For every credibility gap there is a gullibility fill.
        —Richard Clopton

Seeing is deceiving. It's eating that's believing.
        —James Thurber

He who proselytizes in the cause of unbelief is basically a man in need of belief.   —Eric Hoffer

Reading made Don Quixote a gentleman, but believing what he read made him mad.   —George Bernard Shaw

Why abandon a belief merely because it ceases to be true? Cling to it long enough and . . . it will turn true again, for so it goes. Most of the change we think we see in life is due to truths being in and out of favor.   —Robert Frost

What matters today is not the difference between those who believe and those who do not believe, but the difference between those who care and those who don't.   —Abbé Pire

The essence of belief is the establishment of a habit.
        —Charles S. Pearce

A belief is not true because it is useful.
—Henri Frédéric Amiel (1821–1881)

There are two ways to slide easily through life; to believe everything or to doubt everything; both ways save us from thinking.
—Alfred Korzybski

The race of men, while sheep in credulity, are wolves for conformity.
—Carl Van Doren

Credulity is the man's weakness, but the child's strength.
—Charles Lamb (1775–1834)

The happiness of credulity is a cheap and dangerous quality of happiness, and by no means a necessity of life.
—George Bernard Shaw

Nothing is so firmly believed as that which is least known.
—Michel de Montaigne (1533–1592)

* *

A man must not swallow more beliefs than he can digest.
—Brooks Adams

The most costly of all follies is to believe passionately in the palpably not true. —H. L. Mencken

* *

Every man prefers belief to the exercise of judgment.
—Seneca (4 B.C.–A.D. 65)

It is a far, far better thing to have a firm anchor in nonsense than to put out on the troubled seas of thought.
—John Kenneth Galbraith

* *

A man lives by believing something, not by debating and arguing about many things. —Thomas Carlyle (1795–1881)

Modern man . . . has not ceased to be credulous . . . the need to believe haunts him. —William James

* *

The one serious conviction that a man should have is that nothing is to be taken too seriously. —Nicholas Murray Butler

Convictions are more dangerous enemies of truth than lies.
—Friedrich Nietzsche (1844–1900)

Belief is a wise wager. Granted that faith cannot be proved, what harm will come to you if you gamble on its truth and it proves false? . . . If you gain, you gain all; if you lose, you lose nothing. Wager, then, without hesitation, that He exists.
—Blaise Pascal (1623–1662)

Belief is desecrated when given to unproved and unquestioned statements for the solace and private pleasure of the believer . . . It is wrong always, everywhere, and for every one, to believe anything upon insufficient evidence.   —William James

THE BIBLE

It ain't those parts of the Bible that I can't understand that bother me, it is the parts that I do understand.   —Mark Twain

The Bible tells us to love our neighbors, and also to love our enemies; probably because they are generally the same people.
—G. K. Chesterton

I am somewhat surprised to hear a member of your Church quote so essentially a Protestant document as the Bible.
—George Bernard Shaw

Scriptures, n. The sacred books of our holy religion, as distinguished from the false and profane writings on which all other faiths are based.   —Ambrose Bierce

There is hardly a book of either Old or New Testament that has not been questioned, either wholly or in part, by some reputable scholar.
—Curtis D. MacDougall (On the other hand, the Bible contains much that is relevant today, like Noah taking forty days to find a place to park.)

———

The scriptures teach us the best way of living, the noblest way of suffering, and the most comfortable way of dying.
—John Flavel (1630?–1691)

The Bible is God's revelation to man, his guide, his light.
—Alfred Armand Montapert

*   *

The total absence of humor from the Bible is one of the most singular things in all literature.   —Alfred North Whitehead

The Good Book—one of the most remarkable euphemisms ever coined.   —Ashley Montagu

*   *

The Bible is God's chart for you to steer by, to keep you from the bottom of the sea, and to show you where the harbor is, and how to reach it without running on rocks or bars.

—Henry Ward Beecher (1813–1887)

A thorough knowledge of the Bible is worth more than a college education.   —Theodore Roosevelt

*   *

There can be no doubt that the Bible . . . became a stumbling-block in the path of progress, scientific, social and even moral. It was quoted against Copernicus as it was against Darwin.

—Preserved Smith

So far as I can remember, there is not one word in the Gospels in praise of intelligence.   —Bertrand Russell

*   *

The question turns mainly on whether the strange Greek in which the four Gospels are written is simply the work of Jews thinking in Aramaic though writing in Greek, or whether it represents rather an effort to translate literally into Greek original Aramaic Gospels now lost.   —Ernest Sutherland Bates

It is a curious thing that God learned Greek when he wished to turn author—and that he did not learn it better.

—Friedrich Nietzsche (1844–1900)

The inspiration of the Bible depends upon the ignorance of the gentleman who reads it.   —Robert G. Ingersoll (1833–1899)

I have read it [the Bible] carefully. And if Bob Ingersoll isn't in hell, God is a liar and the Bible isn't worth the paper it is printed on.
—Billy Sunday (Unless, of course, it's an original Gutenberg.)

*   *

Nobody ever outgrows Scripture; the book widens and deepens with our years.   —Charles Haddon Spurgeon (1834–1892)

The Old Testament is tribal in its provinciality; its god is a local god, and its village police and sanitary regulations are erected into eternal laws.   —John (Albert) Macy

*   *

Whenever we read the obscene stories, the voluptuous debaucheries, the cruel and tortuous executions, the unrelenting vindictiveness with which more than half the Bible is filled, it would be more consistent that we call it the word of a demon than the word of God. It is a history of wickedness that has served to corrupt and brutalize mankind.   —Thomas Paine (1737–1809)

The Bible is the most thought-suggesting book in the world. No other deals with such grand themes.   —Herrick Johnson

*   *

One does well to put on gloves when reading the New Testament; the proximity of so much impurity almost compels to this . . . I have searched in it vainly for even a single congenial trait . . . everything in it is cowardice and self-deception.
    —Friedrich Nietzsche

If we abide by the principles taught by the Bible, our country will go on prospering.   —Daniel Webster (1782–1852)

*   *

The dogma of the infallibility of the Bible is no more self-evident than is that of the infallibility of the popes.
    —Thomas Henry Huxley (1825–1895)

When you have read the Bible, you will know it is the word of God, because you will have found it the key to your own heart, your own happiness and your own duty.   —Woodrow Wilson

BIOGRAPHY

Biography is to give a man some kind of shape after his death.
    —Virginia Woolf

A biographer is an artist upon oath.
    —Sir Desmond MacCarthy

Every great man nowadays has his disciples, and it is always Judas who writes the biography.   —Oscar Wilde (1854–1900) (Some men have been immortalized in biography, while others have been immoralized.)

A well-written life is almost as rare as a well-spent one.
—Thomas Carlyle (1795–1881) (Dead men tell no tales, but many have biographers who do.)

BIRTH AND BIRTH CONTROL

We all worry about the population explosion, but we don't worry about it at the right time.   —Arthur Hoppe (It's a pity that birth control cannot be made retroactive.)

Whenever I hear people discussing birth control, I always remember
that I was the fifth.   —Clarence Darrow

No woman can call herself free who does not own and control her
body. No woman can call herself free until she can choose con-
sciously whether she will or will not be a mother.

—Margaret Sanger

A society which practices death control must at the same time practice birth control.   —John Rock

You should have thought of all this before you were born.
—N. F. Simpson (On second thought, everybody in favor of birth
control has already been born.)

Abortion doesn't belong in the political arena. It's a private right,
like many other rights concerning the family.   —Bella Abzug

To my embarrassment I was born in bed with a lady.

—Wilson Mizner

Birth is the beginning of death.

—Thomas Fuller (1608–1661)

The wailing of the newborn infant is mingled with the dirge for
the dead.   —Lucretius (96?–55 B.C.)

Any use whatsoever of matrimony exercised in such a way that the
act is deliberately frustrated in its natural power to generate life is
an offense against the law of God and of nature, and those who
indulge in such are branded with the guilt of a grave sin.

—Pope Pius XI

Catholics use their political influence to prevent Protestants from
practicing birth control, and yet they must hold that the great majority of Protestant children whom their political action causes to exist
will endure eternal torments in the next world.

—Bertrand Russell

BLACKS

I have a dream that one day on the red hills of Georgia, the sons
of former slaves and the sons of former slave-owners will be able
to sit together at the table of brotherhood . . . that one day even
the State of Mississippi, a state sweltering with the heat of injustice,
sweltering with the heat of oppression, will be transformed into an
oasis of freedom and justice . . . that my four little children will

one day live in a nation where they will not be judged by the color of their skin but by the content of their character.

—Martin Luther King, Jr.

The haughty American nation . . . makes the Negro clean its boots and then proves the moral and physical inferiority of the Negro by the fact that he is a bootblack.

—George Bernard Shaw

A liberal Southerner is someone who wouldn't mind going to see *Green Pastures* provided it had an all-white cast.

—Dick Gregory

The Man ain't prejudiced. He doesn't care what color his slaves are.   —Chester Anderson (History reveals that in 1670 the Virginia Assembly made it illegal for blacks to own white servants.)

The system conceded to black people the right to sit in the front of the bus—a hollow victory when one's longest trip is likely to be from the feudal South to the mechanized poverty of the North.

—Julian Bond

I want to be the white man's brother, not his brother-in-law.

—Martin Luther King, Jr.

We have allowed death to change its name from Southern rope to Northern dope. Too many black youths have been victimized by pushing dope into their veins instead of hope into their brains.

—Jesse Jackson

They put Negroes in the schools, and now they've driven God out.

—George Andrews

If it wasn't for Abe [Lincoln], I'd still be on the open market.

—Dick Gregory

When someone screams "Nigger! Nigger!" the opulent Black says, "Where?"   —E. Franklin Frazier

If they really believe there is danger from the Negro, it must be because they do not intend to give him justice.

—Booker T. Washington

Injustice always breeds fear . . . the main difficulty of the race question does not lie so much in the actual condition of the blacks as it does in the mental attitude of the whites.

—James Weldon Johnson

You cannot have law and order and niggers, too.   —J. B. Stoner

Some people have a wonderful way of looking at things. Like the ones who hire one of us to babysit—so they can go to a Ku Klux Klan meeting.   —Dick Gregory

Whenever the Constitution comes between me and the virtue of white women in South Carolina, I say, "to hell with the Constitution!"   —Coleman L. Blease

When George Jessel took Lena Horne to a famous restaurant, the doorman asked, "Who made your reservations?" Jessel replied, "Abraham Lincoln."   —Earl Wilson

An illustration of the craving that people have to attach favorable symbols to themselves is seen in the community where white people banded together to force out a Negro family that had moved in. They called themselves *Neighborly Endeavor* and chose as their motto the Golden Rule.   —Gordon W. Allport

No niggah's good as a white man, because the niggah's only a few shawt yeahs from cannibalism.   —Eugene Talmadge

If you could just be a nigger one Saturday night, you wouldn't never want to be a white man again as long as you live.
    —William Faulkner

You can't hold a man down without staying down with him.
    —Booker T. Washington

This country was formed for the *white,* not for the black man. And looking upon African slavery from the same viewpoint held by the noble framers of our Constitution, I for one have ever considered it one of the greatest blessings (both for themselves and us) that God ever has bestowed upon a favored nation.
    —John Wilkes Booth (1838–1865)

There are two ways of exerting one's strength: one is pushing down, the other is pulling up.   —Booker T. Washington

In all things that are purely social we can be as separate as the fingers, yet one as the hand in all things essential to mutual progress.
    —Booker T. Washington

To like an individual because he's black is just as insulting as to dislike him because he isn't white.   —e. e. cummings

———————

For your race, in its poverty, has unquestionably one really effective weapon—laughter. Power, money, persuasion, supplication, persecution—these can laugh at a colossal humbug—push it a little—weaken it a little, century by century; but only laughter can blow it to rags and atoms at a blast.   —Mark Twain

Humor is laughing at what you haven't got when you ought to have it.   —Langston Hughes

*   *

Beware of Greeks bearing gifts, colored men looking for loans, and whites who understand the Negro.   —Adam Clayton Powell

A racially integrated community is a chronological term timed from the entrance of the first black family to the exit of the last white family.   —Saul Alinsky

                    *   *

Until justice is blind to color, until education is unaware of race, until opportunity is unconcerned with the color of men's skins, emancipation will be a proclamation but not a fact.
                                        —Lyndon B. Johnson

. . . another Negro hung naked from a tree. In the background a Klansman held aloft a large American flag.   —Jacob Javits

                    *   *

We are all citizens of one world, we are all of one blood. To hate a man because he was born in another country, because he speaks a different language, or because he takes a different view on this subject or that, is a great folly. Desist, I implore you, for we are all equally human . . . Let us have but one end in view, the welfare of humanity.   —John Comenius (1592–1670)

We are all descendants of Adam and we are all products of racial miscegenation.   —Lester B. Pearson

---

Busing is an artificial and inadequate instrument of change which should be abandoned just as soon as we can afford to do so. But we must not take the risk of returning to the kind of segregation, fear and misunderstanding which produced the very problem in the first place.   —Reubin Askew

It is my conviction that God ordained segregation.
                                        —Reverend Billy James Hargis

                    *   *

I believe in white supremacy until the blacks are educated to a point of responsibility.   —John Wayne

Those who deny freedom to others deserve it not for themselves.
                            —Abraham Lincoln (1809–1865)

                    *   *

Negroes . . . must not make the mistake of the German Jews, who assumed that if the German nation received some of them as intellectual and social equals, the whole group would be safe. It took only a psychopathic criminal like Hitler to show them their tragic mistake. *American Negroes may yet face a similar tragedy.* They should prepare for such an eventuality.   —W. E. B. Dubois

The Americans ought to be ashamed of themselves for letting their medals be won by Negroes.   —Adolf Hitler

BOOKS AND READING

Mr. [Irvin] Cobb took me into his library and showed me his books, of which he has a complete set.   —Ring Lardner

Sartor Resartus is simply unreadable, and for me that always sort of spoils a book.   —Will Cuppy (Literature and vocabulary don't go together, otherwise a dictionary would be the greatest literary masterpiece.)

Some men borrow books; some men steal books; and others beg presentation copies from the author.   —James Jeffrey Roche

Book—what they make a movie out of for television.
          —Leonard Louis Levinson

These are not books, lumps of lifeless paper, but *minds* alive on the shelves. From each of them goes out its own voice . . . and just as the touch of a button on our set will fill the room with music, so by taking down one of these volumes and opening it, one can call into range the voice of a man far distant in time and space, and hear him speaking to us, mind to mind, heart to heart.
          —Gilbert Highet

My education was the liberty I had to read indiscriminately and all the time, with my eyes hanging out.   —Dylan Thomas

There is more treasure in books than in all the pirates' loot on Treasure Island . . . and best of all, you can enjoy these riches every day of your life.   —Walt Disney

An ordinary man can . . . surround himself with two thousand books . . . and thenceforward have at least one place in the world in which it is possible to be happy.   —Augustine Birrell

I am a part of all that I have read.   —John Kieran

The novel is the highest example of subtle interrelatedness that man has discovered.   —D. H. Lawrence

The walls of books around him, dense with the past, formed a kind of insulation against the present world and its disasters.
—Ross Macdonald (A good book on your shelf is a friend that turns its back on you and remains a friend.)

Show me the books he loves and I shall know/The man far better than through mortal friends.　　—S. Weir Mitchell

The last thing that we find in making a book is to know what we must put first.　　—Blaise Pascal (1623–1662)

The man who does not read good books has no advantage over the man who can't read them.　　—Mark Twain

I wonder whether what we are publishing now is worth cutting down trees to make paper for the stuff.　　—Richard Brautigan

The things I want to know are in books; my best friend is the man who'll get me a book I ain't read.　　—Abraham Lincoln (According to his cousin, Dennis Hanks, Abe made books tell him more than they told other people.)

Hemingway's remarks are not literature.　　—Gertrude Stein

A best seller is the gilded tomb of a mediocre talent.
　　　　　　　　　　　　　　　　—Logan Pearsall Smith

In literature as in love, we are astonished at what is chosen by others.
　　　　　　　　　　　　　　　　—André Maurois

The worst thing about new books is that they keep us from reading the old ones.　　—Joseph Joubert (1754–1824)

There is a great deal of difference between an eager man who wants to read a book and the tired man who wants a book to read.
　　　　　　　　　　　　　　　　—G. K. Chesterton

A book is the only place in which you can examine a fragile thought without breaking it, or explore an explosive idea without fear it will go off in your face . . . It is one of the few havens remaining where a man's mind can get both provocation and privacy.
　　　　　　　　　　　　　　　　—Edward P. Morgan

———————

Never lend books, for no one ever returns them; the only books I have in my library are books that other folk have lent me.
　　　　　　　　　　　　　　　　—Anatole France

You loan a hard-covered book to a friend and when he doesn't return it you get mad at him. It makes you mean and petty. But twenty-five-cent books are different.　　—John Steinbeck (But where today can anyone purchase a twenty-five-cent book?)

*　　　*

When I get a little money, I buy books; and if any is left, I buy food and clothes.　　—Desiderius Erasmus (1465–1536)

Where is human nature so weak as in the bookstore?
                    —Henry Ward Beecher (1813–1887)

*   *

The multitude of books is making us ignorant.
            —Voltaire (François Marie Arouet) (1694–1778)

We live in an age that reads too much to be wise.
                        —Oscar Wilde (1854–1900)

*   *

Some people read because they are too lazy to think.
                    —G. C. Lichtenberg (1742–1799)

Who knows if Shakespeare might not have thought less if he had
read more?   —Edward Young (1683–1765)

*   *

He has left off reading altogether, to the great improvement of his
originality.   —Charles Lamb (1775–1834)

The road to ignorance is paved with good editions.
                        —George Bernard Shaw

*   *

When we read too fast or too slowly, we understand nothing.
                    —Blaise Pascal (1623–1662)

To read without reflecting is like eating without digesting.
                    —Edmund Burke (1729–1797)

*   *

A bad book is as much a labor to write as a good one, it comes as
sincerely from the author's soul.   —Aldous Huxley

'Tis pleasant, sure, to see one's name in print;/A book's a book,
though there's nothing in't.
                —George Gordon, Lord Byron (1788–1824)

*   *

In a very real sense, people who have read good literature have
lived more than people who cannot or will not read . . . It is not
true that we have only one life to live; if we can read, we can live
as many more lives and as many kinds of lives as we wish.
                        —S. I. Hayakawa

The way a book is read—which is to say, the qualities a reader
brings to a book—can have as much to do with its worth as any-

thing the author puts into it . . . Anyone who can read can learn how to read deeply and thus live more fully.

—Norman Cousins

*   *

Every man who knows how to read has it in his power to magnify himself, to multiply the ways in which he exists, to make his life full, significant and interesting.   —Aldous Huxley

The end of reading is not more books but more life.

—Holbrook Jackson

In the march up to the heights of fame there comes a spot close to the summit in which man reads nothing but detective stories.

—Heywood Broun

With so many fine books to be read, so much to be studied and known, there is no need to bore ourselves with this rubbish.

—Edmund Wilson

*   *

A man may as well expect to grow stronger by always eating as wiser by always reading.   —Jeremy Collier (1650–1726)

Reading is to the mind what exercise is to the body.

—Sir Richard Steele (1672–1729)

*   *

If I had read as much as other men I should have known no more than they.   —Thomas Hobbes (1588–1679)

If we encounter a man of rare intellect, we should ask him what books he reads.   —Ralph Waldo Emerson (1803–1882)

*   *

Book love . . . is your pass to the greatest, the purest, and the most perfect pleasure that God has prepared for His creatures.

—Anthony Trollope (1815–1882)

Books . . . are the curse of the human race.

—Benjamin Disraeli (1804–1881)

*   *

When you read a classic, you do not see more in the book than you did before; you see more in *you* than there was before.

—Clifton Fadiman

Every man with a belly full of classics is an enemy of the human race.   —Henry Miller

* *

. . . that peculiar disease of intellectuals, that infatuation with ideas at the expense of experience that compels experience to conform to bookish preconceptions. —Archibald MacLeish

The best effect of any book is that it excites the reader to self activity. —Thomas Carlyle (1795–1881)

BORES

Every improvement in communication makes the bore more terrible. —Frank Moore Colby

A bore is a man who, when you ask him how he is, tells you. —Bert Leston Taylor

No one really listens to anyone else, and if you try it for a while you'll see why. —Mignon McLaughlin

Bore—a guy with a cocktail glass in one hand and your lapel in the other. —Henny Youngman (The worst thing about a bore is not that he won't stop talking, but that he won't let you stop listening.)

He is an old bore; even the grave yawns for him. —Sir Herbert Beerbohm Tree

He's the kind of bore who's here today and here tomorrow. —Binnie Barnes

A bore is a person who talks when you want him to listen. —Ambrose Bierce

A bore is a fellow talker who can change the subject to his topic of conversation faster than you can change it back to yours. —Laurence J. Peter

Bores can be divided into two classes; those who have their own particular subject, and those who do not need a subject. —A. A. Milne

Nothing is interesting if you're not interested. —Helen MacInness

We often forgive those who bore us; we cannot forgive those whom we bore. —Duc de La Rochefoucauld (1613–1680) (A bore is someone endowed with more patience than his listeners.)

Boredom is a vital problem for the moralist since half the sins of mankind are caused by fear of it. —Bertrand Russell

Boredom results from a deficit of sensory responsiveness to the external world.   —Dr. Estelle R. Ramey

No one could be rich enough to buy the right to be such a bore.
          —John Kenneth Galbraith

Somebody's boring me . . . I think it's me.   —Dylan Thomas

A subject for a great poet would be God's boredom after the seventh day of Creation.   —Friedrich Nietzsche (1844–1900)

The average man who does not know what to do with his life, wants another one which will last forever.   —Anatole France

Bores bore each other too; but it never seems to teach them anything.   —Don Marquis

---

Is not life a hundred times too short for us to bore ourselves?
          —Friedrich Nietzsche

"What'll we do with ourselves this afternoon?" cried Daisy, "and the day after that, and the next thirty years?"
          —F. Scott Fitzgerald

*   *

I am never bored anywhere: being bored is an insult to oneself.
          —Jules Renard

A person who deprives you of solitude without providing you with company.   —Gian Vincenzo Lavina (A person who lights up a room simply by leaving it.)

BROTHERHOOD

I love my country better than my family; but I love humanity better than my country.   —François Fénelon

The world has narrowed into a neighborhood before it has broadened into a brotherhood.   —Lyndon B. Johnson

The mystic bond of brotherhood makes all men one.
          —Thomas Carlyle (1795–1881)

Until you have become really in actual fact a brother of everyone, brotherhood will not come to pass. Only by brotherhood will liberty be saved.   —Feodor Dostoevski (1821–1881)

It is easier to love humanity as a whole than to love one's neighbor.
          —Eric Hoffer

To correct the evils, great and small, which spring from want of sympathy and from positive enmity among strangers, as nations or as individuals, is one of the highest functions of civilization.

—Abraham Lincoln (1809–1865)

BUREAUCRACY

The nearest thing to immortality in this world is a government bureau. —General Hugh S. Johnson (A bureaucrat's idea of cleaning up his files is to make a copy of every paper before he destroys it.)

Bureaucracy defends the status quo long past the time when the quo has lost its status. —Laurence J. Peter

A bureaucrat is a Democrat who holds some office that a Republican wants. —Alben W. Barkley

There is very little to admire in bureaucracy, but you have got to hand it to the Internal Revenue Service. —James L. Rogers

We trained hard . . . but every time we were beginning to form up into teams, we would be reorganized. I was to learn later in life that we tend to meet any new situation by reorganizing . . . and a wonderful method it can be for creating the illusion of progress while producing inefficiency and demoralization.

—Petronius (d. A.D. 66)

It is hard to feel individually responsible with respect to the invisible processes of a huge and distant government.

—John Gardner

But it is not by the consolidation, or concentration, of powers, but by their distribution that good government is effected.

—Thomas Jefferson (1743–1826)

The hallmark of our age is the tension between related aspirations and sluggish institutions. —John Gardner

Bureaucracy is a giant mechanism operated by pygmies.

—Honoré de Balzac (1799–1850)

Guidelines for Bureaucrats: (1) When in charge ponder. (2) When in trouble delegate. (3) When in doubt mumble.

—James H. Boren

We can lick gravity, but sometimes the paperwork is overwhelming.

—Wernher von Braun

I've been nitpicked to pieces by the goddamn bureaucracy.
—Travis Reed

*   *

The work of internal government has become the task of controlling the thousands of fifth-rate men.   —Henry Adams

I do not rule Russia; ten thousand clerks do.
—Nicholas I (1796–1855)

BUSINESS

The business of government is to keep the government out of business—that is, unless business needs government aid.
—Will Rogers

I think any man in business would be foolish to fool around with his secretary. If it's somebody else's secretary, fine!
—Senator Barry Goldwater

Statistics indicate that, as a result of overwork, modern executives are dropping like flies on the nation's golf courses.
—Ira Wallach

Business will be better or worse.   —Calvin Coolidge

Some see private enterprise as a predatory target to be shot, others as a cow to be milked, but few are those who see it as a sturdy horse pulling the wagon.   —Winston Churchill

A great society is a society in which men of business think greatly of their functions.   —Alfred North Whitehead

There is more credit and satisfaction in being a first-rate truck driver than a tenth-rate executive.   —B. C. Forbes

Monopoly is business at the end of its journey.
—Henry Demarest Lloyd

The executive exists to make sensible exceptions to general rules.
—Elting E. Morison (An executive is a man who is always annoying the hired help by asking them to do something.)

Since passage of the Federal Reports Act of 1942, information vital for public regulation of business abuse has been controlled by business itself.   —Mark J. Green

Lobbyists are the touts of protected industries.
—Winston Churchill

I think that maybe in every company today there is aways at least one person who is going crazy slowly.   —Joseph Heller

A banker is a person who is willing to make a loan if you present sufficient evidence to show you don't need it.
—Herbert V. Prochnow

Question: Do you consider ten dollars a week enough for a long-shoreman with a family to support?
Answer: If that's all he can get, and he takes it, I should say it's enough.   —J. Pierpont Morgan

Corporation: An ingenious device for obtaining individual profit without individual responsibility.   —Ambrose Bierce

The rushed existence into which industrialized, commercialized man has precipitated himself is actually a good example of an inexpedient development caused entirely by competition between members of the same species. Human beings of today are attacked by so-called *manager diseases,* high blood pressure, renal atrophy, gastric ulcers, and torturing neuroses: they succumb to barbarism because they have no more time for cultural interests.
—Konrad Lorenz

There is no room for the kind of blind speculation that produces booms and blights.   —Art Seidenbaum

Banking may well be a career from which no man really recovers.
—John Kenneth Galbraith

I think that there is nothing, not even crime, more opposed to poetry, to philosophy, ay, to life itself than this incessant business.
—Henry David Thoreau (1817–1862)

There are an enormous number of managers who have retired on the job.   —Peter Drucker

Management by objectives works if you know the objectives. Ninety percent of the time you don't.   —Peter Drucker (Fools rush in where wise men fear to trade.)

The modern corporation is a political institution; its purpose is the creation of legitimate power in the industrial sphere.
—Peter Drucker

The only things that evolve by themselves in an organization are disorder, friction, and malperformance.   —Peter Drucker (How about corruption, nonresponsiveness, and hostility?)

"Absorption of overhead" is one of the most obscene terms I have ever heard.   —Peter Drucker

Capital formation is shifting from the entrepreneur who invests in the future to the pension trustee who invests in the past.

—Peter Drucker

Production is not the application of tools to materials, but logic to work.　—Peter Drucker

Promotion should not be more important than accomplishment, or avoiding instability more important than taking the right risk.

—Peter Drucker

Business has only two basic functions—marketing and innovation.

—Peter Drucker

. . . corporations have at different times been so far unable to distinguish freedom of speech from freedom of lying that their freedom has to be curbed.　—Carl Becker

American business needs a lifting purpose greater than the struggle of materialism.　—Herbert Hoover

There is no suggestion here that networks or individual stations would operate as philanthropies. But I can find nothing in the Bill of Rights or the Communications Act, which says that they must increase their net profits each year lest the Republic collapse.

—Edward R. Murrow

I have always thought it would be easier to redeem a man steeped in vice and crime than a greedy, narrow-minded, pitiless merchant.

—Albert Camus

The society of money and exploitation has never been charged, so far as I know, with assuring the triumph of freedom and justice.

—Albert Camus

There is now scarcely any outlet for energy in this country except business . . . But it was men of another stamp than this that made England what it is; and men of another stamp will be needed to prevent its decline.　—John Stuart Mill (1806–1873)

Most are engaged in business the greater part of their lives, because the soul abhors a vacuum and they have not discovered any continuous employment for man's nobler faculties.

—Henry David Thoreau

Enthusiasm for conservation can be fashioned into a nasty weapon for those who dislike business on general principles.

—William F. Buckley, Jr.

One of the greatest failings of today's executive is his inability to do what he's supposed to do.　—Malcolm Kent

It is probably safe to say that over a long period of time, political morality has been as high as business morality.

—Henry Steele Commager

I niver knew a pollytician to go wrong ontil he's been contaminated by contact with a business man.

—Finley Peter Dunne (Mr. Dooley)

* *

. . . when the corruption of American politics was laid on the threshold of business—like a bastard on the doorstep of his father —a tremendous disturbance resulted.

—Vernon Louis Parrington

I do not dislike but I certainly have no especial respect or admiration for and no trust in, the typical big moneyed men of my country. I do not regard them as furnishing sound opinion as respects either foreign or domestic business.

—Theodore Roosevelt

* *

Every great man of business has got somewhere a touch of the idealist in him.   —Woodrow Wilson

Do other men for they would do you. That's the true business precept.   —Charles Dickens (1812–1870)

* *

In business, the earning of profit is something more than an incident of success. It is an essential condition of success. It is an essential condition of success because the continued absence of profit itself spells failure.   —Justice Louis D. Brandeis

Profitability is the sovereign criterion of the enterprise.

—Peter Drucker

* *

Money-getters are the benefactors of our race. To them . . . are we indebted for our institutions of learning, and of art, our academies, colleges and churches.   —P. T. Barnum (1810–1891)

As John D. Rockefeller explained to a fortunate Sunday School class: "The growth of a large business is merely the survival of the fittest . . . The American Beauty rose can be produced in the splendor and fragrance which bring cheer to its beholder only by sacrificing the early buds which grow up around it."

—John Kenneth Galbraith

* *

A great deal of the so-called government encroachment in the area of business, labor, and the professions has been asked for by the people misusing their freedom.   —J. Irwin Miller

If business leaders had channeled one tenth of the energy they devoted to fighting this bill [Nader's consumer protection bill] into improving their products and services they would not find themselves in this fix. The subcommittee had analyzed the warranties of fifty-one leading manufacturers. Only one of them provided the customers with a warranty free of loopholes.

—James J. Kilpatrick

The business of America is business.   —Calvin Coolidge

When nations grow old the Arts grow cold/And Commerce settles on every tree.   —William Blake (1757–1827)

*   *

On CBS Radio the news of his [Ed Murrow's] death, reportedly from lung cancer, was followed by a cigarette commercial.

—Alexander Kendrick

Business without profit is not business any more than a pickle is a candy.   —Charles F. Abbott

*   *

Business succeeds rather better than the state in imposing its restraints upon individuals, because its imperatives are disguised as choices.   —Walton Hamilton

The percentage of student activists who regard business as overly concerned with profits as against social responsibility has increased sharply in just one year.   —John D. Rockefeller III

*   *

To be a success in business, be daring, be first, be different.

—Marchant

Nobody talks more of free enterprise and competition and of the best man winning than the man who inherited his father's store or farm.   —C. Wright Mills

*   *

Businessmen are notable for a peculiarly stalwart character, which enables them to enjoy without loss of self-reliance the benefits of tariffs, franchises, and even outright government subsidies.

—Herbert J. Muller

If the government was as afraid of disturbing the consumer as it is of disturbing business, this would be some democracy.
——Frank McKinney Hubbard ("Kin Hubbard")

*   *

The egalitarianism of the present tax structure is thought to be seriously dampening individual effort, initiative, and inspiration . . . [it] destroys ambition, penalizes success, discourages investment to create new jobs, and may well turn a nation of risk-taking entrepreneurs into a nation of softies.   ——Fred Maytag II

There are two times in a man's life when he should not speculate: when he can't afford it and when he can.   ——Mark Twain

C

CANADA

Canada needs hewers of water and haulers of wood.
—J. J. Greene

A Canadian is somebody who knows how to make love in a canoe.
—Pierre Berton

The beaver is a good national symbol for Canada. He's so busy chewing he can't see what's going on.   —Howard Cable

"I'm world famous," Dr. Parks said, "all over Canada."
—Mordecai Richler

Quebec is one of the ten provinces against which Canada is defending itself.   —Carl Dubuc

In Canada we don't ban demonstrations, we re-route them.
—Alan Borovoy

Canada is a collection of ten provinces with strong governments loosely connected by fear.   —Dave Broadfoot

I have to spend so much time explaining to Americans that I am not English and to Englishmen that I am not American that I have little time left to be Canadian.   —Laurence J. Peter (On second thought, I am a true cosmopolitan—unhappy anywhere.)

Even when Canadian humor is awful it just lies there being awful in its own fresh way.   —Robert Thomas Allen

If the national mental illness of the United States is megalomania that of Canada is paranoid schizophrenia.

—Margaret Atwood

It is a peculiar Canadian trait to be able to spot an inequity better at a distance, especially if facing south, than close up.

—George Bain

Let the fight come if it must; I don't care whether our sea coast cities are bombarded or not; we would take Canada.

—Theodore Roosevelt

Canada helps make our napalm and then takes in our deserters. Canada has both ends of a dirty stick and ends up with both hands dirty.   —Daniel Berrigan

When the white man came we had the land and they had the Bibles; now they have the land and we have the Bibles.

—Chief Dan George

I see a Serpent in Canada who courts me to his love.

—William Blake (1757–1827)

The Arctic expresses the sum of all wisdom: Silence.

—Walter Bauer

When Columbus made his well-remembered voyage to the Caribbean, Canada had been known to Europeans for more than five hundred years.   —R. A. J. Phillips

John Kenneth Galbraith and Marshall McLuhan are the two greatest modern Canadians the United States has produced.

—Anthony Burgess

Americans are benevolently ignorant about Canada, while Canadians are malevolently well informed about the United States.

—J. Bartlet Brebner

The real friend of this country is the guy who believes in excellence, seeks for it, fights for it, defends it, and tries to produce it.

—Morley Callaghan

Canadians are concerned about the rape of our country by the Americans. And I say that it is not true—how can you rape a prostitute?   —Dave Broadfoot

Canadians represent, as it were, the least militant North American minority group. The white, Protestant, heterosexual ghetto of the north.   —Mordecai Richler

The only way to get away from the influence of the American economy would be to float our half of the continent off somewhere else.   —John Kenneth Galbraith

There has never been a war of Canadian origin, nor for a Canadian cause.   —William Arthur Deacon

---

Perhaps the most striking thing about Canada is that it is not part of the United States.   —J. Bartlet Brebner

A Canadian is a fellow who has become a North American without becoming an American.   —Arthur L. Phelps

*   *

Canada has never been a melting pot; more like a tossed salad.
    —Arnold Edinborough

In any world menu, Canada must be considered the vichyssoise of nations—it's cold, half-French, and difficult to stir.
    —Stuart Keate

*   *

Canada—a triumph of politics over geography and economics— and sometimes it seems over common sense.
    —Robert T. Elson

To agree to disagree, to harness diversity, to respect dissent; perhaps this is the real essence of Canada.   —Robert L. Perry

*   *

My generation of Canadians grew up believing that, if we were very good or very smart, or both, we would someday graduate from Canada.   —Robert Fulford

My theory is that if you can make it in Canada, you can make it anywhere.   —Bernard Slade

*   *

When they said Canada, I thought it would be up in the mountains somewhere.   —Marilyn Monroe

I don't even know what street Canada is on.   —Al Capone

Canada's climate is nine months winter and three months late in the fall.   —Evan Esar (Man wants but little here below— zero.)

Oh, no, it is not always winter in Canada.   —William Parker
Greenough (Would you believe, they have four seasons in one day
—I was wearing out my body changing clothes.)

*   *

All the yachts you could build with your Canadian royalties you
could sail in your bathtub.   —Ernest Buckler

Canadian books may occasionally have had a mild impact outside
Canada; Canadian literature has had none.   —E. K. Brown

*   *

You have a great country up here. And a great people too.
                                 —William Jennings Bryan

Gentlemen, I give you Upper Canada; because I don't want it
myself.   —Artemus Ward

*   *

I have no desire to bolster the sagging ˈcultural economy of this
country.   —Brendan Behan

If Canada is underdeveloped, so is Brigitte Bardot.
                                 —H. R. MacMillan

*   *

Canada is a good country to be from. It has a gentler slower pace
—it lends perspective.   —Paul Anka

I wish the British Government would give you Canada at once. It
is fit for nothing but to breed quarrels.   —Lord Ashburton

*   *

Canada is the only country in the world that knows how to live
without an identity.   —Marshall McLuhan

Canada has no cultural unity, no linguistic unity, no religious unity,
no economic unity, no geographic unity. All it has is unity.
                                 —Kenneth Boulding

CAPITALISM

Under capitalism man exploits man; under socialism the reverse is
true.   —Polish Proverb

Put God to work for you and maximize your potential in our
divinely ordered capitalist system.   —Norman Vincent Peale

The oppressed are allowed once every few years to decide which particular representatives of the oppressing class are to represent and repress them.   —Karl Marx (1818–1883)

The cure for capitalism's failing would require that a government would have to rise above the interests of one class alone.
—Robert L. Heilbroner

The real fight today is against inhuman, relentless exercise of capitalistic power . . . The present struggle in which we are engaged is for social and industrial justice.   —Justice Louis D. Brandeis

Capitalism . . . is outrageously unjust; it requires a continuing maldistribution of wealth in order to exist . . . We live in the twilight of an epoch . . . I am absolutely convinced that we are moving toward some kind of planned economy.
—Michael Harrington

The fear of capitalism has compelled socialism to widen freedom, and the fear of socialism has compelled capitalism to increase equality.   —Will and Ariel Durant

Capitalism in the United States has undergone profound modification, not just under the New Deal but through a consensus that continued to grow after the New Deal . . . Government in the U. S. today is a senior partner in every business in the country.
—Norman Cousins

Social Democracy rests on the assumption that it is desirable to preserve the capitalist system of private enterprise, and that the evils of this system can be sufficiently corrected by the democratic method of procedure.   —Carl Becker

One of the things capitalism brought into the world was democracy, though I do not think the two are inseparable.
—Michael Harrington

If all I'm offered is a choice between monopolistic privilege with regulation and monopolistic privilege without regulation, I'm afraid I have to opt for the former.   —Nicholas Johnson

When the government talks about "raising capital" it means printing it. That's not very creative, but it's what we're going to do.
—Peter Drucker

The inherent vice of capitalism is the unequal sharing of blessings; the inherent virtue of socialism is the equal sharing of miseries.
—Winston Churchill

Uneven economic and political development is an absolute law of capitalism.   —Nikolai Lenin

*   *

Capital as such is not evil; it is its wrong use that is evil.
                                        —Mohandas Gandhi

The forces of a capitalist society, if left unchecked, tend to make
the rich richer and the poor poorer.   —Jawaharlal Nehru

*   *

Only in time of peace can the wastes of capitalism be tolerated.
                                        —F. R. Scott

Man is demolishing nature . . . We are killing things that keep
us alive.   —Thor Heyerdahl

*   *

Corrupt, stupid grasping functionaries will make at least as big a
muddle of socialism as stupid, selfish and acquisitive employers can
make of capitalism.   —Walter Lippmann (To justify his theft,
one trade union official, caught with his hand in the till, explained
that he was using the money to fight Communism.)

Capitalism did not arise because capitalists stole the land . . . but
because it was more efficient than feudalism. It will perish because
it is not merely less efficient than socialism, but actually self-
destructive.   —J. B. S. Haldane

CENSORSHIP / CENSORS

What is good literature, what has educational value, what is refined
public information, what is good art, varies with individuals as it
does from one generation to another. There doubtless would be a
contrariety of views concerning Cervantes' *Don Quixote,* Shakespeare's *Venus and Adonis* or Zola's *Nana.* But a requirement that
literature or art conform to some norm prescribed by an official
smacks of an ideology foreign to our system . . . to withdraw the
second-class rate from this publication today because its contents
seemed to one official not good for the public, would sanction with-
drawal of the second-class rate tomorrow from another periodical
whose social or economic views seemed harmful to another official.
—Unanimous U. S. Supreme Court opinion, U. S. Post Office v. Es-
quire Inc. (1946)

I never knew a girl who was ruined by a bad book.   —Jimmy
Walker (Some people wouldn't read a book even if it were banned.)

The fact is that censorship always defeats its own purpose, for it
creates, in the end, the kind of society that is incapable of exercising
real discretion . . . In the long run it will create a generation

incapable of appreciating the difference between independence of thought and subservience. —Henry Steele Commager (A censor is an expert in cutting remarks.)

To limit the press is to insult a nation; to prohibit reading of certain books is to declare the inhabitants to be either fools or slaves. —Claude Adrien Helvétius (1715–1771)

I have the same confidence in the ability of our people to reject noxious literature as I have in their capacity to sort out the true from the false in theology, economics, or any other field. —Justice William O. Douglas

We can never be sure that the opinion we are endeavoring to stifle is a false opinion; and if we were sure, stifling it would be an evil still. —John Stuart Mill (1806–1873)

The only freedom deserving the name is that of pursuing our own good in our own way, so long as we do not attempt to deprive others of theirs . . . Mankind are greater gainers by suffering each other to live as seems good to themselves, than by compelling each to live as seems good to the rest. —John Stuart Mill

The sooner we all learn to make a distinction between disapproval and censorship, the better off society will be . . . Censorship cannot get at the real evil, and it is an evil in itself. —Granville Hicks (A censor is a man who knows more than he thinks you ought to.)

False views, if supported by some evidence, do little harm, for everyone takes a salutary pleasure in proving their falseness; and when this is done, one path towards error is closed and the road to truth is often at the same time opened. —Charles Darwin (1809–1882)

If in other lands the press and books and literature of all kinds are censored, we must redouble our efforts here to keep them free. —Franklin Delano Roosevelt

They [the dictatorships] know that literacy is a liberating factor in society only where the press is free . . . Where the press is under strict and efficient control, literacy can become a weapon for the support of a universal tyranny. This constitutes one of the remarkable achievements of twentieth century despotism. —George S. Counts

I am going to introduce a resolution to have the Postmaster General stop reading dirty books and deliver the mail. —Gale McGee

A man walking at night . . . sees a light in the window and says, "A mother praying for the safe return of her boy." A second man

sees the light and says, "Oh boy, hanky-panky going on up there!"
The second man is a censor.   —Goodman Ace

The books that the world calls immoral are the books that show the
world its own shame.   —Oscar Wilde (1854–1900)

There is no such thing as a moral or an immoral book. Books are
well written or badly written.   —Oscar Wilde

Assassination is the extreme form of censorship.
                                        —George Bernard Shaw

Censorship, like charity, should begin at home; but, unlike charity,
it should end there.   —Clare Boothe Luce

In Florida, Henry Balch, columnist for the *Orlando Sentinel,* thun-
dered that a children's book telling about the marriage of a white
and a black rabbit was a plot of the *integrating desegregationist,*
and hounded the volume off the shelves of the public library.
—Jacob K. Javits (Censors make up for their lack of awareness
of what is suitable by their extra censory perception.)

———————————

I see no objection in principle to censorship of the mass entertain-
ment of the young.   —Walter Lippmann

I had to censor everything my sons watched . . . even on the Mary
Tyler Moore show I heard the word *damn!*   —Mary Lou Bax

*   *

You have a right to burn books or destroy books if you can prove
they can do harm.   —Professor Thomas Devine

The burning of an author's books, imprisonment for opinion's sake,
has always been the tribute that an ignorant age pays to the genius
of its time.   —Joseph Lewis

Literature should not be suppressed merely because it offends the
moral code of the censor.   —Justice William O. Douglas

A sodomite got very excited looking at a zoology text. Does this
make it pornography?   Stanislaw J. Lec

*   *

Like most censors he [Dr. Thomas Bowdler] was perfectly convinced that his own tastes were somehow in tune with the music of
the spheres . . . behind his complacency lay the assumption of a
Deity who had chosen to infuse into the Best People a practically
infallible sense of what was right, what wrong.
                                        —E. M. Halliday

The dirtiest book of all is the expurgated book.
—Walt Whitman (1819–1892)

*   *

Give me the liberty to know, to utter, and to argue freely according to conscience, above all liberties.
—John Milton (1608–1674)

Any country that has sexual censorship will eventually have political censorship.   —Kenneth Tynan

---

He [Molière] should be burned at the stake as a foretaste of the fires of hell.   —Pierre Roullé

It is impossible for ideas to compete in the marketplace if no forum for their presentation is provided or available.   —Thomas Mann

*   *

No member of a society has a right to teach any doctrine contrary to what the society holds to be true.
—Samuel Johnson (1709–1784)

The best test of truth is the power of the thought to get itself accepted in the competition of the market . . . We should be eternally vigilant against attempts to check the expression that we loathe.   —Oliver Wendell Holmes, Jr.

*   *

We are going to monitor every minute of your broadcast news, and if this kind of bias continues . . . you just might find yourself having a little trouble getting some of your licenses renewed.
—Frank Shakespeare

The ultimate censorship is the flick of the dial.
—Tom Smothers

CHANGE

There is nothing permanent except change.
—Heraclitus (540–475? B.C.)

Just because everything is different doesn't mean anything has changed.   —Irene Peter

The more the change the more it is the same thing.
—Alphonse Karr (1808–1890)

I reject get-it-done, make-it-happen thinking. I want to slow things down so I understand them better.   —Governor Jerry Brown

Let a man proclaim a new principle. Public sentiment will surely be on the other side.   —Thomas B. Reed

It is the nature of a man as he grows older . . . to protest against change, particularly change for the better.   —John Steinbeck

The philosophers have only interpreted the world; the thing, however, is to change it.   —Karl Marx (1818–1883)

It's the most unhappy people who most fear change.
                                        —Mignon McLaughlin

The art of progress is to preserve order amid change and to preserve change amid order.   —Alfred North Whitehead

Progress is a nice word. But change is its motivator and change has its enemies.   —Robert F. Kennedy

Society can only pursue its normal course by means of a certain progression of changes.   —John, Viscount Morley

The moral world is as little exempt as the physical world from the law of ceaseless change, of perpetual flux.   —Sir James Frazer

Man has a limited biological capacity for change. When this capacity is overwhelmed, the capacity is in future shock.
                                        —Alvin Toffler

Things do change. The only question is that since things are deteriorating so quickly, will society and man's habits change quickly enough?   —Isaac Asimov

The only sense that is common in the long run, is the sense of change—and we all instinctively avoid it.   —E. B. White

What we need is a flexible plan for an everchanging world.
                                        —Governor Jerry Brown

CHARACTER

Every man has three characters—that which he exhibits, that which he has, and that which he thinks he has.
                                        —Alphonse Karr (1808–1890)

A man never discloses his own character so clearly as when he describes another's.   —Jean Paul Richter (1763–1825)

Underneath this flabby exterior is an enormous lack of character.
                                        —Oscar Levant

A man's reputation is the opinion people have of him; his character is what he really is.   —Jack Miner

During my eighty-seven years I have witnessed a whole succession of technological revolutions. But none of them has done away with the need for character in the individual or the ability to think.
—Bernard M. Baruch

Character is destiny.   —Heraclitus (540–475? B.C.)

The measure of a man's real character is what he would do if he knew he never would be found out.
—Thomas Babington Macaulay (1800–1859)

Integrity has no need of rules.   —Albert Camus

The discipline of desire is the background of character.
—John Locke (1632–1704)

When some English moralists write about the importance of having character, they appear to mean only the importance of having a dull character.   —G. K. Chesterton

Even polished brass will pass upon more people than rough gold.
—Earl of Chesterfield (1694–1773)

The happiness of every country depends upon the character of its people, rather than the form of its government.
—Thomas Chandler Haliburton (1796–1865)

History is the record of an encounter between character and circumstance.   —Donald Creighton

---

No man knows of what stuff he is made until prosperity and ease try him.   —A. P. Gouthey

No man knows his true character until he has run out of gas, purchased something on the installment plan and raised an adolescent.
—Mercelene Cox

CHILDHOOD / CHILDREN

My mother loved children—she would have given anything if I had been one.   —Groucho Marx

The persons hardest to convince they're at the retirement age are children at bedtime.   —Shannon Fife (Infant care has to be learned from the bottom up.)

The best way to keep children home is to make the home atmosphere pleasant—and let the air out of the tires.

—Dorothy Parker

You can learn many things from children. How much patience you have, for instance.   —Franklin P. Jones (A characteristic of the normal child is he doesn't act that way very often.)

Children are unpredictable. You never know what inconsistency they're going to catch you in next.   —Franklin P. Jones

The modern child will answer you back before you've said anything.

—Laurence J. Peter

If a growing object is both fresh and spoiled at the same time, chances are it is a child.   —Morris Goldfischer (When a mother hasn't enough will power to discipline her children, she calls her weakness child psychology.)

Heredity is what a man believes in until his son begins to behave like a delinquent.   —*Presbyterian Life*

People who say they sleep like a baby usually don't have one.

—Leo J. Burke

Before I got married I had six theories about bringing up children; now I have six children and no theories.

—John Wilmot, Earl of Rochester (1647–1680)

I was not a child prodigy, because a child prodigy is a child who knows as much when it is a child as it does when it grows up.
—Will Rogers (A child prodigy is one with highly imaginative parents.)

"Handle this child carefully," the child specialist said to the mother. "Remember, you're dealing with a sensitive, high-strung little stinker."   —*L. & N.* magazine

By the time the youngest children have learned to keep the house tidy, the oldest grandchildren are on hand to tear it to pieces.

—Christopher Morley

The thing that impresses me most about America is the way parents obey their children.   —Duke of Windsor (On the other hand, some children never disobey because they are never told what to do.)

We've had bad luck with our kids—they've all grown up.

—Christopher Morley

In every child who is born, under no matter what circumstances, and of no matter what parents, the potentiality of the human race is born again; and in him, too, once more, and of each of us, our terrific responsibility towards human life; towards the utmost idea of goodness, of the horror of error, and of God.

—James Agee

Mankind owes to the child the best it has to give.

—U. N. Declaration

There are only two lasting bequests we can hope to give our children. One of these is roots; the other, wings.

—Hodding Carter

You know children are growing up when they start asking questions that have answers.   —John J. Plomp

We must have . . . a place where children can have a whole group of adults they can trust.   —Margaret Mead

As the twig is bent the tree inclines.   —Virgil (70–19 B.C.)

Children enjoy the present because they have neither a past nor a future.   —Jean de La Bruyère (1645–1696) (This may explain why everyone is in awe of the lion tamer in a cage with half a dozen lions—everyone but a school bus driver.)

Remember when your mother used to say, "Go to your room—"? This was a terrible penalty. Now when a mother says the same thing, a kid goes to his room. There he's got an air-conditioner, a TV set, an inter-com, a shortwave radio—he's better off than he was in the first place.   —Sam Levenson

The first idea that the child must acquire, in order to be actively disciplined, is that of the difference between good and evil; and the task of the educator lies in seeing that the child does not confound good with immobility, and evil with activity . . . our aim is to discipline for activity, for work, for good; not for immobility, not for passivity, not for obedience.   —Maria Montessori

You can do anything with children if you only play with them.

—Prince Otto von Bismarck (1815–1898)

By the year 2000 we will, I hope, raise our children to believe in human potential, not God.   —Gloria Steinem

If a child lives with approval, he learns to live with himself.

—Dorothy Law Nolte

———

Separating Negro children from others of similar age and qualifications because of their race generates a feeling of inferiority that may affect their hearts and minds in a way unlikely ever to be undone.

—Chief Justice Earl Warren

Kids lead a tough life . . . Kids and my people have a lot in common . . . Only our problems aren't solved by getting older.

—Dick Gregory

*   *

A three-year-old child is a being who gets almost as much fun out of a fifty-six dollar set of swings as it does out of finding a small green worm.   —Bill Vaughan

If you want to see what children can do, you must stop giving them things.   —Norman Douglas

*   *

When asked why he did not become a father, Thales answered, "Because I am fond of children."

—Diogenes Laertius (c. 150 B.C.)

A son of my own! Oh, no, no, no! Let my flesh perish with me, and let me not transmit to anyone the boredom and the ignominiousness of life.   —Gustave Flaubert (1821–1880)

*   *

Give me the children until they are seven and anyone may have them afterwards.   —Saint Francis Xavier (1506–1552)

Give me half a dozen healthy infants and my own world to bring them up in, and I will guarantee to turn each one of them into any kind of man you please.   —Professor John B. Watson

*   *

Parents are the last people on earth who ought to have children.

—Samuel Butler

The secret of dealing successfully with a child is not to be its parent.

—Mell Lazarus

*   *

All children are essentially criminal.

—Denis Diderot (1713–1784)

I must have been an insufferable child; all children are.

—George Bernard Shaw

*   *

In every real man a child is hidden that wants to play.

—Friedrich Nietzsche (1844–1900)

Everyone is the Child of his past.   —Edna G. Rostow

*   *

Mothers of prejudiced children, far more often than mothers of unprejudiced children, held that obedience is the most important thing a child can learn. —Gordon W. Allport

Too often we give children answers to remember rather than problems to solve. —Roger Lewin

* *

Children are a great comfort in your old age—and they help you reach it faster, too. —Lionel Kauffman

Insanity is hereditary; you can get it from your children.
—Sam Levenson

You are to have as strict a guard upon yourself amongst your children, as if you were amongst your enemies.
—Lord Halifax (George Savile) (1633–1695)

Children need love, especially when they do not deserve it.
—Harold S. Hulbert (In bringing up children, spend on them half as much money and twice as much time.)

* *

A man's destiny stands not in the future but in the past. That, rightly considered, is the most vital of all vital facts. Every child thus has a right to choose his own ancestors.
—Havelock Ellis

'Tis education forms the common mind:/Just as the twig is bent, the tree's inclined. —Alexander Pope (1688–1744)

* *

Most of us become parents long before we have stopped being children. —Mignon McLaughlin (A child psychologist starts out with learning what's wrong with his parents, and ends up with learning what's wrong with their parents.)

* *

Children are our most valuable natural resource.
—Herbert Hoover

The noblest works and foundation have proceeded from childless men. —Francis Bacon (Who gave no hostages to fortune.)

* *

The moment the little boy is concerned with which is a jay and which is a sparrow, he can no longer see the birds or hear them sing. —Eric Berne

A boy may be a brilliant mathematician . . . at the age of thirteen. But I never knew a child of that age who had much that was useful to say about the ends of human life.
—Robert Maynard Hutchins

*   *

The fault no child ever loses is the one he was most punished for.
—Cesare Beccaria (1738?–1794)

Every child should have an occasional pat on the back as long as it is applied low enough and hard enough.
—Bishop Fulton J. Sheen

*   *

Likely as not, the child you can do the least with will do the most to make you proud.   —Mignon McLaughlin

Reasoning with a child is fine, if you can reach the child's reason without destroying your own.   —John Mason Brown (Give a child enough rope and he will trip you up.)

CHRISTIAN / CHRISTIANITY

To be like Christ is to be a Christian.
—William Penn (1644–1718)

Ethical man—a Christian holding four aces.   —Mark Twain

When I mention religion I mean the Christian religion: and not only the Christian religion but the Protestant religion: and not only the Protestant religion but the Church of England.
—Henry Fielding (1707–1754)

I maintain Christianity is a life much more than a religion.
—R. M. Moberly

The government of the United States is not in any sense founded upon the Christian religion.   —John Adams (1735–1826)

Christian life consists of faith and charity.
—Martin Luther (1483–1546)

Science has done more for the development of western civilization in one hundred years than Christianity did in eighteen hundred years.   —John Burroughs

I have now disposed of all my property to my family. There is one thing more I wish I could give them, and that is the Christian religion.   —Patrick Henry (1736–1799)

What I got in Sunday-School . . . was simply a firm conviction that the Christian faith was full of palpable absurdities, and the Christian God preposterous . . . The act of worship, as carried on by Christians, seems to me to be debasing rather than ennobling. It involves grovelling before a Being who, if He really exists, deserves to be denounced instead of respected.

—H. L. Mencken

Christianity, above all, has given a clear-cut answer to the demands of the human soul. —Alexis Carrel

I call Christianity the one great curse, the one enormous and innermost perversion, the one great instinct of revenge, for which no means are too venomous, too underhand, too underground and too petty—I call it the one immortal blemish of mankind.

—Friedrich Nietzsche (1844–1900)

There is no real difference between worldly and heavenly wisdom. For religion consecrates daily life.

—John Lubbock (1803–1865)

The memory of my own suffering has prevented me from ever shadowing one young soul with the superstitions of the Christian religion. —Elizabeth Cady Stanton

The Christian religion not only was at first attended with miracles, but even at this day cannot be believed by any reasonable person without one. —David Hume (1711–1776)

People in general are equally horrified at hearing the Christian religion doubted, and at seeing it practiced. —Samuel Butler

The world is equally shocked at hearing Christianity criticized and seeing it practiced. —D. Elton Trueblood

*　　*

To raise society to a higher level is the chief business of the Church. To overcome evil with good is the genius of Christianity.

—A. P. Gouthey

Christianity might be a good thing if anyone ever tried it.

—George Bernard Shaw

*　　*

When once the Apostle Paul had posited universal love between men as the foundation of his Christian community, extreme intolerance on the part of Christendom towards those who remained outside it became the inevitable consequence.

—Sigmund Freud

The First Crusade . . . set off on its two-thousand mile jaunt by massacring Jews, plundering and slaughtering all the way from the Rhine to the Jordan. "In the temple of Solomon," wrote the ecstatic cleric, Raimundus de Agiles, "one rode in blood up to the knees and even to the horses' bridles, by the just and marvelous Judgment of God!"   —Herbert J. Muller

* *

The test of Christian character should be that a man is a joy-bearing agent to the world.   —Henry Ward Beecher (1813–1887)

Being a Christian is more than just an instantaneous conversion— it is a daily process whereby you grow to be more and more like Christ.   —Billy Graham

* *

A Christian is a man who feels repentance on a Sunday for what he did on Saturday and is going to do on Monday.
     —Thomas R. Ybarra

Most of us spend the first six days of each week sowing wild oats, then we go to church on Sunday and pray for a crop failure.
     —Fred Allen

* *

I consider Christian theology to be one of the great disasters of the human race . . . it would be impossible to imagine anything more un-Christlike than theology. Christ probably couldn't have understood it.   —Alfred North Whitehead

Christian theology is not only opposed to the scientific spirit; it is opposed to every other form of rational thinking.
     —H. L. Mencken

———————

The most glorious thing in life is to be a Christian. The most exalted privilege in life is to have intimate daily, hourly fellowship with God.   —A. P. Gouthey

He who begins by loving Christianity better than Truth, will proceed by loving his sect or church better than Christianity, and end in loving himself better than all.
     —Samuel Taylor Coleridge (1772–1834)

* *

There never was found in any age of the world, either philosopher or sect, or law, or discipline which did so highly exalt the public good as the Christian faith.   —Francis Bacon (1561–1626)

It can do truth no service to blink the fact . . . that a large portion of the noblest and most valuable teaching has been the work, not only of men who did not know, but of men who knew and rejected, the Christian faith. —John Stuart Mill (1806–1873)

* *

Man is raw and wild, that is one of the reasons why he needs the Christian teaching. —Alfred Armand Montapert

For Shakespeare, in the matter of religion, the choice lay between Christianity and nothing. He chose nothing.

—George Santayana

* *

All diseases of Christians are to be ascribed to demons.
—Saint Augustine (354–430)

The age of ignorance commenced with the Christian system.
—Thomas Paine (1737–1809)

* *

Organized Christianity has probably done more to retard the ideals that were its founder's than any other agency in the world.
—Richard Le Gallienne

Mothers and Dads that take their children to church never get into trouble. —J. Edgar Hoover (But going to church doesn't make you a Christian any more than going to the garage makes you a car.)

CITIES

All cities are mad, but the madness is gallant. All cities are beautiful, but the beauty is grim. —Christopher Morley

The individual who pollutes the air with his factory and the ghetto kid who breaks store windows both represent the same thing. They don't care about each other—or what they do to each other.
—Daniel Patrick Moynihan

In a real estate man's eye, the most exclusive part of the city is wherever he has a house to sell. —Will Rogers

A hick town is one where there is no place to go where you shouldn't go. —Alexander Woollcott (It's a place where it's no sooner done than said.)

There are just three big cities in the United States that are *story cities*—New York, of course, New Orleans, and best of the lot, San Francisco.   —Frank Norris

Hollywood—a place where people from Iowa mistake each other for movie stars.   —Fred Allen

Hollywood—a place where the inmates are in charge of the asylum.
—Laurence Stallings

Hollywood: They know only one word of more than one syllable here, and that is *fillum*.   —Louis Sherwin

Behind the phony tinsel of Hollywood lies the real tinsel.
—Oscar Levant

Boston—a festering mud puddle.   —Ellis Arnall

Boston is a moral and intellectual nursery always busy applying first principles to trifles.   —George Santayana (It has also been called the Athens of America and the place where the tide goes out and never comes back.)

Chicago has a strange metaphysical elegance of death about it.
—Claes Oldenburg

Chicago—a pompous Milwaukee.   —Leonard Louis Levinson

That's great advertising when you can turn Chicago into a city you'd want to spend more than three hours in.
—Jerry Della Femina

A hundred years ago Cincinnati was often called *Porkopolis* because so many hogs were butchered and processed there.
—J. C. Furnas

Cleveland—Two Hobokens back to back.   —Joan Holman (Contest Announcement: First prize—one week in Cleveland. Second prize—two weeks in Cleveland.)

This dismal Cairo [Illinois], an ugly sepulchre, a grave uncheered by any gleam of promise.   —Charles Dickens (1812–1870)

Beverly Hills—a pool's paradise.   —Leonard Louis Levinson (And Pasadena—a cemetery with lights.)

Oh to be in L.A. when the polyethyl-vinyl trees are in bloom!
—Herb Gold

Los Angeles—a town where you can watch night baseball almost any afternoon.   —*Changing Times* (And where the neon lights go when they die. One hundred communities in search of a city. The Big Orange.)

[Los Angeles] a city no worse than others, a city rich and vigorous and full of pride, a city lost and beaten and full of emptiness.
—Raymond Chandler

I don't like the life here in New York. There is no greenery. It would make a stone sick.   —Nikita S. Khrushchev (When a New Yorker looks as if he has a suntan, it's probably rust.)

Purple-robed and pauper-clad,/Raving, rotten, money-mad;/A squirming herd in Mammon's mesh,/A wilderness of human flesh; /Crazed with avarice, lust, and rum,/New York, thy name's delirium.   —Byron Rufus Newton (New York is also called Fun City, The Big Apple, and a place halfway between Sodom and Gomorrah.)

On the whole I'd rather be in Philadelphia.   —W. C. Fields (We arrived in Philadelphia on Sunday but it wasn't open.)

San Diego is as close to Utopia as any American city of metropolitan size is likely to come.   —Jack Smith

San Diego didn't look like the kind of town where people get born.
—Steve Ellman

Two days brought us to San Pedro, and two days more (to our no small joy), gave us our last view of that place.
—Richard Henry Dana (1815–1882)

The pneumatic noisemaker is becoming the emblematic Sound of New York, the way the bells of Big Ben are the Sound of London.
—Horace Sutton

Cities are growing so fast their arteries are showing through their outskirts.   —Clyde Moore

*   *

The government of cities is the one conspicuous failure of the United States.   —James Bryce

The serious problems of the cities are largely insoluble now and will be for the foreseeable future.   —Edward C. Banfield

*   *

Only the modern city offers the mind the grounds on which it can achieve awareness of itself.
—Georg Wilhelm Hegel (1770–1831)

The city is not obsolete; it's the center of our civilization.
—Edward Logue

I'd rather wake up in the middle of nowhere than in any city on earth.
—Steve McQueen

I have never felt salvation in nature. I love cities above all.
—Michelangelo Antonioni

*   *

When you get there [Oakland], there isn't any there there.
—Gertrude Stein

The trouble with Oakland is that when you get there it's there!
—Herb Caen

*   *

I always seem to suffer from loss of faith on entering cities.
—Ralph Waldo Emerson (1803–1882)

The country only has charms for those not obliged to stay there.
—Édouard Manet

CITIZENS

The health of a democratic society may be measured by the quality of functions performed by private citizens.
—Alexis de Tocqueville (1805–1859)

Citizens pay their taxes, and then they abdicate. They have lost their skills as citizens; they have contracted them out to public employees.
—E. S. Savas

We are all citizens of history.   —Clifton Fadiman

People who develop the habit of thinking of themselves as world citizens are fulfilling the first requirement of sanity in our time . . . More and more, the choice for the world's people is between becoming world warriors or world citizens.   —Norman Cousins

The worth of a state, in the long run, is the worth of the individuals composing it.   —John Stuart Mill (1806–1873) (This includes the naturalized citizen, that is, one who becomes a citizen with his clothes on.)

I am a citizen, not of Athens or Greece, but of the world.
—Socrates (470?–399 B.C.)

CIVILIZATION

Civilization is a stream with banks. The stream is sometimes filled with blood from people killing, stealing, shouting and doing things historians usually record, while on the banks, unnoticed, people build homes, make love, raise children, sing songs, write poetry and even whittle statues. The story of civilization is the story of what happened on the banks. Historians are pessimists because they ignore the banks for the river.   —Will and Ariel Durant

We're born princes and the civilizing process turns us into frogs.
          —Eric Berne

The history of man is a graveyard of great cultures that came to catastrophic ends because of their incapacity for planned, rational, voluntary reaction to challenge.   —Erich Fromm

We live in a Newtonian world of Einsteinian physics ruled by Frankenstein logic.   —David Russell

Civilization is progress from an indefinite, incoherent homogeneity toward a definite, coherent heterogeneity.   —Herbert Spencer

The bones, sinews and nerves of modern civilization are coal, steel, cotton and wheat. He who controls these is mightier than the Lord.
          —B. Traven

Speech is civilization itself . . . It is silence which isolates.
          —Thomas Mann

The notion of primitive man possessing some inner peace which we civilized people have somehow lost, and need to regain, is a lot of nonsense. Your average New Guinea native lives not only in fear of his enemies, but in terror-struck dread of the unknown.
          —Gordon Linsley

Perfection of means and confusion of ends seem to characterize our age.   —Albert Einstein

To correct the evils, great and small, which spring from want of sympathy and from positive enmity among strangers, as nations or as individuals, is one of the highest functions of civilization.
          —Abraham Lincoln (1809–1865)

The only true hope for civilization—the conviction of the individual that his inner life can affect outward events and that, whether or not he does so, he is responsible for them.   —Stephen Spender

Intelligent discontent is the mainspring of civilization.
          —Eugene V. Debs

Civilization advances by extending the number of important operations which we can perform without thinking of them.
          —Alfred North Whitehead

To be able to fill leisure intelligently is the last product of civilization.
          —Arnold Toynbee

To have doubted one's own first principles is the mark of a civilized man.   —Oliver Wendell Holmes, Jr.

The inventor tries to meet the demand of a crazy civilization. —Thomas Alva Edison (Nowadays civilization is not at the cross-roads; it's at the cloverleaves.)

———————

Civilization is a race between education and catastrophe.
                —H. G. Wells

Education is the transmission of civilization.
          —Will and Ariel Durant

*   *

This strange disease of modern life with its brisk hurry and divided aims.   —Matthew Arnold (1822–1888)

No man who is in a hurry is quite civilized.
          —Will and Ariel Durant

*   *

The People, though we think of a great entity when we use the word, means nothing more than so many millions of individual men.
              —James Bryce

Society in its full sense . . . is never an entity separable from the individuals who compose it. No individual can arrive even at the threshold of his potentialities without a culture in which he partici-pates. Conversely, no civilization has in it any element which in the last analysis is not the contribution of an individual.
              —Ruth Benedict

*   *

Civilization is nothing else but the attempt to reduce force to being the last resort.   —José Ortega y Gasset

Civilization—the victory of persuasion over force.
              —Palmer Wright

*   *

You can't say that civilization don't advance, for in every war they kill you a new way.   —Will Rogers

Whatever fosters militarism makes for barbarism; whatever fosters peace makes for civilization.   —Herbert Spencer

*   *

Civilization is the encouragement of differences. Civilization thus becomes a synonym of democracy. Force, violence, pressure, or compulsion with a view to conformity, is both uncivilized and un-democratic.   —Mohandas Gandhi

Commandment Number One of any truly civilized society is this: Let people be different.　—David Grayson

*　　*

The end of the human race will be that it will eventually die of civilization.　—Ralph Waldo Emerson (1803–1882)

We can destroy ourselves by cynicism and disillusion just as effectively as by bombs.　—Kenneth Clark

*　　*

If all the perverted ingenuity which was put into making automobiles had only gone into improving the breed of horses, we might be a lot better off today.　—Joe Gould

I have always considered that the substitution of the internal combustion engine for the horse marked a very gloomy milestone in the progress of mankind.　—Winston Churchill

---

Civilization is a method of living, an attitude of equal respect for all men.　—Jane Addams

A visitor from Mars could easily pick out the civilized nations. They have the best implements of war.　—Herbert V. Prochnow

*　　*

Civilization and profits go hand in hand.　—Calvin Coolidge

What has destroyed every previous civilization has been the tendency to the unequal distribution of wealth and power.
—Henry George (1839–1897)

*　　*

It is impossible to overlook the extent to which civilization is built up upon a renunciation of instinct, how much it presupposes precisely the nonsatisfaction (by suppression, repression or some other means) of powerful instincts.　—Sigmund Freud

The flush toilet is the basis of Western civilization.
—Alan Coult

CIVIL RIGHTS

The 1964 Civil Rights Act was the best thing that ever happened to the South in my lifetime.　—James Earl Carter

Nothing then is unchangeable but the inherent and inalienable rights of man.　—Thomas Jefferson (1743–1826)

With every civil right there has to be a corresponding civil obligation.
—Edison Haines

The obligation to endure gives us the right to know.
—Jean Rostand

The population-environment movement is absolutely inseparable from the antiwar movement, the drive for urban rehabilitation, prison reform, and—most importantly—the civil rights movement.
—Dr. Paul R. Ehrlich

Many today seem to be demanding for themselves the unlimited right to disobey the law . . . an essential concomitant of civil disobedience is the actor's willingness to accept the punishment that follows.   —Earl Morris

Behind the phrase law and order many conceal their opposition to civil rights enforcement and to dissent.   —Ramsey Clark (On second thought, civil liberties are always safe as long as their exercise doesn't bother anyone.)

I will not load or fire any weapon except when authorized by an officer under specific conditions, or when required to save my life.
—Order No. 3 of the *Special Orders for Members of the Armed Forces Engaged in Civil Disturbance Operations*

If some people got their rights they would complain of being deprived of their wrongs.   —Oliver Herford

---

Law enforcement is a protecting arm of civil liberties. Civil liberties cannot exist without law enforcement; law enforcement without civil liberties is a hollow mockery.   —J. Edgar Hoover

Of all the tasks of government the most basic is to protect its citizens against violence.   —John Foster Dulles

*   *

What men value in this world is not rights but privileges.
—H. L. Mencken

The suppression of civil liberties is to many less a matter for horror than the curtailment of the freedom to profit.   —Marya Mannes

---

The rights you have are the rights given you by this Committee (HUAC). *We* will determine what rights you have and what rights you have not got.   —J. Parnell Thomas

I am the inferior of any man whose rights I trample underfoot.
—Horace Greeley (1811–1872)

*   *

I've voted against them [civil rights] . . . What you're doing is creating rights at the expense of other people.

—Benjamin R. Blackburn

The single overriding cause of rioting in the cities was . . . the insidious and pervasive white sense of the inferiority of black men.

—Report of the National Advisory Commission on Civil Disorders

COLLEGES / UNIVERSITIES

A man who has never gone to school may steal from a freight car; but if he has a university education, he may steal the whole railroad.

—Theodore Roosevelt

A university is what a college becomes when the faculty loses interest in students.   —John Ciardi

When a subject becomes totally obsolete we make it a required course.   —Peter Drucker

Our educational system disqualifies people for honest work.

—Peter Drucker

In business school classrooms they construct wonderful models of a nonworld.   —Peter Drucker

College professor—someone who talks in other people's sleep.

—Bergen Evans

The things taught in schools and colleges are not an education, but the means of education.

—Ralph Waldo Emerson (1803–1882)

It takes me several days, after I get back to Boston, to realize that the reference "the president" refers to the president of Harvard and not to a minor official in Washington.

—Oliver Wendell Holmes, Jr.

Socrates gave no diplomas or degrees, and would have subjected any disciple who demanded one to a disconcerting catechism on the nature of true knowledge.   —G. M. Trevelyan

I adore Rochdale College. It's exactly like Paris during the riots. Garbage everywhere.   —Fernando Arrabal

In my college days seniors used to vote on a number of questions, among them whether *education* or *contacts* had been the most valuable gain of the past four years. *Contacts* always won.

—Barrows Dunham

Freedom of inquiry, freedom of discussion, and freedom of teaching —without these a university cannot exist.
—Robert Maynard Hutchins

A university does great things, but there is one thing it does not do; it does not intellectualize its neighborhood.
—John Henry, Cardinal Newman (1801–1890)

If the median scores made by college graduates on the Army General Classification Test are a reliable criterion, our best brains go into the physical sciences, including engineering; our second best into law; and our third best into English . . . At the bottom, in this order: Education, Home Economics, and Physical Education.
—Joseph Wood Krutch

The university exists only to find and to communicate the truth.
—Robert Maynard Hutchins

The university is the only institution in Western society whose business it is to search for and transmit truth regardless of all competing or conflicting pressures and demands; pressures for immediate usefulness, for social approval, pressures to serve the special interests of government, a class, a professional group, a race, a faith, even a nation.   —Henry Steele Commager

*   *

Fathers send their sons to college either because they went to college or because they didn't.   —L. L. Hendren (It took a college education for a parent to afford a son's college education. The son's diploma is the receipt for the bills his father paid.)

Economists report that a college education adds many thousands of dollars to a man's lifetime income—which he then spends sending his son to college.   —Bill Vaughan (The best way to keep the wolf from the door is with a sheepskin.)

*   *

Colleges teach the dead languages as if they were buried and the living ones as if they were dead.   —Frank Moore Colby (Latin is used on tombstones because it's a dead language.)

It is possible for a student to win twelve letters at a university without his learning how to write one.
—Robert Maynard Hutchins

*   *

Education does not mean a college education. The author of the Gettysburg Address and the Second Inaugural could hardly be called uneducated.   —Bergen Evans

The typical liberal-arts college . . . . merely offers a smorgasbord of courses.   —John Fischer

---

The college no longer exists to produce men qua men, men prepared for life in a society of men, but men as specialized experts, men prepared for employment in an industry or a profession. But the educated man, the man capable not of providing specialized answers, but of asking the great and liberating questions by which humanity makes its way through time, is not more frequently encountered than he was two hundred years ago.

—Archibald MacLeish

It is evident that in democratic communities the interest of individuals, as well as the security of the commonwealth, demands that the education of the greater number should be scientific, commercial, and industrial, rather than literary.

—Alexis de Tocqueville (1805–1859)

*   *

I also believe that academic freedom should protect the right of a professor or student to advocate Marxism, socialism, communism, or any other minority viewpoint—no matter how distasteful to the majority, provided . . .   —Richard M. Nixon (Honesty, like liberty, will not survive in statutes if it has died in the hearts of men.)

What are our schools for if not indoctrination against Communism?

—Richard M. Nixon

*   *

The chief value in going to college is that it's the only way to learn it really doesn't matter.   —George Edwin Howes

Those who worry about radicalism in our schools and colleges are often either reactionaries who themselves do not bear allegiance to the traditional American principles, or defeatists who despair of the success of our own philosophy in an open competition.

—James Bryant Conant

*   *

A liberal education . . . frees a man from the prison-house of his class, race, time, place, background, family and even his nation.

—Robert Maynard Hutchins

I don't believe in education for most people. Teach them how to use a lathe and let it go at that.   —Kevin P. Phillips

COMMITTEES

Committee—a group of men who individually can do nothing but as a group decide that nothing can be done.   —Fred Allen (To kill time, a committee meeting is the perfect weapon.)

Committee—a group of the unfit, appointed by the unwilling, to do the unnecessary.   —Stewart Harrol (To get something done, a committee should consist of no more than three men, two of them absent.)

You'll find in no park or city/A monument to a committee. —Victoria Pasternak (Committees have become so important nowadays that subcommittees have to be appointed to do the work.)

Committee—a group of men who keep minutes and waste hours.
—Milton Berle

A committee is a thing which takes a week to do what one good man can do in an hour.   —Elbert Hubbard

A camel looks like a horse that was planned by a committee.
—*Vogue* magazine, July, 1958

No committee could ever come up with anything as revolutionary as a camel—anything as practical and as perfectly designed to perform effectively under such difficult conditions.
—Laurence J. Peter

COMMUNICATION

Silence gives consent, or a horrible feeling that nobody's listening.
—Franklin P. Jones

I have never been able to understand why it is that just because I am unintelligible nobody understands me.   —Milton Mayer

The ancient sage who concocted the maxim, "Know Thyself" might have added, "Don't Tell Anyone!"   —H. F. Henrichs

"The Medium is the Message" because it is the medium that shapes and controls the search and form of human associations and action.
—Marshall McLuhan

The marvels—of film, radio, and television—are marvels of one-way communication, which is not communication at all.
—Milton Mayer (On second thought, the advantage of modern means of communication is that they enable you to worry about things in all of the world.)

The purpose of all higher education is to make men aware of what was and what is; to incite them to probe into what may be. It seeks to teach them to understand, to evaluate, to communicate.
—Otto Kleppner

Extremists think "communication" means agreeing with them.
—Leo Rosten

It is a luxury to be understood.
—Ralph Waldo Emerson (1803–1882)

What a man really says when he says that someone else can be persuaded by force, is that he himself is incapable of more rational means of communication.   —Norman Cousins

Good communication is as stimulating as black coffee, and just as hard to sleep after.   —Anne Morrow Lindbergh

---

To work through an interpreter is like hacking one's way through a forest with a feather.   —James Evans

"Out of sight, out of mind," when translated into Russian [by computer], then back again into English, became "invisible maniac."
—Arthur Calder-Marshall

*   *

Be obscure clearly.   —E. B. White

The *Mets* has come along slow, but fast!   —Casey Stengel

*   *

The prime purpose of eloquence is to keep other people from speaking.   —Louis Vermeil

Though I'm anything but clever,/I could talk like that forever.
—W. S. Gilbert

*   *

The most immutable barrier in nature is between one man's thoughts and another's.   —William James

You'll never really know what I mean and I'll never know exactly what you mean.   —Mike Nichols

What this country needs is more free speech worth listening to.
—Hansell B. Duckett

To say the right thing at the right time, keep still most of the time.
—John W. Roper

*   *

The older I grow, the more I listen to people who don't say much.
—Germain G. Glidden

A lecture is an occasion when you numb one end to benefit the other.   —John Gould

*   *

Communication is something so simple and difficult that we can never put it in simple words.   —T. S. Matthews

The best argument is that which seems merely an explanation.
—Dale Carnegie

*   *

To say what you think will certainly damage you in society; but a free tongue is worth more than a thousand invitations.
—Logan Pearsall Smith

Repartee: What a person thinks of after he becomes a departee.
—Dan Bennett

COMMUNISM / SOCIALISM

Any pitcher who throws at a batter and deliberately tries to hit him is a Communist.   —Alvin Dark

Eisenhower told me never to trust a Communist.
—Lyndon B. Johnson (U-2, Ike?)

The theory of the Communists may be summed up in the single sentence: Abolition of private property.
—*The Communist Manifesto*

Socialism is nothing but the capitalism of the lower classes.
—Oswald Spengler

The youth of today and of those to come after them would assess the work of the revolution in accordance with values of their own . . . a thousand years from now, all of them, even Marx, Engels, and Lenin, would possibly appear rather ridiculous.
—Mao Tse-tung

The Communist system must be based on the will of the people, and if the people should not want that system, then that people should establish a different system.   —Nikita S. Khrushchev (Democracy can learn some things from Communism: for example, when a Communist politician is through, he is through.)

Authoritarian socialism has failed almost everywhere, but you will not find a single Marxist who will say it has failed because it was wrong or impractical. He will say it has failed because nobody went far enough with it. So failure never proves that a myth is wrong. —Jean-François Revel (Socialism works, but nowhere as efficiently as in the beehive and the anthill.)

I would call the Democratic Left in Latin America the group which secures social advances for all the people in a framework of freedom and consent.   —Luis Muñoz Marin (Socialism is bureaucracy of the people, by the people, and for the people.)

The Russian dictatorship of the proletariat has made a farce of the whole Marxist vision: developing a powerful, privileged ruling class to prepare for a classless society, setting up the most despotic state in history so that the state may *wither away,* establishing by force a colonial empire to combat imperialism and unite the workers of the world.   —Herbert J. Muller

One does not have to keep bad governments in to keep Communists out.   —John Kenneth Galbraith

We should have had socialism already, but for the socialists.
—George Bernard Shaw

The inherent vice of capitalism is the unequal sharing of blessings; the inherent virtue of socialism is the equal sharing of miseries.
—Winston Churchill

The function of socialism is to raise suffering to a higher level.
—Norman Mailer

*   *

I am a firm believer in socialism and I know that the quicker you have monopoly in this country the quicker you will have socialism.
—Charles P. Steinmetz

The alternative to the totalitarian state is the cooperative commonwealth.   —Norman Thomas

---

In the economic sense, our socialism was more like state capitalism . . . Marx had never dreamed of anything of the sort . . . Soviet

Russia had broken with everything in her history that was revolutionary, and had got onto the usual rails of great-power imperialism.
—Svetlana Alliluyeva

Socialism is workable only in heaven where it isn't needed, and in hell where they've got it.   —Cecil Palmer

* *

There are as many Communists in the freedom movement as there are Eskimos in Florida.   —Martin Luther King, Jr.

Martin Luther King is the most notorious liar in the country.
—J. Edgar Hoover

* *

Communism is a society where each one works according to his ability and gets according to his needs.
—Pierre Joseph Proudhon (1809–1865)

Socialism will never destroy poverty and the injustice and inequality of capacities.   —Count Leo Tolstoy

* *

The rich experience of history teaches that *up to now* not a single class has voluntarily made way for another class.
—Joseph Stalin

A proletarian dictatorship is never proletarian.
—Will and Ariel Durant

* *

The Communist Party cannot be neutral toward religion. It stands for science, and all religion is opposed to science.
—Joseph Stalin

Communism, like any other revealed religion, is largely made up of prophecies.   —H. L. Mencken

COMPETENCE / INCOMPETENCE

Public office is the last refuge of the incompetent.   —Boies Penrose (The incompetent with nothing to do can still make a mess of it.)

So much of what we call management consists in making it difficult for people to work.   —Peter Drucker

Whenever a man's failure can be traced to management's mistakes, he has to be kept on the payroll.   —Peter Drucker

Job enrichment has been around for sixty years. It's been successful every time it has been tried, but industry is not interested.
—Peter Drucker

In a hierarchy every employee tends to rise to his level of incompetence.   —Laurence J. Peter

Work is achieved by those employees who have not yet reached their level of incompetence.   —Laurence J. Peter

Competence, like truth, beauty and a contact lens, is in the eye of the beholder.   —Laurence J. Peter

If you don't know where you are going, you will probably end up somewhere else.   —Laurence J. Peter

There are some days when I think I'm going to die from an overdose of satisfaction.   —Salvador Dali

Walking isn't a lost art—one must, by some means, get to the garage.   —Evan Esar

Even if you're on the right track, you'll get run over if you just sit there.   —Will Rogers

When you get right down to the root of the meaning of the word "succeed," you find that it simply means to follow through.
—F. W. Nichol (The customer who's always right probably waits on himself.)

As I grow older, I pay less attention to what men say. I just watch what they do.   —Andrew Carnegie

The various admirable movements in which I have been engaged have always developed among their members a large lunatic fringe.
—Theodore Roosevelt (There is a difference between being not able and notable.)

CONCEIT

Conceit causes more conversation than wit.
—Duc de La Rochefoucauld (1613–1680)

When I went to America I had two secretaries, one for autographs, the other for locks of hair. Within six months the one had died of writer's cramp, the other was completely bald.
—Oscar Wilde (1854–1900)

There are people who say I have never really done anything wrong in my life; of course, they only say it behind my back.
—Oscar Wilde

Failures are usually the most conceited of men.

—D. H. Lawrence

If other people are going to talk, conversation becomes impossible.

—James McNeill Whistler

I can't tell you if genius is hereditary, because heaven has granted me no offspring.   —James McNeill Whistler

My specialty is being right when other people are wrong.

—George Bernard Shaw

If I had not been born Perón, I would have liked to be Perón.

—Juan Perón

The books I haven't written are better than the books other people have.   —Cyril V. Connolly

I am responsible only to God and history.

—Generalissimo Francisco Franco y Bahamonde

When an attorney characterized Frank Lloyd Wright as America's greatest architect, Wright confessed to his wife that he could not deny it because he was under oath.

It is hard to think at the top.   —Stringfellow Barr

I forgot they were talking about me. They sound so wonderfully convincing.   —Jean Giradoux

Perfection is such a nuisance that I often regret having cured myself of using tobacco.   —Émile Zola

Had I been present at the creation, I would have given some useful hints for the better ordering of the universe.

—King Alfonso X of Spain (1252–1284)

A self-made man? Yes—and worships his creator.

—William Cowper (1731–1800)

To my extreme mortification, I grow wiser every day.

—George Gordon, Lord Byron (1788–1824)

The finest steel has to go through the hottest fire.

—Richard M. Nixon

*   *

Compared to Velazquez I am nothing, but compared to contemporary painters, I am the most big genius of modern times . . . but modesty is not my specialty.   —Salvador Dali

One of my chief regrets during my years in the theater is that I couldn't sit in the audience and watch me.   —John Barrymore

*   *

I conceived at least one great love in my life, of which I was always the object.   —Albert Camus

To love oneself is the beginning of a lifelong romance.
—Oscar Wilde

When God invented man, he wanted him to look like me.
—Brian Oldfield

There cannot be a God because, if there were one, I would not believe that I was not He.
—Friedrich Nietzsche (1844–1900)

The British are very consistent. They were just as calm about my arrival tonight as they were back in 1924.   —Casey Stengel

I am incredibly eager . . . that the history which you are writing should give prominence to my name and praise it frequently.
—Marcus Tullius Cicero (106–43 B.C.)

I have written so accurately and honestly that my overall contribution will have to be considered by future students of my time.
—John O'Hara

To give an accurate and exhaustive account of that period would need a pen far less brilliant than mine.   —Max Beerbohm

CONFORMITY / NONCONFORMITY

You won't skid if you stay in a rut.   —Frank McKinney Hubbard ("Kin Hubbard") (A rut is a grave with the ends knocked out.)

If there is anything the nonconformist hates worse than a conformist it's another nonconformist who doesn't conform to the prevailing standards of nonconformity.   —Bill Vaughan

Force, violence, pressure, or compulsion with a view to conformity, are both uncivilized and undemocratic.   —Mohandas Gandhi

What is the new loyalty? It is, above all, conformity. It is the uncritical and unquestioning acceptance of America as it is . . . It rejects inquiry into the race question or socialized medicine, or public housing . . . regards as heinous any challenge to what is called *the system of private enterprise,* identifying that system with Americanism. It abandons evolution, repudiates the once popular concept of progress, and regards America as a finished product, perfect and complete.   —Henry Steele Commager

Avoid revolution or expect to get shot. Mother and I will grieve, but we will gladly buy a dinner for the National Guardsman who shot you.
                —Dr. Paul Williamson, father of a Kent State student

The race of men, while sheep in credulity, are wolves for conformity.   —Carl Van Doren

Every society honors its live conformists and its dead troublemakers.
                —Mignon McLaughlin

I believe that that community is already in process of dissolution where each man begins to eye his neighbor as a possible enemy, where nonconformity with the accepted creed, political as well as religious, is a mark of disaffection.   —Judge Learned Hand

The strongest bulwark of authority is uniformity; the least divergence from it is the greatest crime.   —Emma Goldman

Comedy is the last refuge of the nonconformist mind.
                —Gilbert Seldes

CONSCIENCE

Conscience was born when man had shed his fur, his tail, his pointed ears.   —Sir Richard Burton (1821–1890)

The unknown is an ocean. What is conscience? The compass of the unknown.   —Joseph Cook

Conscience is the inner voice that warns us that someone may be looking.   —H. L. Mencken (A clear conscience begins with a poor memory.)

. . . to forge in the smithy of my soul the uncreated conscience of my race.   —James Joyce (Conscience is something that tells you that instinct is wrong.)

I am more afraid of my own heart than of the pope and all his cardinals. I have within me the great pope, Self.
                —Martin Luther (1483–1546)

Conscience: A small, still voice that makes minority reports.
—Franklin P. Jones (It's also what makes a boy tell his mother before his sister does.)

The world has achieved brilliance without conscience. Ours is a world of nuclear giants and ethical infants.

—General Omar Bradley

His conscience always drove him on to an excess of geniality when he was conscious of feeling none.   —John Fowles (Conscience is the still, small voice which tells a candidate that what he is doing is likely to lose votes.)

The Anglo-Saxon conscience doesn't keep you from doing what you shouldn't; it just keeps you from enjoying it.

—Salvador de Madariaga

The New England conscience doesn't stop you from doing what you shouldn't; it just stops you from enjoying it.

—Cleveland Amory

Pop used to say about the Presbyterians, it don't prevent them committing all the sins there are, but it keeps them from getting any fun out of it.   —Christopher Morley

------

In matters of conscience, the law of the majority has no place.

—Mohandas Gandhi

How could a state be governed . . . if every individual remained free to obey or not to obey the law according to his private opinion?

—Thomas Hobbes (1588–1679)

CONSERVATION

Things are not as bad as they seem. They are worse.

—Bill Press

All of a sudden all these conservationists are coming out of the woodwork to tell us how to save Alaska.   —Ted Stevens

The only means of conservation is innovation.   —Peter Drucker (Conservation today is a grim synonym for survival.)

What are we to make of the flurry of industrial ads depicting everything from Standard Oil to Dow Chemical to the American Rifle Association as conservation-minded people?

—Barry Weisberg

His [Walter Heller's] idea: levy stiff taxes on the discharge of effluents . . . reward companies that did most to clean up the environment.   —*Time* magazine

European countries . . . treat timber as a crop. We treat timber resources as if they were a mine.   —Franklin Delano Roosevelt

Government cannot close its eyes to the pollution of waters, to the erosion of soil, to the slashing of forests any more than it can close its eyes to the need for slum clearance and schools.
        —Franklin Delano Roosevelt

It becomes increasingly obvious to all countries that the uneven distribution and consumption of resources . . . is morally, ethically, and practically unacceptable.   —Moshe Safdie

Man is a complex being: he makes deserts bloom—and lakes die.
        —Gil Stern

China has four times the population of the U. S. within a land area of roughly the same size. With intensive labor, scrupulous conservation of resources and recycling of human and animal wastes, the Chinese are feeding and supporting themselves without outside aid.
        —Donald MacInnis

People are easily anesthetized by overstatement, and there is a danger that the environmental movement will fall flat on its face when it is most needed, simply because it has pitched its tale too strongly.
        —John Maddox

Such prosperity as we have known it up to the present is the consequence of rapidly spending the planet's irreplaceable capital.
        —Aldous Huxley

Our ideals, laws and customs should be based on the proposition that each generation in turn becomes the custodian rather than the absolute owner of our resources—and each generation has the obligation to pass this inheritance on to the future.
        —Alden Whitman

CONSERVATIVES

The very word conservative means that we conserve all that is good, that we reject all that is bad, and we must use our intelligence, our intellect, our training for the purpose of determining what we shall reject and what we shall conserve and retain.   —R. B. Bennett

A conservative is a man who does not think that anything should be done for the first time.   —Frank Vanderlip (On second thought, he could be a Liberal who went into a holding pattern.)

Traditionalists are pessimists about the future and optimists about the past.   —Lewis Mumford

The conservative is led by disposition, not unmixed with pecuniary self-interest, to adhere to the familiar and the established.
—John Kenneth Galbraith (A conservative is like a player trying to steal second base while keeping his foot on first.)

Conservative, n. a statesman who is enamored of existing evils, as distinguished from the Liberal, who wishes to replace them with others.   —Ambrose Bierce

Conservatism . . . means not trusting to one's reasoning powers.
                                              —Charles S. Pearce

The conservatives want to lay off civil servants when it's the uncivil servants we should get rid of.   —Irene Peter

The most dangerous thing in the world is to leap a chasm in two jumps.   —David Lloyd George

Liberalism is trust of the people tempered by prudence; Conservatism is distrust of the people tempered by fear.
                                   —William Ewart Gladstone (1809–1898)

If a man is right he can't be too radical; if he is wrong, he can't be too conservative.
                          —Josh Billings (Henry Wheeler Shaw) (1818–1885)

Conservatism is the worship of dead revolutions.
                                              —Clinton Rossiter

Conservatism had to make universal the "why worry" technique.
                                              —Denton Massey

Conservatism is the maintenance of conventions already in force.
                                              —Thorstein Veblen

Their very conservatism is secondhand, and they don't know what they are conserving.   —Robertson Davies (A true conservative is one who can't see any difference between radicalism and an idea.)

The soul of most conservatism is sentimentality, and sentimentality preserves the good and the bad with indiscriminate relish.
                                              —Gwyn Thomas

I believe that the essential characteristic which identifies the Conservative is his belief that there is and must be an underlying moral and spiritual content to all political philosophy and action if it is to have lasting value.   —Fulton E. Davis

---

A man who is not a Liberal at sixteen has no heart; a man who is not a Conservative at sixty has no head.
                                   —Benjamin Disraeli (1804–1881)

I never dared be radical when young/For fear it would make me conservative when old.   —Robert Frost

*   *

The older generation almost always fails to understand the younger one—they think their own immutable values the only ones . . . And so the older generation barks like a dog at what they don't understand.   —Count Leo Tolstoy

The Conservatives do not believe it necessary, and, even if it were, we should oppose it.   —Quentin Hogg, M.P.

*   *

The modern conservative is engaged in one of man's oldest exercises in moral philosophy, that is the search for a superior moral justification for selfishness. It is an exercise which always involves a certain number of internal contradictions and even a few absurdities. The conspicuously wealthy turn up urging the character-building value of privation for the poor.   —John Kenneth Galbraith

This conservatism of the wealthy class is so obvious a feature that it has even come to be recognized as a mark of respectability . . . Conservatism, being an upper-class characteristic, is decorous; and conversely, innovation, being a lower-class phenomenon, is vulgar.
                                                    —Thorstein Veblen

*   *

A conservative is a man who is too cowardly to fight and too fat to run.   —Elbert Hubbard

No man can cause more grief than that one clinging blindly to the vices of his ancestors.   —William Faulkner

*   *

The middle of the road is where the white line is—and that's the worst place to drive.   —Robert Frost

The desire for safety stands against every great and noble enterprise.
                                                    —Tacitus (55?–130?)

Conservatism offers no redress for the present, and makes no preparation for the future.   —Benjamin Disraeli

The conservative who resists change is as valuable as the radical who proposes it.   —Will and Ariel Durant

*   *

A conservative is a man with two perfectly good legs who, however, has never learned how to walk forward.
                                                    —Franklin Delano Roosevelt

The conservative is the realist, taking over the side of all that is real, abiding, basic, fundamental.   —E. Merrill Root

*   *

A conservative is a man who just sits and thinks, mostly sits.
                                                —Woodrow Wilson

Stability is not immobility.
                    —Prince Klemens von Metternich (1773–1859)

*   *

We know what happens to people who stay in the middle of the road —they get run over.   —Aneurin Bevan

The middle of the road is all of the usable surface. The extremes, right and left, are in the gutters.   —Dwight D. Eisenhower

*   *

Conservatives are not necessarily stupid, but most stupid people are conservatives.   —John Stuart Mill (1806–1873)

But the world does move, and its motive power under God is the fearless thought and speech of those who dare to be in advance of their time . . . They are the masts and sails of the ship to which conservatism answers as ballast. The ballast is important—at times indispensable—but it would be of no account if the ship were not bound to go ahead.   —Horace Greeley (1811–1872)

*   *

But in this country [Canada] what is there for Conservatives to conserve or for Reformers to reform?   —Goldwin Smith

In most countries, people grow fiercely possessive of their property. It is a bastion of conservatism.   —Gordon W. Allport

CONSISTENCY

Consistency is the last refuge of the unimaginative.
                                    —Oscar Wilde (1854–1900)

The foolish and the dead alone never change their opinion.
                            —James Russell Lowell (1819–1891)

The only completely consistent people are the dead.
                                            —Aldous Huxley

Like all weak men he laid an exaggerated stress on not changing one's mind.   —Somerset Maugham

Nothing that isn't a real crime makes a man appear so contemptible and little in the eyes of the world as inconsistency.
                                —Joseph Addison (1672–1719)

If a politician murders his mother, the first response of the press or of his opponents will likely be not that it was a terrible thing to do, but rather that in a statement made six years before he had gone on record as being opposed to matricide.   —Meg Greenfield

Consistency requires you to be as ignorant today as you were a year ago.   —Bernard Berenson

A foolish consistency is the hobgoblin of little minds.
                         —Ralph Waldo Emerson (1803–1882)

Consistency is a paste jewel that only cheap men cherish.
                         —William Allen White

The only man who can change his mind is a man that's got one.
                         —Edward Noyes Westcott (1846–1898)

CONSTITUTION / BILL OF RIGHTS

The United States Constitution is law, the Declaration of Independence is not; and it is the Declaration of Independence, not the Constitution, that *legalizes* the overthrow of the government.
                         —Milton Mayer

The Constitution gives every American the inalienable right to make a damn fool of himself.   —John Ciardi.

The Constitution . . . speaks of liberty and prohibits the deprivation of liberty without due process of law. In prohibiting that deprivation the Constitution does not recognize an absolute and uncontrollable liberty.   —Chief Justice Charles Evans Hughes
(Some lawyers are clever enough to convince you that the Constitution is unconstitutional.)

We don't want nothing but the Constitution, no more, no less.
                         —Dick Gregory

It is very doubtful whether man is enough of a political animal to produce a good, sensible, serious and efficient constitution. All the evidence is against it.   —George Bernard Shaw

Taken to the streets, conflict is a destructive force; taken to the courts, conflict can be a creative force.   —Richard M. Nixon, discussing the Constitution at the National Conference on the Judiciary, March 11, 1971

The average citizen expresses pride in the American Bill of Rights and then seeks to protect his real estate by restrictive covenants.
                         —H. A. Overstreet

The Constitution not only is, but ought to be, what the judges say it is. —Chief Justice Charles Evans Hughes

The difficulty in modification of the Constitution makes the Supreme Court a very powerful body in shaping the course of our civilization.
—F. D. G. Ribble

*   *

An act of the legislature, repugnant to the constitution, is void.
—John Marshall (1755–1835) (When a corrupt official hasn't a leg to stand on, he stands on his constitutional rights.)

One who belongs to the most vilified and persecuted minority in history is not likely to be insensible to the freedom guaranteed by our Constitution.   —Justice Felix Frankfurter

*   *

The Constitution of the United States was made not merely for the generation that then existed, but for posterity—unlimited, undefined, endless, perpetual posterity.
—Henry Clay (1777–1852)

Constitutions should consist only of general provisions; the reason is that they must necessarily be permanent, and that they cannot calculate for the possible change of things.
—Alexander Hamilton (1757–1804)

If a State can prescribe, as a rule of civil conduct, that whites and blacks shall not travel as passengers in the same railroad coach, why may it not so regulate the use of the streets of its cities and towns as to compel white citizens to keep on one side of the street and black citizens to keep on the other?
—Justice John Marshall Harlan

The question before us is, whether the class of persons described in the plea in abatement compose a portion of this people, and are constituent members of this sovereignty. We think they are not . . . They were at that time considered as a subordinate and inferior class of beings . . . they had no rights which the white man was bound to respect.   —Chief Justice Roger B. Taney (1777–1864)

*   *

However you might feel about the Bill of Rights and the Constitution, they make you a beneficiary in perpetuity in principles, ideals, and they place an obligation on you.   —John Henry Faulk

Your Constitution is all sail and no anchor.
—Thomas Babington Macaulay (1800–1859)

CONVERSATION

The trouble with her is that she lacks the power of conversation but not the power of speech.   —George Bernard Shaw

If you think before you speak, the other fellow gets in his joke first.
—Ed Howe

Don't talk unless you can improve the silence.
—Vermont Proverb

To speak ill of others is a dishonest way of praising ourselves.
—Will and Ariel Durant

The real art of conversation is not only to say the right thing in the right place but to leave unsaid the wrong thing at the tempting moment.   —Dorothy Nevill

A good conversationalist is not one who remembers what was said, but says what someone wants to remember.   —John Mason Brown (On second thought, the world beats a path to your door if you produce better claptrap.)

Conversation means being able to disagree and still continue the conversation.   —Dwight MacDonald

Inject a few raisins of conversation into the tasteless dough of existence.   —O. Henry (William Sydney Porter) (Ignorance has its virtues: without it there would be mighty little conversation.)

One of the reasons that we find so few persons rational and agreeable in conversation is that there is hardly a person who does not think more of what he wants to say than of his answer to what is said.   —Duc de La Rochefoucauld (1613–1680)

No man would listen to you talk if he didn't know it was his turn next.   —Ed Howe

The misfortune of Goldsmith in conversation is this: he goes on without knowing how he is to get off.
—Samuel Johnson (1709–1784)

It is all right to hold a conversation but you should let go of it now and then.   —Richard Armour

---

Beware of the man who goes to cocktail parties not to drink but to listen.   —Pierre Daninos

It takes a great man to make a good listener.
                              —Sir Arthur Helps (1813–1875)

* *

If you don't say anything, you won't be called on to repeat it.
                              —Calvin Coolidge

Think twice before you speak—and you'll find everyone talking about something else.   —Francis Rodman

COURAGE / COWARDICE

A coward is a hero with a wife, kids, and a mortgage.   —Marvin Kitman (First or second mortgage? Wife?)

Bravery is being the only one who knows you're afraid.
                              —Franklin P. Jones

A timid person is frightened before a danger, a coward during the time, and a courageous person afterwards.
                              —Jean Paul Richter (1763–1825)

The bitter part of discretion is valor.   —Henry W. Nevinson

Courage is grace under pressure.   —Ernest Hemingway

Perfect valor is to do unwitnessed what we should be capable of doing before all the world.
                              —Duc de La Rochefoucauld (1613–1680)

No call alligator long mouth till you pass him.
                              —Jamaican Proverb

If you are brave too often, people will come to expect it of you.
                              —Mignon McLaughlin (A frightening idea!)

The nation had the lion's heart. I had the luck to give the roar.
                              —Winston Churchill

One man with courage makes a majority.
                              —Andrew Jackson (1767–1845)

Have the courage to live. Anyone can die.   —Robert Cody

Often the test of courage is not to die but to live.
                              —Conte Vittorio Alfieri (1749–1803)

* *

It is to the interest of the commonwealth of mankind that there should be some one who is unconquered, some one against whom fortune has no power.   —Seneca (4 B.C.–A.D. 65)

It is a blessed thing that in every age some one has had the individuality enough and courage enough to stand by his own convictions.   —Robert G. Ingersoll (1833–1899)

*   *

Coward, n. one who in a perilous emergency thinks with his legs.
—Ambrose Bierce

If God wanted us to be brave, why did he give us legs?
—Marvin Kitman

*   *

Courage is walking naked through a cannibal village.
—Leonard Louis Levinson

The only courage that matters is the kind that gets you from one moment to the next.   —Mignon McLaughlin

*   *

The more wit the less courage.
—Thomas Fuller (1608–1661)

This bosom friend of senators and congressmen was about as daring as an early Shirley Temple movie.
—James Thurber, speaking of Will Rogers

Coward: A man in whom the instinct of self-preservation acts normally.   —Sultana Zoraya

Pacifism is simply undisguised cowardice.   —Adolf Hitler

*   *

We must have courage to bet on our ideas, to take the calculated risk, and to act. Everyday living requires courage if life is to be effective and bring happiness.   —Maxwell Maltz

I dip my pen in the blackest ink, because I am not afraid of falling into my inkpot.   —Ralph Waldo Emerson (1803–1882)

*   *

Courage is a quality so necessary for maintaining virtue that it is always respected, even when it is associated with vice.
—Samuel Johnson (1709–1784)

It is courage the world needs, not infallibility . . . courage is always the surest wisdom.   —Sir Wilfred Grenfell

CREATIVITY

Creative intelligence in its various forms and activities is what makes man.   —James Harvey Robinson

The great creative individual . . . is capable of more wisdom and virtue than collective man ever can be.
                                    —John Stuart Mill (1806–1873)

Abstract ideas are the patterns two or more memories have in common. They are born whenever someone realizes that similarity . . . Creative thinking may mean simply the realization that there's no particular virtue in doing things the way they always have been done.   —Rudolf Flesch

Anxiety is the essential condition of intellectual and artistic creation . . . and everything that is finest in human history.
                                    —Charles Frankel

Now I really make the little idea from clay, and I hold it in my hand. I can turn it, look at it from underneath, see it from one view, hold it against the sky, imagine it any size I like, and really be in control almost like God creating something.
                                    —Henry Moore

Discipline and focused awareness . . . contribute to the act of creation.   —John Poppy

There is a correlation between the creative and the screwball. So we must suffer the screwball gladly.   —Kingman Brewster

The difference between a top-flight creative man and the hack is his ability to express powerful meanings indirectly.
                                    —Vance Packard

Personally, I would sooner have written *Alice in Wonderland* than the whole *Encyclopedia Britannica*.   —Stephen Leacock

To be willing to suffer in order to create is one thing; to realize that one's creation necessitates one's suffering, that suffering is one of the greatest of God's gifts, is almost to reach a mystical solution of the problem of evil.   —J. W. N. Sullivan

If you see in any given situation only what everybody else can see, you can be said to be so much a representative of your culture that you are a victim of it.   —S. I. Hayakawa

---

When I am . . . completely myself, entirely alone . . . or during the night when I cannot sleep, it is on such occasions that my ideas flow best and most abundantly. Whence and how these come I know not nor can I force them . . . Nor do I hear in my imagination the parts successively, but I hear them *gleich alles zusammen* (at the same time all together).

—Wolfgang Amadeus Mozart (1756–1791)

Somebody once asked Anton Bruckner: "Master, how, when, where did you think of the divine motif of your Ninth Symphony?" "Well, it was like this," Bruckner replied. "I walked up the Kahlenberg, and when it got hot and I got hungry, I sat down by a little brook and unpacked my Swiss cheese. And just as I open the greasy paper, that darn tune pops into my head!"

—Anton Bruckner (1825–1896)

*   *

One must not lose desires. They are mighty stimulants to creativeness, to love, and to long life.

—Alexander A. Bogomoletz

No matter how old you get, if you can keep the desire to be creative, you're keeping the man-child alive.   —John Cassavetes

*   *

The past is but the beginning of a beginning.   —H. G. Wells

Every beginning is a consequence—every beginning ends something.   —Paul Valéry

*   *

It is the function of creative men to perceive the relations between thoughts, or things, or forms of expression that may seem utterly different, and to be able to combine them into some new forms—the power to connect the seemingly unconnected.

—William Plomer

Research is to see what everybody else has seen, and to think what nobody else has thought.   —Albert Szent-Györgyi

---

For after the object is removed or the eye shut, we still retain an image of the things seen, though more obscure than when we see it . . . Imagination, therefore, is nothing but decaying sense.

—Thomas Hobbes (1588–1679)

The nature of artistic attainment is psychologically inaccessible to us.   —Sigmund Freud

*   *

Creativeness often consists of merely turning up what is already there. Did you know that right and left shoes were thought up only a little more than a century ago?   —Bernice Fitz-Gibbon

An idea is a feat of association.   —Robert Frost

*   *

Creativity is so delicate a flower that praise tends to make it bloom, while discouragement often nips it in the bud. Any of us will put out more and better ideas if our efforts are appreciated.
—Alex F. Osborn

Creative minds always have been known to survive any kind of bad training.   —Anna Freud

CRIME AND PUNISHMENT

You can get much farther with a kind word and a gun than you can with a kind word alone.   —Al Capone (It's strange that men should take up crime when there are so many legal ways to be dishonest.)

I'm convinced that every boy, in his heart, would rather steal second base than an automobile.   —Justice Tom Clark (The reason crime doesn't pay is that when it does it is called by a more respectable name.)

The professional arsonist builds vacant lots for money.
—Jimmy Breslin

Any company executive who overcharges the government more than $5 million will be fined $50 or have to go to traffic school three nights a week.   —Art Buchwald

If England treats her criminals the way she has treated me, she doesn't deserve to have any.   —Oscar Wilde (1854–1900)

When I came back to Dublin I was courtmartialed in my absence and sentenced to death in my absence, so I said they could shoot me in my absence.   —Brendan Behan

A kleptomaniac can't help helping himself.   —Henry Morgan

Prisons don't rehabilitate, they don't punish, they don't protect, so what the hell do they do?   —Governor Jerry Brown (Prison reform will not work until we start sending a better class of people there.)

For my part I think it a less evil that some criminals should escape than that the government should play an ignoble part.

—Oliver Wendell Holmes, Jr.

There are only two places in our world where time takes precedence over the job to be done: school and prison.   —William Glasser (Time is money, but not when you're doing it in jail.)

Only the man who has enough good in him to feel the justice of the penalty can be punished; the others can only be hurt.

—William Ernest Hocking

Under a government which imprisons any unjustly, the true place for a just man is also a prison.   —Henry David Thoreau (1817–1862) (The only man who should not be judged by the company he keeps is a warden.)

Penology . . . has become torture and foolishness, a waste of money and a cause of crime . . . a blotting out of sight and heightening of social anxiety.   —Paul Goodman

The vilest deeds like poison weeds/Bloom well in prison-air:/It is only what is good in Man/That wastes and withers there.

—Oscar Wilde

*   *

The reformative effect of punishment is a belief that dies hard, chiefly, I think, because it [punishment] is so satisfying to our sadistic impulses.   —Bertrand Russell

Our emotions cry for vengeance in the wake of a horrible crime, but we know that killing the criminal cannot undo the crime, will not prevent similar crimes by others, does not benefit the victim, destroys human life, and brutalizes society. If we are to still violence, we must cherish life.   —Ramsey Clark

*   *

Capital punishment . . . has always been a religious punishment and is irreconcilable with humanism.   —Albert Camus

Capital punishment is as fundamentally wrong as a cure for crime as charity is wrong as a cure for poverty.   —Henry Ford

*   *

Examination of the number of murders before and after the abolition of the death penalty does not support the theory that capital punishment has a unique deterrent effect.

—Capital Punishment, published by the UN, 1968

Let us call it by the name which, for lack of any other nobility, will at least give the nobility of truth, and let us recognize it for what it essentially is: a revenge.   —Albert Camus

*   *

The crime problem is in part an overdue debt that the country must pay for ignoring for decades the conditions that breed lawlessness.
—Chief Justice Earl Warren

Poverty is the mother of crime.
—Marcus Aurelius (121–180)

*   *

Juvenile delinquency starts in the high chair and ends in the death chair.   —James D. C. Murray

When I see the *Ten Most Wanted Lists* . . . I always have this thought: If we'd made them feel wanted earlier, they wouldn't be wanted now.   —Eddie Cantor

*   *

Crime is contagious. If the government becomes a lawbreaker, it breeds contempt for the law.   —Justice Louis D. Brandeis

Nothing so upholds the laws as the punishment of persons whose rank is as great as their crime.
—Cardinal Richelieu (1585–1642)

We have to condemn publicly the very *idea* that some people have the right to repress others. In keeping silent about evil, in burying it so deep within us that no sign of it appears on the surface, we are *implanting* it, and it will rise up a thousandfold in the future. When we neither punish nor reproach evildoers . . . we are ripping the foundations of justice from beneath new generations.
—Alexander I. Solzhenitsyn

Distrust all men in whom the impulse to punish is powerful.
—Friedrich Nietzsche (1844–1900)

*   *

The death penalty will seem to the next generation, as it seems to many even now, an anachronism too discordant to be suffered, mocking with grim reproach all our clamorous professions of the sanctity of life.   —Justice Benjamin N. Cardozo

The long and distressing controversy over capital punishment is very unfair to anyone meditating murder.   —Geoffrey Fisher

CRITICISM / CRITICS

The actual definition of reviewmanship is now, I think, stabilized. In its shortest form it is "How to be one-up on the author without actually tampering with the text." In other words, how, as a critic, to show that it is really you yourself who should have written the book, if you had had the time, and since you hadn't you are glad that someone else has, although obviously it might have been done better.   —Stephen Potter

I was so long writing my review that I never got around to reading the book.   —Groucho Marx

A critic is a legless man who teaches running.
                                            —Channing Pollock

A critic is a man who knows the way but can't drive the car.
                                            —Kenneth Tynan

Criticism is a study by which men grow important and formidable at very small expense.   —Samuel Johnson (1709–1784)

Never answer a critic, unless he's right.   —Bernard M. Baruch

To escape criticism—do nothing, say nothing, be nothing.
                                            —Elbert Hubbard

Can't a critic give his opinion of an omelette without being asked to lay an egg?   —Clayton Rawson (Should one refrain from criticizing Shakespeare unless one can write like Shakespeare?)

I had another dream the other day about music critics. They were small and rodent-like with padlocked ears, as if they had stepped out of a painting by Goya.   —Igor Stravinsky

A critic is a man created to praise greater men than himself, but he is never able to find them.   —Richard Le Gallienne

---

Criticism comes easier than craftsmanship.
                                            —Zeuxis (c. 400 B.C.)

One of the greatest creations of the human mind is the art of reviewing books without having read them.
                                            —G. C. Lichtenberg (1742–1799)

*   *

Criticism—a big bite out of someone's back.   —Elia Kazan

If the critics were always right we should be in deep trouble.
—Robert Morley

*   *

People ask you for criticism but they only want praise.
—Somerset Maugham

I love criticism just so long as it's unqualified praise.
—Noel Coward

*   *

When I dislike what I see on the stage, I can be vastly amusing, but when I write about something I like, I am appallingly dull.
—Max Beerbohm

Impersonal criticism is like an impersonal fist fight or an impersonal marriage, and as successful.   —George Jean Nathan

---

Miss Truman is a unique American phenomenon with a pleasant voice of little size and fair quality . . . There are few moments during her recital when one can relax and feel confident she will make her goal, which is the end of the song.   —Paul Hume

I have read your lousy review of Margaret's concert. I've come to the conclusion that you are "an eight ulcer man on four ulcer pay" . . . Some day I hope to meet you. When that happens you'll need a new nose, a lot of beefsteak for black eyes, and perhaps a supporter below.   —Harry S Truman

*   *

The stones that Critics hurl with Harsh Intent/A Man may use to build a Monument.   —Arthur Guiterman

Pay no attention to what the critics say; no statue has ever been put up to a critic.   —Jean Sibelius

*   *

One of the first and most important things for a critic to learn is how to sleep undetected at the theatre.   —William Archer

To many people dramatic criticism must be like trying to tattoo soap bubbles.   —John Mason Brown

*   *

He is forced to be literate about the illiterate, witty about the witless and coherent about the incoherent.   —John Crosby

Critics are like eunuchs in a harem: they know how it's done, they've seen it done every day, but they're unable to do it themselves.
—Brendan Behan

CULTURE

Culture is the sum of all the forms of art, of love and of thought, which, in the course of centuries, have enabled man to be less enslaved.   —André Malraux

Culture is what your butcher would have if he were a surgeon.
—Mary Pettibone Poole

Culture is to know the best that has been said and thought in the world.   —Matthew Arnold (1822–1888) (A cultured person is one who can entertain himself, entertain guests, and entertain ideas.)

Politically I believe in democracy, but culturally, not at all . . . Whenever a cultural matter rolls up a majority, I know it is wrong.
—John Sloan

You will always find it [hatred] strongest and most violent where there is the lowest degree of culture.
—Johann W. von Goethe (1749–1832)

The great law of culture: let each become all that he was created capable of being.   —Thomas Carlyle (1795–1881)

Culture is on the horns of this dilemma: if profound and noble, it must remain rare, if common it must become mean.
—George Santayana

When two cultures collide is the only time when true suffering exists.
—Hermann Hesse

In the destinies of the several Cultures that follow upon one another, grow up with one another, touch, overshadow, and suppress one another, is compressed the whole content of human history.
—Oswald Spengler

Colonialism reduces the culture of the colonized person to the level of folklore and propaganda.   —André d'Allemagne

As a rule high culture and military power go hand in hand, as evidenced in the cases of Greece and Rome.
—Baron Kolmar von der Goltz

CUSTOMS / HABITS / FOLKWAYS

The decent moderation of today will be the least human of things tomorrow. At the time of the Spanish Inquisition, the opinion of good

sense and of the good medium was certainly that people ought not to burn too large a number of heretics; extreme and unreasonable opinion obviously demanded that they should burn none at all.
—Maurice Maeterlinck

In a democracy only those laws which have their bases in folkways or the approval of strong groups have a chance of being enforced.
—Abraham Myerson

Habit with him was all the test of truth;/"It must be right: I've done it from my youth." —George Crabbe (1754–1832) (Besides, habit is the easiest way to be wrong again.)

The unfortunate thing about this world is that good habits are so much easier to give up than bad ones. —Somerset Maugham

That which seems the height of absurdity in one generation often becomes the height of wisdom in another. —Adlai Stevenson

Men will sooner surrender their rights than their customs.
—Moritz Guedemann

The perpetual obstacle to human advancement is custom.
—John Stuart Mill (1806–1873)

Custom will often blind one to the good as well as to the evil effects of any long-established system. —Bishop Richard Whately

Never suffer an exception to occur till the new habit is securely rooted in your life. Each lapse is like the letting fall of a ball of string which one is carefully winding up; a single slip undoes more than a great many turns will wind again. —William James

Custom does often reason overrule/And only serves for reason to the fool. —John Wilmot, Earl of Rochester (1647–1680)

The chains of habit are too weak to be felt until they are too strong to be broken. —Samuel Johnson (1709–1784)

There is no possible line of conduct which has not at some time and place been condemned, and which at some other time and place been enjoined as a duty. —William Lecky

. . . persons who would be placed outside the pale of society with contempt are not those who would be placed there by another culture. —Ruth Benedict

CYNICISM / CYNICS

A cynic is a man who, when he smells flowers, looks around for a coffin. —H. L. Mencken

Cynic: n. a blackguard whose faulty vision sees things as they are, not as they ought to be.   —Ambrose Bierce

Cynicism is an unpleasant way of saying the truth.
                                        —Lillian Hellman

The power of accurate observation is commonly called cynicism by those who have not got it.   —George Bernard Shaw

Everything is worth precisely as much as a belch, the difference being that a belch is more satisfying.   —Ingmar Bergman

Cynicism is disappointed idealism.   —Harry Kemelman

Cynicism is humour in ill-health.   —H. G. Wells

Cynicism—the intellectual cripple's substitute for intelligence. —Russell Lynes (The cynic who doesn't believe in anything still wants you to believe him.)

A cynic is a man who knows the price of everything and the value of nothing.   —Oscar Wilde (1854–1900) (Or one who will laugh at anything so long as it isn't funny.)

A cynic is a person searching for an honest man, with a stolen lantern.   —Edgar A. Shoaff

We can destroy ourselves by cynicism and disillusion, just as effectively as by bombs.   —Kenneth Clark

Stoicism is the wisdom of madness and cynicism the madness of wisdom.   —Bergen Evans

Watch what people are cynical about, and one can often discover what they lack.   —Harry Emerson Fosdick (Cynicism is disillusioned idealism.)

DEATH

Death: The penultimate commercial transaction finalized by probate.   —Bernard Rosenberg

If I could drop dead right now, I'd be the happiest man alive!
          —Samuel Goldwyn

It is impossible to experience one's death objectively and still carry a tune.   —Woody Allen

I'm not afraid to die. I just don't want to be there when it happens.
          —Woody Allen

Since we have to speak well of the dead, let's knock them while they're alive.   —John Sloan

If you don't go to other men's funerals they won't go to yours.
          —Clarence Day

My uncle is a Southern planter. He's an undertaker in Alabama.
          —Fred Allen

If, after I depart this vale, you ever remember me and have thought to please my ghost, forgive some sinner and wink your eye at some homely girl.   —H. L. Mencken

And our hearts . . . like muffled/drums, are beating funeral marches to the grave.
—Henry Wadsworth Longfellow (1807–1882)

A single death is a tragedy, a million deaths is a statistic.
—Joseph Stalin

Man weeps to think that he will die so soon; woman, that she was born so long ago.   —H. L. Mencken

Life does not cease to be funny when people die any more than it ceases to be serious when people laugh.
—George Bernard Shaw

Once you accept your own death all of a sudden you are free to live. You no longer care about your reputation . . . you no longer care except so far as your life can be used tactically—to promote a cause you believe in.   —Saul Alinsky

How gaily a man wakes in the morning to watch himself keep on dying.   —Henry S. Haskins

She made a ravishing corpse.   —Ronald Firbank

I never wanted to see anybody die, but there are a few obituary notices I have read with pleasure.   —Clarence Darrow (On the other hand, according to obituary notices, a mean and useless citizen never dies.)

Sleep is lovely, death is better still, not to have been born is of course the miracle.   —Heinrich Heine (1797–1856)

The rain has such a friendly sound/To one who's six feet underground.   —Edna St. Vincent Millay

In the long run we are all dead.   —John Maynard Keynes (Death is nature's warning to slow down.)

When one considers just what man is,/Happy it be that short his span is.   —James Cagney

The more complete one's life is, the more . . . one's creative capacities are fulfilled, the less one fears death . . . People are not afraid of death per se, but of the incompleteness of their lives.
—Lisl Marburg Goodman (On second thought, to the atheist, death is the end; to the believer, the beginning; to the agnostic, the sound of silence.)

There is no constitutional right to choose to die.
—Chief Justice Joseph Weintraub, New Jersey Supreme Court

I warmed both hands before the fire of life;/It sinks, and I am ready to depart.   —Walter Savage Landor (1775–1864)

The long habit of living indisposeth us for dying.
      —Sir Thomas Browne (1605–1682)

One thing is certain and the rest is Lies;/The Flower that once has blown forever dies. —Edward FitzGerald (1809–1883)

One short sleep past, we wake eternally,/And Death shall be no more:/Death, thou shalt die! —John Donne (1572–1631)

When I am dead, my dearest,/Sing no sad songs for me.
      —Christina Rossetti (1830–1894)

Death tugs at my ear and says: "Live, I am coming."
      —Oliver Wendell Holmes, Sr. (1809–1894)

The riders in a race do not stop when they reach the goal. There is a little finishing canter before coming to a standstill. There is time to hear the kind voices of friends and say to oneself, "The work is done." —Oliver Wendell Holmes, Sr.

We should weep for men at their birth, not at their death.
      —Baron de Montesquieu (1689–1755)

But at my back I always hear/Time's wingéd chariot hurrying near.
      —Andrew Marvell (1621–1678)

To die is landing on some distant shore.
      —John Dryden (1631–1700)

Old man, exhausted by ordeal, detached from human deeds, feeling the approach of the eternal cold, but always watching in the shadows for the gleam of hope. —Charles de Gaulle

The wailing of the newborn infant is mingled with the dirge for the dead. —Lucretius (96?–55 B.C.)

I gave my life to learning how to live./Now that I have organized it all . . . It is just about over. —Sandra Hochman

I remember those happy days and often wish I could speak into the ears of the dead the gratitude which was due to them in life and so ill-returned. —Gwyn Thomas

---

Fear death?—to feel the fog in my throat,/The mist in my face.
      —Robert Browning (1812–1889)

. . . the fog is rising.
      —Emily Dickinson's last words (1830–1886)

* *

When the cancer that later took his life was first diagnosed, Senator Richard L. Neuberger remarked upon his "new appreciation of things I once took for granted—eating lunch with a friend, scratching my cat Muffet's ears and listening for his purrs, the company of my wife, reading a book or magazine in the quiet of my bed lamp at night, raiding the refrigerator for a glass of orange juice or a slice of toast. For the first time, I think I actually am savoring life."   —*Better Homes and Gardens* magazine

Good-by world . . . Good-by to clocks ticking . . . and Mama's sunflowers. And food and coffee. And new-ironed dresses and hot baths . . . and sleeping and waking up. Oh, earth, you're too wonderful for anybody to realize you.   —Thornton Wilder

*   *

Such men as come Proud, open-eyed and laughing to the tomb.
                                    —William Butler Yeats

To the Gay Laugh of my Mother at the Gate of the Grave.
                                    —Sean O'Casey

*   *

Death can make even triviality momentous.   —Edward Le Comte (And obituaries are the last writes.)

Die, my dear Doctor, that's the last thing I shall do!
                                    —Lord Palmerston (1784–1865)

*   *

Death is not the greatest loss in life. The greatest loss is what dies inside us while we live.   —Norman Cousins

Those who welcome death have only tried it from the ears up.
                                    —Wilson Mizner

*   *

Man is the only animal that contemplates death, and also the only animal that shows any sign of doubt of its finality.
                                    —William Ernest Hocking

The night approaches . . . Bringing dread/Of that irrevocable journey to Eternal Sleep./Is it so awesome? Ask the Dead.
                                    —Lloyd Hartley

———————

This is my death . . . and it will profit me to understand it.
                                    —Anne Sexton

A man's dying is more the survivors' affair than his own.
                                    —Thomas Mann

*   *

The beginnings and endings of all human undertakings are untidy.
—John Galsworthy

And all I ask is a merry yarn from a laughing fellow-rover,/And quiet sleep and a sweet dream when the long trick's over.
—John Masefield

*   *

A dying man needs to die, as a sleepy man needs to sleep, and there comes a time when it is wrong, as well as useless, to resist.
—Stewart Alsop

Between grief and nothing I will take grief.
—William Faulkner

DEMOCRACY

Democracy is that form of society, no matter what its political classification, in which every man has a chance and knows that he has it.   —James Russell Lowell (1819–1891)

Democracy is the art of running the circus from the monkey cage.
—H. L. Mencken

Democracy is a form of government you have to keep for four years no matter what it does.   —Will Rogers (Democracy is just stumbling along to the right decision instead of going straight forward to the wrong one.)

As I would not be a slave, so I would not be a master. This expresses my idea of democracy.
—Abraham Lincoln (1809–1865)

A democratic society might be defined . . . as one in which the majority is always prepared to put down a revolutionary minority.
—Walter Lippmann

Man's capacity for justice makes democracy possible, but man's inclination to injustice makes democracy necessary.
—Reinhold Niebuhr

Democracy is finding proximate solutions to insoluble problems.
—Reinhold Niebuhr

Democracy substitutes selection by the incompetent many for appointment by the corrupt few.   —George Bernard Shaw (The chief defect of a democracy is that only the political party out of office knows how to run the government.)

The evidence is overwhelming that the Framers used the term "Republic" as we now use the term democracy to describe a state in which the majority governs.   —Henry Steele Commager

The idea that you can merchandise candidates for high office like breakfast cereal . . . is the ultimate indignity to the democratic process.   —Adlai Stevenson

On one occasion I remarked . . . that democracy had at least one merit, namely, that a Member of Parliament cannot be stupider than his constituents, for the more stupid he is, the more stupid they were to elect him.   —Bertrand Russell (Democracy is a process by which the people are free to choose the man who will get the blame.)

If one man offers you democracy and another offers you a bag of grain, at what stage of starvation will you prefer the grain to the vote?   —Bertrand Russell

There is no form of Government but what may be a blessing to the people if well administered . . . this [government] is likely to be well administered for a course of years, and can only end in Despotism as other forms have done before it, when the people shall become so corrupted as to need despotic Government, being incapable of any other.   —Benjamin Franklin (1706–1790)

Law, in a democracy, means the protection of the rights and liberties of the minority.   —Alfred E. Smith (In a democracy the majority rules, but the minority tries to show the majority how.)

Democracy alone, of all forms of government, enlists the full force of men's enlightened will . . . It is the most humane, the most advanced and in the end the most unconquerable of all forms of human society. The democratic aspiration is no mere recent phase of human history. It is human history.
                                      —Franklin Delano Roosevelt

Democracy is based on the conviction that man has the moral and intellectual capacity, as well as the inalienable right, to govern himself with reason and justice.   —Harry S Truman

If you want to understand democracy, spend less time in the library with Plato and more time in the buses with people.   —Simeon Strunsky (Popular government is still only a theory because no one has yet found a government that is popular.)

Democracy accepts in theory, and realizes in practice better than other forms of government, the humane and rational values of life.
                                      —Carl Becker

A democracy is predicated on the idea that ordinary men and women are capable of governing themselves. —Adolf Berle

Only a country that is rich and safe can afford to be a democracy, for democracy is the most expensive and nefarious kind of government ever heard of on earth. —H. L. Mencken (A democracy is a form of government in which the people often vote for someone different but seldom if ever get something different.)

Democracy is a kingless regime infested by many kings who are sometimes more exclusive, tyrannical, and destructive than one, if he be a tyrant. —Benito Mussolini

The happiest thing that can be said about democracy . . . is that it is one of the few systems that has even been willing to risk a long period of confusion and mixed purposes for the sake of giving man a chance to grow up in mind and responsibility.
—H. A. Overstreet

Democracy will not be salvaged by men who talk fluently, debate forcefully and quote aptly. —Lancelot Hogben

Our real disease—which is Democracy.
—Alexander Hamilton (1757–1804)

A democracy is no more than an aristocracy of orators. The people are so readily moved by demagogues that control must be exercised by the government over speech and press.
—Thomas Hobbes (1588–1679)

Democracy is the art of thinking independently together.
—Alexander Meiklejohn (On the other hand, it can be a government where you can say what you think even if you don't think.)

Democracy is not a way of governing . . . but primarily a way of determining who shall govern and, broadly, to what ends.
—R. M. MacIver (Democracy decides matters by counting heads instead of breaking them.)

Democracy is the recurrent suspicion that more than half of the people are right more than half of the time. —E. B. White

Democracy is the worst system of all forms of government.
—Robert Welch

There can be no daily democracy without daily citizenship.
—Ralph Nader

An adult who ceases after youth to unlearn and relearn his facts and to reconsider his opinions . . . is a menace to a democratic community. —Edward Thorndike

*   *

Our inequality materializes our upper classes, vulgarizes our middle class, brutalizes our lower class.

—Matthew Arnold (1822–1888)

No class of Americans, so far as I know, has ever objected . . . to any amount of governmental meddling if it appeared to benefit that particular class.   —Carl Becker

*   *

Democracy arose from men's thinking that if they are equal in any respect, they are equal absolutely.   —Aristotle (384–322 B.C.)

A democracy is a government in the hands of men of low birth, no property, and unskilled labor.   —Aristotle

*   *

Democracy is direct self-government, over all the people, for all the people, by all the people.

—Theodore Parker (1810–1860)

. . . that government of the people, by the people, for the people, shall not perish from the earth.

—Abraham Lincoln (1809–1865)

*   *

One thing that made their [Labor's] struggle so hard was that those men of exceptional ability who might have been their leaders almost always made fortunes of their own and then turned their strength against their former comrades.   —Preserved Smith

Beware of the man who rises to power from one suspender.

—Edgar Lee Masters

*   *

The difficulty for a democracy is, how to find and keep high ideals. The individuals who compose it are . . . persons who need to follow an ideal, not to set one; and one ideal of greatness, high feeling and fine culture, which an aristocracy once supplied to them, they lose by the very fact of ceasing to be a lower order and becoming a democracy.   —Matthew Arnold

Democracy means government by the uneducated, while aristocracy means government by the badly educated.   —G. K. Chesterton

*   *

I know not how better to describe our form of government in a single phrase than by calling it a government by the chairmen of the Standing Committees of Congress.   —Woodrow Wilson

Because of our Congressional committee system, our government is closer to a gerontocracy than a democracy.

—Charles Frankel

*   *

Democracy is the worst system devised by the wit of man, except for all the others.   —Winston Churchill

Democracy is good. I say this because other systems are worse.

—Jawaharlal Nehru

All the ills of democracy can be cured by more democracy.

—Alfred E. Smith

The doctrine that the cure for the evils of democracy is more democracy is like saying that the cure of crime is more crime.

— H. L. Mencken

*   *

There is no greater farce than to talk of democracy. To begin with, it is a lie; it has never existed in any great country.

—Henri Bourassa

Democracy to me is liberty *plus* economic security.

—Maury Maverick

*   *

The House of Representatives is by far the most *representative* component in the federal government . . . yet the House has been the most illiberal . . . The poor and powerless have more often been befriended by Presidents than by congressmen, and . . . the Senate, an institution that is an affront to majoritarianism, has been far more liberal than the House. And the Supreme Court, which has always been beyond the reach of the franchised voter, has been—in recent times, at any rate—by far the most liberal of all.

—Richard Rovere

The tendencies of democracies are, in all things, to mediocrity, since the tastes, knowledge and principles of the majority form the tribunal of appeal.   —James Fenimore Cooper (1789–1851)

*   *

Democracy means not "I'm as good as you are," but "you're as good as I am."   —Theodore Parker (1810–1860)

The worst form of inequality is to try to make unequal things equal.

—Aristotle (384–322 B.C.)

*   *

The upper classes are . . . a nation's past; the middle class is its future.   —Ayn Rand

In every well-governed state wealth is a sacred thing; in democracies it is the only sacred thing.   —Anatole France

*   *

Where the earth is underpopulated and there is an economic demand for men, democracy is inevitable. That state of things cannot be permanent. Therefore, democracy cannot last. It contains no absolute and *eternal* truths.   —William Graham Sumner

I have the happiness to know that it [democracy] is a rising, and not a setting sun.   —Benjamin Franklin (1706–1790)

*   *

We have watched American democracy at close hand for many years and we believe few governments are institutionally so susceptible to dictatorship as this one.   —Gerald Johnson

Democracy is a device that insures we shall be governed no better than we deserve.   —George Bernard Shaw

DEMOCRATIC PARTY / DEMOCRATS

Thomas Jefferson founded the Democratic Party; Franklin Roosevelt dumbfounded it.   —Dewey Short

Republicans sleep in twin beds—some even in separate rooms. That is why there are more Democrats.   —Will Stanton

The Democratic Party is like a mule—without pride of ancestry or hope of posterity.   —Edmund Burke (1729–1797)

I belong to no organized political party—I am a Democrat.
                                                    —Will Rogers

Its [the Democratic Party's] leaders are always troubadors of trouble; crooners of catastrophe . . . A Democratic President is doomed to proceed to his goals like a squid, squirting darkness all about him.
                                                    —Clare Boothe Luce

If the person you are trying to diagnose politically is some sort of intellectual, the chances are two to one he is a Democrat.
                                                    —Vance Packard

The Democratic Party can always be relied on to make a damn fool of itself at the critical time.   —Ben "Pitchfork" Tillman

When a leader is in the Democratic Party he's a boss; when he's in the Republican Party he's a leader.　　—Harry S Truman

If the Republicans will stop telling lies about the Democrats, we will stop telling the truth about them.　　—Adlai Stevenson

DESTINY

Destiny is not a matter of chance, it is a matter of choice; it is not a thing to be waited for, it is a thing to be achieved.
　　　　　　　　　　　—William Jennings Bryan

There is a destiny that makes us brothers, none goes his way alone. All that we send into the lives of others comes back into our own.
　　　　　　　　　　　—Edwin Markham

I am the master of my fate;/I am the captain of my soul.
　　　　　　　　　　　—William E. Henley

Anatomy is destiny.　　—Sigmund Freud

Trend is not destiny.　　—Lewis Mumford

Man knows at last that he is alone in the universe's unfeeling immensity. His destiny is nowhere spelled out, nor is his duty.
　　　　　　　　　　　—Jacques Monod

There is no fate that cannot be surmounted by scorn.
　　　　　　　　　　　—Albert Camus

Fate is nonawareness.　　—Jan Kott

Man blames fate for other accidents, but feels personally responsible when he makes a hole in one.　　—*Horizons* magazine

Intellect annuls fate. So far as a man thinks, he is free.
　　　　　　　　　—Ralph Waldo Emerson (1803–1882)

He that is born to be hanged shall never be drowned.
　　　　　　　　　—Thomas Fuller (1608–1661)

We have mastered a destiny which broke another man [Napoleon] a hundred and thirty years ago.
　　　　—Adolf Hitler (Owner of a somewhat clouded crystal ball)

The future is hidden even from the men who made it.
　　　　　　　　　　　—Anatole France

DEVIL

May you get to Heaven a half hour before the Devil knows you're dead.　　—Irish Proverb

Whenever science makes a discovery, the devil grabs it while the angels are debating the best way to use it.   —Alan Valentine

The world is all the richer for having the devil in it, so long as we keep our foot upon his neck.   —William James (But when a man says, "Get thee behind me, Satan," he's probably ashamed to have even the devil see what he's up to.)

It is so stupid of modern civilization to have given up believing in the devil when he is the only explanation of it.   —Ronald Knox (Did the devil really create the world when God wasn't looking?)

The Christians were the first to make the existence of Satan a dogma of the church.
—Madame Elena Blavatsky (founder of Theosophy) (1831–1891)

In all systems of theology the devil figures as a male person. Yet, it is women who keep the church going.   —Don Marquis (The devil could change. He was once an angel and may be evolving still.)

———

An apology for the devil: it must be remembered that we have heard only one side of the case. God has written all the books.
        —Samuel Butler

Satan hasn't a single salaried helper; the Opposition employs a million.   —Mark Twain

*   *

The devil is a gentleman who never goes where he is not welcome.
        —John A. Lincoln

The devil is easy to identify. He appears when you're terribly tired and makes a very reasonable request which you know you shouldn't grant.   —Fiorello La Guardia (When a man is between the devil and the deep blue sea, his fear of drowning generally triumphs.)

*   *

A religion can no more afford to degrade its Devil than to degrade its God.   —Havelock Ellis

God and the devil are an effort after specialization and division of labor.   —Samuel Butler

*   *

The devil can cite scripture for his purpose.
        —William Shakespeare (1564–1616)

The devil hath power to assume a pleasing shape.
—William Shakespeare

*   *

Few people now believe in the devil; but very many enjoy behaving
as their ancestors behaved when the Fiend was a reality as unquestionable as his Opposite Number.   —Aldous Huxley

Talk of the devil, and his horns appear.
—Samuel Taylor Coleridge (1772–1834)

*   *

The Devil does not stay where music is.
—Martin Luther (1483–1546)

Why should the devil have all the good tunes?   —Rowland Hill

*   *

The Devil is making his pitch!   —Billy Graham (Get thee
behind me, Satan, and push me along.)

There never was a devil who didn't advise people to keep out of hell.
—Ed Howe

DICTATORS

A dictatorship is a country where they have taken the politics out
of politics.   —Sam Himmell

The dictatorships of our time are the greatest examples of direct
actionists that the world has ever seen.   —M. M. Coady

Whenever you have an efficient government you have a dictatorship.
—Harry S Truman

It is a paradox that every dictator has climbed to power on the ladder of free speech. Immediately on attaining power each dictator
has suppressed all free speech except his own.   —Herbert
Hoover (The country that has only one man who can save it is not
worth saving.)

Any doctrine that . . . weakens personal responsibility for judgment and for action . . . helps create the attitudes that welcome
and support the totalitarian state.   —John Dewey

I am of the opinion that the dictatorships gave far more thought to
education than the democratic states . . . Where the press is under

strict and efficient control, literacy can become a weapon for the support of universal tyranny.   —George S. Counts (In a democracy, you believe it or not; in a dictatorship, you believe it or else.)

The alternative to the totalitarian state is the cooperative commonwealth.   —Norman Thomas

Almost certainly we are moving into an age of totalitarian dictatorships. An age in which freedom of thought will be at first a deadly sin and later on a meaningless abstraction. The autonomous individual is going to be stamped out of existence.
      —George Orwell (And we shall all come to love Big Brother.)

Contrary to the prevalent opinion . . . I indicated that wars and revolutions were not disappearing but would grow in the twentieth century to an absolutely unprecedented height . . . that democracies were declining, giving place to various kinds of despotisms.
      —P. A. Sorokin

*   *

The danger of social upheaval now may well be universal . . . I feel building up in this country enormous resentment, mostly political, waiting to be captured.   —David Riesman

I have a feeling that at any time about three million Americans can be had for any militant reaction against law, decency, the Constitution, the Supreme Court, compassion and the rule of reason.
      —John Kenneth Galbraith

*   *

The bourgeoisie, during its rule of scarce one hundred years, has created more massive and more colossal productive forces than have all preceding generations together.
      —The Communist Manifesto

If our economy of freedom fails to distribute wealth as ably as it has created it, the road to dictatorship will be open to any man who can persuasively promise security to all.
      —Will and Ariel Durant

*   *

The great strength of the totalitarian state is that it forces those who fear it to imitate it.   —Adolf Hitler

No one man can terrorize a whole nation unless we are all his accomplices.   —Edward R. Murrow

*   *

God help the nation where self-caricature and satire are verboten.
—Evan Esar

Dictatorship: A place where public opinion can't even be expressed privately.   —Walter Winchell (In a dictatorship, suppression is nine points of the law.)

*   *

A society of sheep must in time beget a government of wolves.
—Bertrand de Jouvenel

It is useless for the sheep to pass resolutions in favor of vegetarianism while the wolf remains of a different opinion.
—Dean William R. Inge

I will believe in the right of one man to govern a nation despotically when I find a man born into the world with boots and spurs, and a nation with saddles on their backs.
—Algernon Sidney (1622–1683)

If men cannot agree on how to rule themselves, someone else must rule them.   —Theodore H. White (Under a dictatorship the people have to follow their leader when they should be chasing him instead.)

*   *

A decisive victory of the revolution over tsarism is the revolutionary-democratic dictatorship of the proletariat and the peasantry.
—Nikolai Lenin

Today's rebel is tomorrow's tyrant.   —Will and Ariel Durant

DIGNITY

Where is there dignity unless there is honesty?
—Marcus Tullius Cicero (106–43 B.C.)

She balanced her dignity on the tip of her nose.   —Heywood Broun (The first thing in the human personality that dissolves in alcohol is dignity.)

But if a man happens to find himself . . . he has a mansion which he can inhabit with dignity all the days of his life.
—James Michener

In his private heart no man much respects himself.
—Mark Twain

Perhaps the only true dignity of man is his capacity to despise himself.   —George Santayana

*   *

The truly American sentiment recognizes the dignity of labor and the fact that honor lies in honest toil.   —Grover Cleveland

Scrubbing floors and emptying bedpans has as much dignity as the Presidency.   —Richard M. Nixon

———————

To behave with dignity is nothing less than to allow others freely to be themselves.   —Sol Chaneles

It is only people of small moral stature who have to stand on their dignity.   —Arnold Bennett (When a person stands on his dignity, it's probably because he has a very insecure footing.)

DIPLOMACY

Diplomacy is the art of saying "Nice doggie!" till you can find a rock.   —Wynn Catlin

Diplomacy is to do and say/the nastiest thing in the nicest way.
—Isaac Goldberg

The art of acceptance is the art of making someone who has just done you a small favor wish that he might have done you a greater one.   —Russell Lynes

Diplomacy—lying in state.   —Oliver Herford

One function of diplomacy is to dress realism in morality.
—Will and Ariel Durant

A diplomat is a person who can tell you to go to hell in such a way that you actually look forward to the trip.   —Caskie Stinnett

A diplomat's life is made up of three ingredients: protocol, Geritol, and alcohol.   —Adlai Stevenson

A diplomat is a man who always remembers a woman's birthday but never remembers her age.   —Robert Frost

Diplomats are just as essential to starting a war as soldiers are for finishing it . . . You take diplomacy out of war, and the thing would fall flat in a week.   —Will Rogers

I presented myself as the most amateur of diplomats. He [Nehru] proclaimed himself an amateur prime minister. I think that truth will not be a barrier to our association.

—John Kenneth Galbraith

Diplomacy has rarely been able to gain at the conference table what cannot be gained or held on the battlefield.

—General Walter Bedell Smith

A diplomat and a stage magician are the two professions that have to have a high silk hat. All the tricks that either one of them have are in the hat, and are all known to other diplomats and magicians.

—Will Rogers

We're eyeball to eyeball and the other fellow just blinked.

—Dean Rusk

Alliances have no absolute virtues, whatever may be the sentiments on which they are based.　　—Charles de Gaulle

It is our policy to steer clear of permanent alliances with any portion of the foreign world.　　—George Washington (1732–1799)

Close alliances with despots are never safe for free states.

—Demosthenes (385?–322 B.C.)

The reason for having diplomatic relations is not to confer a compliment, but to secure a convenience.　　—Winston Churchill

To say nothing, especially when speaking, is half the art of diplomacy.

　　—Will and Ariel Durant (Think twice before saying nothing.)

My advice to any diplomat who wants to have a good press is to have two or three kids and a dog.　　—Carl Rowan

In order to be a diplomat one must speak a number of languages, including double-talk.　　—Carey McWilliams

---

Diplomacy is the art of fishing tranquilly in troubled waters.

—J. Christopher Herold

Diplomacy: The art of jumping into troubled waters without making a splash.　　—Art Linkletter

*　　*

An appeaser is one who feeds a crocodile—hoping it will eat him last.　　—Winston Churchill

Appeasers believe that if you keep on throwing steaks to a tiger, the tiger will become a vegetarian.　　—Heywood Broun

*　　*

In politics, as in high finance, duplicity is regarded as a virtue.
　　　　　　　—Mikhail A. Bakunin (1814–1876)

Sincere diplomacy is no more possible than dry water or wooden iron.　—Joseph Stalin

*　　*

Sometimes in the world of diplomacy it is very important to have a pretext to return after having said goodbye.　—Peter Ustinov

Don't ever slam a door; you might want to go back.
　　　　　　　—Don Herold

*　　*

Diplomacy is the art of letting someone else have your way.
　　　　　　　—Daniele Vare

A diplomat is a fellow that lets you do all the talking while he gets what he wants.
　　　　　　　—Frank McKinney Hubbard ("Kin Hubbard")

Diplomacy—the patriotic art of lying for one's country.
　　　　　　　—Ambrose Bierce

I have discovered the art of fooling diplomats: I speak the truth and they never believe me.
　　　　　　　—Camillo Di Cavour (1810–1861)

*　　*

Diplomat: A person who can be disarming even though his country isn't.　—Sidney Brody

American diplomacy is easy on the brain but hell on the feet.
　　　　　　　—Charles G. Dawes

*　　*

A real diplomat is one who can cut his neighbor's throat without having his neighbor notice it.　—Trygve Lie

America never lost a war or won a conference.　—Will Rogers

*　　*

All discussion, all debate, all dissidence tends to question, and in consequence, to upset existing convictions; that is precisely its purpose and its justification.　—Judge Learned Hand

In international politics, the union of two thieves who have their hands so deeply inserted in each other's pocket that they cannot separately plunder a third.   —Ambrose Bierce

*   *

Peace, commerce and honest friendship with other nations—entangling alliances with none.

—Thomas Jefferson (1743–1826)

Any alliance whose purpose is not the intention to wage war is senseless and useless.   —Adolf Hitler

DOUBT

I respect faith but doubt is what gets you an education.

—Wilson Mizner

If only God would give me some clear sign! Like making a large deposit in my name at a Swiss bank.   —Woody Allen

If you would be a real seeker after truth, it is necessary that at least once in your life you doubt, as far as possible, all things.

—René Descartes (1596–1650)

The important thing is not to stop questioning.

—Albert Einstein

Doubt 'til thou canst doubt no more . . . doubt is thought, and thought is life. Systems which end doubt are devices for drugging thought.   —Albert Guérard

There are two ways to slide easily through life: to believe everything or to doubt everything; both ways save us from thinking.

—Alfred Korzybski

To have doubted one's own first principles is the mark of a civilized man.   —Oliver Wendell Holmes, Jr.

The certainties of one age are the problems of the next.

—R. H. Tawney

Doubt is not a pleasant mental state but certainty is a ridiculous one.

—Voltaire (François Marie Arouet) (1694–1778)

Men become civilized, not in proportion to their willingness to believe, but in proportion to their readiness to doubt.

—H. L. Mencken

DREAMS

I like the dreams of the future better than the history of the past.
— Thomas Jefferson (1743–1826)

An era can be said to end when its basic illusions are exhausted.
— Arthur Miller

I have learned this at least by my experiment: that if one advances
confidently in the direction of his dreams, and endeavors to live the
life which he has imagined, he will meet with a success unexpected
in common hours.   — Henry David Thoreau (1817–1862)

Dreams are the touchstones of our characters.
— Henry David Thoreau

He's a man out there in the blue, ridin' on a smile and a shoeshine
. . . a salesman has got to dream, boys.   — Arthur Miller

DRINK

A woman drove me to drink and I never even had the courtesy to
thank her.   — W. C. Fields

What contemptible scoundrel stole the cork from my lunch?
— W. C. Fields

I always keep a supply of stimulant handy in case I see a snake—
which I also keep handy.   — W. C. Fields

We lived for days on nothing but food and water.
— W. C. Fields

Anybody who hates dogs and loves whiskey can't be all bad.
— W. C. Fields

Wouldn't it be terrible if I quoted some reliable statistics which
prove that more people are driven insane through religious hysteria
than by drinking alcohol?   — W. C. Fields

No animal ever invented anything so bad as drunkenness—or so
good as drink.   — G. K. Chesterton (People who insist on
drinking before driving, are putting the quart before the hearse.)

I am a prohibitionist. What I propose to prohibit is the reckless use
of water.   — Bob Edwards

There are two things that will be believed of any man whatsoever, and one of them is that he has taken to drink.   —Booth Tarkington (An alcoholic spends his life committing suicide on the installment plan, that is, he drinks like a fish but not the same thing.)

I drink to make other people interesting.

—George Jean Nathan

Prohibition makes you want to cry into your beer, and denies you the beer to cry into.   —Don Marquis (The only advantage of having lived through the Age of Prohibition is that any liquor tastes good.)

I really don't drink, but I'll split a quart with you.

—Johnston Peter

ECOLOGY

Ecologists believe that a bird in the bush is worth two in the hand.
—Stanley C. Pearson (On second thought, a bird in the hand is fingerlicking good.)

The sun, the moon and the stars would have disappeared long ago, had they happened to be within reach of predatory human hands.
—Havelock Ellis

The most alarming of all man's assaults upon the environment is the contamination of air, earth, rivers, and sea . . . this pollution is for the most part irrecoverable.   —Rachel Carson

We won't have a society if we destroy the environment.
—Margaret Mead

If the prospect for human freedom in the last half of this twentieth century is to become any brighter, we have got to find a better way to develop and use the riches of this earth.
—Oscar L. Chapman

Whoever could make two ears of corn . . . grow upon a spot of ground where only one grew before, would deserve better of mankind . . . than the whole race of politicians put together.
—Jonathan Swift (1667–1745)

*   *

The more we strive to reach the political science future, the more
likely we are to achieve the ecological disaster.

—Garrett De Bell

Should we allow environmental deterioration to continue, man's
fate may be worse than extinction.   —Ron S. Boster

The confrontation will be between those who are committed to
making our presently inadequate social, economic, and political
institutions equal to the task of repairing our ravaged environment as against those whose first and enduring allegiance is to
private profit and corporate power and the political institutions
which stand guard to protect and preserve that profit and power.

—*The Progressive* magazine

Ecology has become the political substitute for the word "mother."

—Jesse Unruh

*   *

He [the strip-mining engineer] has a well-defined purpose, which
is to get the coal out by the most efficient means; that these should
involve the brutalization of Nature and the spoiling of the environment is irrelevant.   —Bertrand de Jouvenel

Man shapes himself through decisions that shape his environment.

—René Dubos

EDUCATION

The object of education is to prepare the young to educate themselves throughout their lives.   —Robert Maynard Hutchins

It sometimes seems as though we were trying to combine the ideal
of no schools at all with the democratic ideal of schools for everybody by having schools without education.

—Robert Maynard Hutchins

Education: A debt due from present to future generations.

—George Peabody (1795–1869)

"Whom are you?" said he, for he had been to night school.

—George Ade

The advantage of a classical education is that it enables you to
despise the wealth which it prevents you from achieving.

—Russell Green

A school should not be a preparation for life. A school should be life.   —Elbert Hubbard

Education is what survives when what has been learnt has been forgotten.   —B. F. Skinner

Education is helping the child realize his potentialities.

—Erich Fromm

The great end of education is to discipline rather than to furnish the mind; to train it to the use of its own powers, rather than fill it with the accumulation of others.

—Tryon Edwards (1809–1894)

Sixty years ago I knew everything; now I know nothing; education is a progressive discovery of our own ignorance.

—Will Durant

To be able to be caught up into the world of thought—that is being educated.   —Edith Hamilton

Education is the transmission of civilization.

—Will and Ariel Durant

The man who has ceased to learn ought not to be allowed to wander around loose in these dangerous days.   —M. M. Coady

What we want is to see the child in pursuit of knowledge, and not knowledge in pursuit of the child.   —George Bernard Shaw

Education today, more than ever before, must see clearly the dual objectives: education for living and educating for making a living.

—James Mason Wood

Education is the instruction of the intellect in the laws of Nature.
—Thomas Henry Huxley (1825–1895)

A child miseducated is a child lost.   —John F. Kennedy

Perhaps the most valuable result of all education is the ability to make yourself do the thing you have to do, when it ought to be done, whether you like it or not.   —Thomas Henry Huxley

The average Ph.D. thesis is nothing but a transference of bones from one graveyard to another.   —J. Frank Dobie

All who have meditated on the art of governing mankind have been convinced that the fate of empires depends on the education of youth.   —Aristotle (384–322 B.C.)

It is no longer correct to regard higher education solely as a privilege. It is a basic right in today's world.   —Norman Cousins

My idea of education is to unsettle the minds of the young and inflame their intellects.   —Robert Maynard Hutchins

Why should society feel responsible only for the education of children, and not for the education of all adults of every age?
—Erich Fromm

If there is anything education does not lack today, it is critics.
—Nathan M. Pusey

The one real object of education is to have a man in the condition of continually asking questions.   —Bishop Mandell Creighton

The aim of education is the knowledge not of fact, but of values.
—Dean William R. Inge

Since a democratic society repudiates the principle of external authority, it must find a substitute in voluntary disposition and interest; these can be created only by education.
—John Dewey

The primary purpose of a liberal education is to make one's mind a pleasant place in which to spend one's leisure.
—Sydney J. Harris

The ink of the scholar is more sacred than the blood of the martyr.
—Mohammed (570–632)

When asked how much educated men were superior to those un-educated, Aristotle answered, "As much as the living are to the dead."   —Diogenes Laertius (c. 150 B.C.)

I call a complete and generous education that which fits a man to perform justly, skilfully, and magnanimously all the offices, both private and public, of peace and war.
—John Milton (1608–1674)

I question whether we can afford to teach mother macramé when Johnny still can't read.   —Governor Jerry Brown

Why should we subsidize intellectual curiosity?
—Ronald Reagan

In the education of children there is nothing like alluring the interest and affection; otherwise you only make so many asses laden with books.   —Michel de Montaigne (1533–1592)

The secret of education is respecting the pupil.
—Ralph Waldo Emerson (1803–1882)

America is the only country left where we teach languages so that no pupil can speak them.   —John Erskine

Education belongs pre-eminently to the church . . . neutral or lay schools from which religion is excluded are contrary to the fundamental principles of education.   —Pope Pius XI

Education has in America's whole history been the major hope for improving the individual and society.   —Gunnar Myrdal

Nothing in education is so astonishing as the amount of ignorance it accumulates in the form of inert facts.   —Henry Adams

The education of a man is never completed until he dies.
—Robert E. Lee (1807–1870)

The whole drift of my education goes to persuade me that the world of our present consciousness is only one out of many worlds of consciousness that exist.   —William James

I've over-educated myself in all the things I shouldn't have known at all.   —Noel Coward

The greatest challenges facing both the arts and education are how to navigate the perilous course between adventure and discipline; how to respond to tradition without either rejecting it or becoming its slave.   —Robert W. Corrigan

Today, educational levels are replacing class structures as the significant vertical stratification of society . . . Possibly—and this may be the hardest task of the next fifty years—we may even discover how to preserve and enhance the self-respect of those who fall far behind in the education race.   —Max Ways

The chief object of education is not to learn things but to unlearn things.   —G. K. Chesterton

Education is a method by which one acquires a higher grade of prejudices.   —Laurence J. Peter

At the desk where I sit, I have learned one great truth. The answer for all our national problems—the answer for all the problems of the world—comes to a single word. That word is "education." —Lyndon B. Johnson (There is no substitute for education, unless it is the American public school system.)

If a prolonged education does nothing else it gives the mind a sort of shyness and induces either a perfect sensitivity to words, or it induces silence, the conviction that nothing can ever again be said better than it has been said before.   —Gwyn Thomas

The business of education is not to make the young perfect in any one of the sciences, but so to open and dispose their minds as may best make them capable of any, when they shall apply themselves to it.   —John Locke (1632–1704)

In the long run of history, the censor and the inquisitor have always lost. The only sure weapon against bad ideas is better ideas. The source of better ideas is wisdom. The surest path to wisdom is a liberal education.   —A. Whitney Griswold

The main thing needed to make men happy is intelligence . . . and it can be fostered by education.   —Bertrand Russell

*   *

The ultimate victory of tomorrow is democracy, and through democracy with education, for no people in all the world can be kept eternally ignorant or eternally enslaved.

—Franklin Delano Roosevelt

Education makes a people easy to lead, but difficult to drive; easy to govern, but impossible to enslave.

—Henry Peter, Lord Brougham (1778–1868)

*   *

The traditional educational theory [is] to the effect that the way to bring up children is to keep them *innocent* (i.e., believing in biological, political, and socioeconomic fairy tales) as long as possible . . . that students should be given the best possible maps of the territories of experience in order that they may be prepared for life, is not as popular as might be assumed.   —S. I. Hayakawa

The logic of all this seems to be that it is all right for young people in a democracy to learn about any civilization or social theory that is not dangerous, but that they should remain entirely ignorant of any civilization or social theory that might be dangerous on the ground that what you don't know can't hurt you . . . a complete denial of the democratic principle that the general diffusion of knowledge and learning through the community is essential to the preservation of free government.   —Carl Becker

*   *

Intelligence appears to be the thing that enables a man to get along without education. Education enables a man to get along without the use of his intelligence.   —Albert Edward Wiggam

Education can train, but not create, intelligence.

—Edward McChesney Sait

The supreme end of education is expert discernment in all things— the power to tell the good from the bad, the genuine from the counterfeit, and to prefer the good and the genuine to the bad and the counterfeit.   —Samuel Johnson (1709–1784)

The aim of a college education is to teach you to know a good man when you see one.   —William James

The purpose of all higher education is to make men aware of what was and what is; to incite them to probe into what may be. It seeks to teach them to understand, to evaluate, to communicate.

—Otto Kleppner

I prefer the company of peasants because they have not been educated sufficiently to reason incorrectly.

—Michel de Montaigne (1533–1592)

*   *

If I had learned education I would not have had time to learn anything else.   —Cornelius Vanderbilt (1794–1877)

All of us learn to write in the second grade . . . most of us go on to greater things.   —Bobby Knight

*   *

We must open the doors of opportunity. But we must also equip our people to walk through those doors.   —Lyndon B. Johnson

America is the best half-educated country in the world.

—Nicholas Murray Butler

EGOTISM

One nice thing about egotists: They don't talk about other people. —Lucille S. Harper (Perhaps that's because they're always me-deep in conversation.)

Don't talk about yourself; it will be done when you leave.

—Wilson Mizner

There are two kinds of egotists: Those who admit it, and the rest of us.   —Laurence J. Peter

It is a curious fact that of all the illusions that beset mankind none is quite so curious as that tendency to suppose that we are mentally and morally superior to those who differ from us in opinion.

—Elbert Hubbard

Take egotism out, and you would castrate the benefactors.

—Ralph Waldo Emerson (1803–1882)

An egotist is a man who thinks that if he hadn't been born, people would have wondered why.   —Dan Post

Religion is a monumental chapter in the history of human egotism.

—William James

Egotism is nature's compensation for mediocrity.

—L. A. Safian

Egotism is the anesthetic that dulls the pains of stupidity.

—Frank Leahy

There's only one thing that can keep growing without nourishment: the human ego. —Marshall Lumsden

ENGLAND / ENGLISH

This royal throne of kings, this scepter'd isle,/This earth of majesty, this seat of Mars,/This other Eden, demi-paradise/ . . . This happy breed of men, this little world,/This precious stone set in a silver sea/ . . . This blessed plot, this earth, this realm, this England . . . —William Shakespeare (1564–1616)

Those comfortable padded lunatic asylums which are known euphemistically as the stately homes of England. —Virginia Woolf

We were not fairly beaten, my lord. No Englishman is ever fairly beaten. —George Bernard Shaw

If a playwright is funny, the English look for a serious message, and if he's serious, they look for the joke. —Sacha Guitry

We are the first race in the world, and the more of the world we inherit the better it is for the human race. —Cecil Rhodes

The Englishman respects your opinions, but he never thinks of your feelings. —Sir Wilfred Laurier

Englishman: A creature who thinks he is being virtuous when he is only being uncomfortable. —George Bernard Shaw

I've discovered that what we in England call drafts you in America call cross-ventilation. —Hermione Gingold

You English, you *play* politics. But we French, we *fight* politics.

—Adrien Arcand

Where there is one Englishman there will be a garden. Where there are two Englishmen there will be a club. But this does not mean any falling off in the number of gardens. There will be three. The club will have one too. —A. W. Smith

Deploring change is the unchangeable habit of all Englishmen.

—Raymond Postgate

The maxim of the British people is "Business as usual."

—Winston Churchill

* *

England is the paradise of individuality, eccentricity, heresy, anomalies, hobbies, and humors.   —George Santayana

England has civilization but no culture.   —Robin Mathews

The climate of England has been the world's most powerful colonizing impulse.   —Russell Green

Oh, to be in England/Now that April's there.
—Robert Browning (1812–1889)

* *

In England I would rather be a man, a horse, a dog or a woman, in that order. In America I think the order would be reversed.
—Bruce Gould

Contrary to popular belief, English women do not wear tweed nightgowns.   —Hermione Gingold

EQUALITY / INEQUALITY

I reckon there's as much human nature in some folks as there is in others, if not more.   —Edwards Noyes Westcott (1846–1898)

Greater health, wealth, freedom, fairness, and educational opportunity are not going to give us the egalitarian society of our philosophical heritage. It will instead give us a society sharply graduated, with ever greater innate separation between the top and bottom, and ever more uniformity within families as far as inherited abilities are concerned . . . making the social ladder even steeper for those left at the bottom.   —Richard Herrnstein

The orthodox environmental theories have been accepted not because they have stood up under proper scientific investigations, but because they harmonize so well with our democratic belief in human equality.   —Arthur Jensen

It is the mark of the cultured man that he is aware of the fact that equality is an ethical and not a biological principle.
—Ashley Montagu

Equality of opportunity is an equal opportunity to prove unequal talents.   —Sir Herbert Samuel

Wherever there is great property, there is great inequality . . . for one very rich man, there must be at least five hundred poor.
—Adam Smith (1723–1790)

Inequality of rights and power proceeds from the very Author of nature, from whom all paternity in heaven and earth is named.
—Pope Leo XIII

Our new government's foundations are laid, its cornerstone rests, upon the great truth that the Negro is not equal to the white man, that slavery—subordination to the superior race—is his natural and normal condition.   —Alexander H. Stephens (1812–1883)

The defect of equality is that we only desire it with our superiors.
—Henry Becque (1837–1899)

Your levellers wish to level down as far as themselves, but they cannot bear levelling up to themselves.
—Samuel Johnson (1709–1784)

By law of nature all men are equal.
—Domitius Ulpian (170?–228)

All animals are equal, but some animals are more equal than others.   —George Orwell

*   *

Let us be very clear on this matter: if we condemn people to inequality in our society we also condemn them to inequality in our economy.   —Lyndon B. Johnson

Real equality is not to be decreed by law. It cannot be given and it cannot be forced.   —Raymond Moley

*   *

Americans are so enamored of equality that they would rather be equal in slavery than unequal in freedom.
—Alexis de Tocqueville (1805–1859)

Would it not be better for everyone to realise that there are differences in heredity and environment which have to be recognized?
—William Ross

ERROR

The fellow who never makes a mistake takes his orders from one who does.   —Herbert V. Prochnow (On the other hand, if you don't learn from your mistakes, there's no sense making them.)

The habitually punctual make all their mistakes right on time.
—Laurence J. Peter

A blunderer is a man who starts a meat market during Lent.
—James Montgomery Bailey

When everyone is in the wrong, everyone is in the right.
—Pierre de La Chausée (1692–1754)

An old error is always more popular than a new truth.
—German Proverb

Truth will sooner come out of error than from confusion.
—Francis Bacon (1561–1626)

If error is corrected whenever it is recognized as such, the path of error is the path of truth.   —Hans Reichenbach

Admitting Error clears the Score/And proves you Wiser than before.   —Arthur Guiterman

*   *

The world always makes the assumption that the exposure of an error is identical with the discovery of the truth—that error and truth are simply opposite. They are nothing of the sort. What the world turns to, when it has been cured of one error, is usually simply another error, and maybe one worse than the first one.
—H. L. Mencken

An error is the more dangerous in proportion to the degree of truth which it contains.   —Henri Frédéric Amiel (1821–1881)

I have made mistakes but I have never made the mistake of claiming that I never made one.   —James Gordon Bennett

They defend their errors as if they were defending their inheritance.
—Edmund Burke (1729–1797)

*   *

Wise men learn by other men's mistakes, fools by their own.
—H. G. Bohn

The man who makes no mistakes does not usually make anything.
—Bishop W. C. Magee

*   *

A life spent in making mistakes is not only more honorable but more useful than a life spent in doing nothing.
—George Bernard Shaw

To err is human, but when the eraser wears out ahead of the pencil, you're overdoing it.   —J. Jenkins

ETHICS AND MORALS

Failure seems to be regarded as the one unpardonable crime, success 'as the all-redeeming virtue, the acquisition of wealth as the single worthy aim of life. The hair-raising revelations of skullduggery and grand-scale thievery merely incite others to surpass by yet bolder outrages and more corrupt combinations.
          —Charles Francis Adams (1807–1886)

I would rather be the man who bought the Brooklyn Bridge than the man who sold it.   —Will Rogers

An ethical man is a Christian holding four aces.   —Mark Twain

First secure an independent income, then practice virtue.
          —Greek Proverb

What is moral is what you feel good after.
          —Ernest Hemingway

France fell because there was corruption without indignation.
          —Romain Rolland

Science presented us first with normative ethics, then with relativistic ethics, and at last with no ethics at all.
          —George Faludy

When you prevent me from doing anything I want to do, that is persecution; but when I prevent you from doing anything you want to do, that is law, order and morals.
          —George Bernard Shaw

All the religion we have is the ethics of one or another holy person.
          —Ralph Waldo Emerson (1803–1882)

Moral judgments can't be made any more . . . the most important evidence that God is dead is the hopelessness in today's world.   —Thomas J. J. Altizer

The so-called new morality is too often the old immorality condoned.   —Lord Shawcross

A man is ethical only when life, as such, is sacred to him, that of plants and animals as well as that of his fellowman, and when he devotes himself helpfully to all life that is in need of help.
          —Albert Schweitzer

Ethics stays in the prefaces of the average business science book.
          —Peter Drucker

There is no more purpose or meaning in the world than you put into it . . . The answer to the quest for moral directives is therefore the same as the answer to the quest for certainty: both are demands for unattainable aims.   —Hans Reichenbach

In morals, always do as others do; in art, never.

—Jules Renard

What are we faced with in the nineteenth century? An age where woman was sacred; and where you could buy a thirteen-year-old girl for a few pounds . . . if you wanted her for only an hour or two . . . where more churches were built than in the whole previous history of the country; and where one in sixty houses in London was a brothel . . . where it was universally maintained that women do not have orgasms; and yet every prostitute was taught to simulate them. Where there was an enormous progress and liberation in every other field of human activity; and nothing but tyranny in the most personal and fundamental.

—John Fowles

It is the duty of the free man to live for his own sake, and not for others . . . Exploitation does not belong to a depraved or an imperfect and primitive state of society . . . it is a consequence of the intrinsic Will to Power, which is just the Will to Live.

—Friedrich Nietzsche (1844–1900)

My attitude to the world? I view it as a mess in which the clowns are paid more than they are worth, so I respectfully suggest that when we get going, we get our full share.

—George Jean Nathan

*   *

There is perhaps no phenomenon which contains so much destructive feeling as *moral indignation,* which permits envy or hate to be acted out under the guise of *virtue.*   —Erich Fromm

Moral indignation is jealousy with a halo.   —H. G. Wells

*   *

The justification of majority rule in politics is not to be found in its ethical superiority.   —Walter Lippmann

No one should expect the government to act in accordance with the moral code appropriate to the conduct of the individual.

—Baruch Spinoza (1632–1677)

*   *

Morality is the custom of one's country and the current feeling of one's peers. Cannibalism is moral in a cannibal country.

—Samuel Butler

There is no possible line of conduct which has at some time and place been condemned, and which has not at some other time and place been enjoined as a duty. —William Lecky

* *

The old view that the principles of right and wrong are immutable and eternal is no longer tenable. The moral world is as little exempt as the physical world from the law of ceaseless change, of perpetual flux. —Sir James Frazer

What is morality in any given time or place? It is what the majority then and there happen to like and immorality is what they dislike. —Alfred North Whitehead

---

Two things fill the mind with ever new and increasing wonder and awe—the starry heavens above me, and the moral law within me. —Immanuel Kant (1724–1804)

Without doubt the greatest injury . . . was done by basing morals on myth, for sooner or later myth is recognized for what it is, and disappears. Then morality loses the foundation on which it has been built. —Sir Herbert Samuel

* *

The paramount virtue of religion is that it has lighted up morality. —Matthew Arnold (1822–1888)

Divine morality is the absolute negation of human morality. —Mikhail A. Bakunin (1814–1876)

* *

War alone brings up to its highest tension all human energy and puts the stamp of nobility upon the peoples who have the courage to face it. —Benito Mussolini

No morality can be founded on authority, even if the authority were divine. —A. J. Ayer

EXPERIENCE

We should be careful to get out of an experience only the wisdom that is in it—and stop there; lest we be like the cat that sits down on a hot stove-lid. She will never sit down on a hot stove-lid again —and that is well; but also she will never sit down on a cold one anymore. —Mark Twain

Experience enables you to recognize a mistake when you make it again.   —Franklin P. Jones

Experience is the worst teacher; it gives the test before presenting the lesson.   —Vernon Law

Experience is not what happens to a man; it is what a man does with what happens to him.   —Aldous Huxley (Experience is the one thing you have plenty of when you're too old to get the job.)

If history repeats itself, and the unexpected always happens, how incapable must man be of learning from experience.
—George Bernard Shaw

. . . that peculiar disease of intellectuals, that infatuation with ideas at the expense of experience that compels experience to conform to bookish preconceptions.   —Archibald MacLeish (There's only one thing more painful than learning from experience, and that is not learning from experience.)

A proverb is a short sentence based on long experience.
—Miguel de Cervantes (1547–1616) (He who has burned his mouth blows his soup.—German Proverb)

There are many truths of which the full meaning cannot be realized until personal experience has brought it home.
—John Stuart Mill (1806–1873)

Experience is the comb that Nature gives us when we are bald.
—Belgian Proverb

Experience: A comb life gives you after you lose your hair.
—Judith Stern

*   *

Life is a series of experiences, each one of which makes us bigger, even though sometimes it is hard to realize this.   —Henry Ford

Experience is awareness of encompassing the totality of things.
—Sidney Hook (If humanity profits from its mistakes, we have a glorious future coming up.)

To most men, experience is like the stern lights of a ship which illumine only the track it has passed.
—Samuel Taylor Coleridge (1772–1834)

We learn from experience. A man never wakes up his second baby just to see it smile.   —Grace Williams

*   *

Nothing can take the place of practical experience out in the world.
                                        —A. B. Zu Tavern

The best substitute for experience is being sixteen.
                                        —Raymond Duncan

F

FACTS

There are no eternal facts as there are no absolute truths.
—Friedrich Nietzsche (1844–1900)

Facts do not cease to exist because they are ignored.
—Aldous Huxley (*As a matter of fact* is an expression that precedes many an expression that isn't.)

The degree of one's emotion varies inversely with one's knowledge of the facts—the less you know the hotter you get.
—Bertrand Russell

Get your facts first, and then you can distort them as much as you please. —Mark Twain (Facts are stubborn, but statistics are more pliable.)

Facts are stupid until brought into connection with some general law. —Louis Agassiz (1807–1873)

Every man has a right to his opinion, but no man has a right to be wrong in his facts. —Bernard M. Baruch

To some lawyers all facts are created equal.
—Justice Felix Frankfurter

Generally the theories we believe we call facts, and the facts we disbelieve we call theories.   —Felix Cohen

To treat your facts with imagination is one thing, but to imagine your facts is another.   —John Burroughs

*   *

The truth is more important than the facts.

—Frank Lloyd Wright

Facts and truth are often cousins—not brothers.

—Edward Bunker

FAILURE

Success is not a harbor but a voyage with its own perils to the spirit. The game of life is to come up a winner, to be a success, or to achieve what we set out to do. Yet there is always the danger of failing as a human being. The lesson that most of us on this voyage never learn, but can never quite forget, is that to win is sometimes to lose.   —Richard M. Nixon (Many a man gets to the top of the ladder, and then finds out it has been leaning against the wrong wall.)

Success makes us intolerant of failure, and failure makes us intolerant of success.   —William Feather (There are two kinds of failures: those who thought and never did, and those who did and never thought.)

Show me a thoroughly satisfied man—and I will show you a failure.

—Thomas Alva Edison

Men can suck the heady juice of exalted self-importance from the bitter weed of failure—failures are usually the most conceited of men.   —D. H. Lawrence

Whenever one finds oneself inclined to bitterness, it is a sign of emotional failure.   —Bertrand Russell (Success goes to your head, failure to your heart.)

How far high failure overleaps the bounds of low success.

—Lewis Morris

The fault, dear Brutus, is not in our stars,/But in ourselves that we are underlings.   —William Shakespeare (1564–1616) (The great question is not whether you have failed, but whether you are content with failure.)

Good people are good because they've come to wisdom through failure.   —William Saroyan

I cannot give you the formula for success, but I can give you the formula for failure—which is: Try to please everybody.
—Herbert Bayard Swope

When a man blames others for his failures, it's a good idea to credit others with his successes. —Howard W. Newton

You never know where bottom is until you plumb for it.
—Frederick Laing

In the game of life it's a good idea to have a few early losses, which relieves you of the pressure of trying to maintain an undefeated season. —Bill Vaughan

The difference between failure and success is doing a thing nearly right and doing a thing exactly right. —Edward Simmons

I am concerned with the cracking up that is happening all over . . . I have tried to touch the feeling of people who have self-propelled themselves in life and have been successful in attaining something they find they don't really want. —Elia Kazan

---

If at first you don't succeed, try, try, again. Then quit. There's no use being a damn fool about it. —W. C. Fields

There is no failure except in no longer trying.
—Elbert Hubbard

FAITH

Christians hold that their faith does good, but other faiths do harm . . . What I wish to maintain is that *all* faiths do harm. We may define *faith* as a firm belief in something for which there is no evidence. When there is evidence, no one speaks of *faith*. We do not speak of faith that two and two are four or that the earth is round. We only speak of faith when we wish to substitute emotion for evidence . . . We are told that faith could remove mountains, but no one believed it; we are now told that the atomic bomb can remove mountains, and everyone believes it. —Bertrand Russell

Hereafter I'll be able to understand everything, taking all on trust.
—Tristan Corbière

Faith is one of those words that connotes, however irrationally, some kind of virtue in itself. —Louis J. Halle

We have not lost faith, but we have transferred it from God to the medical profession. —George Bernard Shaw

Treat the other man's faith gently; it is all he has to believe with.
—Henry S. Haskins

Faith, n. Belief without evidence in what is told by one who speaks, without knowledge, of things without parallel.
—Ambrose Bierce

Faith means belief in something concerning which doubt is theoretically possible.   —William James

Faith—an illogical belief in the occurrence of the improbable.
—H. L. Mencken

Faith means intense, usually confident, belief that is not based on evidence sufficient to command assent from every reasonable person.
—Walter Kaufmann

Bid, then, the tender light of faith to shine/By which alone the mortal heart is led/Unto the thinking of the thought divine.
—George Santayana

Faith in a holy cause is to a considerable extent a substitute for the lost faith in ourselves.   —Eric Hoffer

Life is doubt, and faith without doubt is nothing but death.
—Miguel de Unamuno

Faith is never identical with piety.   —Karl Barth

The faith in which I was brought up assured me that I was better than other people; I was *saved,* they were *damned* . . . Our hymns were loaded with arrogance—self-congratulation on how cozy we were with the Almighty and what a high opinion he had of us, what hell everybody else would catch come Judgment Day.
—Robert Heinlein

Evidently God can cure cancer and tuberculosis, but cannot grow a new leg . . . this is blasphemy, but not mine—the priests and faith healers are guilty of limiting God's powers.
—Abraham Myerson

Action and faith enslave thought, both of them in order not to be troubled or inconvenienced by reflection, criticism, and doubt.
—Henri Frédéric Amiel (1821–1881)

The word *faith* is not generally regarded as a primary term in the scientist's lexicon, yet . . . faith is the vital ingredient in the Cyclops project (i.e., communicating with extraterrestrial races via microwave transmission).   —Norman Cousins

To believe only possibilities is not faith but mere Philosophy.
—Sir Thomas Browne (1605–1682)

A faith that cannot survive collision with the truth is not worth many regrets. —Arthur C. Clarke

Faith must trample under foot all reason, sense, and understanding.
—Martin Luther (1483–1546)

Question with boldness even the existence of God; because, if there be one, he must more approve of the homage of reason than that of blindfolded fear. —Thomas Jefferson (1743–1826)

Man prefers to believe what he prefers to be true.
—Francis Bacon (1561–1626)

It is not that I think or believe [in spiritualism], but that I *know*.
—Sir Arthur Conan Doyle

* *

I had to set limits to knowledge in order to make place for faith.
—Immanuel Kant (1724–1804)

Faith has need of the whole truth.
—Pierre Teilhard de Chardin

* *

If the work of God could be comprehended by reason, it would be no longer wonderful, and faith would have no merit if reason provided proof.
—Pope Gregory I (Saint Gregory the Great) (540–604)

The process of scientific discovery is, in effect, a continual flight from wonder. —Albert Einstein

* *

Understanding is the reward of faith. Therefore seek not to understand that thou mayest believe, but believe that thou mayest understand. —Saint Augustine (354–430)

Say what you will about the sweet miracle of unquestioning faith, I consider a capacity for it terrifying and absolutely vile!
—Kurt Vonnegut, Jr.

FALSITY

A thing is not necessarily true because badly uttered, nor false because spoken magnificently. —Saint Augustine (354–430)

Any fool can tell the truth, but it requires a man of some sense to know how to lie well. —Samuel Butler

The handwriting on the wall may be a forgery.

—Ralph Hodgson

Sin has many tools, but a lie is the handle that fits them all.

—Oliver Wendell Holmes, Jr.

If one is to be called a liar, one may as well make an effort to deserve the name.   —A. A. Milne

Fraud and falsehood only dread examination. Truth invites it.

—Thomas Cooper (1759–1851)

Desiring to be more than true, you are worse than false.

—Armand Baschet

I have the same confidence in the ability of our people to reject noxious literature as I have in their capacity to sort out the true from the false in theology, economics, or any other field.

—Justice William O. Douglas

A big lie is more plausible than truth.   —Ernest Hemingway

None speak false, when there is none to hear.   —James Beattie

---

A liar needs a good memory.   —Quintilian (35?–95?)

There is nothing so pathetic as a forgetful liar.

—F. M. Knowles

*   *

A halber emez iz a gantzer lign (A half truth is a whole lie).

—Yiddish Proverb

Whatever is only almost true is quite false, and among the most dangerous of errors, because being so near truth, it is the more likely to lead astray.   —Henry Ward Beecher (1813–1887)

*   *

A falsehood is an attempt to withhold the truth from those who have a right to know.   —Laurence J. Peter

And after all what is a lie? 'Tis but the truth in masquerade.

—George Gordon, Lord Byron (1788–1824)

Society can exist only on the basis that there is some amount of polished lying and that no one says exactly what he thinks.

—Lin Yutang

A little inaccuracy saves a world of explanation.   —C. E. Ayres

*   *

I am different from Washington; I have a higher, grander standard
of principle. Washington could not lie. I *can* lie, but I won't.
—Mark Twain

A falsehood once received from a famed writer becomes traditional
to posterity.   —John Dryden (1631–1700)

FAME

There is a famous family named Stein—
There's Gert, and there's Epp, and there's Ein;
Gert's poems are bunk,
Epp's statues are junk,
And no one understands Ein.   —Anon, Jr.

The day will come when everyone will be famous for fifteen minutes.
—Andy Warhol (And eventually the day will come when the fellow
who predicts the end of the world will be famous for fifteen seconds.)

A celebrity is a person who works hard all his life to become well
known, and then wears dark glasses to avoid being recognized.
—Fred Allen

In short, whoever you may be,/To this conclusion you'll agree,/
When everyone is somebodee,/Then no one's anybody!
—W. S. Gilbert

After a fellow gets famous it doesn't take long for someone to bob
up that used to sit by him at school.   —Frank McKinney Hubbard ("Kin Hubbard") (And the other indication will be when
some insane person imagines he is you.)

All the fame I look for in life is to have lived it quietly.
—Michel de Montaigne (1533–1592)

I think immortality is an overrated commodity.   —S. N. Behrman (And so is newspaper fame—a case of hero today and gone
tomorrow.)

Fame has also this great drawback, that if we pursue it we must
direct our lives in such a way as to please the fancy of men, avoiding
what they dislike and seeking what is pleasing to them.
—Baruch Spinoza (1632–1677)

Fame—the aggregate of all the misunderstandings that collect
around a new name.   —Rainer Maria Rilke

Fame creates its own standards. A guy who twitches his lips is just another guy with a lip twitch—unless he's Humphrey Bogart.

           —Sammy Davis, Jr.

Passion for fame: a passion which is the instinct of all great souls.

           —Edmund Burke (1729–1797)

Fame is the spur that the clear spirit doth raise/(That last infirmity of noble mind).   —John Milton (1608–1674)

*   *

If you would not be forgotten as soon as you are dead, either write things worth reading or do things worth writing.

           —Benjamin Franklin (1706–1790)

If fame is to come only after death, I am in no hurry for it.

           —Marcus Valerius Martial (A.D. 40–102)

FAMILY

The Universal Declaration of Human Rights describes the family as the natural and fundamental unit of society. It follows that any choice and decision with regard to the size of the family must irrevocably rest with the family itself and cannot be made by anyone else.   —United Nations

The parent who could see his boy as he really is, would shake his head and say, "Willie is no good; I'll sell him."

           —Stephen Leacock

He that hath wife and children hath given hostages to fortune.

           —Francis Bacon (1561–1626)

Most parents don't worry about a daughter until she fails to show up for breakfast. Then it is too late.   —Frank McKinney Hubbard ("Kin Hubbard") (Only a mother would think her daughter has been a good girl when she returns from a date with a Gideon Bible in her handbag.)

You can say this for these ready-mixes—the next generation isn't going to have any trouble making pies exactly like mother used to make.   —Earl Wilson

If you cannot get rid of the family skeleton, you may as well make it dance.   —George Bernard Shaw

A lot of parents pack up their troubles and send them off to a summer camp.   —Raymond Duncan

The only time a woman wishes she were a year older is when she is expecting a baby. —Mary Marsh

Nobody with that awful wife and those ugly children could be anything but normal. —Gore Vidal

There are no illegitimate children—only illegitimate parents.
—Judge Leon R. Yankwich

Who of us is mature enough for offspring before the offspring themselves arrive? The value of marriage is not that adults produce children but that children produce adults. —Peter De Vries

No matter how many communes anybody invents, the family always creeps back. —Margaret Mead

Some people seem compelled by unkind fate to parental servitude for life. There is no form of penal servitude much worse than this.
—Samuel Butler

Instant availability without continuous presence is probably the best role a mother can play. —Lotte Bailyn

Nothing is so soothing to our self-esteem as to find our bad traits in our forbears. It seems to absolve us. —Van Wyck Brooks

———————

The reason parents no longer lead their children in the right direction is because the parents aren't going that way themselves.
—Frank McKinney Hubbard ("Kin Hubbard")

To bring up a child in the way he should go, travel that way yourself once in a while.
—Josh Billings (Henry Wheeler Shaw) (1818–1885)

*   *

A married man with a family will do anything for money.
—Charles de Talleyrand (1754–1838)

I have certainly known more men destroyed by the desire to have a wife and child and to keep them in comfort than I have seen destroyed by drink and harlots. —William Butler Yeats

*   *

A good family . . . is one that used to be better.
—Cleveland Amory

Our family is not yet so good as to be degenerating.
—Kurt Ewald

*   *

When I was a boy of fourteen, my father was so ignorant I could hardly stand to have the old man around. But when I got to be twenty-one, I was astonished at how much he had learned in seven years.   —Mark Twain (It never occurs to a boy that he will some day be as dumb as his father.)

The children despise their parents until the age of forty, when they suddenly become just like them—thus preserving the system. —Quentin Crewe (By the time a man realizes that his father was usually right, he has a son who thinks he's usually wrong.)

The family is the nucleus of civilization.

—Will and Ariel Durant

As long as the family and the myth of the family . . . have not been destroyed, women will still be oppressed.

—Simone de Beauvoir

*   *

The family you come from isn't as important as the family you're going to have.   —Ring Lardner

We adore titles and heredities in our hearts, and ridicule them with our mouths. This is our democratic privilege.   —Mark Twain (Why pay money to have your family tree traced; go into politics and your opponents will do it for you.)

FANATICISM / FANATICS

A fanatic is one who sticks to his guns whether they're loaded or not.   —Franklin P. Jones

A fanatic is a man that does what he thinks the Lord would do if he knew the facts of the case.

—Finley Peter Dunne (Mr. Dooley)

A fanatic is one who can't change his mind and won't change the subject.   —Winston Churchill (Or a person who is highly enthusiastic about something in which you are not even remotely interested.)

The worst vice of the fanatic is his sincerity.   —Oscar Wilde (1854–1900) (And he goes through life, his mouth open and his mind closed.)

Fanaticism consists in redoubling your effort when you have forgotten your aim.   —George Santayana

The tendency to claim God as an ally for our partisan values and ends is . . . the source of all religious fanaticism.
—Reinhold Niebuhr

Goose pimples rose all over me, my hair stood on end, my eyes filled with tears of love and gratitude for this greatest of all conquerors of human misery and shame, and my breath came in little gasps. If I had not known that the Leader would have scorned such adulation, I might have fallen to my knees in unashamed worship, but instead I drew myself to attention, raised my arm in the eternal salute of the ancient Roman Legions and repeated the holy words, "Heil Hitler!"   —George Lincoln Rockwell

FASCISM

Reactionary concepts plus revolutionary emotion result in Fascist mentality.   —Wilhelm Reich

Fascism is, above all, action and sentiment . . . it is the unconscious reawakening of our profound racial instinct.
—Alfredo Rocco

My private and public feud with Fascism keeps me alive.
—Abraham L. Feinberg

Fascism, which was not afraid to call itself reactionary . . . does not hesitate to call itself illiberal and anti-liberal.
—Benito Mussolini

Fascism is Capitalism in decay.   —Nikolai Lenin

Fascism is nothing but capitalist reaction.   —Leon Trotsky

*   *

The next step [in a Fascist movement] is to fascinate fools and muzzle the intelligent, by emotional excitement on the one hand and terrorism on the other.   —Bertrand Russell

That which the Fascists hate above all else, is intelligence.
—Miguel de Unamuno

Fascist rule prevents worse injustice, and if Fascism goes under, nothing can save the country from chaos: God's cause goes under with it.   —Arthur, Cardinal Hinsley

Because Fascism is a lie, it is condemned to literary sterility. And when it is past, it will have no history, except the bloody history of murder.   —Ernest Hemingway

FAULTS

If we had no faults we should not take so much pleasure in noting those of others.   —Duc de La Rochefoucauld (1613–1680) (Why bother to find fault—there's no reward offered.)

She's generous to a fault—if it's her own.

—Arthur "Bugs" Baer

Faults are thick where love is thin.   —James Howell

Be to her virtues very kind,/Be to her faults a little blind.

—Matthew Prior (1664–1721)

A man's defects are the faults of his time while his virtues are his own.   —Johann W. von Goethe (1749–1832)

Pride has a greater share than goodness of heart in the remonstrances we make to those who are guilty of faults; we reprove not so much with a view to correct them as to persuade them that we are exempt from those faults ourselves.   —Duc de La Rochefoucauld (Rare is the person who can weigh the faults of others without putting his thumb on the scales.)

FEAR

If a man harbors any sort of fear, it . . . makes him landlord to a ghost.   —Lloyd Douglas

I believe that anyone can conquer fear by doing the things he fears to do, provided he keeps doing them until he gets a record of successful experiences behind him.   —Eleanor Roosevelt

To hate and to fear is to be psychologically ill . . . it is, in fact, the consuming illness of our time.   —H. A. Overstreet

---

The only thing we have to fear is fear itself.

—Franklin Delano Roosevelt

Nothing is so much to be feared as fear.

—Henry David Thoreau (1817–1862)

*   *

Nothing is terrible except fear itself.
—Francis Bacon (1561–1626)

The only thing I am afraid of is fear.
—Arthur Wellesley, Duke of Wellington (1759–1852)

* *

The fear of life is the favorite disease of the twentieth century.
—William Lyon Phelps

It is not death that a man should fear, but he should fear never beginning to live. —Marcus Aurelius (121–180)

Who is more foolish, the child afraid of the dark or the man afraid of the light? —Maurice Freehill

The only thing we have to fear on the planet is man.
—Carl Jung

* *

There is perhaps nothing so bad and so dangerous in life as fear.
—Jawaharlal Nehru

A good scare is worth more to a man than good advice.
—Ed Howe

THE FLAG

And the star-spangled banner in triumph shall wave/O'er the land of the free and the home of the brave.
—Francis Scott Key (1779–1843)

Many a bum show has been saved by the flag.
—George M. Cohan

Patriotic societies seem to think that the way to educate school children in a democracy is to stage bigger and better flag-saluting.
—S. I. Hayakawa

I name thee Old Glory.
—Captain William Driver (1803–1886)

"Shoot if you must, this old grey head,/But spare your country's flag," she said. —John Greenleaf Whittier (1807–1892)

These Colors Don't Run. —Bumper sticker

* *

When the flag is unfurled, all reason is in the trumpet.
—Ukrainian Proverb

It seems like th' less a statesman amounts to th' more he loves th' flag.   —Frank McKinney Hubbard ("Kin Hubbard")

*   *

I thought I'd never see the day when Communists and niggers and white niggers and Jews were flying under the banner of the United Nations flag, not the American flag we fought for.   —Matt Murphy (The man who is always waving the flag usually waives what it stands for.)

A person gets from a symbol the meaning he puts into it.
—The United States Supreme Court

*   *

Let us raise a standard to which the wise and honest can repair.
—George Washington (1732–1799)

The flag is a flag of liberty of opinion as well as of political liberty.
—Woodrow Wilson

———————

I am one of those who desire to wash the flag, not burn it.
—Norman Thomas

If any one attempts to haul down the American flag, shoot him on the spot.   —John A. Dix (1798–1879)

FOOD / HUNGER

Gluttony is not a secret vice.   —Orson Welles

Shake and shake/The catsup bottle,/None will come,/And then a lot'll.   —Richard Armour

A gourmet can tell from the flavor whether a woodcock's leg is the one on which the bird is accustomed to roost.   —Lucius Beebe

I feel a recipe is only a theme, which an intelligent cook can play each time with a variation.   —Madame Benoit

I wish my ulcers and I could get together on a mutually satisfactory diet.   —Irvin S. Cobb

Jack Sprat could eat no fat,/His wife could eat no lean. A real sweet pair of neurotics.   —Jack Sharkey

The great companies did not know that the line between hunger and anger is a thin line.   —John Steinbeck

I've never known a country to be starved into democracy.
—Senator George D. Aiken

The food here is so tasteless you could eat a meal of it and belch and it wouldn't remind you of anything. —Redd Foxx

An empty stomach is not a good political adviser.
—Albert Einstein

No man can be a patriot on an empty stomach.
—William Cowper (1731–1800)

Principles have no real force except when one is well fed.
—Mark Twain

No amount of political freedom will satisfy the hungry masses.
—Nikolai Lenin

How long would we remain free in a daily, desperate, overpopulated scramble for bread? —David Brinkley

---

Undoubtedly the desire for food has been, and still is, one of the main causes of great political events. —Bertrand Russell

All forms of government fall when it comes up to the question of bread—bread for the family, something to eat. Bread to a man with a hungry family comes first—before his union, before his citizenship, before his church affiliation. Bread!
—John L. Lewis

* *

A hungry man is not a free man. —Adlai Stevenson

True individual freedom cannot exist without economic security and independence. People who are hungry and out of a job are the stuff of which dictatorships are made.
—Franklin Delano Roosevelt

Obesity is really widespread. —Joseph O. Kern II

Eat, drink and be merry, for tomorrow ye diet.
—Lewis C. Henry

* *

Another good reducing exercise consists in placing both hands against the table edge and pushing back. —Robert Quillen

I'm not going to starve to death just so I can live a little longer.
—Irene Peter

FOOLS / FOLLY

There's a sucker born every minute.
                    —P. T. Barnum (1810–1891)

Every man is a damn fool for at least five minutes every day; wisdom consists of not exceeding the limit.   —Elbert Hubbard

Never let a fool kiss you or a kiss fool you.   —Joey Adams

If fifty million people say a foolish thing, it is still a foolish thing.
                    —Anatole France

Fools rush in where angels fear to tread.
                    —Alexander Pope (1688–1744)

I have great faith in fools; self-confidence my friends call it.
                    —Edgar Allan Poe (1809–1849)

There is nothing by which men display their character so much as in what they consider ridiculous . . . Fools and sensible men are equally innocuous. It is in the half fools and the half wise that the great danger lies.   —Johann W. von Goethe (1749–1832)

———————

Controversy equalizes fools and wise men—and the fools know it.
                    —Oliver Wendell Holmes, Jr.

By dint of railing at idiots we run the risk of becoming idiots ourselves.   —Gustave Flaubert (1821–1880)

*   *

There is no fool like an old fool.   —John Lyly (1554?–1606)

There's no fool like an old fool—you can't beat experience.
                    —Jacob M. Braude

*   *

A fool must now and then be right by chance.
                    —William Cowper (1731–1800)

The greatest lesson in life is to know that even fools are right sometimes.   —Winston Churchill

*   *

You must play the fool a little if you would not be thought wholly a fool . . . Every day I hear stupid people say things that are not stupid.   —Michel de Montaigne (1533–1592)

He dares to be a fool, and that is the first step in the direction of wisdom.   —James Gibbons Huneker (There are two kinds of fools. One says, "This is old, therefore it is good." The other says, "This is new, therefore it is better.")

Let us be thankful for the fools. But for them the rest of us could not succeed.   —Mark Twain

Few of the many wise apothegms which have been uttered have prevented a single foolish action.
                    —Thomas Babington Macaulay (1800–1859)

*   *

A prosperous fool is a grievous burden.
                    —Aeschylus (525–456 B.C.)

A fool and his money are soon parted.   —James Howell (A fool and his money were lucky to get together in the first place.)

FORCE

He who lives by the sword shall perish by the champagne cocktail.
                    —Saul Alinsky

Force rules the world—not opinion; but it is opinion that makes use of force.   —Blaise Pascal (1623–1662)

Justice without force is powerless; force without justice is tyrannical.   —Blaise Pascal

Fraud is the homage that force pays to reason.
                    —Charles P. Curtis

All cruelty springs from weakness.   —Seneca (4 B.C.–A.D. 65)

The most savage controversies are those about matters as to which there is no good evidence either way. Persecution is used in theology, not in arithmetic.   —Bertrand Russell

The infliction of cruelty with a good conscience is a delight to moralists. That is why they invented hell.   —Bertrand Russell

The natural forces crush and destroy man when he transgresses them, as they destroy or neutralize one another.
                    —John Burroughs

Force and right are the governors of this world; force till right is ready.   —Matthew Arnold (1822–1888)

The era of force must give way to that of knowledge, and the policy of the future will be to teach and to lead.   —Henry Gantt

Force is never more operative than when it is known to exist but is not brandished.   —Alfred Thayer Mahan (The appearance of power *is* power; it is the art of making "big sticks" out of little twigs.)

"Force is but might," the teacher said—/"That definition's just." /The boy said nought but thought instead,/Remembering his pounded head:/"Force is not might but must!"
                                                    —Ambrose Bierce

If you admit that to silence your opponent by force is to win an intellectual argument, then you admit the right to silence people by force.   —Hans Eysenck

*   *

We are today in the most literal sense a lawless society, for our *law* has ceased to be law and become instead its opposite—mere force at the disposal of whoever is at the controls.
                                                    —Charles A. Reich

A man convinced against his will is not convinced.
                                                    —Laurence J. Peter

---

There is plenty of law at the end of a nightstick.
                                                    —Grover Whalen

The inclination to aggression . . . constitutes the greatest impediment to civilization.   —Sigmund Freud

*   *

Covenants without swords are but words.
                                    —Thomas Hobbes (1588–1679)

Who overcomes by force hath overcome but half his foe.
                                    —John Milton (1608–1674)

*   *

Nothing multiplies more easily than force . . . In its grossest and most lethal form, force is represented by groupings of people into nations. This makes possible a concentration of collective effort with a minimum of restraint and a maximum of fury.
                                                    —Norman Cousins

In the scale of the destinies, brawn will never weigh as much as brain.   —James Russell Lowell (1819–1891)

FORGIVENESS

I can pardon everyone's mistakes but my own.
                    —Marcus Porcius Cato (234–149 B.C.)

He that cannot forgive others breaks the bridge over which he must pass himself; for every man has need to be forgiven.
                    —Thomas Fuller (1608–1661)

Forgiveness is the key to action and freedom.
                              —Hannah Arendt

For my part I believe in the forgiveness of sin and the redemption of ignorance.   —Adlai Stevenson

To be wronged is nothing unless you continue to remember it.
                    —Confucius (c. 551–479 B.C.)

The offender never pardons.   —George Herbert (1593–1633)

People will sometimes forgive you the good you have done them, but seldom the harm they have done you.
                              —Somerset Maugham

*   *

It's far easier to forgive an enemy after you've got even with him.
                              —Olin Miller

We should forgive our enemies, but only after they have been hanged first.   —Heinrich Heine (1797–1856)

Without forgiveness life is governed by . . . an endless cycle of resentment and retaliation.   —Roberto Assagioli

Never does the human soul appear so strong as when it forgoes revenge, and dares forgive an injury.
                    —E. H. Chapin (1814–1880)

FORTUNE / MISFORTUNE

I was lucky. When God rained manna from heaven, I had a spoon.
                              —Peter Drucker

The worst misfortune that can happen to an ordinary man is to have an extraordinary father.   —Austin O'Malley

It is not my mode of thought that has caused my misfortunes, but the mode of thought of others.

—Marquis de Sade (1740–1814)

When you're down and out, something always turns up—and it's usually the noses of your friends.   —Orson Welles (The only man who sticks closer to you in adversity than a friend is a creditor.)

Let us be of good cheer, remembering that misfortunes hardest to bear are those which never come.

—James Russell Lowell (1819–1891)

If you are too fortunate, you will not know yourself. If you are too unfortunate, nobody will know you.

—Thomas Fuller (1608–1661)

Everyone can master a grief but he that has it.

—William Shakespeare (1564–1616)

Experience has taught me this, that we undo ourselves by impatience. Misfortunes have their life and their limits, their sickness and their health.   —Michel de Montaigne (1533–1592)

If all our misfortunes were laid in one common heap whence everyone must take an equal portion, most people would be contented to take their own and depart.   —Socrates (470?–399 B.C.)

It is to the interest of mankind that there should be some one who is unconquered, some one against whom fortune has no power.

—Seneca (4 B.C.–A.D. 65)

I must complain the cards are ill shuffled till I have a good hand.
—Jonathan Swift (1667–1745) (Fortune knocks but once, but misfortune has much more patience.)

There are many in this old world of ours who hold that things break about even for all of us. I have observed for example that we all get the same amount of ice. The rich get it in the summertime and the poor get it in the winter.   —Bat Masterson

Adversity is the trial of principle. Without it a man hardly knows whether he is honest or not.   —Henry Fielding (1707–1754)

All of us have sufficient fortitude to bear the misfortunes of others.
—Duc de La Rochefoucauld (1613–1680)

I never knew any man in my life who could not bear another's misfortunes perfectly like a Christian.

—Alexander Pope (1688–1744)

*   *

By trying we can easily learn to endure adversity—another man's.
—Mark Twain

Calamities are of two kinds: misfortune to ourselves, and good fortune to others.   —Ambrose Bierce

*   *

Adversity reveals genius, prosperity conceals it.
—Horace (65–8 B.C.)

Prosperity doth best discover vice; but adversity doth best discover virtue.   —Francis Bacon (1561–1626)

We have a degree of delight . . . in the real misfortunes and pains of others.   —Edmund Burke (1729–1797)

Never find your delight in another's misfortune.
—Publilius Syrus (c. 1st century B.C.)

FREEDOM AND LIBERTY

The natural progress of things is for liberty to yield and government to gain ground.   —Thomas Jefferson (1743–1826) (Men fight for freedom; then they begin to accumulate laws to take it away from themselves.)

Freedom is not enough.   —Lyndon B. Johnson

Liberty doesn't work as well in practice as it does in speeches.
—Will Rogers

It is by the goodness of God that in our country we have those three unspeakably precious things: freedom of speech, freedom of conscience, and the prudence never to practice either of them.
—Mark Twain

You are free and that is why you are lost.   —Franz Kafka (Liberty is always unfinished business.)

Order without liberty and liberty without order are equally destructive.   —Theodore Roosevelt

Wherever public spirit prevails, liberty is secure.
—Noah Webster (1758–1843)

We cannot defend freedom abroad by deserting it at home.
—Edward R. Murrow

What is freedom? Freedom is the right to choose: the right to create for yourself the alternatives of choice. Without the possibility of choice and the exercise of choice a man is not a man but a member, an instrument, a thing. —Archibald MacLeish

The price of freedom of religion or of speech or of the press is that we must put up with, and even pay for, a good deal of rubbish.
—Justice Robert Jackson

The Constitution . . . speaks of liberty and prohibits the deprivation of liberty without due process of law. In prohibiting that deprivation the Constitution does not recognize an absolute and uncontrollable liberty. —Chief Justice Charles Evans Hughes

The contest for ages has been to rescue liberty from the grasp of executive power. —Daniel Webster (1782–1852)

The history of liberty is the history of resistance . . . [it is a] history of the limitation of governmental power.
—Woodrow Wilson

By a careful cultural design, we control not the final behavior, but the *inclination* to behave—the motives, the desires, the wishes . . . we *increase* the feeling of freedom. —B. F. Skinner

Whereas each man claims his freedom as a matter of right, the freedom he accords to other men is a matter of toleration.
—Walter Lippmann

Liberty is always dangerous, but it is the safest thing we have.
—Harry Emerson Fosdick

If you accept the necessity for freedom of expression, it follows that in an intellectual controversy any attempt to coerce rather than to persuade . . . is not merely an offense against the person so coerced, but an erosion of the mechanics which make free expression work, and therefore make it possible. —Michael Kinsley

The shepherd drives the wolf from the sheep's throat, for which the sheep thanks the shepherd as his liberator, while the wolf denounces him for the same act as the destroyer of liberty.
—Abraham Lincoln (1809–1865)

While the State exists, there is no freedom. When there is freedom, there will be no State. —Nikolai Lenin

To be free of bondage or restraint, to live under a government based on the consent of the citizens, these are basic among all freedoms . . . and this is the reason why a democracy is from every possible humane point of view the best form of government . . .

What so many human beings in the modern world have failed to understand is that *freedom* is the greatest of all trusts.
—Ashley Montagu

Freedom is nothing else but a chance to be better.
—Albert Camus

There is no conflict between liberty and safety. We will have both or neither.   —Ramsey Clark

Liberty is being free from the things we don't like in order to be slaves of the things we do like.   —Ernest Benn (No one can enjoy freedom unless he is willing to surrender some part of it.)

Man had achieved *freedom from*—without yet having achieved *freedom to*—to be himself, to be productive, to be fully awake.
—Erich Fromm

The history of liberty has largely been the history of the observance of procedural safeguards.   —Justice Felix Frankfurter (Men rattle their chains to show that they are free.)

When people are free to do as they please, they usually imitate each other.   —Eric Hoffer

The spirit of liberty . . . is the spirit which is not too sure it is always right.   —Judge Learned Hand

The greatest dangers to liberty lurk in insidious encroachment by men of zeal, well-meaning but without understanding.
—Justice Louis D. Brandeis

The tree of liberty must be refreshed from time to time with the blood of patriots and tyrants. It is its natural manure.
—Thomas Jefferson (1743–1826)

A free society is one where it is safe to be unpopular.
—Adlai Stevenson

Those who profess to favor freedom, and yet depreciate agitation, are men who want rain without thunder and lightning.
—Frederick Douglass (1817?–1895)

A nation may lose its liberties in a day and not miss them in a century.   —Baron de Montesquieu (1689–1755)

—————

Our liberty depends on freedom of the press, and that cannot be limited without being lost.   —Thomas Jefferson

The loss of liberty in general would soon follow the suppression of the liberty of the press; for it is an essential branch of liberty, so perhaps it is the best preservative of the whole.
—John Peter Zenger (1697–1746)

* *

The notion that the church, the press, and the universities should serve the state is essentially a Communist notion . . . In a free society these institutions must be wholly free—which is to say that their function is to serve as checks upon the state.
—Alan Barth

Man is forbidden to eat from the tree of knowledge of good and evil. He acts against God's command . . . From the standpoint of the Church, which represents authority, this is essentially sin. From the standpoint of man, however, this is the beginning of human freedom.   —Erich Fromm

* *

Liberty means responsibility. That is why most men dread it.
—George Bernard Shaw

In the end more than they wanted freedom, they wanted security. When the Athenians finally wanted not to give to society but for society to give to them, when the freedom they wished for was freedom from responsibility, then Athens ceased to be free.
—Edward Gibbon (1737–1794)

* *

The fact, in short, is that *freedom* to be meaningful in an organized society must consist of an amalgam of hierarchy of freedoms *and* restraints.   —Samuel Hendel

The story of man is the history, first, of the acceptance and imposition of restraints necessary to permit communal life; and second, of the emancipation of the individual within that system of necessary restraints.   —Justice Abe Fortas

* *

Eternal vigilance is the price of liberty.
—Wendell Phillips (1811–1884)

Those who expect to reap the blessings of freedom must, like men, undergo the fatigue of supporting it.
—Thomas Paine (1737–1809)

* *

For we both alike know that into the discussion of human affairs the question of justice enters only where the pressure of necessity is equal, and that the powerful exact what they can, and the weak grant what they must.   —Thucydides (471?–401? B.C.)

Liberty is so much latitude as the powerful choose to accord the weak.   —Judge Learned Hand

*   *

If Negro freedom is taken away, or that of any minority group, the freedom of all the people is taken away.   —Paul Robeson

No Negro American can be free until the lowliest Negro in Mississippi is no longer disadvantaged because of his race.
—Ralph Bunche

*   *

The purpose of freedom is to create it for others.
—Bernard Malamud

Liberty is the one thing you can't have unless you give it to others.
—William Allen White

*   *

Those who suppress freedom always do so in the name of *law and order*.   —John Lindsay

Order is the first requisite of liberty.
—Georg Wilhelm Hegel (1770–1831)

Many politicians . . . are in the habit of laying it down as a self-evident proposition, that no people ought to be free till they are fit to use their freedom. The maxim is worthy of the fool . . . who resolved not to go into the water till he had learned to swim.
—Thomas Babington Macaulay (1800–1859)

Without freedom, no one really has a name.   —Milton Acorda

*   *

Freedom comes from human beings, rather than from laws and institutions.   —Clarence Darrow

To enjoy freedom we have to control ourselves.
—Virginia Woolf

*   *

It is a great and dangerous error to suppose that all people are equally entitled to liberty.   —John C. Calhoun (1782–1850)

Those who deny freedom to others deserve it not for themselves.
    —Abraham Lincoln (1809–1865)

*   *

Restriction of free thought and free speech is the most dangerous of all subversions. It is the one un-American act that could most easily defeat us.   —Justice William O. Douglas

You hear about constitutional rights, free speech and the free press. Every time I hear these words I say to myself, "That man is a Red!" . . . You never hear a *real* American talk like that!
    —Mayor Frank Hague

*   *

The majority of us are for free speech only when it deals with those subjects concerning which we have no intense convictions.
    —Edmund B. Chaffee

At no time is freedom of speech more precious than when a man hits his thumb with a hammer.   —Marshall Lumsden

*   *

Freedom to live one's life with the window of the soul open to new thoughts, new ideas, new aspirations.   —Harold Ickes

Liberty too can corrupt, and absolute liberty can corrupt absolutely.   —Gertrude Himmelfarb

FREE ENTERPRISE

Free enterprise: A huge area of the American economy is still noticeable to observers with peripheral vision after they subtract the public sector, conglomerates, federally supported agriculture, monopolies, duopolies, and oligopolies.   —Bernard Rosenberg

Private enterprise is ceasing to be free enterprise.
    —Franklin Delano Roosevelt

I don't meet competition, I crush it.   —Charles Revson

Free enterprise ended in the United States a good many years ago. Big oil, big steel, big agriculture avoid the open marketplace. Big corporations fix prices among themselves and drive out the small entrepreneur. In their conglomerate forms, the huge corporations have begun to challenge the legitimacy of the state.
    —Gore Vidal

We are locked into a system of "fouling our own nest," so long as we behave as independent, rational free-enterprisers.

—Garrett Hardin

The primary aim of all government regulation of the economic life of the community should be, not to supplant the system of private economic enterprise, but to make it work.   —Carl Becker

Nobody talks more of free enterprise and competition and of the best man winning than the man who inherited his father's store or farm.   —C. Wright Mills

Private enterprise . . . makes OK private action which would be considered dishonest in public action.   —John F. Kennedy

We stand for the maintenance of private property . . . We shall protect free enterprise as the most expedient, or rather the sole possible economic order.   —Adolf Hitler

If we in business cannot put the brakes on this creeping socialism, the free enterprise system will become a thing of the past.

—Barton A. Cummings

Private enterprise, indeed, became too private. It became privileged enterprise, not free enterprise.   —Franklin Delano Roosevelt

No class of Americans, so far as I know, has ever objected . . . to any amount of governmental meddling if it appeared to benefit that particular class.   —Carl Becker (If you rob Peter to pay Paul you can always depend on the support of Paul.)

After I asked him what he meant, he replied that freedom consisted of the unimpeded right to get rich, to use his ability, no matter what the cost to others, to win advancement.   —Norman Thomas

FRIENDSHIP / FRIENDS

True friendship comes when silence between two people is comfortable.   —Dave Tyson Gentry

A friend that ain't in need is a friend indeed.

—Frank McKinney Hubbard ("Kin Hubbard")

You can always tell a real friend: when you've made a fool of yourself he doesn't feel you've done a permanent job.

—Laurence J. Peter

Friendship is an arrangement by which we undertake to exchange small favors for big ones.

—Baron de Montesquieu (1689–1755)

I don't like to commit myself about heaven and hell—you see, I have friends in both places.   —Mark Twain

Friendship among women is only a suspension of hostilities. —Comte de Rivarol (1753–1801) (A woman is never quite so old as her dearest friend says she is.)

He's the kind of man who picks his friends—to pieces.
     —Mae West (With friends such as these, who needs enemies?)

Instead of loving your enemies, treat your friends a little better.
                                                          —Ed Howe

Nothing so fortifies a friendship as a belief on the part of one friend that he is superior to the other.
                                  —Honoré de Balzac (1799–1850)

Mighty proud I am that I am able to have a spare bed for my friends. —Samuel Pepys (1632–1703) (There are no strangers here—only friends we have not met.)

Love thy neighbor as thyself, but choose your neighborhood.
                                                      —Louise Beal

It is more shameful to distrust our friends than to be deceived by them.   —Duc de La Rochefoucauld (1613–1680) (If your friend won't lend you fifty dollars, he's probably a close friend.)

Platonic friendship: The interval between the introduction and the first kiss.   —Sophie Irene Loeb

Love demands infinitely less than friendship.
                                          —George Jean Nathan

The truth that is suppressed by friends is the readiest weapon of the enemy.   —Robert Louis Stevenson (1850–1894) (A true friend will see you through when others see that you are through.)

We cherish our friends not for their ability to amuse us, but for ours to amuse them.   —Evelyn Waugh

One friend in a lifetime is much; two are many; three are hardly possible.   —Henry Adams (There are three kinds of friends: best friends, guest friends, and pest friends.)

Do not use a hatchet to remove a fly from your friend's forehead.
                                                  —Chinese Proverb

True friendship is like sound health, the value of it is seldom known until it be lost.   —Charles Caleb Colton (1780–1832)

Friendships, like marriages, are dependent on avoiding the unforgivable.   —John D. MacDonald

Nine-tenths of the people were created so you would want to be with the other tenth.   —Horace Walpole (1717–1797) (Some people have a large circle of friends while others have only friends they like.)

To find a friend one must close one eye—to keep him, two. —Norman Douglas (Having friends you like who are like you is a form of narcissism.)

One's friends are that part of the human race with which one can be human.   —George Santayana (The best rule of friendship is to keep your heart a little softer than your head.)

In politics . . . shared hatreds are almost always the basis of friendships.   —Alexis de Tocqueville (1805–1859)

There is no stronger bond of friendship than a mutual enemy.
                                        —Frankfort Moore

* *

If we were all given by magic the power to read each other's thoughts, I suppose the first effect would be to dissolve all friendships.   —Bertrand Russell

If all men knew what each said of the other, there would not be four friends in the world.   —Blaise Pascal (1623–1662)

Against a foe I can myself defend,—/But Heaven protect me from a blundering friend!   —D'Arcy W. Thompson

The essence of true friendship is to make allowance for another's little lapses.   —David Storey

* *

If we all said to people's faces what we say behind one another's backs, society would be impossible.
                                        —Honoré de Balzac (1799–1850)

He is a fine friend. He stabs you in the front.
                                        —Leonard Louis Levinson

G

GENETICS / HEREDITY / ENVIRONMENT

I think that the degree of probability with which racial genetic differences can be stated today is not adequate as a basis for policies to deal with racial issues.   —Arthur Jensen

Once the size of the brain is not limited by the size of the pelvis, it might be possible to double the number of fetal brain cells.

—Caryl Rivers

Heredity is what sets the parents of a teen-ager wondering about each other.   —Laurence J. Peter

I don't know who my grandfather was; I am much more concerned to know what his grandson will be.

—Abraham Lincoln (1809–1865)

Heredity is nothing but stored environment.   —Luther Burbank (The traits that a disobedient child gets from the other parent.)

The scientific theory that there are genetically conditioned mental or behavioral differences between races cannot be called racist. It would be just as illogical to condemn the recognition of physical differences between races as racist.   —Arthur Jensen

With a good heredity, nature deals you a fine hand at cards; and with a good environment, you learn to play the hand well.

—Walter C. Alvarez, M.D.

The environmentalists seem to believe that if cats gave birth to kittens in a stove, the offspring would be biscuits.

—Abraham Myerson

Few people are capable of expressing with equanimity opinions which differ from the prejudices of their social environment.

—Albert Einstein

Most of the estimates for the heritability of intelligence in the populations studied indicate that genetic factors are about twice as important as environmental factors as a cause of IQ differences among individuals.   —Arthur Jensen

We can escape from the level of society, but not from the level of intelligence to which we were born.   —Randall Jarrell

---

The IQ difference between Indians and blacks . . . turns out opposite to what one would predict from purely environmental theory, which, of course, assumes complete genetic equality for intelligence.

—Arthur Jensen

The difference between . . . a philosopher and a common street porter . . . arises not so much from nature as from habit, custom, and education.   —Adam Smith (1723–1790)

*   *

The growth of wealth will recruit for the upper classes precisely those from the lower classes who have the edge in native ability. Whatever else this accomplishes, it will also increase the IQ gap between the upper and lower classes, making the social ladder even steeper for those left at the bottom.

—Richard Herrnstein

Intelligence is largely a matter of genes, but *genetic regression* exerts an equalizing pull on IQ . . . Such a fact makes Herrnstein's position untenable. No fixed *caste* of dull, unemployed people is developing.   —Hans Eysenck

GENIUS AND TALENT

Everyone is a genius at least once a year; a real genius has his original ideas closer together.

—G. C. Lichtenberg (1742–1799)

The principal mark of genius is not perfection but originality, the opening of new frontiers.   —Arthur Koestler

In the battle of existence, Talent is the punch; Tact is the clever footwork.   —Wilson Mizner

Genius is the highest type of reason—talent the highest type of understanding.   —L. P. Hickok

Genius, in one respect, is like gold—numbers of persons are constantly writing about both, who have neither.
—Charles Caleb Colton (1780–1832)

Talent is what you possess; genius is what possesses you.
—Malcolm Cowley

Genius does what it must, talent does what it can.
—Edward Bulwer-Lytton (1803–1873)

It is the curse of talent that, although it labors with greater steadiness and perseverance than genius, it does not reach its goal, while genius already on the summit of the ideal, gazes laughingly about.
—Robert Schumann (1810–1856)

True genius resides in the capacity for evaluation of uncertain, hazardous, and conflicting information.   —Winston Churchill

Every man of genius is considerably helped by being dead.
—Robert S. Lynd

The greatest genius is never so great as when it is chastised and subdued by the highest reason.
—Charles Caleb Colton

In the republic of mediocrity, genius is dangerous.
—Robert G. Ingersoll (1833–1899)

———————

In every work of genius we recognize our own rejected thoughts; they come back to us with a certain alienated majesty.
—Ralph Waldo Emerson (1803–1882)

Poetry is the revelation of a feeling that the poet believes to be interior and personal [but] which the reader recognizes as his own.
—Salvatore Quasimodo

*   *

Genius means little more than the faculty of perceiving in an unhabitual way.   —William James

It is the function of creative men to perceive the relations between thoughts, or things, or forms of expression that may seem utterly different, and to be able to combine them into some new forms—the power to connect the seemingly unconnected.
—William Plomer

The world . . . is only beginning to see that the wealth of a nation consists more than anything else in the number of superior men that it harbors . . . Geniuses are ferments; and when they come together, as they have done in certain lands at certain times, the whole population seems to share in the higher energy which they awaken. The effects are incalculable and often not easy to trace in detail, but they are pervasive and momentous.

—William James

Works of genius are the first things in the world.

—John Keats (1795–1821)

* *

It is the great triumph of genius to make the common appear novel.

—Johann W. von Goethe (1749–1832)

Genius is the ability to reduce the complicated to the simple.

—C. W. Ceram

GOD / GODS

God will forgive me; that's his business.

—Heinrich Heine (1797–1856)

An honest God is the noblest work of man.

—Robert G. Ingersoll (1833–1899)

I could not say I believe. I know! I have had the experience of being gripped by something that is stronger than myself, something that people call God.   —Carl Jung

We turn toward God only to obtain the impossible.

—Albert Camus

Who sees with equal eye, as God of all,/A hero perish or a sparrow fall.   —Alexander Pope (1688–1744)

The great god Ra whose shrine once covered acres/Is filler now for crossword-puzzle makers.   —Keith Preston

We must be greater than God, for we have to undo His injustice.

—Jules Renard

For several years more I maintained public relations with the Almighty. But privately, I ceased to associate with him.

—Jean-Paul Sartre

God—the contrapuntal genius of human fate.

—Vladimir Nabokov

It is fear that first brought gods into the world.
—Petronius (d. A.D. 66?)

To believe in God is impossible—not to believe in Him is absurd.
—Voltaire (François Marie Arouet) (1694–1778)

Even God cannot change the past.
—Agathon (447?–401 B.C.)

When a pious visitor inquired sweetly, "Henry, have you made your peace with God?" he [Thoreau] replied, "We have never quarrelled."
—Brooks Atkinson

Impiety: Your irreverence toward my deity.
—Ambrose Bierce

If the average man is made in God's image, then such a man as Beethoven or Aristotle is plainly superior to God.
—H. L. Mencken

I don't know why it is that the religious never ascribe common sense to God.   —Somerset Maugham

Our idea of God implies necessary and eternal existence; the manifest conclusion then is that God does exist . . . That God has foreordained everything is self-evident.
—René Descartes (1596–1650)

Millions of angels are at God's command.   —Billy Graham

It may be that our role on this planet is not to worship God—but to create him.   —Arthur C. Clarke

God—but a word invoked to explain the world.
—Prat de Lamartine (1790–1869)

God loves you. God doesn't want anyone to be hungry and oppressed. He just puts his big arms around everybody and hugs them up against himself.   —Norman Vincent Peale

Herein we see God's great mercy . . . for the slaughter was in all 5,517, *but ten of the enemy's side were slain to one of ours.*
—Nehemiah Wallington

Why would we have different races if God meant us to be alike and associate with each other?   —Lester Maddox

Fascist rule prevents worse injustice, and if Fascism goes under, nothing can save the country from chaos: God's cause goes under with it.   —Arthur Cardinal Hinsley

God ordained segregation.   —Reverend Billy James Hargis

The Divine Law is against Communism.   —Earl F. Landgrebe

Sensible and responsible women do not want to vote. The relative positions to be assumed by man and woman in the working out of our civilization were assigned long ago by a higher intelligence than ours.   —Grover Cleveland

The speech of the Almighty [in the Book of Job] . . . is a parade of power, devoid of moral content . . . positively immoral by any human standards.   —Kenneth Rexroth

---

God is the tangential point between zero and infinity.
                                            —Alfred Jarry

I could prove God statistically.   —George Gallup

*   *

God had a divine purpose in placing this land between two great oceans to be found by those who had a special love of freedom and courage.   —Ronald Reagan

God has marked the American people as His chosen nation to finally lead in the regeneration of the world.
                                    —Senator Albert J. Beveridge

*   *

There never was any remarkable lawgiver amongst any people who did not resort to divine authority.
                            —Niccolò Machiavelli (1469–1527)

Who says I am not under the special protection of God?
                                            —Adolf Hitler

*   *

Concerning the gods, I am not able to know to a certainty whether they exist or not. For there are many things which prevent one from knowing, especially the obscurity of the subject, and the shortness of the life of man.   —Protagoras (5th century B.C.)

In spite of all the yearnings of men, no one can produce a single fact or reason to support the belief in God and in personal immortality.   —Clarence Darrow

*   *

Many a sober Christian would rather admit that a wafer is God than that God is a cruel and capricious tyrant.
                                    —Edward Gibbon (1737–1794)

I've steered clear of God. He was an incredible sadist.
                                            —John Collier

*   *

It is easy to understand God as long as you don't try to explain
him.   —Joseph Joubert (1754–1824)

If the work of God could be comprehended by reason, it would be
no longer wonderful.
                 —Pope Gregory I (Saint Gregory the Great) (540–604)

*   *

The Devil would be the best way out as an excuse for God . . .
But even so, one can hold God responsible for the existence of the
Devil.   —Sigmund Freud

Faith in immortality, like belief in Satan, leaves unanswered the
ancient question: is God unable to prevent suffering and thus not
omnipotent? or is he able but not willing to prevent it and thus
not merciful? And is he just?   —Walter Kaufmann

*   *

The notion of the Trinity of Gods has enfeebled the belief in one
God. A multiplication of beliefs acts as a division of belief; and in
proportion as anything is divided it is weakened.
                 —Thomas Paine (1737–1809)

Trinity is the word for a committee god.
                 —Bishop James A. Pike

In my view, God educates us through our deceptions and mistakes,
in order to make us understand at last that we ought to believe
only in Him, and not in man.   —Jacques Maritain

Man must accept responsibility for himself . . . There is no meaning to life except the meaning man gives his life by the unfolding
of his powers.   —Erich Fromm

*   *

Cursed is everyone who placeth his hope in man.
                 —Saint Augustine (354–430)

In war, when a commander becomes so bereft of reason and perspective that he fails to understand the dependence of arms on
Divine guidance, he no longer deserves victory.
                 —General Douglas MacArthur

The tendency to claim God as an ally for our partisan values and ends is . . . the source of all religious fanaticism.

—Reinhold Niebuhr

* *

I cannot admit that any man born . . . has either the knowledge or authority to tell other men . . . what God's purposes are.

—Judge Ben B. Lindsey

There are scores of thousands of sects who are ready at a moment's notice to reveal the will of God on every possible subject.

—George Bernard Shaw

* *

This doctrine of the material efficacy of prayer reduces the Creator to a cosmic bellhop of a not very bright or reliable kind.

—Herbert J. Muller

God is not a cosmic bellboy. —Harry Emerson Fosdick

* *

Whom the gods wish to destroy they first call promising.

—Cyril Connolly

Whom the gods would destroy they first make mad.

—Euripides (484–406 B.C.)

GOOD AND EVIL

When choosing between two evils, I always like to try the one I've never tried before. —Mae West

The good die young—because they see it's no use living if you've got to be good. —John Barrymore

There ain't any news in being good. You might write the doings of all the convents of the world on the back of a postage stamp, and have room to spare. —Finley Peter Dunne (Mr. Dooley)

Our repentance is not so much regret for the evil we have done, as fear of its consequences.

—Duc de La Rochefoucauld (1613–1680)

The word *good* has many meanings. For example, if a man were to shoot his grandmother at a range of five hundred yards, I should call him a good shot, but not *necessarily* a good man.

—G. K. Chesterton

We are ne'er like angels till our passion dies.
—Thomas Dekker (1572?–1632)

Only a coward or a madman would give good for evil.
—Euripides (484–406 B.C.)

It is almost impossible systematically to constitute a natural moral law. Nature has no principles. She furnishes us with no reason to believe that human life is to be respected. Nature, in her indifference, makes no distinction between good and evil.

—Anatole France

Any man who hates dogs and babies can't be all bad. —Leo Rosten (Or, as W. C. Fields put it, "Any man who hates dogs and loves whiskey can't be all bad.")

Healthy-mindedness is inadequate as a philosophical doctrine, because the evil facts which it refuses positively to account for are a genuine portion of reality; and they may after all be the best key to life's significance. —William James

Most of the evils of life arise from man's being unable to sit still in a room. —Blaise Pascal (1623–1662)

Non-cooperation with evil is as much a duty as is cooperation with good. —Mohandas Gandhi

When it was seen that many of the wicked seemed quite untroubled by evil consciences . . . then the idea of future suffering was advanced. —Lewis Browne

The only thing necessary for the triumph of evil is for good men to do nothing. —Edmund Burke (1729–1797)

The first idea that the child must acquire, in order to be actively disciplined, is that of the difference between good and evil; and the task of the educator lies in seeing that the child does not confound good with immobility, and evil with activity.

—Maria Montessori

Goodness is beauty in the best estate.
—Christopher Marlowe (1564–1593)

Good, the more communicated, more abundant grows.
—John Milton (1608–1674)

What is the real relation between happiness and goodness? It is only within a few generations that men have found courage to say that there is none. —William Graham Sumner

The only good is knowledge and the only evil is ignorance.
—Socrates (470?–399 B.C.)

GOVERNMENT

The legitimate object of government is to do for a community of people whatever they need to have done, but cannot do at all in their separate and individual capacities.
—Abraham Lincoln (1809–1865)

Government is a contrivance of human wisdom to provide for human wants.   —Edmund Burke (1729–1797)

Now I know what a statesman is; he's a dead politician. We need more statesmen.   —Bob Edwards

Politics has got so expensive that it takes a lot of money even to get beat with.   —Will Rogers

I'm not an old, experienced hand at politics. But I am now seasoned enough to have learned that the hardest thing about any political campaign is how to win without proving that you are unworthy of winning.   —Adlai Stevenson

More men have been elected between Sundown and Sunup than ever were elected between Sunup and Sundown.
—Will Rogers

A statesman is any politician it's considered safe to name a school after.   —Bill Vaughan

Greater love hath no man than this, that he lay down his friends for his political life.   —Jeremy Thorpe

Politician: Any citizen with influence enough to get his old mother a job as charwoman in the City Hall.   —H. L. Mencken

It makes no difference who you vote for—the two parties are really one party representing 4 percent of the people.   —Gore Vidal
(There are always too many Democratic congressmen, too many Republican congressmen, and never enough U. S. congressmen.)

There are some politicians who, if their constituents were cannibals, would promise them missionaries for dinner.   —H. L. Mencken
(Never judge presidential timber by its bark.)

An elected official is one who gets 51 percent of the vote cast by 40 percent of the 60 percent of voters who registered.
—Dan Bennett

Political ability is the ability to foretell what is going to happen tomorrow, next week, next month and next year. And to have the ability afterward to explain why it didn't happen.   —Winston Churchill (A politician's idea of an unfair question is one he can't answer.)

A political war is one in which everyone shoots from the lip.
—Raymond Moley

Politics is the gentle art of getting votes from the poor and campaign funds from the rich, by promising to protect each from the other.
—Oscar Ameringer

What is politics but persuading the public to vote for this and support that and endure these for the promise of those?
—Gilbert Highet

We're going to move left and right at the same time.   —Governor Jerry Brown (When in danger or in doubt, run in circles, yell and shout.)

This is the first convention of the space age—when a candidate can promise the moon and mean it.   —David Brinkley

Government is too big and important to be left to the politicians.
—Chester Bowles

The end move in politics is always to pick up a gun.
—Buckminster Fuller

Politicians make strange bedfellows, but they all share the same bunk.
—Edgar A. Shoaff

Einstein's theory of relativity, as practiced by Congressmen, simply means getting members of your family on the payroll.
—James H. Boren

Politics offers yesterday's answers to today's problems.
—Marshall McLuhan

Do you ever get the feeling that the only reason we have elections is to find out if the polls were right?   —Robert Orben (Some problems are so complex that it takes high intelligence just to be undecided about them.)

The government is the only known vessel that leaks from the top.
—James Reston

Since a politician never believes what he says, he is always astonished when others do.   —Charles De Gaulle

Have you ever seen a candidate talking to a rich person on television?
—Art Buchwald

Now and then an innocent man is sent t' th' legislature.
                    —Frank McKinney Hubbard ("Kin Hubbard")

You cannot adopt politics as a profession and remain honest.
                                        —Louis McHenry Howe

This country has come to feel the same when Congress is in session
as when the baby gets hold of a hammer.   —Will Rogers

Congress is so strange. A man gets up to speak and says nothing.
Nobody listens—and then everybody disagrees.   —Boris Mar-
shalov (Congress favors a stable government, judging from the
amount of stalling it does just horsing around.)

Gerald Ford is the first President of the United States to be elected
by a majority of one—and nobody demanded a recount.
                                        —Laurence J. Peter

In politics one frequently hears it said that so-and-so may be a s.o.b.
but he is our s.o.b. and therefore deserving of our support.
                                        —George E. Allen

Our local congressman admits his opponent resembles Abraham
Lincoln—if you can imagine a short, fat, dishonest Abraham Lincoln.
                                        —Bill Vaughan

When a fellow you knew in school attains some lofty public office,
you're glad for his sake—but somewhat apprehensive for the future
of the country.   —Bill Vaughan

I once said cynically of a politician, "He'll doublecross that bridge
when he comes to it."   —Oscar Levant

The boys are in such a mood that if someone introduced the Ten
Commandments, they'd cut them down to eight.
                                        —Senator Norris Cotton

Practical politics consists in ignoring facts.   —Henry Adams
(During a campaign the air is full of speeches—and vice versa.)

The citizen does not so much vote for a candidate as make a psychological purchase of him.   —Joe McGinnis

An honest politician is one who, when he is bought, will stay bought.
                                        —Simon Cameron (1799–1889)

Politics make estranged bedfellows.   —Goodman Ace

Because of our Congressional committee system, our government is
closer to a gerontocracy than a democracy.   —Charles Frankel
(Next time a man tells you talk is cheap, ask him if he knows how
much a session of Congress costs.)

Politicians are the same all over. They promise to build a bridge even where there is no river.   —Nikita Khrushchev

God help the nation where self-caricature and satire are verboten.
—Evan Esar

It is simply untrue that all our institutions are evil, that all adults are unsympathetic, that all politicians are mere opportunists, that all aspects of university life are corrupt. Having discovered an illness, it's not terribly useful to prescribe death as a cure.
—Senator George McGovern

I have always given it as my decided opinion that no nation had a right to intermeddle in the internal concerns of another; that every-one had a right to form and adopt whatever government they liked best to live under themselves.
—George Washington (1732–1799)

A silent majority and government by the people is incompatible.
—Tom Hayden

The translation of values into public policy is what politics is about.
—Willard Gaylin (A politician's clarification is harder to understand than his original statement.)

Why should any country continue, forever, to be "great"?
—William F. Buckley, Jr.

Politicians should read science fiction, not westerns and detective stories.   —Arthur C. Clarke

The path to political preferment lies through orthodoxy.
—Walter Bagehot (1826–1877) (On second thought, so does the path to corporate preferment.)

The politicians of our time might be characterized by their vain attempts to change the world and by their inability to change them-selves.   —George Faludy

There is a myth that government can do the job cheaply because it doesn't have to make a profit.   —E. S. Savas (There is no such thing as a cheap politician.)

Political campaigns are designedly made into emotional orgies which endeavor to distract attention from the real issues involved, and they actually paralyze what slight powers of cerebration man can normally muster.   —James Harvey Robinson

A constitutional statesman is in general a man of common opinions and uncommon abilities.   —Walter Bagehot

In the last decade, politics has gone from the age of "Camelot," when all things were possible, to the age of "Watergate" when all things are suspect.   —William Hungate

For in reason, all government without the consent of the governed is the very definition of slavery.   —Jonathan Swift (1667–1745) (Affairs of state are operated so that one generation pays the debts of the last generation by issuing bonds payable by the next generation.)

The justification of majority rule in politics is not to be found in its ethical superiority.   —Walter Lippmann

No country today has an effective government.

—Peter Drucker

The real division in the world today is not between socialism and capitalism, it's between freedom and totalitarianism.

—Frank H. Underhill

Government is necessary, not because man is naturally bad . . . but because man is by nature more individualistic than social.

—Thomas Hobbes (1588–1679)

The median number of years for the survival of governments without violence is eleven years.   —Daniel Patrick Moynihan

There is no worse heresy than that the office sanctifies the holder of it.   —Lord Acton

There is no right government except good government.

—George Santayana

Governments will always misuse the machinery of the law as far as the state of public opinion permits.   —Emile Capouya (It is every citizen's duty to support his government, but not necessarily in the style to which it has been accustomed.)

A new science of politics is needed for a new world.

—Alexis de Tocqueville (1805–1859)

A government is free in proportion to the rights it guarantees to the minority.   —Alfred Landon

An act repugnant to the Constitution is void.

—John Marshall (1755–1835)

I'm not a leftist; I'm where the righteous ought to be.

—M. M. Coady

Every nation has the government that it deserves.   —Joseph Marie de Maistre (1753–1821) (The only race in which most people pick the winner is an election.)

The great difficulty with politics is that there are no established principles.   —Napoleon Bonaparte (1769–1821) (A liberal politician calls it share-the-wealth; a conservative calls it soak-the-rich.)

Congress is a middle-aged, middle-class, white male power structure . . . no wonder it's been so totally unresponsive to the needs of this country.   —Bella Abzug (In politics the only occupational ailment is bad posture.)

Governments last as long as the under-taxed can defend themselves against the over-taxed.   —Bernard Berenson

If men were angels, no government would be necessary.
                              —James Madison (1751–1836)

The disclosure mania will make for more cliques that meet privately beforehand to agree on concerted actions subsequently revealed only at the public meeting.   —Warren Bennis

To rule is easy, to govern difficult.
                              —Johann W. von Goethe (1749–1832)

Applause, mingled with boos and hisses, is about all that the average voter is able or willing to contribute to public life.
                              —Elmer Davis

Here is my first principle of foreign policy: good government at home.   —William Ewart Gladstone (1809–1898)

Many people consider the things which government does for them to be social progress, but they consider the things government does for others as socialism.   —Chief Justice Earl Warren

Our task now is not to fix the blame for the past, but to fix the course for the future.   —John F. Kennedy

Political power grows out of the barrel of a gun.
                              —Mao Tse-tung

Any party which takes credit for the rain must not be surprised if its opponents blame it for the drought.   —Dwight W. Morrow

---

A state is better governed which has but few laws, and those laws strictly observed . . .   —René Descartes (1596–1650)

That government is best which governs the least, because its people discipline themselves.   —Thomas Jefferson (1743–1826)

*   *

The difference between politics and statesmanship is philosophy.
                              —Will and Ariel Durant

The difference between a politician and a statesman is: a politician thinks of the next election and a statesman thinks of the next generation.   —James Freeman Clarke

*   *

Whenever any Form of Government becomes destructive . . . it is the Right of the People to alter or abolish it.
                                        —The Declaration of Independence

The Communist system must be based on the will of the people, and if the people should not want that system, then that people should establish a different system.   —Nikita Khrushchev

*   *

In politics, as in high finance, duplicity is regarded as a virtue.
                              —Mikhail A. Bakunin (1814–1876)

It's the inherent right of the government to lie to save itself.
                                        —Arthur D. Sylvester

*   *

Nobody believes a rumor here in Washington until it's officially denied.   —Edward Cheyfitz

You can always get the truth from an American statesman after he has turned seventy or given up hope of the Presidency.
                              —Wendell Phillips (1811–1884)

*   *

He knows nothing; he thinks he knows everything—that clearly points to a political career.   —George Bernard Shaw

Politics is perhaps the only profession for which no preparation is thought necessary.   —Robert Louis Stevenson (1850–1894)

*   *

Government in the U. S. today is a senior partner in every business in the country.   —Norman Cousins

We must have a political state powerful enough to deal with corporate wealth, but how are we going to keep that state with its augmenting power from being captured by the force we want it to control?   —Vernon Louis Parrington

*   *

Nothing is so admirable in politics as a short memory.
                                        —John Kenneth Galbraith

The short memories of American voters is what keeps our politicians in office.   —Will Rogers

* *

Money is the mother's milk of politics.   —Jesse Unruh

When one may pay out over two million dollars to presidential and Congressional campaigns, the U. S. Government is virtually up for sale.   —John Gardner

---

Public office is the last refuge of the incompetent.

—Boies Penrose

One of the shallowest disdains is the sneer against the professional politician.   —Justice Felix Frankfurter

* *

Why should there not be a patient confidence in the ultimate justice of the people?   —Abraham Lincoln (1809–1865)

The people are not the origin of all just power.

—David Hume (1711–1776)

* *

The business of government is to keep the government out of business—that is, unless business needs government aid.

—Will Rogers

Business is business.   —George Colman, Jr.

* *

The middle of the road is all of the usable surface. The extremes, right and left, are in the gutters.   —Dwight D. Eisenhower

The middle of the road is where the white line is—and that's the worst place to drive.   —Robert Frost

* *

When the President says "Jump!" they only ask, "How high?"
—John Ehrlichman

Voters quickly forget what a man says.   —Richard M. Nixon

* *

If men and women of capacity refuse to take part in politics and government, they condemn themselves, as well as the people, to the punishment of living under bad government.

—Senator Sam J. Ervin

And where are the others that might have stood,/Side by your side in the common good?   —Maurice Ogden

GREATNESS

Behind every great man is a woman with nothing to wear.
—L. Grant Glickman

Calvin Coolidge—the greatest man who ever came out of Plymouth
Corner, Vermont.   —Clarence Darrow

The price of greatness is responsibility.
—Winston Churchill (Where the buck stops.)

A small man can be just as exhausted as a great man.
—Arthur Miller

A great man is made up of qualities that meet or make great occasions.   —James Russell Lowell (1819–1891)

Greatness lies not in being strong, but in the right use of strength.
—Henry Ward Beecher (1813–1887)

The world's great men have not commonly been great scholars, nor
the great scholars great men.   —Oliver Wendell Holmes, Jr.

The great are great only because we are on our knees.
—Pierre Joseph Proudhon (1809–1865)

For you are not to suppose, brethren, that heresies could be produced through any little souls. None save great men have been the
authors of heresies.   —Saint Augustine (354–430)

What makes the difference between a Nation that is truly great and
one that is merely rich and powerful? It is the simple things that
make the difference. Honesty, knowing right from wrong, openness,
self-respect, and the courage of conviction.
—Governor David L. Boren

If my resolution to be a great man was half so strong as it is to
despise the shame of being a little one . . .
—William Cowper (1731–1800)

If I am a great man, then a good many of the great men of history
are frauds.   —Andrew Bonar Law

Democracy is measured not by its leaders doing extraordinary
things, but by its citizens doing ordinary things extraordinarily
well.   —John Gardner

Be not afraid of greatness: some are born great, some achieve
greatness and some have greatness thrust upon 'em.
—William Shakespeare (1564–1616)

Some people may have greatness thrust upon them. Very few have excellence thrust upon them.   —John Gardner

---

I studied the lives of great men and famous women, and I found that the men and women who got to the top were those who did the jobs they had in hand, with everything they had of energy and enthusiasm and hard work.   —Harry S Truman

That man is great who can use the brains of others to carry out his work.   —Donn Piatt

GREED

We're all born brave, trusting and greedy, and most of us remain greedy.   —Mignon McLaughlin

One of the weaknesses of our age is our apparent inability to distinguish our needs from our greeds.   —Don Robinson (As the farmer said, "I'm not greedy, all I want is the land next to mine.")

The miser is as much in want of what he has as of what he has not. —Publilius Syrus (c. 1st century B.C.) (There are some men who, in a fifty-fifty proposition, insist on getting the hyphen, too.)

Callous greed grows pious very fast.   —Lillian Hellman

The bird of paradise alights only upon the hand that does not grasp.
        —John Berry

A miser is a guy who lives within his income. He's also called a magician.   —Alliston Herald (Once upon a time money swore solemnly that nobody who did not love money should have it.)

GROWTH

Everybody wants to be somebody; nobody wants to grow. —Johann W. von Goethe (1749–1832) (Every man must do his own growing, no matter how tall his grandfather was.)

If the shoe fits, you're not allowing for growth.
        —Robert N. Coons

Economic growth is not only unnecessary, but ruinous.
        —Alexander I. Solzhenitsyn

Growth is the only evidence of life.
        —John Henry, Cardinal Newman (1801–1890)

Growth for the sake of growth is the ideology of the cancer cell.
—Edward Abbey

The purpose of learning is growth, and our minds, unlike our bodies, can continue growing as we continue to live.
—Mortimer Adler

When I am grown to man's estate/I shall be very proud and great,/ And tell the other girls and boys/Not to meddle with my toys.
—Robert Louis Stevenson (1850–1894)

Men are but children of a larger growth.
—John Dryden (1631–1700)

GUNS AND GUN CONTROLS

Guns have a way of materializing more readily than the commodities that sustain life.   —Norman Cousins

Show me the man who doesn't want his gun registered, and I will show you a man who shouldn't have a gun.   —Homer Cummings (Everybody is a *law-abiding citizen* until the gun goes off.)

In my opinion, anyone pushing through anti-gun legislation is a bloody traitor and should be sent up for treason.
—N. H. Stuart

By our readiness to allow arms to be purchased at will and fired at whim, we have created an atmosphere in which violence and hatred have become popular pastimes.   —Martin Luther King, Jr.

With all the violence and murder and killings we've had in the United States, I think you will agree that we must keep firearms from people who have no business with guns.   —Robert F. Kennedy (May 1968, five days before his assassination)

What in the name of conscience will it take to pass a truly effective gun-control law? Now in this new hour of tragedy, let us spell out our grief in constructive action.   —Lyndon B. Johnson

HAPPINESS / UNHAPPINESS

Happiness is the interval between periods of unhappiness.
—Don Marquis

My life has no purpose, no direction, no aim, no meaning, and yet I'm happy. I can't figure it out. What am I doing right? —Charles M. Schulz (Happiness is liking what you do as well as doing what you like.)

Happiness is not being pained in body or troubled in mind.
—Thomas Jefferson (1743–1826)

The secret of happiness is this: Let your interests be as wide as possible, and let your reactions to the things and persons that interest you be as far as possible friendly rather than hostile.
—Bertrand Russell

Mankind has become so much one family that we cannot insure our own prosperity except by insuring that of everyone else. If you wish to be happy yourself, you must resign yourself to seeing others also happy . . . Contempt for happiness is usually contempt for other people's happiness, and is an elegant disguise for hatred of the human race.   —Bertrand Russell

There is only one honest impulse at the bottom of Puritanism, and that is the impulse to punish the man with a superior capacity for happiness.   —H. L. Mencken

Happiness is a way station between too little and too much.
—Channing Pollock

A person is never happy except at the price of some ignorance.
—Anatole France

Happiness lies in the taste, and not in the things; and it is from having what we desire that we are happy—not from having what others think desirable.   —Duc de La Rochefoucauld (1613–1680) (Not even the Joneses?)

The formula for complete happiness is to be very busy with the unimportant.   —A. Edward Newton

Renown is a source of toil and sorrow; obscurity is a source of happiness.   —Johann L. von Mosheim (1694–1755)

All happiness depends on a leisurely breakfast.
—John Gunther

Good friends, good books and a sleepy conscience: this is the ideal life.   —Mark Twain (The conviction of the rich that the poor are happy is no more foolish than the conviction of the poor that the rich are.)

Happiness is a stock that doubles in a year.   —Ira U. Cobleigh

Happiness? That's nothing more than health and a poor memory.
—Albert Schweitzer

There is nothing which has yet been contrived by man by which so much happiness is produced as by a good tavern.
—Samuel Johnson (1709–1784)

Happiness makes up in height for what it lacks in length.
—Robert Frost

If happiness truly consisted in physical ease and freedom from care, then the happiest individual would not be either a man or a woman; it would be, I think, an American cow.
—William Lyon Phelps (Cud be.)

What everyone wants from life is continuous and genuine happiness. Happiness is the rational understanding of life and the world. —Baruch Spinoza (1632–1677) (The secret of happiness is the exploration and enjoyment of genius untainted by your own lack of it.)

The happiest man is he who learns from nature the lesson of worship.   —Ralph Waldo Emerson (1803–1882)

The only really happy folk are married women and single men.
—H. L. Mencken

If a man has important work, and enough leisure and income to enable him to do it properly, he is in possession of as much happiness as is good for any of the children of Adam.

—R. H. Tawney

What can be added to the happiness of a man who is in health, out of debt, and has a clear conscience?   —Adam Smith (1723–1790) (May his happiest days of the past be his saddest days of the future.)

The happy do not believe in miracles.

—Johann W. von Goethe (1749–1832)

What a wonderful life I've had! I only wish I'd realized it sooner.

—Colette

Happiness is not a state to arrive at, but a manner of traveling.

—Margaret Lee Runbeck

Wandering seemed no more than the happiness of an anxious man.

—Albert Camus

Once you have heard of the lark, known the swish of feet through hill-top grass and smelt the earth made ready for the seed, you are never again going to be fully happy about the cities and towns that man carries like a crippling weight upon his back.

—Gwyn Thomas

Many people are extremely happy, but are absolutely worthless to society.   —Charles Gow

Happiness is like coke—something you get as a by-product in the process of making something else.   —Aldous Huxley

Happiness is the only sanction of life; where happiness fails, existence remains a mad and lamentable experiment.

—George Santayana

Most of us believe in trying to make other people happy only if they can be happy in ways which we approve.

—Robert S. Lynd

Prudence keeps life safe, but does not often make it happy.

—Samuel Johnson (1709–1784)

We cannot get grace from gadgets. In the bakelite house of the future, the dishes may not break, but the heart can. Even a man with ten shower baths may find life flat, stale and unprofitable.

—J. B. Priestley

The only power a god can teach is the power of doing without happiness.   —George Bernard Shaw

The greatest happiness you can have is knowing that you do not necessarily require happiness.   —William Saroyan

*   *

There is no greater sorrow than to recall, in misery, the time when we were happy.   —Dante Alighieri (1265–1321)

No greater grief than to remember days of gladness when sorrow is at hand.   —Friedrich Schiller (1729–1805)

*   *

How many things are there which I do not want.
                    —Socrates (470?–399 B.C.)

To be without some of the things you want is an indispensable part of happiness.   —Bertrand Russell

*   *

It is the chiefest point of happiness that a man is willing to be what he is.   —Desiderius Erasmus (1466?–1536)

Happy the man who early learns the wide chasm that lies between his wishes and his powers!
                    —Johann W. von Goethe (1749–1832)

There is no cure for birth or death save to enjoy the interval.
                    —George Santayana

Man, unlike the animals, has never learned that the sole purpose of life is to enjoy it.   —Samuel Butler

*   *

I have diligently numbered the days of pure and genuine happiness which have fallen to my lot: they amount to fourteen.
                    —Abd-El-Raham (912–961)

A feverish, selfish little clod of ailments and grievances complaining that the world will not devote itself to making you happy.
                    —George Bernard Shaw

*   *

Happiness is the natural flower of duty.   —Phillips Brooks

The pursuit of happiness is a most ridiculous phrase: if you pursue happiness you'll never find it.   —C. P. Snow

*   *

Many people push a burden of inexplicable sadness through half a lifetime like Sisyphus . . . and try to believe that they are happy.

—Peter Stoler

Sisyphus was basically a happy man.   —Albert Camus

*   *

One of the indictments of civilizations is that happiness and intelligence are so rarely found in the same person.

—William Feather

The main thing needed to make men happy is intelligence.

—Bertrand Russell

HATRED

All men kill the thing they hate, too, unless, of course, it kills them first.   —James Thurber

The mayor was a man you had to know to dislike.

—Jim Bishop

Hating people is like burning down your own house to get rid of a rat.   —Harry Emerson Fosdick

I never hated a man enough to give him his diamonds back.

—Zsa Zsa Gabor

Malice is like a game of poker or tennis; you don't play it with anyone who is manifestly inferior to you.   —Hilde Spiel

I don't like her. But don't misunderstand me: my dislike is purely platonic.   —Sir Herbert Beerbohm Tree

Never in this world can hatred be stilled by hatred; it will be stilled only by non-hatred—this is the law Eternal.

—Buddha (563?–483? B.C.)

Always remember others may hate you but those who hate you don't win unless you hate them. And then you destroy yourself.

—Richard M. Nixon

America needs fewer men obsessed with erecting fences of hate, suspicion and name calling.   —William Arthur Ward

Rather perish than hate and fear, and twice rather perish than make oneself hated and feared—this must some day become the highest maxim for every single commonwealth.

—Friedrich Nietzsche (1844–1900)

Hated by fools, and fools to hate,/Be that my motto and my fate.
                              —Jonathan Swift (1667–1745)

Hatred is the coward's revenge for being intimidated.
                              —George Bernard Shaw

Hatred is like fire; it makes even light rubbish deadly.
                    —George Eliot (Mary Ann Evans) (1819–1880)

To hate and to fear is to be psychologically ill . . . it is, in fact, the consuming illness of our time.   —H. A. Overstreet

No man has ever been born a Negro hater, a Jew hater, or any other kind of hater. Nature refuses to be involved in such suicidal practices.   —Harry Bridges

Any kiddies in school can love like a fool,/But hating, my boy, is an art.   —Ogden Nash

Why is propaganda so much more successful when it stirs up hatred than when it tries to stir up friendly feeling?
                              —Bertrand Russell

We have just enough religion to make us hate, but not enough to make us love one another.   —Jonathan Swift

HEART AND HEAD

In each human heart are a tiger, a pig, an ass and a nightingale. Diversity of character is due to their unequal activity.
                              —Ambrose Bierce

There is only one quality worse than hardness of heart and that is softness of head.   —Theodore Roosevelt

I love thee for a heart that's kind—/Not for the knowledge in thy mind.   —W. H. Davies

An advantage of having a hard heart is that it will take a lot to break it.   —W. Burton Baldry

Emotion has taught mankind to reason.
                              —Marquis de Vauvenargues (1715–1747)

When I was one-and-twenty/I heard a wise man say,/"Give crowns and pounds and guineas/But not your heart away."
                              —A. E. Housman

The world is a comedy to those that think, a tragedy to those that feel.   —Horace Walpole (1717–1797)

The heart has its reasons which reason does not understand.
                                    —Blaise Pascal (1623–1662)

The head is always the dupe of the heart.
                          —Duc de La Rochefoucauld (1613–1680)

*   *

The head never rules the heart, but just becomes its partner in crime.   —Mignon McLaughlin

Some people feel with their heads and think with their hearts.
                          —G. C. Lichtenberg (1742–1799)

The pleasures of the intellect are permanent, the pleasures of the heart are transitory.   —Henry David Thoreau (1817–1862)

All great discoveries are made by men whose feelings run ahead of their thinking.   —C. H. Parkhurst

HEAVEN AND HELL

Of the delights of this world man cares most for sexual intercourse, yet he has left it out of his heaven.   —Mark Twain

There are lots of good women who, when they get to heaven, will watch to see if the Lord goes out nights.   —Ed Howe

What a pity that the only way to heaven is in a hearse!
                                    —Stanislaw J. Lec

Probably no invention came more easily to man than when he thought up heaven.   —G. C. Lichtenberg

My idea of heaven is eating foie gras to the sound of trumpets.
                                    —Sydney Smith (1771–1845)

The road to Hell is paved with good intentions.   —Samuel Johnson (1709–1784) (In which case, the road to Heaven must be paved with bad ones.)

Maybe this world is another planet's Hell.   —Aldous Huxley (One man's idea of hell is to be forced to remain in another man's idea of heaven.)

Christ believed in hell. I do not myself feel that any person who is really profoundly humane can believe in everlasting punishment.
—Bertrand Russell (Hell is a place where the motorists are French, the policemen are German, and the cooks are English.)

Hell is not to love anymore.   —Georges Bernanos

I believe in heaven and hell—on earth.
                                        —Abraham L. Feinberg

Many might go to heaven with half the labor they go to hell.
                                —Ben Jonson (1572?–1637)

The wicked often work harder to go to hell than the righteous do to enter heaven.
                —John Billings (Henry Wheeler Shaw) (1818–1885)

This that you have heard is the case of everyone of you that are out of Christ. The world of misery, that lake of burning brimstone, is extended abroad under you. There is the dreadful pit of the glowing flames of the wrath of God; there is hell's wide gaping mouth open.
                        —Jonathan Edwards (1703–1758)

Hell is given up so reluctantly by those who don't expect to go there.
                                —Harry Leon Wilson

*   *

Hold most firmly and doubt not that not only all the pagans, but also all Jews, heretics, and schismatics who depart from their present life outside the Catholic Church, are about to go into eternal fire prepared for the devil and his angels.
                            —Saint Fulgentius (468–533)

Men have fiendishly conceived a heaven only to find it insipid, and a hell only to find it ridiculous.   —George Santayana

HEROES

Every hero becomes a bore at last.
                        —Ralph Waldo Emerson (1803–1882)

We can't all be heroes because someone has to sit on the curb and clap as they go by.   —Will Rogers

In the theatre, a hero is one who believes that all women are ladies, a villain one who believes that all ladies are women.
                                —George Jean Nathan

The true heroes are those who die for causes they cannot quite take seriously.   —Murray Kempton

There is not a more unhappy being than a superannuated idol.
                                          —Joseph Addison (1672–1719)

Show me a hero and I will write you a tragedy.
                                          —F. Scott Fitzgerald

Jesse James shot children, but only in fact, not in folklore.
                                          —John Greenway

One murder makes a villain, millions a hero.
                                          —Bishop Beilby Porteus (1731–1808)

Hero-worship is strongest where there is least regard for human freedom.   —Herbert Spencer

I would rather be a philosopher and a coward than a hero and a fool.   —Ambrose Pratt

---

There is nothing so nice as doing good by stealth and being found out by accident.   —Charles Lamb (1775–1834)

It is nice to make heroic decisions and to be prevented by "circumstances beyond your control" from ever trying to execute them.
                                          —William James

*   *

No man is a hero to his valet. This is not because the hero is no hero, but because the valet is a valet.
                                          —Georg Wilhelm Hegel (1770–1831)

There are a lot of men who are heroes only to their valets.
                                          —Murray Kempton

A light supper, a good night's sleep, and a fine morning have often made a hero of the same man who by indigestion, a restless night, and a rainy morning, would have proved a coward.
                                          —Earl of Chesterfield (1694–1773)

Self-trust is the essence of heroism.
                                          —Ralph Waldo Emerson

*   *

This thing of being a hero, about the main thing to it is to know when to die.   —Will Rogers

A hero is no braver than an ordinary man, but he is braver five minutes longer.   —Ralph Waldo Emerson

HISTORY

History: A nearly defunct field of study that is of value only to the extent that it glorifies everything previously debased, and vice versa.
—Bernard Rosenberg

History is a bucket of ashes.   —Carl Sandburg

God cannot alter the past, but historians can.
—Samuel Butler

History is a set of lies agreed upon.
—Napoleon Bonaparte (1769–1821)

History is an account, mostly false, of events, mostly unimportant, which are brought about by rulers, mostly knaves, and soldiers, mostly fools.   —Ambrose Bierce

History is the great dust-heap . . . a pageant and not a philosophy.
—Augustine Birrell

Any event, once it has occurred, can be made to appear inevitable by a competent historian.   —Lee Simonson

History is indeed little more than the register of the crimes, follies, and misfortunes of mankind.   —Edward Gibbon (1737–1794)

History is philosophy teaching by examples.
—Henry St. John Bolingbroke (1678–1751)

History is the discovering of the constant and universal principles of human nature.   —David Hume (1711–1776)

History is a nightmare from which we are trying to awaken.
—James Joyce

History is a record of human progress, a record of the struggle of the advancement of the human mind, of the human spirit, toward some known or unknown objective.   —Jawaharlal Nehru

History is only a confused heap of facts.
—Earl of Chesterfield (1694–1773)

History is a pact between the dead, the living, and the yet unborn.
—Edmund Burke (1729–1797)

History is mostly guessing; the rest is prejudice.
—Will and Ariel Durant

History is bunk!   —Henry Ford

History is the science of man.   —José Ortega y Gasset

History is the product of vast, amorphous and indecipherable social movements.   —Count Leo Tolstoy

The history of the world is the record of a man in quest of his daily bread and butter.   —Hendrik Willem van Loon

History is a cyclic poem written by Time upon the memories of man.
—Percy Bysshe Shelley (1792–1822)

History balances the frustration of "how far we have to go" with the satisfaction of "how far we have come." It teaches us tolerance for the human shortcomings and imperfections which are not uniquely of our generation, but of all time.   —Lewis F. Powell, Jr.

Men make history and not the other way round. In periods where there is no leadership, society stands still. Progress occurs when courageous, skillful leaders seize the opportunity to change things for the better.   —Harry S Truman

When great changes occur in history, when great principles are involved, as a rule the majority are wrong.   —Eugene V. Debs

History makes us some amends for the shortness of life.
—Philip Skelton (History repeats itself because nobody listens.)

The memories of men are too frail a thread to hang history from.
—John Still (1543–1608)

History must not be written with bias, and both sides must be given, even if there is only one side.   —John Betjeman

Not to know the events which happened before one was born, that is to remain always a boy.   —Marcus Tullius Cicero (106–43 B.C.)(We study history not to be clever in another time, but to be wise always.)

History is the ship carrying living memories to the future.
—Stephen Spender

The study of history is the beginning of political wisdom.
—Jean Bodin (1530–1596) (History teaches us the mistakes we are going to make.)

The rich experience of history teaches that up to now not a single class has voluntarily made way for another class.
—Joseph Stalin

We Americans are the best informed people on earth as to the events of the last twenty-four hours; we are not the best informed as to the events of the last sixty centuries.
—Will and Ariel Durant

History is the biography of great men.
> —Thomas Carlyle (1795–1881)

There is properly no history, only biography.
> —Ralph Waldo Emerson (1803–1882)

* *

A page of history is worth a volume of logic.
> —Oliver Wendell Holmes, Jr.

History's lessons are no more enlightening than the wisdom of those who interpret them.   —David Schoenbrun

* *

When I want to understand what is happening today or try to decide what will happen tomorrow, I look back.
> —Oliver Wendell Holmes, Jr.

* *

What history teaches us is that men have never learned anything from it.   —Georg Wilhelm Hegel (1770–1831)

History repeats itself. That's one of the things wrong with history.
> —Clarence Darrow

* *

History is the science of what never happens twice.
> —Paul Valéry

"History repeats itself" and "History never repeats itself" are about equally true . . . We never know enough about the infinitely complex circumstances of any past event to prophesy the future by analogy.   —G. M. Trevelyan

---

I recommend you to leave the battle of Waterloo as it is.
> —Arthur Wellesley, Duke of Wellington (1759–1852)

History is always best written generations after the event, when clouded fact and memory have all fused into what can be accepted as truth, whether it be so or not.   —Theodore H. White

* *

The men who make history have no time to write about it.
> —Prince Klemens von Metternich (1773–1859)

Anyone can make history. Only a great man can write it.
> —Oscar Wilde (1854–1900)

HOME

A House is not a Home.   —Polly Adler

The strength of a nation is derived from the integrity of its homes.
—Confucius (c. 551–479 B.C.)

I want a house that has got over all its troubles; I don't want to
spend the rest of my life bringing up a young and inexperienced
house.   —Jerome K. Jerome (Nothing modernizes a home so
completely as an ad offering it for sale.)

The fellow that owns his own home is always just coming out of a
hardware store.
—Frank McKinney Hubbard ("Kin Hubbard")

The modern idea of home has been well expressed as the place one
goes from the garage.   —George Wickersham

Home is where the college student home for the holidays isn't.
—Laurence J. Peter

Nobody shoulders a rifle in defense of a boarding house.
—Bret Harte

HONESTY / DISHONESTY

I hope I shall possess firmness and virtue enough to maintain what
I consider the most enviable of all titles, the character of an honest
man.   —George Washington (1732–1799)

Honesty is the first chapter of the book of wisdom.   —Thomas
Jefferson (1743–1826) (Some are born good, some make good,
and some are caught with the goods.)

There's one way to find out if a man is honest—ask him. If he says,
"Yes," you know he is a crook.   —Groucho Marx

A commentary on the times is that the word "honesty" is now pre-
ceded by "old-fashioned."   —Larry Wolters

It's strange that men should take up crime when there are so many
legal ways to be dishonest.   —*Sunshine* magazine

Honesty: The most important thing in life. Unless you really know
how to fake it, you'll never make it.   —Bernard Rosenberg

And whether you're an honest man or whether you're a thief/De-
pends on whose solicitor has given me my brief.
—W. S. Gilbert

It is easier to be dishonest for two than for one.

—John Fowles

We must make the world honest before we can honestly say to our children that honesty is the best policy.

—George Bernard Shaw

"Honesty is the best policy," but he who acts on that principle is not an honest man.   —Bishop Richard Whately (1787–1863)

HONOR

If somebody throws a brick at me, I can catch it and throw it back. But when somebody awards a decoration to me, I am out of words.

—Harry S Truman

The louder he talked of his honor, the faster we counted our spoons.

—Ralph Waldo Emerson (1803–1882)

I have a lantern. You steal my lantern. What, then, is your honor worth no more to you than the price of my lantern?   —Epictetus (c. 1st century A.D.) (But, sir, I am looking for an honest man!)

If you live long enough, the venerability factor creeps in; you get accused of things you never did and praised for virtues you never had.   —I. F. Stone

I could not love thee, Dear, so much/Lov'd I not honour more.

—Richard Lovelace (1618–1658)

———

I would rather men should ask why no statue has been erected in my honor, than why one has.

—Marcus Porcius Cato (234–149 B.C.)

I would rather that the people should wonder why I wasn't President than why I am.   —Salmon P. Chase (1808–1873)

*   *

It is better to be hated for what you are than loved for what you are not.   —André Gide

Dignity does not consist in possessing honors, but in deserving them.   —Aristotle (384–322 B.C.)

*   *

It is better to deserve honors and not have them than to have them and not deserve them.   —Mark Twain

No person was ever honored for what he received. Honor has been the reward for what he gave.   —Calvin Coolidge

*   *

If it be a sin to covet honor, I am the most offending soul.
                    —William Shakespeare (1564–1616)

Glory's no compensation for a belly-ache.   —Rudyard Kipling

HOPE

Hope springs eternal in the human breast.
                    —Alexander Pope (1688–1744)

There is no medicine like hope, no incentive so great, and no tonic so powerful as expectation of something tomorrow.
                    —O. S. Marden

If one truly has lost hope, one would not be on hand to say so.
                    —Eric Bentley

Hope is independent of the apparatus of logic.
                    —Norman Cousins

Hope is the pillar that holds up the world./Hope is the dream of a waking man.   ——Pliny the Elder (23–79)

It is not necessary to hope in order to undertake, nor to succeed in order to persevere.   —Charles the Bold (1433–1477)

Old man exhausted by ordeal, detached from human deeds, feeling the approach of the eternal cold, but always watching in the shadows for the gleam of hope!   —Charles De Gaulle

To travel hopefully is better than to arrive.   —Sir James Jeans

How deceitful hope may be, yet she carries us on pleasantly to the end of life.   —Duc de La Rochefoucauld (1613–1680)

We hope vaguely but dread precisely.   —Paul Valéry

Hope is the most treacherous of human fancies.
                    —James Fenimore Cooper (1789–1851)

It is certainly wrong to despair; and if despair is wrong hope is right.
                    —John Lubbock (1803–1865)

All our lives we are putting pennies—our most golden pennies—into penny-in-the-slot machines that are almost always empty.
                    —Logan Pearsall Smith

Hope is merely disappointment deferred.   —W. Burton Baldry

Waiting and hoping are the whole of life, and as soon as a dream is realized it is destroyed.   —Gian-Carlo Menotti

The hopeful man sees success where others see failure, sunshine where others see shadows and storm.   —O. S. Marden

HUMANITY

In every child who is born, under no matter what circumstances, and of no matter what parents, the potentiality of the human race is born again.   —James Agee

Such is the human race. Often it does seem such a pity that Noah . . . didn't miss the boat.   —Mark Twain

I know of no rights of race superior to the rights of humanity.
      —Frederick Douglass (1817?–1895)

Our humanity were a poor thing were it not for the divinity which stirs within us.   —Francis Bacon (1561–1626)

Only on paper has humanity yet achieved glory, beauty, truth, knowledge, virtue, and abiding love.   —George Bernard Shaw

Scientific and humanist approaches are not competitive but supportive, and both are ultimately necessary.   —Robert C. Wood

We are healthy only to the extent that our ideas are humane.
      —Kurt Vonnegut, Jr.

When any man is more stupidly vain and outrageously egotistic than his fellows, he will hide his hideousness in humanitarianism.
      —George Moore

A humanitarian is always a hypocrite.   —George Orwell

Let us have but one end in view, the welfare of humanity; and let us put aside all selfishness in consideration of language, nationality, or religion.   —John Comenius (1592–1670)

The more humanity advances, the more it is degraded.
      —Gustave Flaubert (1821–1880)

HUMAN NATURE

No doubt Jack the Ripper excused himself on the grounds that it was human nature.　　—A. A. Milne

It is easier to denature plutonium than to denature the evil spirit of man.　　—Albert Einstein

If the State acts in ways abhorrent to human nature, it is the lesser evil to destroy it.　　—Baruch Spinoza (1632–1677)

There is one psychological peculiarity in the human being that always strikes one: to shun even the slightest signs of trouble on the outer edge of your existence at times of well-being . . . to try not to know about the sufferings of others and your own or one's own future sufferings, to yield in many situations, even important spiritual and central ones—as long as it prolongs one's well-being.
　　—Alexander I. Solzhenitsyn

There is no crime of which one cannot imagine oneself to be the author.　　—Johann W. von Goethe (1749–1832)

It is human nature to think wisely and act foolishly.
　　—Anatole France

If we are not ashamed to think it, we should not be ashamed to say it.　　—Marcus Tullius Cicero (106–43 B.C.)

Human action can be modified to some extent, but human nature cannot be changed.　　—Abraham Lincoln (1809–1865)

It is not necessary to get away from human nature but to alter its inner attitude of mind and heart.　　—J. F. Newton

HUMILITY

Humility is not renunciation of pride but the substitution of one pride for another.　　—Eric Hoffer (Humility is the embarrassment you feel when you tell people how wonderful you are.)

They are proud in humility, proud in that they are not proud.
　　—Robert Burton (1577–1640)

I believe the first test of a truly great man is humility.
　　—John Ruskin (1819–1900)

The more humble a man is before God, the more he will be exalted; the more humble he is before man, the more he will get rode rough-shod.   —Josh Billings (Henry Wheeler Shaw) (1818–1885)

Anybody can be Pope; the proof of this is that I have become one.
—Pope John XXIII

Humility is to make a right estimate of one's self.
—Charles Haddon Spurgeon

The fact that people do not understand and respect the very best things, such as Mozart's concertos, is what permits men like us to become famous.   —Johannes Brahms (1833–1897)

HUSBANDS

The most popular labor-saving device today is still a husband with money.   —Joey Adams

A husband is what is left of a man after the nerve is extracted.
—Helen Rowland (All husbands are alike, but they have different faces so you can tell them apart.)

An archeologist is the best husband any woman can have; the older she gets, the more interested he is in her.   —Agatha Christie

Grandchildren don't make a man feel old; it's the knowledge that he's married to a grandmother.   —G. Norman Collie

The husband who doesn't tell his wife everything probably reasons that what she doesn't know won't hurt him.   —Leo J. Burke (When a woman hires a detective to follow her husband, it's probably to learn what the other woman sees in him.)

There is only one thing for a man to do who is married to a woman who enjoys spending money, and that is to enjoy earning it.
—Ed Howe

HYPOCRISY

The wolf in sheep's clothing is a fitting emblem of the hypocrite. Every virtuous man would rather meet an open foe than a pretended friend who is a traitor at heart.   —H. F. Kletzing

"I grant you that he's not two-faced," I said, "but what's the use of that when the one face he has got is so peculiarly unpleasant?"
—C. P. Snow

Hypocrisy—prejudice with a halo.   —Ambrose Bierce

One may smile, and smile, and be a villain.
                          —William Shakespeare (1564–1616)

I hope you have not been leading a double life, pretending to be
wicked, and being really good all the time. That would be hypocrisy.
                          —Oscar Wilde (1854–1900)

The fawning, sneaking, and flattering hypocrite, that will do or be
anything, for his own advantage.   —Edward Stillingfleet

A conservative government is an organized hypocrisy.
                          —Benjamin Disraeli (1804–1881)

Hypocrisy can afford to be magnificent in its promises; for never
intending to go beyond promises, it costs nothing.
                          —Edmund Burke (1729–1797)

He blam'd and protested, but join'd in the plan;/He shared in the
plunder, but pitied the man.   —William Cowper (1731–1800)

When I sell liquor, it's called bootlegging; when my patrons serve
it on silver trays on Lake Shore Drive, it's called hospitality.
                          —Al Capone

My method is basically the same as Masters and Johnson, only they
charge thousands of dollars and it's called therapy. I charge fifty
dollars and it's called prostitution.   —Xaviera Hollander

I will have nought to do with a man who can blow hot and cold
with the same breath.   —Aesop (c. 6th century B.C.)

If it were not for the intellectual snobs who pay, the arts would
perish with their starving practitioners—let us thank heaven for
hypocrisy.   —Aldous Huxley

I

IDEALS / IDEALISM

Ideals are like stars: you will not succeed in touching them with your hands, but like the seafaring man on the desert of waters, you choose them as your guides, and following them you reach your destiny.   —Carl Schurz

I am an idealist. I don't know where I'm going but I'm on my way.
                              —Carl Sandburg

Each time a man stands up for an ideal, or acts to improve the lot of others, or strikes out against injustice, he sends forth a tiny ripple of hope . . . and crossing each other from a million different centers of energy and daring those ripples build a current that can sweep down the mightiest walls of oppression and resistance.
                              —Robert F. Kennedy

An idealist is one who, on noticing that a rose smells better than a cabbage, concludes that it will also make better soup.
                              —H. L. Mencken

Every dogma has its day, but ideals are eternal.
                              —Israel Zangwill

Living up to ideals is like doing everyday work with your Sunday clothes on.   —Ed Howe

If you are not an idealist by the time you are twenty you don't have a heart, but if you are still an idealist by thirty you don't have a head.   —Randolph Bourne

Idealists . . . foolish enough to throw caution to the winds . . . have advanced mankind and have enriched the world.
                                              —Emma Goldman

We are all inclined to judge ourselves by our ideals; others by their acts.   —Harold Nicholson (A visionary is an impractical person whose thoughts are based on ideals in a world whose actions are based on deals.)

Idealism increases in direct proportion to one's distance from the problem.   —John Galsworthy

---

The instinctive need to be the member of a closely knit group fighting for common ideals may grow so strong that it becomes inessential what these ideals are.   —Konrad Lorenz

I've heard him [Konrad Lorenz] say that you can appeal to human beings in the name of the thing they value most to do things that are terrible. One of the traps of idealism and patriotism is this appeal.   —Margaret Mead

---

We are not steering by forms of government, we are steering by principles of government.   —Woodrow Wilson

Idealism is the noble toga that political gentlemen drape over their will to power.   —Aldous Huxley

IDEAS

Neither man nor nation can exist without a sublime idea.
                              —Feodor Dostoevski (1821–1881)

There are well-dressed foolish ideas just as there are well-dressed fools.   —Nicolas Chamfort

No one has ever had an idea in a dress suit.
                                  —Sir Frederick G. Banting

No grand idea was ever born in a conference, but a lot of foolish ideas have died there.   —F. Scott Fitzgerald

Every composer knows the anguish and despair occasioned by forgetting ideas which one has not time to write down.   —Hector Berlioz (Of all sad words of the writer's pen, saddest are these, "I didn't jot it when!")

The most powerful factors in the world are clear ideas in the minds of energetic men of good will.   —J. Arthur Thomson (But man can live without air for seconds, without water for days, without food for weeks, and without ideas for years.)

Ideas shape the course of history.   —John Maynard Keynes

When an idea is wanting a word can always be found to take its place.   —Johann W. von Goethe (1749–1832)

To die for an idea is to place a pretty high price upon conjecture.
—Anatole France

Man is ready to die for an idea, provided that idea is not quite clear to him.   —Paul Eldridge

*   *

The value of an idea has nothing whatsoever to do with the sincerity of the man who expresses it.
—Oscar Wilde (1854–1900)

An idea isn't responsible for the people who believe in it.
—Don Marquis

*   *

All great ideas are controversial, or have been at one time.
—George Seldes

Anyone who has begun to think places some portion of the world in jeopardy.   —John Dewey

*   *

Crank—a man with a new idea until it succeeds.
—Mark Twain

The vast majority of human beings dislike and even actually dread all notions with which they are not familiar . . . Hence it comes about that at their first appearance innovators have . . . always been derided as fools and madmen.   —Aldous Huxley

*   *

The ideas I stand for are not mine. I borrowed them from Socrates. I swiped them from Chesterfield. I stole them from Jesus. And I put them in a book. If you don't like their rules, whose would you use?   —Dale Carnegie

The ideas gained by men before they are twenty-five are practically the only ideas they shall have in their lives.   —William James

*   *

There is only one way in which a person acquires a new idea: by
the combination or association of two or more ideas he already has
into a new juxtaposition in such a manner as to discover a relationship among them of which he was not previously aware.

—Francis A. Cartier

An idea is a feat of association.   —Robert Frost

There is one thing stronger than all the armies in the world: and
that is an idea whose time has come.

—Victor Hugo (1802–1885)

It's just as sure a recipe for failure to have the right idea fifty years
too soon as five years too late.   —J. R. Platt

*   *

The ultimate good is better reached by free trade in ideas. The best
test of truth is the power of the thought to get itself accepted in the
competition of the market.   —Oliver Wendell Holmes, Jr.

It is impossible for ideas to compete in the marketplace if no forum
for their presentation is provided or available.

—Thomas Mann

IGNORANCE

Ignorance is the primary source of all misery and vice.   —Victor Cousin (If ignorance is bliss, there should be more happy
people.)

'Tain't what a man don't know that hurts him; it's what he knows
that just ain't so.

—Frank McKinney Hubbard ("Kin Hubbard")

Everybody is ignorant, only on different subjects.   —Will
Rogers (An ignorant person is one who doesn't know what you
have just found out.)

To the small part of ignorance that we arrange and classify we give
the name knowledge.   —Ambrose Bierce (There's nothing new
under the sun, but there are lots of old things we don't know.)

A great deal of intelligence can be invested in ignorance when the
need for illusion is deep.   —Saul Bellow

The little I know I owe to my ignorance.   —Sacha Guitry

I would rather have my ignorance than another man's knowledge,
because I have got so much more of it.   —Mark Twain

Gross Ignorance: 144 times worse than ordinary ignorance.
—Bennett Cerf

Most ignorance is vincible ignorance: we don't know because we don't want to know.   —Aldous Huxley (Nothing is so ignorant as the ignorance of certainty.)

That there should one man die ignorant who had capacity for knowledge, this I call a tragedy.   —Thomas Carlyle (1795–1881) (A man doesn't know what he knows until he knows what he doesn't know.)

Joe . . . was ignorant enough to feel superior to everything.
—John Ciardi

No man can be a pure specialist without being in the strict sense an idiot.   —George Bernard Shaw

The sheer weight of accumulated knowledge . . . inflicts a paralyzing sense of importance. The mind is overwhelmed by a constant fear of its ignorance.   —George W. Morgan

It's innocence when it charms us, ignorance when it doesn't.
—Mignon McLaughlin

A man must have a certain amount of intelligent ignorance to get anywhere.   —Charles F. Kettering (Ignorance is the mother of research.)

Genuine ignorance is . . . profitable because it is likely to be accompanied by humility, curiosity, and open mindedness; whereas ability to repeat catch-phrases, cant terms, familiar propositions, gives the conceit of learning and coats the mind with varnish waterproof to new ideas.   —John Dewey

Let us not be a generation recorded in future histories as destroying the irreplaceable inheritance of life formed through eons past.
—Charles A. Lindbergh, Jr.

One part of knowledge consists in being ignorant of such things as are not worthy to be known.   —Crates (4th century B.C.)

Discussion is an exchange of knowledge; argument an exchange of ignorance.   —Robert Quillen

---

Beware of the man who works hard to learn something, learns it, and finds himself no wiser than before.   —Kurt Vonnegut, Jr.

And here, poor fool, with all my lore/I stand no wiser than before.
—Johann W. von Goethe (1749–1832)

*   *

To be ignorant of one's ignorance is the malady of the ignorant.
—A. B. Alcott (1799–1888)

Not ignorance, but ignorance of ignorance, is the death of knowledge.   —Alfred North Whitehead

*   *

Nothing is so firmly believed as that which is least known.
—Francis Jeffrey (1773–1850)

The more ignorant the authority, the more dogmatic it is. In the fields where no real knowledge is even possible, the authorities are the fiercest and most assured and punish non-belief with the severest of penalties.   —Abraham Myerson

*   *

Wise men learn more from fools than fools from wise men.
—Marcus Porcius Cato (234–149 B.C.)

I have never met a man so ignorant that I couldn't learn something from him.   —Galileo Galilei (1564–1642)

It is impossible to defeat an ignorant man in argument.
—William G. McAdoo

Ignorance once dispelled is difficult to reestablish.
—Laurence J. Peter

*   *

Your ignorance cramps my conversation.   —Anthony Hope

Ignorance is no excuse—it's the real thing.   —Irene Peter

IMMORTALITY

Immortality—a fate worse than death.   —Edgar A. Shoaff

To desire immortality is to desire the eternal perpetuation of a great mistake.   —Arthur Schopenhauer (1788–1860)

Our existence is but a brief crack of light between two eternities of darkness.   —Vladimir Nabokov

The chief problem about death . . . is the fear that there may be no afterlife, a depressing thought, particularly for those who have bothered to shave . . . I do not believe in an afterlife, although I am bringing a change of underwear.   —Woody Allen

I don't want to achieve immortality through my work, I want to achieve it through not dying.   —Woody Allen

Spring—an experience in immortality.
                              —Henry David Thoreau (1817–1862)

A man has only one way of being immortal on this earth: he has to forget he is mortal.   —Jean Giraudoux

As to posterity, I may ask what has it ever done for us?
                              —Thomas Gray (1716–1771)

Posterity is just around the corner.   —George S. Kaufman

We are made to be immortal, and yet we die. It's horrible, it can't be taken seriously.   —Eugène Ionesco

You lose your immortality when you lose your memory.
                              —Vladimir Nabokov

When we are planning for posterity, we ought to remember that virtue is not hereditary.   —Thomas Paine (1737–1809)

Us, the most transient./Everyone once, once only. Just once and no more.   —Rainer Maria Rilke

Neither can I believe that the individual survives the death of his body, although feeble souls harbor such thoughts through fear or ridiculous egotism.   —Albert Einstein

One of the proofs of the immortality of the soul is that myriads have believed it—they also believed the world was flat.
                              —Mark Twain

Infinity converts that which is possible into the inevitable
                              —Norman Cousins

Up, sluggard, and waste not life; in the grave will be sleeping enough.   —Benjamin Franklin (1706–1790)

Suns may rise and set; we, when our short day has closed, must sleep on during one perpetual night.   —Catullus (84?–54 B.C.)

*   *

When I die I shall be content to vanish into nothingness . . . No show, however good, could conceivably be good forever . . . I do not believe in immortality, and have no desire for it.
                              —H. L. Mencken

I will have nothing to do with your immortality; we are miserable enough in this life, without the absurdity of speculating upon another . . . The basis of your religion is injustice; the Son of God, the pure, the immaculate, the innocent, is sacrificed for the guilty.
                    —George Gordon, Lord Byron (1788–1824)

*   *

Whoever participates with confidence in the adventure of men has his portion of immortality.   —Elie Faure

If there is a sin against life, it lies perhaps less in despairing of it than in hoping for another and evading the implacable grandeur of the one we have.   —Albert Camus

*   *

The average man, who does not know what to do with his life, wants another one which will last forever.   —Anatole France

Millions long for immortality who do not know what to do with themselves on a rainy Sunday afternoon.   —Susan Ertz

---

Never did Christ utter a single word attesting to a personal resurrection and a life beyond the grave.   —Count Leo Tolstoy

Jesus said to her [Martha], "I am the resurrection and the life; he who believes in me, though he die, yet shall he live, and whoever lives and believes in me shall never die."   —The Bible (John 11:25)

*   *

We have always held to the hope, the belief, the conviction that there is a better life, a better world, beyond the horizon.
                    —Franklin Delano Roosevelt

In spite of all the yearnings of men, no one can produce a single fact or reason to support the belief in God and in personal immortality.   —Clarence Darrow

*   *

Surely God would not have created such a being as man . . . to exist only for a day! No, no, man was made for immortality.
                    —Abraham Lincoln (1809–1865)

It's our mortality that terrifies us, because what we're really seeking is immortality—that is, after all, a fool's errand.
                    —Roger Caras

INDIANS

When asked by an anthropologist what the Indians called America
before the white man came, an Indian said simply, "Ours."
—Vine Deloria, Jr.

We used to root for the Indians against the cavalry, because we
didn't think it was fair in the history books that when the cavalry
won it was a great victory, and when the Indians won it was a
massacre. —Dick Gregory

I love the idea of God tempering the wind to the shorn lamb, but
I'd hate to have to sell it to an American Indian.
—Mignon McLaughlin

Before I judge my neighbor, let me walk a mile in his moccasins.
—Sioux Proverb

Treat all men alike. Give them all the same laws. Give them all an
even chance to live and grow. —Chief Joseph

INDIVIDUALITY / INDIVIDUALS

Be Yourself is the worst advice you can give to some people.
—Tom Masson

Every individual has a place to fill in the world and is important in
some respect whether he chooses to be so or not.
—Nathaniel Hawthorne (1804–1864)

I am one individual on a small planet in a little solar system in one
of the galaxies. —Roberto Assagioli

All men are forced into one of two categories; those with eleven
fingers and those without. —Ned Rorem

The image-managers encourage the individual to fashion himself
into a smooth coin, negotiable in any market. —John Gardner

Society attacks early when the individual is helpless.
—B. F. Skinner

The race advances only by the extra achievements of the individual.
You are the individual. —Charles Towne

In heaven an angel is nobody in particular.
—George Bernard Shaw

The things that are wrong with the country today are the sum total
of all the things that are wrong with us as individuals.
                                                    —Charles W. Tobey

The People, though we think of a great entity when we use the
word, means nothing more than so many millions of individual men.
                                                    —James Bryce

Society in its full sense . . . is never an entity separable from the
individuals who compose it. No individual can arrive even at the
threshold of his potentialities without a culture in which he participates. Conversely, no civilization has in it any element which
in the last analysis is not the contribution of an individual.
                                                    —Ruth Benedict

It is an absolute perfection . . . to know how . . . to get the
very most out of one's own individuality.
                                    —Michel de Montaigne (1533–1592)

At bottom every man knows well enough that he is a unique being,
only once on this earth; and by no extraordinary chance will such a
marvelously picturesque piece of diversity in unity as he is, ever be
put together a second time.   —Friedrich Nietzsche (1844–
1900) (Unless scientists start cloning around.)

The higher the individualism, the higher must be the socialism. The
resultant of these opposing forces . . . must be determined by each
age for itself.   —Henry Demarest Lloyd

It is a blessed thing that in every age some one has had the individuality enough and courage enough to stand by his own convictions.   —Robert G. Ingersoll (1833–1899)

It is because of the devotion or sacrifice of individuals that causes
become of value.   —Julian Huxley

The best things and best people rise out of their separateness; I'm
against a homogenized society because I want the cream to rise.
                                                    —Robert Frost

When we lose our individual independence in the corporateness of
a mass movement, we find a new freedom—freedom to hate, bully,
lie, torture, murder and betray without shame and remorse. Herein
undoubtedly lies part of the attractiveness of a mass movement.
                                                    —Eric Hoffer

Everything one does enough of eventually generates its own interest
and one then begins to believe in it.   —Alan Dunn

I think all of our human experience shows that no one with absolute power can be trusted to give it up even in part.
                                            —Justice Louis D. Brandeis

We may sum up much that is significant about inner-direction by saying that, in a society where it is dominant, its tendency is to protect the individual against the others at the price of leaving him vulnerable to himself . . . Within himself he must find justification not only in what he does but in what he is.

—David Riesman

Do you imagine that a state can submit and not be overthrown, in which the decisions of law have no power, but are set aside and trampled upon by individuals?   —Socrates (470?–399 B.C.)

How could a state be governed, or protected in its foreign relations if every individual remained free to obey or not to obey the law according to his private opinion?

—Thomas Hobbes (1588–1679)

*   *

Whatever you may be sure of, be sure of this—that you are dreadfully like other people.

—James Russell Lowell (1819–1891)

There is as much difference between us and ourselves as between us and others.   —Michel de Montaigne (1533–1592)

*   *

It is largely because of the traditional acceptance of conflict between society and the individual that emphasis upon cultural behaviour is so often interpreted as a denial of the autonomy of the individual . . . The problem of the individual is not clarified by stressing the antagonisms between culture and the individual, but by stressing their mutual reinforcement . . . Society in its full sense . . . is never an entity separable from the individuals who compose it.   —Ruth Benedict

It is one of mankind's dilemmas that the humane claims made for the individual are in proportion to the interests of mankind as a whole.   —Konrad Lorenz

Government is necessary, not because man is naturally bad . . . but because man is by nature more individualistic than social.

—Thomas Hobbes

We forfeit three-fourths of ourselves in order to be like other people.   —Arthur Schopenhauer (1788–1860)

*   *

I believe the State exists for the development of individual lives, not individuals for the development of the State.
                                        —Julian Huxley

If you insist that individual rights are the *summum bonum,* then the whole structure of society falls down.   —B. F. Skinner

INSTITUTIONS

In the infancy of societies, the chiefs of the state shape its institutions; later the institutions shape the chiefs of state.
                    —Baron de Montesquieu (1689–1755)

An institution is the lengthened shadow of one man.
                    —Ralph Waldo Emerson (1803–1882)

We despair of changing the habits of men, still we would alter institutions, the habits of millions of men.   —George Iles

All of our institutions must now turn their full intention to the great task ahead—to humanize our lives and thus to humanize our society.   —James Perkins

Most human organizations that fall short of their goals do so not because of stupidity or faulty doctrines, but because of internal decay and rigidification. They grow stiff in the joints. They get in a rut. They go to seed.   —James Gardner

The working of great institutions is mainly the result of a vast mass of routine, petty malice, self-interest, carelessness, and sheer mistake. Only a residual fraction is thought.   —George Santayana

INTEGRATION / SEGREGATION

Segregation is the offspring of an illicit intercourse between injustice and immorality.   —Martin Luther King, Jr.

To like an individual because he's black is just as insulting as to dislike him because he isn't white.   —e. e. cummings

A racially integrated community is a chronological term timed from the entrance of the first black family to the exit of the last white family.   —Saul Alinsky

Busing is an artificial and inadequate instrument of change which should be abandoned just as soon as we can afford to do so. But we must not take the risk of returning to the kind of segregation, fear and misunderstanding which produced the very problem in the first place.   —Reubin Askew

In all things that are purely social we can be as separate as the fingers, yet one as the hand in all things essential to mutual progress.
—Booker T. Washington

I am in favor of integration but not solely for the purpose of busing.
—Irene Peter

INTELLIGENCE / INTELLECTUALS

An intellectual is a man who takes more words than necessary to tell more than he knows. —Dwight D. Eisenhower

If an animal does something, we call it instinct; if we do the same thing for the same reason, we call it intelligence.
—Will Cuppy

We forgot to make ourselves intelligent when we made ourselves sovereign. —Will Durant

An "egghead" is a person who stands firmly on both feet in mid-air on both sides of an issue. —Senator Homer Ferguson

Eggheads, unite! You have nothing to lose but your yolks.
—Adlai Stevenson

It would take only one generation of forgetfulness to put us back intellectually several thousand years. —Dean Tollefson

If the Aborigine drafted an IQ test, all of Western civilization would presumably flunk it. —Stanley Garn (An intelligence test sometimes shows a man how smart he would have been not to have taken it.)

I do not feel obliged to believe that that same God who has endowed us with sense, reason, and intellect has intended us to forego their use. —Galileo Galilei (1564–1642)

Intellect . . . is the critical, creative, and contemplative side of mind . . . intelligence seeks to grasp, manipulate, re-order, adjust; intellect examines, ponders, wonders, theorizes, criticizes, imagines . . . —Richard Hofstadter

Intellect distinguishes between the possible and the impossible; reason distinguishes between the sensible and the senseless. Even the possible can be senseless. —Max Born

Recent discoveries in the physiology of the brain suggest that there may be two different kinds of intelligence—analytic, conceptual, verbal intelligence, located in the left hemisphere of the brain, and intuitive, artistic intelligence in the right hemisphere.
—*Newsweek* magazine

Intelligent discontent is the mainspring of civilization.
—Eugene V. Debs

College professors are suspect because whenever emotion is in control, anti-intellectualism prevails.   —Gordon W. Allport

The intelligence is proved not by ease of learning but by understanding what we learn.   —Joseph Whitney

Every child ought to be more intelligent than his parents.
—Clarence Darrow

Superior intellect is a large development of the faculty of association by similarity.   —Alexander Bain

---

There is nobody so irritating as somebody with less intelligence and more sense than we have.   —Don Herold

Do not always assume that the other fellow has intelligence equal to yours. He may have more.   —Terry-Thomas

*   *

The difference between intelligence and education is this: intelligence will make you a good living.   —Charles F. Kettering

Intelligence appears to be the thing that enables a man to get along without education. Education enables a man to get along without the use of his intelligence.   —Albert Edward Wiggam

*   *

. . . that peculiar disease of intellectuals, that infatuation with ideas at the expense of experience that compels experience to conform to bookish preconceptions.   —Archibald MacLeish

If everybody contemplates the infinite instead of fixing the drains, many of us will die of cholera.   —John Rich

---

It is only intellect that keeps me sane; perhaps this makes me overvalue intellect against feeling.   —Bertrand Russell

No one who lives among intellectuals is likely to idealize them unduly.   —Richard Hofstadter

*   *

Those who desire to rise as high as our human condition allows, must renounce intellectual pride . . . the omnipotence of clear thinking . . . belief in the absolute power of logic.
—Alexis Carrel

The decisive events of the world take place in the intellect.
—Henri Frédéric Amiel (1821–1881)

*   *

An intellectual is someone whose mind watches itself.
—Albert Camus

It hinders the creative work of the mind if the intellect examines too closely the ideas as they pour in.
—Friedrich Schiller (1759–1805)

INVENTION

Inventing is a combination of brains and materials. The more brains you use, the less material you need.   —Charles F. Kettering

Want is the mistress of invention.
—Susanna Centlivre (1667?–1723)

Invention breeds invention.
—Ralph Waldo Emerson (1803–1882)

He who builds a better mousetrap these days runs into material shortages, patent-infringement suits, work stoppages, collusive bidding, discount discrimination—and taxes.   —H. E. Martz (Fortunately the wheel was invented before the car, otherwise the scraping noise would be terrible!)

High heels were invented by a woman who had been kissed on the forehead.   —Christopher Morley

If necessity is the mother of invention, what was papa doing?
—Ruth Weekley

Invention is the mother of necessity.   —Thorstein Veblen

J

JEWS

The Jew is like anyone else only more so.   —Arnold Forster

In Israel, in order to be a realist you must believe in miracles.
—David Ben-Gurion

The Jews and Arabs should settle their dispute in the true spirit of Christian charity.   —Senator Alexander Wiley

We Jews have a secret weapon in our struggle with the Arabs— we have no place to go.   —Golda Meir

All share in the government of the world was denied for centuries to perhaps the ablest, certainly the most tenacious race that had ever lived in it.   —James Russell Lowell (1819–1891)

After I decided to become a Jew only then did I learn the Jews don't really have all the money. When I found out Rockefeller and Ford were goyim I almost resigned.   —Sammy Davis, Jr.

For others a knowledge of the history of their people is a civic duty, while for Jews it is a sacred duty.   —Maurice Samuel

The paradox is that those people who left only monuments behind as a record of their existence have vanished with time, whereas the Jews who left ideas have survived . . . a society without ideas has no history.   —Max I. Dimont

*   *

The greatest danger of Jewish power lies in their large ownership and influence in our motion pictures, our press, our radio, and our government.   —Charles A. Lindbergh, Jr.

Jews own the banks in this country [and] the newspapers.
—General George S. Brown (Navy), Chairman, Joint Chiefs of Staff (Anti-Semitism—the Gentile art of making enemies.)

His Majesty's Government views with favour the establishment in Palestine of a national home for the Jewish people . . . it being clearly understood that nothing shall be done which shall prejudice the civil and religious rights of existing non-Jewish communities in Palestine, or the rights and political status enjoyed by the Jews in any other country.   —Arthur J. Balfour

When Arthur Balfour launched his scheme for peopling Palestine with Jewish immigrants, I am credibly informed that he did not know there were Arabs in the country.
                                           —Dean William R. Inge

*   *

Christ cannot possibly have been a Jew. I don't have to prove that scientifically. It is a fact!   —Joseph Paul Goebbels

I determine who is a Jew.   —Hermann Goering

*   *

If my theory of relativity is proven successful, Germany will claim me as a German . . . Should my theory prove untrue . . . Germany will declare that I am a Jew.   —Albert Einstein

Hitler had the best answers to everything.   —Charles Manson

JUDGMENT

Our duty is to believe that for which we have sufficient evidence, and to suspend our judgment when we have not.
                                           —John Lubbock (1803–1865)

Here is the beginning of philosophy: a recognition of the conflicts between men, a search for their cause, a condemnation of mere opinion . . . and the discovery of a standard of judgment.
—Epictetus (c. 1st century A.D.) (Any man can prove he has good judgment by saying you have.)

Each morning puts a man on trial and each evening passes judgment.   —Roy L. Smith

Judgment is not the knowledge of fundamental laws; it is knowing how to apply a knowledge of them.   —Charles Gow

Give your decisions, never your reasons; your decisions may be right, your reasons are sure to be wrong.   —Earl of Mansfield (1705–1793) (The man who says he is willing to meet you half-way is usually a poor judge of distance.)

A smattering of philosophy had liberated his [Nero's] intellect without maturing his judgment.   —Tacitus (55?–130?)

What shall we do to be saved? In politics, establish a constitutional cooperative society of world government. In economics, find working compromises between free enterprise and socialism. —Arnold Toynbee (A compromise is the art of dividing a cake in such a way that each one thinks he is getting the biggest piece.)

We should all be obliged to appear before a board every five years, and justify our existence . . . on pain of liquidation.
—George Bernard Shaw

Judge a tree from its fruit; not from the leaves.
—Euripides (484–406 B.C.)

Examine the contents, not the bottle.   —The Talmud

*   *

Better bend than break.   —Scottish Proverb

Better Red than dead.   —Bertrand Russell

Let us train our minds to desire what the situation demands.
—Seneca (4 B.C.–A.D. 65)

Compromise makes a good umbrella but a poor roof; it is a temporary expedient.   —James Russell Lowell (1819–1891)

JURY

My idea of the ideal jury is twelve Irish unionists deciding the case of my client, Patrick O'Brien, a union bricklayer, who was run over by Chauncy Marlborough's Rolls-Royce while Marlborough was on his way to deposit $50,000 in the bank.   —Melvin Belli

Jury service honorably performed is as important in defense of our country, its Constitution and laws, and the ideals and standards for which they stand, as the service rendered by the soldier on the field of battle in time of war.   —Judge George H. Boldt

A fox should not be of the jury at a goose's trial.
                    —Thomas Fuller (1608–1661)

A jury is composed of twelve men of average ignorance.
                    —Herbert Spencer

The most important reason jurors rarely use their theoretical power
is that they are constantly told they have none.
                    —Jon M. Van Dyke

A jury consists of twelve persons chosen to decide who has the
better lawyer.   —Robert Frost

Jury: A group of twelve men who, having lied to the judge about
their hearing, health and business engagements, have failed to fool
him.   —H. L. Mencken

A jury too often has at least one member who is more ready to hang
the panel than the traitor.   —Abraham Lincoln (1809–1865)

JUSTICE / INJUSTICE

Why should there not be a patient confidence in the ultimate justice
of the people?   —Abraham Lincoln (1809–1865)

Liberty! Liberty! In all things let us have justice, and then we shall
have enough liberty.   —Joseph Joubert (1754–1824)

I have always believed that to have true justice we must have equal
harassment under the law.   —Paul Krassner

Justice is my being allowed to do whatever I like. Injustice is whatever prevents my doing so.   —Samuel Johnson (1709–1784)
(Justice is when the decision is in our favor.)

Let justice be done, though the heavens fall!
                    —Earl of Mansfield (1705–1793)

Justice is truth in action.   —Benjamin Disraeli (1804–1881)

Justice delayed is justice denied.
                    —William Ewart Gladstone (1809–1898)

Fairness is what justice really is.   —Justice Potter Stewart

Justice . . . is so subtle a thing that to interpret it one has only
need of a heart.   —José Garcia Oliver

Justice is incidental to law and order.   —J. Edgar Hoover

Justice discards party, friendship, kindred, and is always, therefore,
represented as blind.   —Joseph Addison (1672–1719)

For we both alike know that into the discussion of human affairs the question of justice enters only where the pressure of necessity is equal, and that the powerful exact what they can, and the weak grant what they must.   —Thucydides (471?–401? B.C.)

Peace without justice is tyranny.   —William Allen White

The sword of the law should never fall but on those whose guilt is so apparent as to be pronounced by their friends as well as foes.
—Thomas Jefferson (1743–1826)

Unless justice be done to others it will not be done to us.
—Woodrow Wilson

This is a court of law, young man, not a court of justice.
—Oliver Wendell Holmes, Jr.

I have a secret passion for mercy . . . but justice is what keeps happening to people.   —Ross Macdonald

In times when the government imprisons any unjustly, the true place for a just man is also the prison.
—Henry David Thoreau (1817–1862)

Every human being has a responsibility for injustice anywhere in the community.   —Scott Buchanan

So long as society is founded on injustice, the function of the laws will be to defend injustice. And the more unjust they are the more respectable they will seem.   —Anatole France

National injustice is the surest road to national downfall.
—William Ewart Gladstone (1809–1898)

People are, if anything, more touchy about being thought silly than they are about being thought unjust.   —E. B. White

Since when do you have to agree with people to defend them from injustice?   —Lillian Hellman

---

How invincible is justice if it be well spoken.
—Marcus Tullius Cicero (106–43 B.C.)

The price of justice is eternal publicity.   —Arnold Bennett

*   *

Use every man after his desert and who should 'scape whipping?
—William Shakespeare (1564–1616)

Justice, though due to the accused, is due to the accuser too.
—Justice Benjamin N. Cardozo

God would prefer to suffer the government to exist no matter how evil, rather than allow the rabble to riot, no matter how justified they are in doing so.   —Martin Luther (1483–1546)

I think the first duty of society is justice.
                              —Alexander Hamilton (1757–1804)

K

KINDNESS

I expect to pass through life but once. If therefore, there be any kindness I can show, or any good thing I can do to any fellow being, let me do it now, and not defer or neglect it, as I shall not pass this way again.   —William Penn (1644–1718)

He was so benevolent, so merciful a man that he would have held an umbrella over a duck in a shower of rain.

—Douglas Jerrold (1803–1857)

Kindness in words creates confidence. Kindness in thinking creates profoundness. Kindness in giving creates love.

—Lao-tzu (604?–531 B.C.)

Let us open up our natures, throw wide the doors of our hearts and let in the sunshine of good will and kindness.   —O. S. Marden

Wise sayings often fall on barren ground; but a kind word is never thrown away.   —Sir Arthur Helps (1813–1875)

Life is mostly froth and bubble,/Two things stand like stone—/ Kindness in another's trouble,/Courage in our own.

—Adam L. Gordon

KNOWLEDGE

Where there is the tree of knowledge, there is always Paradise: so say the most ancient and the most modern serpents.
—Friedrich Nietzsche (1844–1900)

Learned men are the cisterns of knowledge, not the fountain-heads.
—James Northcote

Knowledge is power, if you know it about the right person.
—Ethel Watts Mumford

I think this is the most extraordinary collection of talent, of human knowledge, that has ever been gathered together at the White House—with the possible exception of when Thomas Jefferson dined here alone.
—John F. Kennedy (to his Nobel Prize-winning guests)

Knowledge is of two kinds. We know a subject ourselves, or we know where we can find information upon it.
—Samuel Johnson (1709–1784)

Of all men's miseries the bitterest is this, to know so much and to have control over nothing.   —Herodotus (484–432 B.C.)

Mediocre men often have the most acquired knowledge.
—Claude Bernard (1813–1878)

An heretic . . . is a fellow who disagrees with you regarding something neither of you knows anything about.
—William Cowper Brann (1855–1898)

Who Knows what he is Told, must know a Lot of Things that Are Not So.   —Arthur Guiterman

The first step to knowledge is to know that we are ignorant.
—Lord David Cecil

We can be knowledgeable with other men's knowledge, but we cannot be wise with other men's wisdom.
—Michel de Montaigne (1533–1592)

The obligation to endure gives us the right to know.
—Jean Rostand

It's what you learn after you know it all that counts.
—John Wooden

In formal logic, a contradiction is the signal of a defeat; but in the evolution of real knowledge it marks the first step in progress towards a victory.   —Alfred North Whitehead

I want to know if I can live with what I know, and only that.
—Albert Camus

All our knowledge has its origins in our perceptions.
—Leonardo da Vinci (1452–1519)

The general diffusion of knowledge and learning through the community is essential to the preservation of free government.
—Carl Becker

Wonder rather than doubt is the root of knowledge.
—Abraham Joshua Heschel

I find that a great part of the information I have was acquired by looking up something and finding something else on the way.
—Franklin P. Adams

Knowledge is the only instrument of production that is not subject to diminishing returns.   —J. M. Clark

We do not know one millionth of one percent about anything.
—Thomas Alva Edison

The world is governed more by appearance than by realities, so that it is fully as necessary to seem to know something as it is to know it.
—Daniel Webster (1782–1852)

It is no good to try to stop knowledge from going forward. Ignorance is never better than knowledge.   —Enrico Fermi

Never try to tell everything you know. It may take too short a time.
—Norman Ford

Man's business here is to know for the sake of living, not to live for the sake of knowing.   —Frederic Harrison

---

What can I know? What ought I to do? What may I hope?
—Immanuel Kant (1724–1804)

What do I know?   —Michel de Montaigne (1533–1592)

*   *

A specialist is one who knows everything about something and nothing about anything else.   —Ambrose Bierce

The man we call a specialist today was formerly called a man with a one-track mind.   —Endre Balogh

*   *

Knowledge without conscience is the ruination of the soul.
—François Rabelais (1495?–1553)

Knowledge is ruin to my young men.   —Adolf Hitler

*   *

There is far greater peril in buying knowledge than in buying meat
and drink.   —Plato (427?-347? B.C.)

Beware of false knowledge; it is more dangerous than ignorance.
                                        —George Bernard Shaw

Try to know everything of something, and something of everything.
                        —Henry Peter, Lord Brougham (1778-1868)

To know all things is not permitted.   —Horace (65-8 B.C.)

*   *

Since we cannot know all that is to be known of everything, we
ought to know a little about everything.
                                        —Blaise Pascal (1623-1662)

Better know nothing than half-know many things.
                                —Friedrich Nietzsche (1844-1900)

L

LABOR

Some are bent with toil, and some get crooked trying to avoid it.
—Herbert V. Prochnow

I believe in the dignity of labor, whether with head or hand; that the world owes every man an opportunity to make a living.
—John D. Rockefeller, Jr.

My mistake was buying stock in the company. Now I worry about the lousy work I'm turning out.   —Marvin Townsend

Labor in a white skin cannot be free as long as labor in a black skin is branded.   —Karl Marx (1818–1883)

Invariably right things get done for the wrong reasons. So the [labor] organizer looks for wrong reasons to get right things done.
—Saul Alinsky

Like all other contracts, wages should be left to the fair and free competition of the market and should never be controlled by the interference of the legislatures.
—David Ricardo (1772–1823)

One thing that made their struggle so hard was that those men of exceptional ability who might have been their leaders almost always made fortunes of their own and then turned their strength against their former comrades.   —Preserved Smith

Long ago we stated the reason for labor organizations. We said that union was essential to give laborers opportunity to deal on an equality with their employer. —U. S. Supreme Court

We all belong t' th' union when it comes t' wantin' more money and less work. —Frank McKinney Hubbard ("Kin Hubbard")

Fight labor's demands to the last ditch and there will come a time when it seizes the whole of power, makes itself sovereign and takes what it used to ask. —Walter Lippmann

I would like to see a fair division of profits between capital and labor, so that the toiler could save enough to mingle a little June with the December of his life.
—Robert G. Ingersoll (1833–1899)

LANGUAGE

For more than forty years I have been speaking prose without knowing it. —Molière (1622–1673)

Slang is a language that rolls up its sleeves, spits on its hands and goes to work. —Carl Sandburg

The English tongue is rapidly spreading and bids fair to become the general language of the human race.
—John Lubbock (1803–1865)

Language—a form of organized stutter. —Marshall McLuhan

If you scoff at language study . . . how, save in terms of language, will you scoff? —Mario Pei

In Paris they simply stared when I spoke to them in French; I never did succeed in making those idiots understand their own language.
—Mark Twain

The American arrives in Paris with a few French phrases he has culled from a conversational guide or picked up from a friend who owns a beret. —Fred Allen

Great literature is simply language charged with meaning to the utmost possible degree. —Ezra Pound

I cannot learn languages; men of ordinary capacity can learn Sanskrit in less time than it takes me to buy a German dictionary.
—George Bernard Shaw

One of the difficulties in the language is that all our words from loose using have lost their edge.   —Ernest Hemingway

I'd rather be caught holding up a bank than stealing so much as a two-word phrase from another writer; but . . . when someone has the wit to coin a useful word, it ought to be acclaimed and broadcast or it will perish.   —Jack Smith

If names are not correct, language will not be in accordance with the truth of things.   —Confucius (c. 551–479 B.C.)

If only everyone talked the way we do in my household. I mean . . . if only everyone . . . like . . . talked . . . you know . . . the way we do . . . right? It would be so much . . . like . . . easier . . . you know . . . understand . . . right?
—Robert Nordell

I am referred to in that splendid language [Urdu] as "Fella belong Mrs. Queen."   —Prince Philip, Duke of Edinburgh

*   *

If thought corrupts language, language can also corrupt thought.
—George Orwell

The purpose of *Newspeak* . . . is to make all other modes of thought impossible.   —George Orwell

---

Language is the light of the mind.
—John Stuart Mill (1806–1873)

Philosophy is language idling.   —Ludwig Wittgenstein

*   *

Men . . . employ speech only to conceal their thoughts.
—Voltaire (François Marie Arouet) (1694–1778)

The chief virtue that language can have is clearness, and nothing detracts from it so much as the use of unfamiliar words.
—Hippocrates (460?–370? B.C.)

LAUGHTER

We are all here for a spell, get all the good laughs you can.
—Will Rogers

In a comedy, laughs don't hurt.   —David Picker

Laughter is the sensation of feeling good all over and showing it principally in one place.
—Josh Billings (Henry Wheeler Shaw) (1818–1885)

Nobody ever died of laughter.   —Max Beerbohm

Incongruity is the mainspring of laughter.   —Max Beerbohm

Laughter is a tranquilizer with no side effects.
—Arnold Glasow

Life does not cease to be funny when people die, any more than it ceases to be serious when people laugh.
—George Bernard Shaw

If you don't learn to laugh at trouble, you won't have anything to laugh at when you grow old.   —Ed Howe

The test of a real comedian is whether you laugh at him before he opens his mouth.   —George Jean Nathan

One must have a heart of stone to read the death of Little Nell without laughing.   —Oscar Wilde (1854–1900)

And if I laugh at any mortal thing,/'Tis that I may not weep.
—George Gordon, Lord Byron (1788–1824)

I hasten to laugh at everything, for fear of being obliged to weep.
—Pierre Augustin de Beaumarchais (1732–1799)

*   *

If you're not allowed to laugh in heaven, I don't want to go there.
—Martin Luther (1483–1546)

God cannot be solemn, or he would not have blessed man with the incalculable gift of laughter.   —Sydney Harris

It better befits a man to laugh at life than to lament over it.
—Seneca (4 B.C.–A.D. 65)

But let me laugh awhile, I've mickle time to grieve.
—John Keats (1795–1821)

No one is more profoundly sad than he who laughs too much.
Jean Paul Richter (1763–1825)

A good laugh is sunshine in a house.
—William Makepeace Thackeray (1811–1863)

*   *

If you would succeed in life, you must be solemn, solemn as an ass.
All great monuments are built over solemn asses.

—Thomas Corwin

An individual is as strong as his or her prejudice. Two things reduce
prejudice—education and laughter. —Laurence J. Peter

LAW / LAWYERS / JUDGES / SUPREME COURT

It ain't no sin if you crack a few laws now and then, just so long as
you don't break any. —Mae West

An appeal is when ye ask wan court to show its contempt for another court. —Finley Peter Dunne (Mr. Dooley)

I care not who makes the laws of a nation if I can get out an injunc-
tion. —Finley Peter Dunne (Mr. Dooley) (In most law courts
a man is assumed guilty until he is proven influential.)

A verbal contract isn't worth the paper it's written on.

—Samuel Goldwyn

It is illegal in England to state in print that a wife can and should
derive sexual pleasure from intercourse. —Bertrand Russell

He didn't know the right people. That's all a police record means.
—Raymond Chandler (When a mob attacked Bertrand Russell in
1918 for his unpopular pacifist views, a friend pleaded with the
police to intervene, to no avail. "But he is an eminent philosopher,"
the friend pleaded. The police shrugged. "But he is famous all over
the world," the friend insisted. The police were unimpressed. "But
he is the brother of an earl," the friend cried desperately. The police
rushed to the rescue.)

There are not enough jails, not enough policemen, not enough
courts to enforce a law not supported by the people.

—Hubert H. Humphrey

Of course there's a different law for the rich and the poor; otherwise, who would go into business? —E. Ralph Stewart

A man may as well open an oyster without a knife, as a lawyer's
mouth without a fee. —Barten Holyday

Reading isn't an occupation we encourage among police officers.
We try to keep paper work down to a minimum. —Joe Orton

If police efficiency were an end in itself, the police would be free to put an accused on the rack. Police efficiency must yield to constitutional rights.   —Judge John Minor Wisdom (Who will guard the guardians?)

Have you noticed how much those who deal in absolutes—magistrates, policemen, priests—are generally quite humorless?
                                           —Hubert Monteilhet

I'm not *against* the police; I'm just afraid of them.
                                           —Alfred Hitchcock

The rookie [policeman] is faced with the situation where it is easier for him to become corrupt than to remain honest.
                                           —Knapp Commission Report

What society fails to realize is that the tension between the police and the judiciary has always been fundamental to our constitutional system. It is intentional and healthy and constitutes the real difference between a free society and a police state.
                                           —Nicholas Katzenbach

Most middle-class whites have no idea what it feels like to be subjected to police who are routinely suspicious, rude, belligerent, and brutal.   —Dr. Benjamin Spock

Where law ends, tyranny begins.
                                           —William Pitt the Elder (1708–1778)

Law never made men a whit more just.
                                           —Henry David Thoreau (1817–1862)

Courtroom: A place where Jesus Christ and Judas Iscariot would be equals, with the betting odds in favor of Judas.
                                           —H. L. Mencken

Our court dockets are so crowded today it would be better to refer to it as the overdue process of law.   —Bill Vaughan

This won't be the first time I've arrested somebody and then built my case afterward.   —James Garrison

A witness cannot give evidence of his age unless he can remember being born.   —Judge Blagden

These detective series on TV always end at precisely the right moment—after the criminal is arrested and before the court turns him loose.   —Robert Orben

Ignorance of the law does not prevent the losing lawyer from collecting his bill.   —*Puck* magazine (Lawyers help those who help themselves.)

You're an attorney. It's your duty to lie, conceal and distort everything, and slander everybody.   —Jean Giraudoux (A lawyer is a man who helps you get what is coming to him.)

No poet ever interpreted nature as freely as a lawyer interprets truth.
—Jean Giraudoux

To some lawyers all facts are created equal.   —Justice Felix Frankfurter (And are clever enough to convince you that the Constitution is unconstitutional.)

A lawyer starts life giving five hundred dollars' worth of law for five dollars, and ends giving five dollars' worth for five hundred dollars.   —Benjamin H. Brewster (He becomes case-hardened.)

"In my youth," said his father, "I took to the law,/And argued each case with my wife;/And the muscular strength which it gave to my jaw/Has lasted the rest of my life."   —Lewis Carroll (Charles Lutwidge Dodgson) (1832–1898)

The United States is the greatest law factory the world has ever known.   —Chief Justice Charles Evans Hughes

Under current law, it is a crime for a private citizen to lie to a government official, but not for the government official to lie to the people.   —Donald M. Fraser

The violation of some laws is a normal part of the behavior of every citizen.   —Stuart Chase

The Lord Chief Justice of England recently said that the greater part of his judicial time was spent investigating collisions between propelled vehicles, each on its own side of the road, each sounding its horn and each stationary.   —Philip Guedalla

There are a lot of mediocre judges and people and lawyers, and they are entitled to a little representation.
—Senator Roman L. Hruska

The Supreme Court has handed down the Eleventh Commandment: "Thou shalt not, in thy classrooms, read the first ten."
—Fletcher Knebel

If you think that you can think about a thing, inextricably attached to something else, without thinking of the thing it is attached to, then you have a legal mind.   —Thomas Reed Powell (The public must learn to obey the laws like everybody else.)

Lawyers spend a great deal of their time shoveling smoke.
—Oliver Wendell Holmes, Jr.

The law is reason free from passion.
—Aristotle (384–322 B.C.)

Law is experience developed by reason and applied continually to further experience.   —Roscoe Pound

Laws not enforced cease to be laws, and rights not defended may wither away.   —Thomas Moriarty

To quote me the authority of *precedents* leaves me quite unmoved. All human progress has been made by ignoring precedents. If mankind had continued to be the slave of precedent we should still be living in caves and subsisting on shellfish and wild berries.
                                                                  —Viscount Philip Snowden

Those terrifying verbal jungles called *laws* are simply such directives, accumulated, codified, and systematized through the centuries . . . The decision finally rests not upon appeals to past authority, but upon *what people want*.   —S. I. Hayakawa

The law that will work is merely the summing up in legislative form of the moral judgment that the community has already reached.
                                                                  —Woodrow Wilson

The law itself is on trial in every case as well as the cause before it.
                                                                  —Justice Harlan F. Stone

The laws of a nation form the most instructive portion of its history.
                                                                  —Edward Biggon

Law is nothing unless close behind it stands a warm living public opinion.   —Wendell Phillips (1811–1884)

If men recognize no law superior to their desires, then they must fight when their desires collide.   —R. H. Tawney

Under our constitutional system, courts stand against any winds that blow as havens of refuge for those who might otherwise suffer because they are helpless, weak, outnumbered, or because they are non-conforming victims of prejudice and public excitement.
                                                                  —Justice Hugo L. Black

The law is not an end in itself, nor does it provide ends. It is pre-eminently a means to serve what we think is right.
                                                                  —Justice William J. Brennan, Jr.

The life of the law has not been logic; it has been experience.
                                                                  —Oliver Wendell Holmes, Jr.

While unconstitutional exercise of power by the executive and legislative branches is subject to judicial restraint, the only check upon our own exercise of power is our own sense of self-restraint.
                                                                  —Justice Harlan F. Stone

Where the weak or oppressed assert the rights that have been so long denied them, those in power inevitably resist on the basis of the necessity for tranquility.　—Chief Justice Earl Warren

The people can change Congress but only God can change the Supreme Court.　—George W. Norris

We want a Supreme Court which will do justice under the Constitution—not over it. In our courts we want a government of laws and not of men.　—Franklin Delano Roosevelt

When you break the big laws, you do not get liberty; you do not even get anarchy. You get the small laws.　—G. K. Chesterton

Law is merely the expression of the will of the strongest for the time being.　—Brooks Adams

We have to find ways to clear the courts of the endless stream of "victimless crimes" that get in the way of serious consideration of serious crimes. There are more important matters for highly skilled judges and prosecutors than minor traffic offenses, loitering and drunkenness.　—Richard M. Nixon

Law is not justice and a trial is not a scientific inquiry into truth. A trial is the resolution of a dispute.　—Edison Haines

But it is foolishness for the party of *law and order* to imagine that these *forces of public authority* created to preserve order are always going to be content to preserve order that that party desires. Inevitably they will end by themselves defining and deciding on the order they are going to impose—which, naturally, will be that which suits them best.　—José Ortega y Gasset (Men fight for freedom; then they begin to accumulate laws to take it away from themselves.)

Laws and institutions must go hand in hand with the progress of the human mind.　—Thomas Jefferson (1743–1826)

Of the faults traditionally attributed to democracy one only is fairly chargeable on the United States . . . the disposition to be lax in enforcing laws disliked by any large part of the population.
　　　　　　　—James Bryce

The law's final justification is in the good it does or fails to do to the society of a given place and time.　—Albert Camus

It is not our freedom that is in jeopardy, in the first instance; it is our public order. If that breaks down, freedom will be lost and so . . . will the prospect for greater justice.　—Eric Sevareid

When a legal distinction is determined . . . between night and day, childhood and maturity, or any other extremes, a point has to be fixed or a line has to be drawn . . . the line or point seems arbitrary . . . but when it is seen that a line or point there must be, and that there is no mathematical or logical way of fixing it precisely, the decision of the legislature must be accepted unless we can say that it is very wide of any reasonable mark.

—Oliver Wendell Holmes, Jr.

If you have the right eye for these things, you can see that accused men are often attractive.   —Franz Kafka

---

The more corrupt the state, the more numerous the laws.

—Tacitus (55?–130?)

The greater the number of laws and enactments, the more thieves and robbers there will be.   —Lao-tzu (c. 604–531 B.C.)

*   *

In a democracy only those laws which have their bases in folkways or the approval of strong groups have a chance of being enforced.

—Abraham Myerson

A state is better governed which has but few laws, and those laws strictly observed.   —René Descartes (1596–1650)

*   *

We must observe the moralistic attitude toward law in America, expressed in the common belief that there is a higher law.

—Gunnar Myrdal

Higher laws are unilaterally determined.   —Eric Sevareid

*   *

I don't want a lawyer to tell me what I cannot do; I hire him to tell me how to do what I want to do.   —J. Pierpont Morgan

What do I care about the law? Hain't I got the power?

—Cornelius Vanderbilt (1794–1877)

*   *

It is difficult to imagine any grounds, other than our own personal economic predilections, for holding a minimum wage law void.

—Justice Harlan F. Stone

The decisions of the courts on economic and social questions depend on their economic and social philosophy.

—Theodore Roosevelt

*   *

Fidelity to the public requires that the laws be as plain and explicit as possible, that the less knowing may understand, and not be ensnared by them, while the artful evade their force.
—Samuel Cooke

The minute you read something you can't understand, you can almost be sure it was drawn up by a lawyer.   —Will Rogers
(A lawyer is a man who prevents someone else from getting your money.)

*   *

Laws are spider webs through which the big flies pass and the little ones get caught.   —Honoré de Balzac (1799–1850)

Laws are like cobwebs, for any trifling or powerless thing falls into them, they hold it fast; but if a thing of any size falls into them, it breaks the mesh and escapes.   —Anacharsis (c. 600 B.C.)

*   *

Many today seem to be demanding for themselves the unlimited right to disobey the law . . . an essential concomitant of civil disobedience is the actor's willingness to accept the punishment that follows.   —Earl Morris

By God, I will not obey this filthy enactment!
—Ralph Waldo Emerson (1803–1882), of the Fugitive Slave Act

*   *

What I cannot live with may not bother another man's conscience. The result is that conscience will stand against conscience.
—Hannah Arendt

Every actual state is corrupt. Good men must not obey laws too well.   —Ralph Waldo Emerson (1803–1882)

*   *

Justice is too good for some people and not good enough for the rest.   —Norman Douglas

Law and order are always and everywhere the law and order which protect the established hierarchy.   —Herbert Marcuse

*   *

Crime is contagious. If a government becomes a lawbreaker, it breeds contempt for the law; it invites every man to become a law unto himself.   —Justice Louis D. Brandeis

Who will protect the public when the police violate the law?
—Ramsey Clark

* *

No matter how many litanies we intone, we will not induce our people to obey laws that those in authority do not themselves obey.
—Henry Steele Commager

Nobody has a more sacred obligation to obey the law than those who make the law. —Sophocles (496?–406 B.C.)

We cannot, by total reliance on law, escape the duty to judge right and wrong . . . There are good laws and there are occasionally bad laws, and it conforms to the highest traditions of a free society to offer resistance to bad laws, and to disobey them.
—Alexander Bickel

Disobedience is the worst of evils. This it is that ruins a nation.
—Jean Anouilh

* *

From Antigone through Martin Luther to Martin Luther King the issue of liberty has turned on the existence of a higher law than that of The State. —Milton Mayer

How could a state be governed, or protected in its foreign relations if every individual remained free to obey or not to obey the law according to his private opinion?
—Thomas Hobbes (1588–1679)

* *

Those who uphold the law must be wiser and calmer than those who seek to repudiate it. —John Lindsay

Bad laws are the worst sort of tyranny.
—Edmund Burke (1729–1797)

* *

Much hindrance in dealing with problems of social control is rendered by the use of the word *lawlessness*. —Stuart Chase

Law is a reflection and source of prejudice. It both enforces and suggests forms of bias. —Diane Schulder

* *

Order is the first requisite of liberty.
—Georg Wilhelm Hegel (1770–1831)

There is no crueler tyranny than that which is perpetuated under the shield of law and in the name of justice.
—Baron de Montesquieu (1689–1755)

"LAWS"

Ade's Law—Anybody can win—unless there happens to be a second entry. —George Ade

Barnum's Law—You can fool most of the people most of the time.
—P. T. Barnum

Berra's Law—You can observe a lot just by watching.
—Yogi Berra

Billings' Law—Live within your income, even if you have to borrow to do so. —Josh Billings (Henry Wheeler Shaw) (1818–1885)

Clopton's Law—For every credibility gap there is a gullibility fill.
—Richard Clopton

Coolidge's Law—Anytime you don't want anything, you get it.
—Calvin Coolidge

Coolidge's 2nd Law—A lost article invariably shows up after you replace it. —Calvin Coolidge

Coughlin's Law—Don't talk unless you can improve the silence.
—Laurence C. Coughlin

Ettore's Law—The other line moves faster.
—Barbara Ettore

Gates' Law—If there isn't a law, there will be.
—W. I. E. Gates

Gomez' Law—If you don't throw it, they can't hit it.
—Lefty Gomez

Lec's Immutable Law—The first requisite for immortality is death.
—Stanislaw J. Lec

Levenson's Law—No matter how well a toupee blends in back, it always looks like hell in front. —Sam Levenson

Levenson's 2nd Law—Insanity is hereditary—you can get it from your children. —Sam Levenson

Lippmann's Law—Where all think alike, no one thinks very much.
—Walter Lippmann

Maier's Law—If facts do not conform to theory, they must be disposed of. —N. R. F. Maier

Ms. Peter's Law—Today if you're not confused you're just not thinking clearly. —Irene Peter

Peter's Law—The unexpected always happens.
—Laurence J. Peter

Pope's Law—All looks yellow to a jaundiced eye.
—Alexander Pope

Roos' Law—If there's a harder way of doing something, someone will find it.   —Ralph E. Roos

Runyon's Law—The race is not always to the swift, nor the battle to the strong, but that's the way to bet.   —Damon Runyon

Truman's Law—If you can't convince them, confuse them.
—Harry S Truman

Tuchman's Law—If power corrupts, weakness in the seat of power, with its constant necessity of deals and bribes and compromising arrangements, corrupts even more.   —Barbara Tuchman

LEADERSHIP / LEADERS

The question, "Who ought to be boss?" is like asking "Who ought to be the tenor in the quartet?" Obviously, the man who can sing tenor.   —Henry Ford

If the blind lead the blind, both shall fall into the ditch.
—The Bible (Matthew 15:14)

It is hard to look up to a leader who keeps his ear to the ground.
—James H. Boren

He led his regiment from behind—/He found it less exciting./But when away his regiment ran,/His place was at the fore, O.
—W. S. Gilbert

Leadership is action, not position.
—Donald H. McGannon

In all legislative assemblies, the greater the number composing them may be, the fewer will be the men who will in fact direct their proceedings.   —Alexander Hamilton (1757–1804)

It is frequently a misfortune to have very brilliant men in charge of affairs; they expect too much of ordinary men.
—Thucydides (471?–401 B.C.)

If you would be leader of men, you must lead your own generation, not the next.   —Woodrow Wilson

Leaders have a significant role in creating the state of mind that is society.   —John Gardner

Not to decide is to decide.   —Harvey Cox

Leaders are the custodians of a nation's ideals, of the beliefs it cherishes, of its permanent hopes, of the faith which makes a nation out of a mere aggregation of individuals.   —Walter Lippmann

---

I must follow the people. Am I not their leader?
                              —Benjamin Disraeli (1804–1881)

There go my people. I must find out where they are going so I can lead them.   —Alexandre Ledru-Rollin (1807–1874)

*   *

Reason and judgment are the qualities of a leader.
                              —Tacitus (55?–130?)

Charlatanism of some degree is indispensable to effective leadership.
                              —Eric Hoffer

LEARNING

He not only overflowed with learning, but stood in the slop.
                              —Sydney Smith (1771–1845)

Anyone who stops learning is old, whether at twenty or eighty. Anyone who keeps learning stays young. The greatest thing in life is to keep your mind young.   —Henry Ford

Never learn to do anything: if you don't learn, you'll always find someone else to do it for you.   —Mark Twain

Learning preserves the errors of the past, as well as its wisdom. For this reason, dictionaries are public dangers, although they are necessities.   —Alfred North Whitehead

He learned the arts of riding, fencing, gunnery,/And how to scale a fortress—or a nunnery.
                              —George Gordon, Lord Byron (1788–1824)

Personally I'm always ready to learn, although I do not always like being taught.   —Winston Churchill

The brighter you are, the more you have to learn.
                                                    —Don Herold

Learned men are the cisterns of knowledge, not the fountainheads.
                              —James Northcote (1746–1831)

We see then how far the monuments of wit and learning are more durable than the monuments of power, or of the hands. For have not the verses of Homer continued twenty-five hundred years or more, without the loss of a syllable or letter; during which time infinite palaces, temples, castles, cities have been decayed and demolished?   —Francis Bacon (1561–1626)

I am defeated, and know it, if I meet any human being from whom I find myself unable to learn anything.

—George Herbert Palmer

If a little knowledge is dangerous, where is a man who has so much as to be out of danger?

—Thomas Henry Huxley (1825–1895)

A little learning is not a dangerous thing to one who does not mistake it for a great deal.   —William Allen White

*   *

It is surely harmful to souls to make it a heresy to believe what is proved.   —Galileo Galilei (1564–1642)

By identifying the new learning with heresy, you make orthodoxy synonymous with ignorance.

—Desiderius Erasmus (1465–1536)

A little learning is a dangerous thing;/Drink deep, or taste not the Pierian spring.   —Alexander Pope (1688–1744)

A little learning is a dangerous thing, but a lot of ignorance is just as bad.   —Bob Edwards

*   *

All that I know I learned after I was thirty.

—Georges Clemenceau

The second half of a man's life is made up of nothing but the habits he has acquired during the first half.

—Feodor Dostoevski (1821–1881)

LEISURE AND RETIREMENT

Increased means and increased leisure are the two civilizers of man.
—Benjamin Disraeli (1804–1881)

Liberty is being free from the things we don't like in order to be slaves of the things we do like.   —Ernest Benn (The best intelligence test is what we do with our leisure.)

Who knows whether in retirement I shall be tempted to the last infirmity of mundane minds, which is to write a book.
—Geoffrey Fisher

A society that gives to one class all the opportunities for leisure, and to another all the burdens of work, dooms both classes to spiritual sterility.   —Lewis Mumford

The thing that I should wish to obtain from money would be leisure with security.   —Bertrand Russell (The time you enjoy wasting is not wasted time.)

Some men are so selfish that they read a book or go to a concert for their own sinister pleasure, instead of doing it to improve social conditions, as the good citizen does when drinking cocktails or playing bridge.   —Jacques Barzun

It is seldom that an American retires from business to enjoy his fortune in comfort . . . He works because he has always worked, and knows no other way.   —Thomas Nichols (Retirement is the time when you never do all the things you intended to do when you'd have the time.)

Few women and fewer men have enough character to be idle.
—E. V. Lucas

The end of labor is to gain leisure.   —Aristotle (384–322 B.C.) (So that you can drink coffee on your own time.)

A perpetual holiday is a good working definition of hell.
—George Bernard Shaw

Let me give a word of advice to you young fellows who have been looking forward to retirement: Have nothing to do with it. Listen: it's like this. Have you ever been out for a late autumn walk in the closing part of the afternoon, and suddenly looked up to realize that the leaves have practically all gone? And the sun has set and the day gone before you knew it—and with that a cold wind blows across the landscape? That's retirement.   —Stephen Leacock

---

If we are dreamers who laud the self-indulgent life, we suspect that we really wish we could buckle down to work. Should we begin to work, however, we must anticipate that we will soon bemoan the lazy life we left behind.   —Harvey Mindess

Retired is being tired twice, I've thought,/First tired of working,/ Then tired of not.   —Richard Armour

*   *

To the man whose senses are alive and alert there is not even the need to stir from one's threshold.   —Henry Miller

Only a person who can live with himself can enjoy the gift of leisure.
—Henry Greber

*   *

If the soul has food for study and learning, nothing is more delightful than an old age of leisure . . . Leisure consists in all those virtuous activities by which a man grows morally, intellectually, and spiritually. It is that which makes a life worth living.
—Marcus Tullius Cicero (106–43 B.C.)

If a man has important work, and enough leisure and income to enable him to do it properly, he is in possession of as much happiness as is good for any of the children of Adam.
—R. H. Tawney

*   *

Leisure is the most challenging responsibility a man can be offered.
—Dr. William Russell

To be able to fill leisure intelligently is the last product of civilization.   —Arnold Toynbee

---

Those who decide to use leisure as a means of mental development, who love good music, good books, good pictures, good plays, good company, good conversation—what are they? They are the happiest people in the world.   —William Lyon Phelps

The only liberty an inferior man really cherishes is the liberty to quit work, stretch out in the sun, and scratch himself.
—H. L. Mencken

*   *

I would not exchange my leisure hours for all the wealth in the world.   —Comte de Mirabeau (1749–1791)

Leisure tends to corrupt, and absolute leisure corrupts absolutely.
—Edgar A. Shoaff

*   *

One ought, every day at least, to hear a little song, read a good poem, see a fine picture, and, if it were possible, to speak a few reasonable words.   —Johann W. von Goethe (1749–1832)

Retirement is the ugliest word in the language.
—Ernest Hemingway

*   *

The gradually declining years are among the sweetest in a man's
life.   —Seneca (4 B.C.–A.D. 65)

To retire is the beginning of death.   —Pablo Casals

LIBERALISM / LIBERALS

The liberal is accustomed to appearing radical to conservatives,
counter-revolutionary to radicals, and as a fink to activists of all
persuasions.   —Harry S. Ashmore

A liberal is a man who leaves the room when the fight begins.
—Heywood Broun

A liberal is a person whose interests aren't at stake at the moment.
—Willis Player

Conservatives and liberals may be defined as those who think that
on the whole things are all right and you better not tinker much
with them, and those who think that there is enormous room for
improvement.   —Justice Felix Frankfurter

The failure to recognize the distinction between heresy and conspiracy is fatal to a liberal civilization.   —Sidney Hook

The worst enemy of the new radicals are the old liberals.
—Nikolai Lenin

America has had gifted conservative statesmen and national leaders
. . . But with few exceptions, only the liberals have gone down
in history as national heroes.   —Gunnar Myrdal

I get very tired of the smug self-satisfaction, the holier-than-thou
attitude, the sneering meticulousness of men and women with whose
outlook on economic and social questions I often regretfully find
myself in accord . . . They rush to the aid of any liberal victor,
and then proceed to stab him in the back when he fails to perform
the mental impossibility of subscribing unconditionally to their
dozen or more conflicting principles . . . they cannot lead, they
will not follow, and they refuse to cooperate.   —Harold Ickes

---

A liberal is a man who is willing to spend somebody else's money.
—Carter Glass

I can remember way back when a liberal was one who was generous
with his own money.   —Will Rogers

*   *

Though I believe in liberalism, I find it difficult to believe in liberals. —G. K. Chesterton

The radical of one century is the conservative of the next. The radical invents the views. When he has worn them out the conservative adopts them. —Mark Twain

---

Liberalism . . . is the supreme form of generosity; it is the right which the majority concedes to minorities and hence it is *the noblest cry* that has ever resounded in this planet.
—José Ortega y Gasset

Criticism also comes from our native Communists . . . and from the fuzzy-minded totalitarian liberals who believe that their creeping collectivism can be adopted without destroying personal liberty and representative government. —Herbert Hoover

* *

I would call the Democratic Left . . . the group which secures social advancement for all the people in a framework of freedom and consent. —Luis Muñoz Marin

Liberal—a power worshipper without the power.
—George Orwell

LIFE

It is not true that life is one damn thing after another—it's one damn thing over and over. —Edna St. Vincent Millay (Life isn't all beer and skittles; few of us have touched a skittle in years.)

Life is easier to take than you'd think; all that is necessary is to accept the impossible, do without the indispensable and bear the intolerable. —Kathleen Norris (In spite of the cost of living, it's still popular.)

Life is just a bowl of pits. —Rodney Dangerfield

Life is like a blanket too short. You pull it up and your toes rebel, you yank it down and shivers meander about your shoulder; but cheerful folks manage to draw their knees up and pass a very comfortable night. —Marion Howard

One learns in life to keep silent and draw one's own confusions.
—Cornelia Otis Skinner

If living conditions don't stop improving in this country, we're going to run out of humble beginnings for our great men.
—Russell P. Askue

The mass of men lead lives of quiet desperation.
—Henry David Thoreau (1817–1862)

When a man has pity on all living creatures then only is he noble.
—Buddha (563?–483? B.C.)

Not a shred of evidence exists in favor of the idea that life is serious.
—Brendan Gill (Scientists are trying to produce life in the laboratory, but it shouldn't be difficult if the laboratory assistant is pretty and willing.)

I am interested in this world, in this life, not some other world or future life.   —Jawaharlal Nehru

I am on the side of the unregenerate who affirm the worth of life as an end in itself.   —Oliver Wendell Holmes, Jr.

Life is not a spectacle or a feast: it is a predicament.
—George Santayana

Let us endeavor so to live that when we come to die even the undertaker will be sorry.   —Mark Twain

Life just is. You have to flow with it. Give yourself to the moment. Let it happen.   —Governor Jerry Brown

Life can only be understood backwards; but it must be lived forwards.   —Sören Kierkegaard (1813–1855)

Life is not a problem to be solved but a reality to be experienced.
—Sören Kierkegaard (When a person puts his best foot forward and gets it stepped on—that's life.)

Life is what happens to us while we are making other plans.
—Thomas La Mance

Life happens too fast for you ever to think about it. If you could just persuade people of this, but they insist on amassing information.   —Kurt Vonnegut, Jr.

I advise you to go on living solely to enrage those who are paying your annuities. It is the only pleasure I have left.
—Voltaire (François Marie Arouet) (1694–1778)

Is not life a hundred times too short for us to bore ourselves?
—Friedrich Nietzsche (1844–1900)

Is not this the true romantic feeling—not the desire to escape life, but to prevent life from escaping you?
—Thomas Clayton Wolfe

No objects of value . . . are worth risking the priceless experience of waking up one more day.   —Jack Smith

My grandfather always said that living is like licking honey off a thorn.   —Louis Adamic

The hardest thing to learn in life is which bridge to cross and which to burn.   —David Russell

The course of life is unpredictable . . . no one can write his autobiography in advance.   —Abraham Joshua Heschel

The first half of our life is ruined by our parents and the second half by our children.   —Clarence Darrow

One's only real life is the life one never leads.
                    —Oscar Wilde (1854–1900)

. . . my sense of my own importance to myself is tremendous. I am all I have, to work with, to play with, to suffer and to enjoy. It is not the eyes of others that I am wary of, but my own.
                    —Noel Coward

There is no wealth but life.   —John Ruskin (1819–1900)

The good life is one inspired by love and guided by knowledge.
—Bertrand Russell (On second thought, the good life starts only when you stop wanting a better one.)

How little we should enjoy life if we never flattered ourselves.
          —Duc de La Rochefoucauld (1613–1680)

I had a lover's quarrel with the world.   —Robert Frost

Pythagoras used to say life resembles the Olympic Games; a few men strain their muscles to carry off a prize; others bring trinkets to sell to the crowd for a profit; and some there are who seek no further advantage than to look at the show and see how and why everything is done. They are spectators of other men's lives in order better to judge and manage their own.
         —Michel de Montaigne (1533–1592)

Isn't your life extremely flat/With nothing to grumble at?
                  —W. S. Gilbert

The less of routine, the more of life.
               —A. B. Alcott (1799–1888)

Life is like playing a violin in public and learning the instrument as one goes on.   —Samuel Butler

What can a man do who doesn't know what to do?
               —Milton Mayer

Life shouldn't be printed on dollar bills.   —Clifford Odets

May you live all the days of your life.

—Jonathan Swift (1667–1745)

My whole life is a movie. It's just that there are no dissolves. I have to live every agonizing moment of it. My life needs editing.

—Mort Sahl

To be free is to have achieved your life.   —Tennessee Williams

The great majority of us are required to live a life of constant duplicity. Your health is bound to be affected if, day after day, you say the opposite of what you feel, if you grovel before what you dislike, and rejoice at what brings you nothing but misfortune.

—Boris Pasternak

Life is a progress from want to want, not from enjoyment to enjoyment.   —Samuel Johnson (1709–1784)

The man who has no inner life is the slave of his surroundings.

—Henri Frédéric Amiel (1821–1881)

The tragedy of life is what dies inside a man while he lives.

—Albert Schweitzer

Late on the third day, at the very moment when, at sunset . . . there flashed upon my mind, unforeseen and unsought, the phrase, *Reverence for Life*.   —Albert Schweitzer

The man who has become a thinking being feels a compulsion to give to every will-to-live the same reverence for life that he gives to his own.   —Albert Schweitzer

Because a work of art does not aim at reproducing natural appearances, it is not, therefore, an escape from life . . . but an expression of the significance of life, a stimulation to greater effort in living.   —Henry Moore.

I gave my life to learning how to live./Now that I have organized it all . . . /It is just about over.   —Sandra Hochman

———————————

Life would be infinitely happier if we could only be born at the age of eighty and gradually approach eighteen.   —Mark Twain

Yes, that's the worst of living—you get older every day.

—Reverend P. F. How

*   *

There are few things easier than to live badly and die well.

—Oscar Wilde (1854–1900)

Those who do not know how to live must make a merit of dying.

—George Bernard Shaw

*   *

The game of life is not so much in holding a good hand as playing a poor hand well.   —H. T. Leslie

Life is like a game of cards. The hand that is dealt you represents determinism; the way you play it is free will.

—Jawaharlal Nehru

*   *

The one serious conviction that a man should have is that nothing is to be taken too seriously.   —Samuel Butler

The whole world is a comedy to those that think, a tragedy to those that feel.   —Horace Walpole (1717–1797)

*   *

Were it offered to my choice, I should have no objections to a repetition of the same life from its beginning, only asking the advantages authors have in a second edition to correct some faults of the first.

—Benjamin Franklin (1706–1790)

I am so far resigned to my lot that I feel small pain at the thought of having to part from what has been called the pleasant habit of existence . . . I would not care to live my wasted life over again . . . let me slip away as quietly and comfortably as I can.

—Frederick Locker Lampson (1821–1895)

*   *

As I grow to understand life less and less, I learn to live it more and more.   —Jules Renard

The longer I live the more beautiful life becomes.

—Frank Lloyd Wright

*   *

The dignity of man lies in his ability to face reality in all its meaninglessness.   —Martin Esslin

The meaningless absurdity of life is the only incontestable knowledge accessible to man.   —Count Leo Tolstoy

---

Life is real! Life is earnest!/And the grave is not its goal;/Dust thou art, to dust returneth,/Was not spoken of the soul.

—Henry Wadsworth Longfellow (1807–1882)

A new question has arisen in modern man's mind, the question, namely, whether life is worth living . . . No sensible answer can be given to the question . . . because the question does not make any sense.   —Erich Fromm

* *

The man who regards his own life and that of his fellow creatures as meaningless is not merely unhappy but hardly fit for life.

—Albert Einstein

It was previously a question of finding out whether or not life had to have a meaning to be lived. It now becomes clear, on the contrary, that it will be lived all the better if it has no meaning.

—Albert Camus

* *

Since all life is futility, then the decision to exist must be the most irrational of all. —Emile M. Cioran

He who asks of life nothing but the improvement of his own nature . . . is less liable than anyone else to miss and waste life.

—Henri Frédéric Amiel (1821–1881)

* *

What the meaning of human life may be I don't know; I incline to suspect that it has none. —H. L. Mencken

When one has great gifts, what answer to the meaning of existence should one require beyond the right to exercise them?

—W. H. Auden

* *

The goal of all life is death. —Sigmund Freud

When people are serving, life is no longer meaningless.

—John Gardner

LOGIC

Logic is like the sword—those who appeal to it shall perish by it.

—Samuel Butler

Logic—an instrument used for bolstering a prejudice.

—Elbert Hubbard

All snakes who wish to remain in Ireland will please raise their right hands. —Attributed to Saint Patrick (c. 373–464)

If love makes the world go 'round,/Why are we going to outer space? —Margaret Gilman

The weather for catching fish is that weather, and no other, in which fish are caught. —W. H. Blake

Logic is the art of going wrong with confidence.
—Joseph Wood Krutch

In formal logic, a contradiction is the signal of defeat: but in the evolution of real knowledge it marks the first step in progress toward a victory.   —Alfred North Whitehead

Logicians have but ill defined/As rational the human kind./Logic, they say, belongs to man,/But let them prove it if they can.
—Oliver Goldsmith (1728–1774)

Logic is the soul of wit, not of wisdom; that's why wit is funny.
—Lincoln Steffens

Walter Shandy attributed most of his son's misfortunes to the fact that at a highly critical moment his wife had asked him if he had wound the clock, a question so irrelevant that he despaired of the child's ever being able to pursue a logical train of thought.
—Laurence Sterne (1713–1768) (Against logic there is no armor like ignorance.)

LOVE

Love doesn't make the world go 'round. Love is what makes the ride worthwhile.   —Franklin P. Jones

He gave her a look you could have poured on a waffle.
—Ring Lardner

If Jack's in love, he's no judge of Jill's beauty.
—Benjamin Franklin (1706–1790) (On second thought, it's a good thing love is blind, otherwise it would see too much.)

God, for two people to be able to live together for the rest of their lives is almost unnatural.   —Jane Fonda

To love is to admire with the heart; to admire is to love with the mind.   —Théophile Gautier (1811–1872)

If two people love each other there can be no happy end to it.
—Ernest Hemingway (People fall in love, but they have to climb out.)

Love is the word used to label the sexual excitement of the young, the habituation of the middle-aged, and the mutual dependence of the old.   —John Ciardi (It's easy to understand love at first sight, but how explain love after two people have been looking at each other for years?)

Many a man has fallen in love with a girl in a light so dim he would not have chosen a suit by it.   —Maurice Chevalier

Make love to every woman you meet; if you get five percent on your outlays it's a good investment.   —Arnold Bennett

Let there be spaces in your Togetherness.   —Kahlil Gibran

Only little boys and old men sneer at love.

—Louis Auchincloss

Platonic love is love from the neck up.

—Thyra Samter Winslow

People who are sensible about love are incapable of it.

—Douglas Yates

Love does not consist in gazing at each other but in looking outward together in the same direction.

—Antoine de Saint Exupéry

Religion has done love a great service by making it a sin.

—Anatole France

The only abnormality is the incapacity to love.   —Anais Nin

Physiological expenditure is a superficial way of self-expression. People who incline towards physical love accomplish nothing at all. —Salvador Dali (It's better to have loved and lost than to do forty pounds of laundry a week.)

And yet, a single night of universal love could save everything.

—Roland Giguère

Take away love and our earth is a tomb.

—Robert Browning (1812–1889)

I never loved another person the way I loved myself.

—Mae West

As soon as you cannot keep anything from a woman, you love her. —Paul Géraldy (The man who worships the ground his girl walks on probably knows her father owns the property.)

No woman ever falls in love with a man unless she has a better opinion of him than he deserves.   —Ed Howe

The voyage of love is all the sweeter for an outside stateroom and a seat at the captain's table.   —Henry S. Haskins (Money can't buy love but it improves your bargaining position.)

Come live with me, and be my Love;/And we will all the pleasures prove.   —Christopher Marlowe (1564–1593)

It's not love's going hurts my days/But that it went in little ways.

—Edna St. Vincent Millay

He was awake a long time before he remembered that his heart was broken. —Ernest Hemingway

Hate the sin and love the sinner. —Mohandas Gandhi

Let me say . . . that the true revolutionary is guided by a great feeling of love. —Che Guevara

LOYALTY

He has every attribute of a dog except loyalty.
—Senator Thomas P. Gore

She's got to be a loyal, frank person if she's got to bitch everyone in the world to do it. —F. Scott Fitzgerald

Schools have always inculcated patriotism, but the terms of allegiances are often narrowly conceived. The fact that loyalty to the nation requires loyalty to all subgroups within the nation is seldom pointed out. —Gordon W. Allport

Loyalty must arise spontaneously from the hearts of people who love their country and respect their government.
—Justice Hugo L. Black

Too often a sense of loyalty depends on admiration, and if we can't admire it is difficult to be loyal. —Aimee Buchanan

Loyalty is the one thing a leader cannot do without.
—A. P. Gouthey

The strongest bulwark of authority is uniformity; the least divergence from it is the greatest crime. —Emma Goldman

LYING / LIARS

A lie can travel half way around the world while the truth is putting on its shoes. —Mark Twain

The only form of lying that is absolutely beyond reproach is lying for its own sake. —Oscar Wilde (1854–1900)

There are a terrible lot of lies going about the world, and the worst of it is that half of them are true. —Winston Churchill (Legend: A lie that has attained the dignity of age.)

It's queer the way the likes of me do be telling the truth, and the wise are lying all times. —John M. Synge

The cruelest lies are often told in silence.
—Robert Louis Stevenson (1850–1894)

The biggest liar in the world is They Say.   —Douglas Malloch

It takes a wise man to handle a lie; a fool had better remain honest.
—Norman Douglas

A liar needs a good memory.   —Quintilian (35?–95?) (If at first you don't succeed, lie, lie again!)

Forgetting that several excuses are always less convincing than one.
—Aldous Huxley

People need good lies. There are too many bad ones.
—Kurt Vonnegut, Jr.

The liar's punishment is not in the least that he is not believed but that he cannot believe anyone else.   —George Bernard Shaw (Two liars are company, three are a crowd, and four or more a chamber of commerce.)

He who cannot lie does not know what the truth is.
—Friedrich Nietzsche (1844–1900)

All political parties die at last of swallowing their own lies.
—John Arbuthnot (1667–1735)

George Washington, as a boy, was ignorant of the commonest accomplishments of youth. He could not even lie.   —Mark Twain

There is no greater lie than a truth misunderstood.
—William James

All the historical books which contain no lies are extremely tedious.
—Anatole France

We lie loudest when we lie to ourselves.   —Eric Hoffer

In the size of the lie is always contained a certain factor of credulity, since the great masses of the people . . . will more easily fall victims to a great lie than to a small one.   —Adolf Hitler

The victor will never be asked if he told the truth.
—Adolf Hitler

A man who won't lie to a woman has very little consideration for her feelings.   —Olin Miller

Lying is an indispensable part of making life tolerable.
—Bergen Evans

*   *

She deceiving, I believing;/What need lovers wish for more?
                              —Sir Charles Sedley (1639?–1701)

When my love swears that she is made of truth,/I do believe her,
though I know she lies.   —William Shakespeare (1564–1616)

He who permits himself to tell a lie once finds it much easier to do
it a second and a third time till at length it becomes habitual.
—Thomas Jefferson (1743–1826) (To an inveterate liar, truth is
stranger than fiction.)

The men the American people admire most extravagantly are the
most daring liars; the men they detest most violently are those who
try to tell them the truth.   —H. L. Mencken

*   *

It is always the best policy to speak the truth, unless, of course, you
are an exceptionally good liar.   —Jerome K. Jerome (Never
believe another liar even when you know he's telling the truth.)

I have nothing to hide. The White House has nothing to hide.
                              —Richard M. Nixon

MADNESS

A little madness in the Spring/Is wholesome even for the King.
—Emily Dickinson (1830–1886)

Sanity is madness put to good use.   —George Santayana

There is a pleasure sure,/In being mad, which none but madmen know!   —John Dryden (1631–1700)

We cannot unthink unless we are insane.   —Arthur Koestler

There nearly always is method in madness. It's what drives men mad, being methodical.   —G. K. Chesterton

It is better to be mad with the rest of the world than to be wise alone.   —Baltasar Gracián (1601–1658)

Today I felt pass over me/A breath of wind from the wings of madness.   —Charles Baudelaire (1821–1867)

I saw the best minds of my generation destroyed by madness.
—Allen Ginsberg

Insanity—a perfectly rational adjustment to an insane world.
—R. D. Laing

Most men are within a finger's breadth of being mad.
—Diogenes (c. 412–323 B.C.)

There is no genius free from some tincture of madness.
—Seneca (4 B.C.–A.D. 65)

Great wits are sure to madness near allied/And thin partitions do their bounds divide. —John Dryden

I suppose it is much more comfortable to be mad and not know it, than to be sane and have one's doubts. —G. B. Burgin

The madman who knows that he is mad is close to sanity.
—Juan Ruiz de Alarcón (1580?–1639)

MAJORITY / MINORITY

The minority is always wrong—at the beginning. —Herbert V. Prochnow (Minority often proves to be the majority because it turns out and votes.)

A significant factor in our history has been the effort, on the one hand, of minority groups to prevent the people from ruling, and, on the other hand, of the people to express their will and to have it applied rationally. —Bernard Smith

The greatest good of a minority of our generation may be the greatest good of the greatest number in the long run.
—Oliver Wendell Holmes, Jr.

The test of courage comes when we are in the minority; the test of tolerance comes when we are in the majority.
—Ralph W. Sockman

Any man more right than his neighbor constitutes a majority of one. —Henry David Thoreau (1817–1862)

One man with courage is a majority. —Thomas Jefferson (1743–1826) (After his Cabinet had voted No on emancipation, Lincoln raised his right hand and said, "The ayes have it!")

If a man is in a minority of one, we lock him up.
—Oliver Wendell Holmes, Jr.

The principle of majority rule is the mildest form in which force of numbers can be exercised. It is a pacific substitute for civil war.
—Walter Lippmann

The rule of 51 percent is a convenience . . . because we do not know any less troublesome method of obtaining a political decision.

But it may easily become an absurd tyranny if we regard it worship-fully, as though it were more than a political device. We have lost all of its true meaning when we imagine the opinion of 51 percent is in some high fashion the true opinion of the whole 100 percent, or indulge in the sophistry that the rule of a majority is based upon the ultimate equality of man.   —Walter Lippmann

*   *

Governments exist to protect the rights of minorities.
          —Wendell Phillips (1811–1884)

Law, in a democracy, means the protection of the rights and liber-ties of the minority.   —Alfred E. Smith

---

The tendencies of democracies are, in all things, to mediocrity, since the tastes, knowledge and principles of the majority form the tribunal of appeal.   —James Fenimore Cooper (1789–1851)

The justification of majority rule in politics is not to be found in its ethical superiority.   —Walter Lippmann

MAN / MANKIND / HUMANKIND

Man is but a reed, the most weak in nature, but he is a thinking reed.
          —Blaise Pascal (1623–1662)

What a man is is the basis of what he dreams and thinks, accepts and rejects, feels and perceives.   —John Mason Brown (But a Man-of-the-hour is the one whose wife told him to wait a minute.)

Man is nature's sole mistake.   —W. S. Gilbert

Ah, how unjust to nature and himself/Is thoughtless, thankless, in-consistent man!   —Edward Young (1683–1765)

Man is Creation's masterpiece; but who says so?
          —Elbert Hubbard

Apart from man, no being wonders at its own existence.
          —Arthur Schopenhauer (1788–1860)

Man—a reasoning rather than a reasonable animal.
          —Alexander Hamilton (1757–1804)

Man is a rope connecting animal and superman—a rope over a precipe . . . What is great in man is that he is a bridge and not a goal.   —Friedrich Nietzsche (1844–1900)

[Man] is a brute, only more intelligent than the other brutes, a blind prey to impulses . . . victim to endless illusions, which make his mental existence a burden, and fills his life with barren toil and trouble.   —H. G. Wells

The tragedy and the magnificence of Homo sapiens together rise from the same smokey truth that we alone among the animal species refuse to acknowledge natural law.   —Robert Ardrey

We never stop investigating. We are never satisfied that we know enough to get by. Every question we answer leads on to another question. This has become the greatest survival trick of our species.
—Desmond Morris

Men can do all things if they will.
—Leon Battista Alberti (1404–1472)

Man is designed to be a comprehensivist.
—Buckminster Fuller

The salvation of mankind lies only in making everything the concern of all.   —Alexander I. Solzhenitsyn

There is nothing commonplace in the world except the mental attitude of man.   —Charles Burchfield

The fall of man stands a lie before Beethoven, a truth before Hitler.
—Gregory Corso

To say that a man is made up of certain chemical elements is a satisfactory description only for those who intend to use him as a fertilizer.   —Herbert J. Muller

His [man's] history is as a tale that is told, and his very monument becomes a ruin.   —Washington Irving (1783–1859)

We must laugh at man to avoid crying for him.
—Napoleon Bonaparte (1769–1821)

All censure of a man's self is oblique praise.
—Samuel Johnson (1709–1784)

Man is not entirely corrupt and depraved but to state that he is, is to come closer to the truth than to state that he is essentially good.
—William McGovern and David Collier

A woman is a woman until the day she dies, but a man's a man only as long as he can.   —Moms Mabley

We must, however, acknowledge, as it seems to me, that man with all his noble qualities . . . still bears in his bodily frame the indelible stamp of his lowly origin.
—Charles Darwin (1809–1882)

No man is an island, entire of itself; every man is a piece of the continent, a part of the main.   —John Donne (1573?–1631)

The lame man who keeps the right road outstrips the runner who takes a wrong one. Nay, it is obvious that the more active and swift the latter is the further he will go astray.
                              —Francis Bacon (1561–1626)

The superior man understands what is right; the inferior man understands what will sell.   —Confucius (c. 551–479 B.C.)

The basic problem is that our civilization, which is a civilization of machines, can teach man everything except how to be a man.
                              —André Malraux

One machine can do the work of fifty ordinary men. No machine can do the work of one extraordinary man.   —Elbert Hubbard

Man is God's highest present development. He is the latest thing in God.   —Samuel Butler

He is a poor creature who does not believe himself to be better than the whole world else no matter how ill we may be, nor how low we may have fallen, we should not change identity with any other person.   —Samuel Butler

---

In nothing do men approach so nearly to the gods as doing good to men.   —Marcus Tullius Cicero (106–43 B.C.)

Every man is worth just so much as the things are worth about which he busies himself.   —Marcus Aurelius (121–180)

*   *

The control man has secured over nature has far outrun his control over himself.   —Ernest Jones

A man is rich in proportion to the things he can afford to let alone.
                              —Henry David Thoreau (1817–1862)

*   *

Whenever two people meet there are really six people present. There is each man as he sees himself, each man as the other person sees him, and each man as he really is.   —William James

Every man has three characters—that which he exhibits, that which he has, and that which he thinks he has.
                              —Alphonse Karr (1808–1890)

*   *

I know of no more encouraging fact than the unquestionable ability of man to elevate his life by a conscious endeavor.
—Henry David Thoreau

The greatest revolution of our generation is the discovery that human beings, by changing the inner attitudes of their minds can change the outer aspects of their lives.   —William James

*   *

Man, biologically considered . . . is the most formidable of all the beasts of prey, and, indeed, the only one that preys systematically on its own species.   —William James

Man is the only animal to whom the torture and death of his fellow creatures is amusing in itself.
—James A. Froude (1818–1894)

*   *

Man—a creature made at the end of the week's work when God was tired.   —Mark Twain

I sometimes think that God in creating man somewhat overestimated His ability.   —Oscar Wilde (1854–1900)

*   *

There is no stigma attached to recognizing a bad decision in time to install a better one.   —Laurence J. Peter

To give up pretensions is as blessed a relief as to get them ratified.
—William James

Man is a social animal.   —Baruch Spinoza (1632–1677)

Man is a political animal.   —Aristotle (384–322 B.C.)

*   *

Man—a being in search of meaning.   —Plato (427?–347 B.C.)

Man is the measure of all things.
—Protagoras (5th century B.C.)

*   *

There is as much difference between us and ourselves as between us and others.   —Michel de Montaigne (1533–1592)

Whatever you may be sure of, be sure of this, that you are dreadfully like other people.   —James Russell Lowell (1819–1891)

* *

The significance of man is that he is insignificant and is aware of it.
—Carl Becker

When a man is wrapped up in himself, he makes a pretty small package.   —John Ruskin (1819–1900)

* *

Compared to what we ought to be, we are only half awake. We are making use of only a small part of our physical and mental resources.   —William James

Nature gave man two ends—one to sit on and one to think with. Ever since then man's success or failure has been dependent on the one he used most.   —George R. Kirkpatrick

* *

Man is a blind, witless, low-brow, anthropocentric clod who inflicts lesions upon the earth.   —Ian McHarg

The more I see of man, the more I like dogs.
—Mme. de Staël (1766–1817)

* *

Cursed is every one who places his hope in man.
—Saint Augustine (354–430)

My aim is the re-establishment of the worship of men.
—Gabriele D'Annunzio

MARRIAGE

When singleness is bliss, it's folly to be wives.
—Bill Counselman

Marriage—a community consisting of a master, a mistress, and two slaves—making in all two.   —Ambrose Bierce

Marriage is a great institution, but I'm not ready for an institution, yet.   —Mae West

The honeymoon is over when he phones that he'll be late for supper —and she has already left a note that it's in the refrigerator.
—Bill Lawrence (Marriage is a good deal like taking a bath—not so hot once you get accustomed to it.)

Marriage is the deep, deep peace of the double bed after the hurly-burly of the chaise longue.   —Mrs. Patrick Campbell

Matrimony is a process by which a grocer acquired an account the florist had.   —Francis Rodman

A man may be a fool and not know it, but not if he is married.
                                                   —H. L. Mencken

One was never married, and that's his hell; another is, and that's his plague.   —Robert Burton (1577–1640)

No matter how happily a woman may be married, it always pleases her to discover that there is a nice man who wishes she were not.
                                                   —H. L. Mencken

Marriage—a book of which the first chapter is written in poetry and the remaining chapters in prose.   —Beverley Nichols (A husband may forget where he went on his honeymoon, but he never forgets why.)

Why does a woman work ten years to change a man's habits and then complain that he's not the man she married?   —Barbra Streisand (A bachelor is a man who is right sometimes.)

The Japanese have a word for it. It's judo—the art of conquering by yielding. The Western equivalent of judo is, "Yes, dear."
—J. P. McEvoy (Marriage is a romance in which the hero dies in the first chapter.)

Love, the quest; marriage, the conquest; divorce, the inquest.
—Helen Rowland (Marriage—the sole cause of divorce.)

When a husband and wife have got each other, the devil only knows which has got the other.   —Honoré de Balzac (1799–1850)

When a girl marries, she exchanges the attentions of many men for the inattention of one.   —Helen Rowland (Marriage is a lottery in which if you lose you can't tear up the ticket.)

Back of every achievement is a proud wife and a surprised mother-in-law.   —Brooks Hays

The critical period in matrimony is breakfast time.
—A. P. Herbert (Divorces are sometimes caused by husbands having dinner with their secretaries, but more often by having breakfast with their wives.)

The great secret of successful marriage is to treat all disasters as incidents and none of the incidents as disasters.
                                                   —Harold Nicholson

Of course there is such a thing as love, or there wouldn't be so many divorces.   —Ed Howe

I shall marry in haste and repeat at leisure.
                                                   —James Branch Cabell

I have a wife, you have a wife, we all have wives, we've had a taste of paradise, we know what it means to be married.
                              —Sholem Aleichem (Solomon J. Rabinowitz)

Marriage is a feast where the grace is sometimes better than the dinner.   —Charles Caleb Colton (1780–1832)

Today, he admits, he gave his sons just one piece of advice. "Never confuse *I love you* with *I want to marry you*."
                              —Cleveland Amory

Nowadays, two can live as cheaply as one large family used to!
                              —Joey Adams

Friendships, like marriages, are dependent on avoiding the unforgivable.   —John D. MacDonald

Often the difference between a successful marriage and a mediocre one consists of leaving about three or four things a day unsaid.
                              —Harlan Miller

Almost all married people fight, although many are ashamed to admit it. Actually a marriage in which no quarreling at all takes place may well be one that is dead or dying from emotional undernourishment. If you care, you probably fight.   —Flora Davis

A sound marriage is not based on complete frankness; it is based on a sensible reticence.   —Morris L. Ernst

As bad as marrying the devil's daughter and living with the old folks.   —G. L. Apperson

Marriage is a mistake every man should make.
                              —George Jessel

The vow of fidelity is an absurd commitment, but it is the heart of marriage.   —Father Robert Capon

———

One should always be in love. That is the reason one should never marry.   —Oscar Wilde (1854–1900)

Dora and I are now married, but just as happy as we were before.
                              —Bertrand Russell

*   *

All marriages are happy. It's the living together afterward that causes all the trouble.   —Raymond Hull

A man in love is incomplete until he has married. Then he's finished.
                              —Zsa Zsa Gabor

*   *

Wedded persons may thus pass over their lives quietly . . . if the husband becomes deaf and the wife blind.

—Richard Taverner

A good marriage would be between a blind wife and a deaf husband.
—Michel de Montaigne (1533–1592)

She said he proposed something on their wedding night her own brother wouldn't have suggested.   —James Thurber

Niagara Falls is only the second biggest disappointment of the standard honeymoon.   —Oscar Wilde (1854–1900)

*   *

A working girl is one who quit her job to get married.

—E. J. Kiefer

Women marry because they don't want to work.

—Mary Garden

*   *

A man marries to have a home, but also because he doesn't want to be bothered with sex and all that sort of thing.

—Somerset Maugham

Marriage always demands the greatest understanding of the art of insincerity possible between two human beings.

—Vicki Baum

MARTYRDOM / MARTYRS

Let others wear the martyr's crown; I am not worthy of this honor.
—Desiderius Erasmus (1465–1536)

The tyrant dies and his rule ends, the martyr dies and his rule begins.   —Sören Kierkegaard (1813–1855)

Martyrs set bad examples.   —David Russell

To die for an idea is to set a rather high price upon conjecture.
—Anatole France

Martyrdom has always been a proof of the intensity, never of the correctness of a belief.   —Arthur Schnitzler

*   *

Martyrdom is the only way in which a man can become famous without ability.   —George Bernard Shaw

They who do not know how to live must make a merit of dying.
                                        —George Bernard Shaw

———————

Christ died for our sins. Dare we make his martyrdom meaningless by not committing them?   —Jules Feiffer

A thing is not necessarily true because a man dies for it.
                                        —Oscar Wilde (1854–1900)

THE MEDIA

If newspapers are useful in overthrowing tyrants, it is only to establish a tyranny of their own.
                                        —James Fenimore Cooper (1789–1851)

Where the press is under strict and efficient control, literacy can become a weapon for the support of a universal tyranny.
                                        —George S. Counts

The art of newspaper paragraphing is to stroke a platitude until it purrs like an epigram.   —Don Marquis

Journalism: A profession whose business it is to explain to others what it personally does not understand.   —Lord Northcliffe

Journalism largely consists in saying "Lord Jones Dead" to people who never knew Lord Jones was alive.   —G. K. Chesterton. (Journalist—a person who works harder than any other lazy person in the world.)

Newspapers always excite curiosity. No one ever lays one down without a feeling of disappointment.
                                        —Charles Lamb (1775–1834)

Along with responsible newspapers we must have responsible readers.   —Arthur Hays Sulzberger

The old nobility would have survived if they had known enough to become masters of printing materials.
                                        —Napoleon Bonaparte (1769–1821)

A newspaper is the lowest thing there is!   —Mayor Richard J. Daley (Politicians will just have to try harder.)

If a newspaper prints a sex crime, it's smut, but when *The New York Times* prints it, it's a sociological study.
                                        —Adolph S. Ochs

Self-government will be the more secure if the editorial page recovers the vigor and stature it had before the businessman took over from the editor as top man in journalism.   —Herbert Brucker

It is well to remember that freedom through the press is the thing that comes first. Most of us probably feel we couldn't be free without newspapers, and that is the real reason we want the newspapers to be free.   —Edward R. Murrow

The American reading his Sunday paper in a state of lazy collapse is perhaps the most perfect symbol of the triumph of quantity over quality . . . Whole forests are being ground into pulp daily to minister to our triviality.   —Irving Babbitt

The day of the printed word is far from ended. Swift as is the delivery of the radio bulletin, graphic as is television's eyewitness picture, the task of adding meaning and clarity remains urgent. People cannot and need not absorb meaning at the speed of light.
    —Erwin Canham

The press, the movies, radio and television bear a large share of the responsibility for the climate of fear . . . which has enveloped our country and which has become such a threat to our freedom.
    —William T. Evjue

Getting an award from TV is like getting kissed by someone with bad breath.   —Mason Williams

The only newspapers that can be bought are the ones not worth buying.   —Lord Liverpool (1770–1828) (A free press is one that prints a dictator's speech but doesn't have to.)

Newspaper editors are men who separate the wheat from the chaff, and then print the chaff.   —Adlai Stevenson

TV performers for the most part fall into two groups—those who have been dropped and those who are going to be dropped.
—Dr. Leslie Bell (Television has changed the American child from an irresistible force into an immovable object.)

An ounce of image is worth a pound of performance.
    —Laurence J. Peter

I feel sorry for them [the press] because they should recognize that to the extent they allow their own hatreds to consume them, they will lose the rationality which is the mark of a civilized man.
    —Richard M. Nixon, to Rabbi Korff

The things that bother a press about a President will ultimately bother the country.   —David Halberstam

Animation is not the art of drawings-that-move, but the art of movements that are drawn.   —Norman McLaren

---

I find television very educating. Every time somebody turns on the set I go into the other room and read a book.

—Groucho Marx

TV—chewing gum for the eyes.   —Frank Lloyd Wright

*   *

News is the first rough draft of history.   —Ben Bradlee

Journalism is literature in a hurry.

—Matthew Arnold (1822–1888)

*   *

Most American television stations reproduce all night long what only a Roman could have seen in the Coliseum during the reign of Nero.

—George Faludy

We're in the same position as a plumber laying a pipe. We're not responsible for what goes through the pipe.   —David Sarnoff

*   *

Children will watch anything, and when a broadcaster uses crime and violence and other shoddy devices to monopolize a child's attention it's worse than taking candy from a baby. It is taking precious time from the process of growing up.   —Newton Minow

We are drowning our youngsters in violence, cynicism and sadism piped into the living room and even the nursery. The grandchildren of the kids who used to weep because the Little Match Girl froze to death now feel cheated if she isn't slugged, raped and thrown into a Bessemer converter.   —Jenkin Lloyd Jones

---

The indispensable requirement for a good newspaper—as eager to tell a lie as the truth.   —Norman Mailer

I keep reading between the lies.   —Goodman Ace

*   *

Journalism is the ability to meet the challenge of filling space.

—Rebecca West

The only authors whom I acknowledge as American are the journalists. They, indeed, are not great writers, but they speak the language of their countrymen, and make themselves heard by them.

—Alexis de Tocqueville (1805–1859)

*   *

Do you realize if it weren't for Edison we'd be watching TV by
candlelight?   —Al Boliska

The vast wasteland of TV is not interested in producing a better
mousetrap but in producing a worse mouse.
                              —Laurence C. Coughlin

MEDICAL

Medicine, the only profession that labours incessantly to destroy the
reason for its existence.   —James Bryce

She got her good looks from her father—he's a plastic surgeon.
                              —Groucho Marx

My doctor is nice; every time I see him I'm ashamed of what I think
of doctors in general.   —Mignon McLaughlin (There was a
time when an apple a day kept the doctor away, but now it's mal-
practice insurance.)

A vasectomy is never having to say you're sorry.   —Rubin
Carson (The kindest cut of all.)

The true physician does not preach repentance; he offers absolution.
—H. L. Mencken (A doctor is a person who still has his adenoids,
tonsils, and appendix.)

I don't see why any man who believes in medicine would shy at the
faith cure.   —Finley Peter Dunne (Mr. Dooley) (When a patient is at death's door, it is the duty of the doctor to pull him
through.)

The principles of Washington's farewell address are still sources of
wisdom when cures for social ills are sought. The methods of Washington's physicians, however, are no longer studied.
                              —Thurman Arnold

The art of medicine consists of amusing the patient while nature
cures the disease.   —Voltaire (François Marie Arouet) (1694–
1778) (On the other hand, if there was no such thing as tennis,
cardiologists would have had to invent it.)

It should be the function of medicine to have people die young as
late as possible.   —Ernst L. Wynder, M.D.

The one thing I dread is affluence. I have a lovely office now, with
pictures on the wall and a swivel chair, and I can't do anything.
                              —Sir Frederick G. Banting

You must begin with an ideal and end with an ideal.
—Sir Frederick G. Banting

You can only cure retail but you can prevent wholesale.
—Brock Chisholm

Painstaking detective work by medical researchers is producing mounting evidence that environmental impurities in man's habitat are the primary cause of most cancer.   —Peter J. Bernstein

There are no such things as incurables; there are only things for which man has not found a cure.   —Bernard M. Baruch

Care more for the individual patient than for the special features of the disease.   —Sir William Osler

The pen is mightier than the sword! The case for prescriptions rather than surgery.   —Marvin Kitman

There are more doctors in a single North Shore medical building than in one entire West Side ghetto.   —Jack Starr

---

I got the bill for my surgery. Now I know what those doctors were wearing masks for.   —James H. Boren

A hospital should also have a recovery room adjoining the cashier's office.   —Francis O'Walsh

*   *

One of the things the average doctor doesn't have time to do is catch up with the things he didn't learn in school, and one of the things he didn't learn in school is the nature of human society, its purpose, its history, and its needs . . . If medicine is necessarily a mystery to the average man, nearly everything else is necessarily a mystery to the average doctor.   —Milton Mayer

A rule of thumb in the matter of medical advice is to take everything any doctor says with a grain of aspirin.   —Goodman Ace

---

Wherever the art of medicine is loved, there also is love of humanity.   —Hippocrates (460?–370? B.C.)

Financial ruin from medical bills is almost exclusively an American disease.   —Roul Turley

MEDIOCRITY

The world is made of people who never quite get into the first team and who just miss the prizes at the flower show.
—J. Bronowski

Only a mediocre person is always at his best.
—Somerset Maugham

Good behavior is the last refuge of mediocrity.
—Henry S. Haskins

In my opinion, we are in danger of developing a cult of the Common Man, which means a cult of mediocrity.
—Herbert Hoover

Great spirits have always found violent opposition from mediocrities.   —Albert Einstein

The general tendency of things throughout the world is to render mediocrity the ascendant power among mankind.
—John Stuart Mill (1806–1873)

The characteristic of the hour is that the commonplace mind, knowing itself to be commonplace, has the assurance to proclaim the rights of the commonplace and to impose them wherever it will . . . I uphold a radically aristocratic interpretation of history . . . For the mass to claim the right to act of itself is then a rebellion against its own destiny.   —José Ortega y Gasset

MEMORY AND IMAGINATION

It's a poor sort of memory that only works backwards.
—Lewis Carroll (Charles Lutwidge Dodgson) (1832–1898)

A good storyteller is a person who has a good memory and hopes other people haven't.   —Irvin S. Cobb

Nothing fixes a thing so intensely in the memory as the wish to forget it.   —Michel de Montaigne (1533–1592)

One thing you will probably remember well is any time you forgive and forget.   —Franklin P. Jones

Quite literally, a man's memory is what he forgets with.
—Odell Shepard (Memory is what makes you wonder what you've forgotten.)

Memory is a crazy woman that hoards colored rags and throws away food.   —Austin O'Malley

There must be at least 500 million rats in the United States; of course, I am speaking only from memory.
—Edgar Wilson Nye (1850–1896)

There is not any memory with less satisfaction than the memory of some temptation we resisted.   —James Branch Cabell (The man with a clear conscience probably has a poor memory.)

We must always have old memories, and young hopes.
—Arsène Houssaye

He is indebted to his memory for his jests and to his imagination for
his facts.   —Richard Brinsley Sheridan (1751–1816) (You
never know how much a man can't remember till he is called as a
witness.)

How is it that our memory is good enough to retain the least triviality that happens to us, and yet not good enough to recollect how
often we have told it to the same person?   —Duc de La Rochefoucauld (1613–1680) (I remember the good old days because
there were so few of them.)

The advantage of a bad memory is that one enjoys several times the
same good things for the first time.
—Friedrich Nietzsche (1844–1900)

I have a bad memory for facts.   —Stendhal (Henri Beyle)
(1783–1842) (Nostalgia isn't what it used to be.)

Every man's memory is his private literature.
—Aldous Huxley

Talking about things that are understandable only weighs down the
mind and falsifies the memory.   —Alfred Jarry

There is nothing like an odour to stir memories.
—William McFee

Memory is what tells a man that his wife's birthday was yesterday.
—Mario Rocco

———

Nothing is so admirable in politics as a short memory.
—John Kenneth Galbraith

Voters quickly forget what a man says.   —Richard M. Nixon

———

God gave us memory that we might have roses in December.
—James M. Barrie

Let us not burden our remembrances with a heaviness that is gone.
—William Shakespeare (1564–1616)

MIDDLE AGE

Middle Age is when your age starts to show around your middle.
—Bob Hope (Middle age is when you still believe you'll feel better
in the morning.)

Middle age is a time of life/That a man first notices in his wife.
—Richard Armour

Middle age is when the best exercise is one of discretion.
—Laurence J. Peter (Middle age is when we can do just as much as ever, but would rather not.)

Middle age is when anything new in the way you feel is most likely a symptom.   —Laurence J. Peter

Don't worry about middle age: you'll outgrow it.
—Laurence J. Peter

When you begin to smile at things that used to cause you to laugh.
—*Puck* magazine (When you change from stud to dud.)

Middle age is the time when a man is always thinking that in a week or two he will feel as good as ever.   —Don Marquis (Middle age is when you are too young to get on Social Security and too old to get another job.)

Middle age is when you're sitting at home on Saturday night and the telephone rings and you hope it isn't for you.   —Ogden Nash (Middle age is when you stop criticizing the older generation and start criticizing the younger one.)

Middle age is when your old classmates are so grey and wrinkled and bald they don't recognize you.   —Bennett Cerf

When a man is warned to slow down by a doctor instead of a policeman.   —Sidney Brody (When you want to see how long your car will last instead of how fast it will go.)

How it rejoices a middle-aged woman when her husband criticizes a pretty girl!   —Mignon McLaughlin (One of the chief pleasures of middle age is looking at the picture of the girl you didn't marry.)

MIDDLE CLASS

A moderately honest man with a moderately faithful wife, moderate drinkers both, in a moderately healthy house: that is the true middle-class unit.   —George Bernard Shaw

The best political community is formed by citizens of the middle class.   —Aristotle (384–322 B.C.)

The upper classes are . . . a nation's past; the middle class is its future.   —Ayn Rand

The one class you do *not* belong to and are not proud of at all is the lower-middle class. No one ever describes himself as belonging to the lower-middle class.   —George Mikes

This picture of a despotic God who wants unrestricted power over men and their submission and humiliation, was the projection of the middle class's own hostility and envy.   —Erich Fromm

Our middle classes who are comfortable and irresponsible at other people's expense, and are neither ashamed of that condition nor even conscious of it.   —George Bernard Shaw

---

The Nazi ideology was ardently greeted by the lower strata of the middle class . . . certain features were characteristic of this part of the middle class throughout history: their love of the strong, hatred of the weak.   —Erich Fromm

The middle class is always a firm champion of equality when it concerns a class above it; but it is its inveterate foe when it concerns elevating a class below it.
                              —Orestes A. Brownson (1803–1876)

MILITARY / MILITARISM

In a free country like our own . . . every male brought into existence should be taught from infancy that the military service of the Republic carries with it honor and distinction, and his very life should be permeated with the ideal that even death itself may become a boon when a man dies that a nation may live and fulfill its destiny.   —General Douglas MacArthur

I have every confidence that you [Lieutenant Calley] are a fine military officer that we can all be proud of!   —Paul Harvey

The Marine Corps . . . have a propaganda machine that is almost equal to Stalin's.   —Harry S Truman

Militarism is the characteristic, not of an army, but of a society.
                              —R. H. Tawney

And, as everyone knows, the army is a poor training corps for democracy, no matter how inspiring its cause.
                              —Pierre Elliott Trudeau

The basic problems facing the world today are not susceptible to a military solution.   —John F. Kennedy

Diplomacy has rarely been able to gain at the conference table what cannot be gained or held on the battlefield.

—General Walter Bedell Smith

I dropped an aerial torpedo right in the center, and the group opened up like a flowering rose. It was most entertaining.

—Vittorio Mussolini

I do like to see the arms and legs fly.

—Colonel George S. Patton III

*   *

Military intelligence is a contradiction in terms.

—Groucho Marx

Military justice is to justice what military music is to music.

—Groucho Marx

*   *

Covenants without swords are but words.

—Thomas Hobbes (1588–1679)

The body of a dead enemy always smells sweet.

—Aulus Vitellius (A.D. 15–69)

Militarism is the great preserver of our ideals of hardihood, and human life with no use for hardihood would be contemptible.

—William James

Military men are the scourges of the world.

—Guy de Maupassant (1850–1893)

*   *

The necessary and wise subordination of the military to civil power [must] be sustained.   —Dwight D. Eisenhower

The military and not the civilian authorities should be in charge of nuclear weapons.   —General Edwin A. Walker (Ret.) (It became necessary to destroy the town—Bentre, South Vietnam— to save it.)

*   *

The atom bomb is not an inhuman weapon.

—Major General Leslie Groves

We'll blast them back into the stone ages!   —General William C. Westmoreland (But what can we do for an encore?)

* *

In the councils of government we must guard against the acquisition of unwarranted influence, whether sought or unsought, by the military-industrial complex. The potential for the disastrous rise of misplaced power exists and will persist.
—Dwight D. Eisenhower

Give me the order to do it and I can break up Russia's five A-bomb nests in a week. And when I go up to meet Christ . . . I think I could explain to Him that I had saved civilization.
—Major General Orvil A. Anderson

MIND

Millions say the apple fell but Newton was the one to ask why.
—Bernard M. Baruch

The brain is as strong as its weakest think.   —Eleanor Doan

When a man knows he is to be hanged in a fortnight, it concentrates his mind wonderfully.   —Samuel Johnson (1709–1784)

He discloses the workings of a mind to which incoherence lends an illusion of profundity.   —T. De Vere White (If a cluttered desk is the sign of a cluttered mind, what is the significance of a clean desk?)

The mind ought sometimes to be amused, that it may the better return to thought, and to itself.   —Phaedrus (5th century B.C.)

Laws and institutions must go hand in hand with the progress of the human mind.   —Thomas Jefferson (1743–1826)

Let us train our minds to desire what the situation demands. —Seneca (4 B.C.–A.D. 65) (William James said that the greatest discovery of his time was that human beings could alter their lives by altering their attitudes of mind.)

As every divided kingdom falls, so every mind divided between many studies confounds and saps itself.   —Leonardo da Vinci (1452–1519) (Leonardo should know—he possessed the ultimate divided mind.)

It requires a very unusual mind to make an analysis of the obvious.
—Alfred North Whitehead

With luck and resolution and good guidance . . . the human mind can survive not only poverty, but even wealth.
—Gilbert Highet

The mind is its own place, and in itself can make a heaven of Hell, a hell of Heaven.   —John Milton (1608–1674) (Great minds discuss ideas, average minds discuss events, small minds discuss people.)

The ability to divorce one's mind from one's actions is a symptom of psychological aberration.   —Walter Goodman

By annihilating desires you annihilate the mind.
                              —Claude Adrien Helvétius (1715–1771)

All paid employments absorb and degrade the mind.
                              —Aristotle (384–322 B.C.)

At a certain age some people's minds close up; they live on their intellectual fat.   —William Lyon Phelps

---

It is well to open one's mind but only as a preliminary to closing it . . . for the supreme act of judgment and selection.
                              —Irving Babbitt

If you keep your mind sufficiently open, people will throw a lot of rubbish into it.   —William A. Orton

---

Faced with the choice between changing one's mind and proving that there is no need to do so, almost everyone gets busy on the proof.   —John Kenneth Galbraith

The growth of the human mind is still high adventure, in many ways the highest adventure on earth.   —Norman Cousins

MODESTY

I wasn't really naked. I simply didn't have any clothes on.
                              —Josephine Baker

I loved them because it is a joy to find thoughts one might have, beautifully expressed . . . by someone . . . wiser than oneself.
                              —Marlene Dietrich

Telling his class that a critic had called him a second Beethoven, Bruckner said, "How can anybody dare to say such a thing!"
                              —Anton Bruckner (1825–1896)

There's no reason why the University [of Chicago] should be stuck with me at fifty-one because I was a promising young man at thirty.
                              —Robert Maynard Hutchins

I'm very proud . . . that I'm smart enough to get the point.
—Harry S Truman, to cartoonist Burr Shafer (Modesty is the practice of withholding from others the high opinion you hold of yourself.)

At least I have the modesty to admit that lack of modesty is one of my failings.   —Hector Berlioz (1803–1869)

What's a Sun-Dial in the Shade?
                              —Benjamin Franklin (1706–1790)

Modesty is a vastly overrated virtue.

                              —John Kenneth Galbraith

Modesty died when clothes were born.   —Mark Twain

Tell me not everything I wrote was bad.
                              —Maurice Ravel, to Roland-Manuel

---

The English instinctively admire any man who has no talent and is modest about it.   —James Agee

False modesty is better than none.   —Vilhjalmur Stefansson

*   *

I have offended God and mankind because my work didn't reach the quality it should have.
                              —Leonardo da Vinci (1452–1519)

Tell me, on your soul and conscience, do you believe that anything of mine will live?   —Alexandre Dumas père (1802–1870), to Dumas fils (1824–1895)

*   *

If Heaven had only granted me five more years I could have become a real painter.   —Katsushika Hokusai (1760–1849)

There will be no proof that I ever was a writer.
                              —Franz Kafka, urging that all of his works be burned

---

My life has been nothing but a failure.   —Claude Monet

People will forgive anything but beauty and talent. So I am doubly unpardonable.   —James McNeill Whistler

"MOD MALAPROPS"

They went at it hammer and tongues.   —Mary Schafer

She's been dwindling in the stock market.
                              —Dr. Maxwell Kurtz

It's time to button down the hatches, or is it batten down the hedges?   —Barbara Straus

He eats like a horse afire.   —Angelina Bicos

I haven't hit a square ball all afternoon.   —Lori Johnson

I resent insinuendoes.   —Mayor Richard J. Daley

She picked a lawyer out of the phone book at ransom.
—Ina Kern

They served the most abdominal cocktails.   —Nellie Norton

Don't cross your bridges until you've burned them.
—Dick Bower

Marge and I are insufferable friends.   —Jane Ace

The chickens have come home to roast.   —Jane Ace

That politician is nothing but a sneak in the grass.
—Clive Bishop

The guards chased the escaped prisoner with a couple of Bagels.
—Leo Kennedy

When we were in Florence we visited the Pizza Palace.
—Gil Pratt

We shall reach greater and greater platitudes of achievement.
—Mayor Richard J. Daley

The doc says I have a slight case of conspicuous consumption.
—Jinnie Lane

We sold our house and are moving into one of those Pandemoniums.   —Marie Aragon

Isn't Beverly Sills a suburb of Los Angeles?   —Dorris King

He's one of those Cretins from the Mediterranean.
—Judy Boggs

If that skunk ever bites you, you'll get claustrophobia.
—Nadine Martin

It looks like a flaw in the ointment.   —Annie Loth

He was just a finger's breath away from success, too.
—Colette Burns

My husband doesn't munch words!   —Mary Carter

What about those endangered species on the Serendipity Plain?
—Charles J. Neugebauer

Stuff like that is a dredge on the market today.

—Andrew Conlin

Everyone has his hangovers. —Dick Dyas, Jr.

Well, shudder my timbers! —Roland Levesque

MONEY

If a man runs after money, he's money-mad; if he keeps it, he's a capitalist; if he spends it, he's a playboy; if he doesn't get it, he's a ne'er-do-well; if he doesn't try to get it, he lacks ambition. If he gets it without working for it, he's a parasite; and if he accumulates it after a lifetime of hard work, people call him a fool who never got anything out of life. —Vic Oliver

Money is what you'd get on beautifully without if only other people weren't so crazy about it. —Margaret Case Harriman (Money doesn't buy happiness, but that's not the reason so many people are poor.)

Money is always there but the pockets change; it is not in the same pockets after a change, and that is all there is to say about money.

—Gertrude Stein

Anyone who thinks there's safety in numbers hasn't looked at the stock market pages. —Irene Peter

There are few ways in which a man can be more innocently employed than in getting money.

—Samuel Johnson (1709–1784)

Here we are sitting in a shower of gold, with nothing to hold up but a pitchfork. —Jules Bertillon

There are poor men in this country who cannot be bought: the day I found that out, I sent my gold abroad.

—Comtesse De Voigrand

If all the rich men in the world divided up their money amongst themselves, there wouldn't be enough to go around.

—Jules Bertillon

I've realized, after fourteen months in this country, the value of money, whether it is clean or dirty. —Nguyen Cao Ky (A little hush money can do a lot of talking.)

Money doesn't always bring happiness. People with ten million dollars are no happier than people with nine million dollars.
—Hobart Brown (Money can't buy happiness, but it can buy you the kind of misery you prefer.)

The safest way to double your money is to fold it over once and put it in your pocket.   —Frank McKinney Hubbard ("Kin Hubbard") .(The only problems money can solve are money problems.)

When a fellow says, "It ain't the money but the principle of the thing," it's the money.
                    —Frank McKinney Hubbard ("Kin Hubbard")

Money won't buy happiness, but it will pay the salaries of a large research staff to study the problem.   —Bill Vaughan

Only one fellow in ten thousand understands the currency question, and we meet him every day.
                    —Frank McKinney Hubbard ("Kin Hubbard")

Never invest your money in anything that eats or needs repairing.
                                        —Billy Rose

It is not the employer who pays wages—he only handles the money. It is the product that pays wages.   —Henry Ford

Money is the symbol of duty, it is the sacrament of having done for mankind that which mankind wanted.   —Samuel Butler

We all know how the size of sums of money appears to vary in a remarkable way according as they are being paid in or paid out.
                                        —Julian Huxley

One of the benefits of inflation is that kids can no longer get sick on a nickel's worth of candy.   —*Journeyman Barber* magazine

Money—in its absence we are coarse; in its presence we are vulgar.
—Mignon McLaughlin (The way some people talk you might think a rich man couldn't be happy unless he made some happy poor man unhappy by giving him all his money.)

If you make money your god, it will plague you like the devil.
                    —Henry Fielding (1707–1754)

When I was young I thought that money was the most important thing in life; now that I am old I know that it is.
                    —Oscar Wilde (1854–1900)

That money talks/I'll not deny,/I heard it once:/It said, "Goodbye."
                                        —Richard Armour

The golden age only comes to men when they have forgotten gold.
                                        —G. K. Chesterton

He had so much money that he could afford to look poor.
—Edgar Wallace

I'd like to live like a poor man with lots of money.
—Pablo Picasso

* *

A disordered currency is one of the greatest political evils.
—Daniel Webster (1782–1852)

Inflation is the most important fact of our time, the single greatest peril to our economic health. —Bernard M. Baruch

* *

Money is a terrible master but an excellent servant.
—P. T. Barnum (1810–1891)

It is physically impossible for a well-educated, intellectual, or brave man to make money the chief object of his thoughts.
—John Ruskin (1819–1900)

* *

Money often costs too much.
—Ralph Waldo Emerson (1803–1882)

Money costs too much. —Ross MacDonald

* *

As a general rule, nobody has money who ought to have it.
—Benjamin Disraeli (1804–1881)

If you would know what the Lord God thinks of money, you have only to look at those to whom he gives it. —Maurice Baring

---

It's a kind of spiritual snobbery that makes people think they can be happy without money. —Albert Camus

To be clever enough to get a great deal of money, one must be stupid enough to want it. —G. K. Chesterton

* *

When it is a question of money, everybody is of the same religion.
—Voltaire (François Marie Arouet) (1694–1778)

There are a handful of people whom money won't spoil, and we count ourselves among them. —Mignon McLaughlin

MOTIVES

Any science, we should insist, better than any other discipline, can hold up to its students and followers an ideal of patient devotion to the search for objective truth, with vision unclouded by personal or political motive.　　—Sir Henry Hallett Dalt

Lord, grant that I may always desire more than I can accomplish.
　　　　　　　—Michelangelo (1475–1564)

The stoical scheme of supplying our wants by lopping off our desires is like cutting off our feet when we want shoes.
　　　　　　　—Jonathan Swift (1667–1745)

We know nothing about motivation. All we can do is write books about it.　　—Peter Drucker

---

One must not lose desires. They are mighty stimulants to creativeness, to love, and to long life.　　—Alexander A. Bogomoletz

Every man without passions has within him no principle of action, nor motive to act.　　—Claude Adrien Helvétius (1715–1771)

*　　*

The biggest gap in the world is the gap between the justice of a cause and the motives of the people pushing it.　　—John P. Grier

However brilliant an action it should not be esteemed great unless the result of a great motive.
　　　　　　　—Duc de La Rochefoucauld (1613–1680)

*　　*

We would often be ashamed of our finest actions if the world understood all the motives which produced them.
　　　　　　　—Duc de La Rochefoucauld

If the outcome is good, what's the difference between motives that sound good and good sound motives?　　—Laurence J. Peter

---

It is a horrible demoralizing thing to be a lawyer. You look for such low motives in everyone and everything.
　　　　　　　—Katherine T. Hinkson

If no action is to be deemed virtuous for which malice can imagine a sinister motive, then there never was a virtuous action.
　　　　　　　—Thomas Jefferson (1743–1826)

MUSIC

I know only two tunes: one of them is "Yankee Doodle," and the other isn't.   —Ulysses S. Grant (1822–1885)

Listen, kid, take my advice, never hate a song that has sold a half-million copies!   —Irving Berlin, to Cole Porter

No good opera plot can be sensible, for people do not sing when they are feeling sensible.   —W. H. Auden

Opera in English is, in the main, just about as sensible as baseball in Italian.   —H. L. Mencken

I've never heard such corny lyrics, such simpering sentimentality, such repetitious, uninspired melody. Man, we've got a hit on our hands!   —Brad Anderson

If an opera cannot be played by an organ-grinder, it is not going to achieve immortality.   —Sir Thomas Beecham (No wonder the most popular operatic composer was nicknamed *Hurdy-gurdy Verdi.*)

I adore art . . . when I am alone with my notes, my heart pounds and the tears stream from my eyes, and my emotion and my joys are too much to bear.   —Giuseppe Verdi

Music and woman I cannot but give way to, whatever my business is.   —Samuel Pepys (1632–1703)

I know that the twelve notes in each octave and the varieties of rhythm offer me opportunities that all of human genius will never exhaust.   —Igor Stravinsky

Brahms was curiously insecure about his work, and appeared to have a nervous dread of seeming to appraise a given piece too highly. Hence this defense mechanism of beating his critics to the punch, as it were, disparaging his music before anyone else had a chance to do so.   —Deems Taylor

Had I learned to fiddle, I should have done nothing else.   —Samuel Johnson (1709–1784)

Berlioz says nothing in his music, but he says it magnificently.   —James Gibbons Huneker

Wagner's music is better than it sounds.   —Mark Twain

Bach opens a vista to the universe. After experiencing him, people feel there is meaning to life after all.   —Helmut Walcha

I occasionally play works by contemporary composers and for two reasons. First to discourage the composer from writing any more and secondly to remind myself how much I appreciate Beethoven.

—Jascha Heifetz

Life can't be all bad when for ten dollars you can buy all the Beethoven sonatas and listen to them for ten years.

—William F. Buckley, Jr.

Mozart is the human incarnation of the divine force of creation.

—Johann W. von Goethe (1749–1832)

Never did Mozart write for eternity, and it is for precisely that reason that much of what he wrote is for eternity.

—Albert Einstein

Every composer knows the anguish and despair occasioned by forgetting ideas which one has no time to write down.

—Hector Berlioz (1803–1869)

People compose for many reasons: to become immortal; because the pianoforte happens to be open; because they want to become a millionaire; because of the praise of friends; because they have looked into a pair of beautiful eyes; for no reason whatsoever.

—Robert Schumann (1810–1856)

I don't want anyone to admire my pants in a museum.

—Frédéric Chopin (1810–1849)

The notes I handle no better than many pianists. But the pauses between the notes—ah, that is where the art resides!

—Artur Schnabel

Conductors must give unmistakable and suggestive signals to the orchestra—not choreography to the audience.   —George Szell

I have my own particular sorrows, loves, delights; and you have yours. But sorrow, gladness, yearning, hope, love, belong to all of us, in all times and in all places. Music is the only means whereby we feel these emotions in their universality.   —H. A. Overstreet

Without music life would be a mistake.

—Friedrich Nietzsche (1844–1900)

Chamber music—a conversation between friends.

—Catherine Drinker Bowen

I haven't understood a bar of music in my life, but I have felt it.

—Igor Stravinsky

A man like Verdi must write like Verdi.   —Giuseppina Verdi

* *

Debussy is like a painter who looks at his canvas to see what more he can take out; Strauss is like a painter who has covered every inch and then takes the paint he has left and throws it at the canvas.
—Ernest Bloch

How much has to be explored and discarded before reaching the naked flesh of feeling.   —Claude Debussy

* *

The most poetic musician who ever lived.
—Franz Liszt (1811–1886), of Franz Peter Schubert (1797–1828)

Everything he touches turns to music.
—Robert Schumann (1810–1856), of Schubert

* *

Bach almost persuades me to be a Christian.   —Roger Fry

Music owes as much to Bach as religion to its founder.
—Robert Schumann

* *

I produce music as an apple-tree produces apples.
—Camille Saint-Saëns

I write [music] as a sow piddles.
—Wolfgang Amadeus Mozart (1756–1791)

* *

After silence, that which comes nearest to expressing the inexpressible is music.   —Aldous Huxley

When words leave off, music begins.   —Heinrich Heine (1797–1856) (Gustav Mahler maintained that if a composer could say what he had to say in words he would not bother trying to say it in music.)

* *

Wagner had some wonderful moments but awful half hours.
—Gioacchino Rossini (1792–1868)

One can't judge Wagner's opera *Lohengrin* after a first hearing, and I certainly don't intend hearing it a second time.
—Gioacchino Rossini

I always wish that the last movement [of the *Regenlieder Sonata*]
might accompany me in my journey from here to the next world.
                    —Clara Schumann (1819–1896), to Brahms

Brahms has very little melodic invention . . . he excites and irri-
tates our musical senses without wishing to satisfy them.
                    —Peter Ilich Tchaikovsky (1840–1893)

                    *   *

In music one must think with the heart and feel with the brain.
                                        —George Szell

I'll play it first and tell you what it is later.   —Miles Davis

N

NAMES

There, I guess King George will be able to read that!   —John
Hancock (1737–1793) (on placing his boldly written signature on
the Declaration of Independence, July 4, 1776)

The first Rotarian was the first man to call John the Baptist, Jack.
—H. L. Mencken

There is everything in a name. A rose by any other name would
smell as sweet, but would not cost half as much during the winter
months.   —George Ade

The Ancient Mariner would not have taken so well if it had been
called The Old Sailor.   —Samuel Butler

Fate tried to conceal him by naming him Smith.
—Oliver Wendell Holmes, Jr.

A self-made man may prefer a self-made name.   —Judge
Learned Hand (on permitting Samuel Goldfish to change his name
to Samuel Goldwyn)

Names are not always what they seem. The common Welsh name
Bzjxxllwcp is pronounced Jackson.   —Mark Twain

A nickname is the hardest stone that the devil can throw at a man.
—William Hazlitt (1778–1830)

NATIONALISM

It is not easy to see how the more extreme forms of nationalism can long survive when men have seen the Earth in its true perspective as a single small globe against the stars.
—Arthur C. Clarke

The U. S. is having the same trouble as Rome in its search for "defensible frontiers."   —Lord Curzon

Nationalism is always an effort in a direction opposite to that of the principle which creates nations . . . nationalism is nothing but a mania, a pretext to escape from the necessity of inventing something new.   —José Ortega y Gasset

Born in iniquity, and conceived in sin, the spirit of nationalism has never ceased to bend human institutions to the service of dissension and distress.   —Thorstein Veblen

The most tragic paradox of our time is to be found in the failure of nation-states to recognize the imperatives of internationalism.
—Chief Justice Earl Warren

The greatest obsolescence of all in the Atomic Age is national sovereignty . . . Nothing multiplies more easily than force . . . In its grossest and most lethal form, force is represented by groupings of people into nations. This makes possible a concentration of collective effort with a minimum of restraint and a maximum of fury.   —Norman Cousins

They [our British forefathers] accepted it as natural and inevitable that nations should be engaged in a ceaseless struggle for survival, prosperity and predominance.   —Correlli Barnett

Every nation ridicules other nations, and all are right.   —Arthur Schopenhauer (1788–1860) (Nationalism and rationalism make estranged bedfellows.)

At this moment, probably the strongest ideology in the world is nationalism. This atmosphere is not favorable to bringing about a world without war.   —Norman Thomas

No other factor in history, not even religion, has produced so many wars as has the clash of national egotisms sanctified by the name of patriotism.   —Preserved Smith

*   *

Ethnocentrism is the technical name in which one's own group is the center of everything. —William Graham Sumner

National Pride is a modern form of tribalism.
—Robert Shnayerson

* *

If there be a God, I think he would like me to paint Africa British-Red as possible. —Cecil Rhodes

If we have to start over again with another Adam and Eve, I want them to be Americans. —Richard Russell

---

The purpose of the United Nations should be to protect the essential sovereignty of nations, large and small.
—Nikita Khrushchev

Nationalism is a silly cock crowing on his own dunghill.
—Richard Aldington

* *

A nation is a society united by a delusion about its ancestry and by a common hatred of its neighbours.
—Dean William R. Inge

I love my country too much to be a nationalist.
—Albert Camus

NATURE

Nature is proving that she can't be beaten—not by the likes of us. She's taking the world away from intellectuals and giving it back to the apes. —Robert E. Sherwood

Nature's laws affirm instead of prohibit. If you violate her laws you are your own prosecuting attorney, judge, jury, and hangman.
—Luther Burbank

Any interference with nature is damnable. Not only nature but also the people will suffer. —Anahario (wife of Grey Owl)

Nature I loved, and next to Nature, Art.
—Walter Savage Landor (1775–1864)

All are but parts of one stupendous whole,/Whose body Nature is, and God the soul. —Alexander Pope (1688–1744)

Let us permit nature to have her way; she understands her business better than we do. —Michel de Montaigne (1533–1592)

Nature, to be commanded, must be obeyed.
—Francis Bacon (1561–1626)

In nature there are neither rewards nor punishments; there are only consequences.   —Robert B. Ingersoll (1833–1899)

Nature has no principles. She furnishes us with no reason to believe that human life is to be respected. Nature, in her indifference, makes no distinction between good and evil.   —Anatole France

---

Nature uses as little as possible of anything.
—Johannes Kepler (1571–1630)

I forget how many thousand eggs go wrong for one codfish that gets hatched. But as Berkeley said long ago, it is idle to censure the creation as wasteful if you believe in a creator who has unlimited stuff to play with.   —Sir Frederick Pollock

*   *

Nature, heartless, witless nature.   —A. E. Housman

Never does nature say one thing and wisdom another.
—Juvenal (60?–140)

NEIGHBORS

A neighborhood is where, when you go out of it, you get beat up.
—Murray Kempton

Give the neighbor's kids an inch and they'll take a yard.
—Helen Castle

The good neighbor looks beyond the external accidents and discerns those inner qualities that make all men human and, therefore, brothers.   —Martin Luther King, Jr.

The impersonal hand of government can never replace the helping hand of a neighbor.   —Hubert H. Humphrey

There is a Law that man should love his neighbor as himself. In a few hundred years it should be as natural to mankind as breathing or the upright gait; but if he does not learn it he must perish.
—Alfred Adler

Your neighbor is the man who needs you.   —Elbert Hubbard

Nothing makes you more tolerant of a neighbor's noisy party than being there.   —Franklin P. Jones

NONSENSE / TRIVIA

If your parents didn't have any children, there's a good chance that you won't have any. —Clarence Day

Nonsense is good only because common sense is so limited.
—George Santayana

Thus so wretched is man that he would weary even without any cause for weariness . . . and so frivolous is he that, though full of a thousand reasons for weariness, the least thing, such as playing billiards or hitting a ball, is sufficient to amuse him.
—Blaise Pascal (1623–1662)

In a museum in Havana there are two skulls of Christopher Columbus, "one when he was a boy and one when he was a man."
—Mark Twain

American freedom consists largely in talking nonsense.
—Ed Howe

Forgive me my nonsense as I also forgive the nonsense of those who think they talk sense. —Robert Frost

A nose that can see is worth two that sniff. —Eugène Ionesco

What happens to the hole when the cheese is gone?
—Bertolt Brecht

Everything serious that he says is a joke and everything humorous that he says is dead serious.
—Clarence Darrow, of Lincoln Steffens

The greatest danger to human beings is their consciousness of the trivialities of their aims. —Gerard Brennan (But ignorance of one's ignorance is the greatest ignorance.)

The true, strong and sound mind is the mind that can embrace equally great things and small.
—Samuel Johnson (1709–1784)

The trouble with being punctual is that nobody's there to appreciate it. —Franklin P. Jones

One truth discovered, one pang of regret at not being able to express it, is better than all the fluency and flippancy in the world.
—William Hazlitt (1778–1830)

People are never so ready to believe you as when you say things in dispraise of yourself; and you are never so much annoyed as when they take you at your word. —Somerset Maugham

Good sense about trivialities is better than nonsense about things
that matter.   —Max Beerbohm

Only exceptionally rational men can afford to be absurd.
                                                —Allan Goldfein

Don't talk to me about a man's being able to talk sense; everyone
can talk sense—can he talk nonsense?
                        —William Pitt the Elder (1708–1778)

*   *

What Cole Porter was truly serious about was not being serious.
                                                —Reed Whittemore

It is almost as important to know what is not serious as to know
what is.   —John Kenneth Galbraith

*   *

It is a very sad thing that nowadays there is so little useless information.   —Oscar Wilde (1854–1900)

There is much pleasure to be gained from useless knowledge.
                                                —Bertrand Russell

*   *

In larger things we are convivial;/What causes trouble is the trivial.
                                                —Richard Armour

It is a far, far better thing to have a firm anchor in nonsense than
to put out on the troubled seas of thought.
                                        —John Kenneth Galbraith

*   *

We find it hard to believe that other people's thoughts are as silly
as our own, but they probably are.
                                        —James Harvey Robinson

If you jot down every silly thought that pops into your mind, you
will soon find out everything you most seriously believe.
                                        —Mignon McLaughlin

He dares to be a fool, and that is the first step in the direction of
wisdom.   —James Gibbons Huneker

No matter how thin you slice it, it's still baloney.
                                                —Alfred E. Smith

ODIUM LITERATIM

He writes his plays for the ages—the ages between five and twelve.
—George Jean Nathan

Ed Sullivan will be around as long as someone else has talent.
—Fred Allen

Brooks Atkinson described a Shubert play as "beautiful, if you are deaf and dumb."

That's not writing, that's typing!
—Truman Capote, of Jack Kerouac

Tennyson is a beautiful half of a poet.
—Ralph Waldo Emerson (1803–1882)

David Merrick, displaying . . . his sneaky knack for extending the life of a production beyond the reasonable expectations of the playwright's mother.   —Walter Kerr

Uhland's poetry is like the famous war horse, Bayard; it possesses all possible virtues and only one fault: it is dead.
—Heinrich Heine (1797–1856)

Cicero's style bores me. When I have spent an hour reading him . . . and try to recollect what I have extracted, I usually find it nothing but wind.   —Michel de Montaigne (1533–1592)

He wasn't exactly hostile to facts, but he was apathetic about them.
— Wolcott Gibbs, of Alexander Woollcott

His imagination resembles the wings of an ostrich.
— Thomas Babington Macaulay (1800–1859), of Dryden (1631–1700)

H. L. Mencken suffers from the hallucination that he is H. L. Mencken — there is no cure for a disease of that magnitude.
— Maxwell Bodenheim

He had occasional flashes of silence that made his conversation perfectly delightful.   — Sydney Smith (1771–1845), of Macaulay

He became mellow before he became ripe.
— Alexander Woollcott, of Christopher Morley

The perfection of rottenness.
— William James, of a book by Santayana

Poor Matt, he's gone to Heaven, no doubt — but he won't like God.
— Robert Louis Stevenson (1850–1894), of Matthew Arnold (1822–1888)

Hard to lay down but easy not to pick up.
— Malcolm Cowley, of John O'Hara's novels

She's genuinely bogus.
— Christopher Hassall, of Dame Edith Sitwell

This novel is not to be tossed lightly aside, but to be hurled with great force.   — Dorothy Parker

His style has the desperate jauntiness of an orchestra fiddling away for dear life on a sinking ship.
— Edmund Wilson, of Evelyn Waugh

The cruelest thing that has happened to Lincoln since he was shot by Booth was to fall into the hands of Carl Sandburg.
— Edmund Wilson

His more ambitious works may be defined as careless thinking carefully versified.   James Russell Lowell (1819–1891), of Alexander Pope (1688–1744)

I am reading Henry James . . . and feel myself as one entombed in a block of smooth amber.   — Virginia Woolf

The gods bestowed on Max the gift of perpetual old age.
— Oscar Wilde (1854–1900), of Max Beerbohm

If its length be not considered a merit, it hath no other.
— Edmund Waller (1606–1687), of *Paradise Lost*

The high-water mark, so to speak, of Socialist literature is W. H. Auden, a sort of gutless Kipling.   — George Orwell

Nobody can read Freud without realizing that he was the scientific
equivalent of another nuisance, George Bernard Shaw.
—Robert Maynard Hutchins

The more I think you over the more it comes home to me what an
unmitigated Middle Victorian ass you are!
—H. G. Wells, to George Bernard Shaw

It is his life work to announce the obvious in terms of the scandalous.   —H. L. Mencken, of George Bernard Shaw

James Joyce—an essentially private man who wished his total indifference to public notice to be universally recognized.
—Tom Stoppard

Mr. Henry James writes fiction as if it were a painful duty.
—Oscar Wilde

Henry James had a mind so fine that no idea could violate it.
—T. S. Eliot

Henry James was one of the nicest old ladies I ever met.
—William Faulkner

Thomas Wolfe has always seemed to me the most overrated, long-
winded and boring of reputable American novelists.
—Edith Oliver

Always willing to lend a helping hand to the one above him.
—F. Scott Fitzgerald, of Hemingway

Your novel has every fault that the English novel can have . . . a
rotten work of genius.
—Ford Madox Ford, to D. H. Lawrence

Hoffer, our resident Peasant Philosopher, is an example of articulate
ignorance.   —John Seelye, of Eric Hoffer

OLD AGE

Of late I appear/To have reached that stage/When people look
old/Who are only my age.   —Richard Armour

You just wake up one morning, and you got it!
—Moms Mabley

I refuse to admit I'm more than fifty-two even if that does make
my sons illegitimate.   —Lady Astor

I've never known a person to live to be one hundred and be remarkable for anything else.
—Josh Billings (Henry Wheeler Shaw) (1818–1885)

The older I grow the more I distrust the familiar doctrine that age brings wisdom.   —H. L. Mencken

There is only one thing age can give you, and that is wisdom.
—S. I. Hayakawa

Giving up is the ultimate tragedy.   —Robert J. Donovan

When a man retires and time is no longer a matter of urgent importance, his colleagues generally present him with a watch.
—R. C. Sherriff

Old age is when you first realize other people's faults are no worse than your own.   —Edgar A. Shoaff

You know you're getting old when the candles cost more than the cake.   —Bob Hope

I'm saving that rocker for the day when I feel as old as I really am.
—Dwight D. Eisenhower

If I'd known I was going to live so long, I'd have taken better care of myself.   —Leon Eldred

First you forget names, then you forget faces, then you forget to pull your zipper up, then you forget to pull your zipper down.
—Leo Rosenberg

I'm sixty-five and I guess that puts me in with the geriatrics, but if there were fifteen months in every year, I'd only be forty-eight.
—James Thurber

To me, old age is fifteen years older than I am.
—Bernard M. Baruch

If God had to give a woman wrinkles, He might at least have put them on the soles of her feet.
—Ninon de Lenclos (1620–1705)

A man is only as old as the woman he feels.
—Groucho Marx

I'm not interested in age. People who tell their age are silly. You're as old as you feel.   —Elizabeth Arden

The best thing about getting old is that all those things you couldn't have when you were young you no longer want.   —L. S. McCandless (That's the problem with old age—there's not much future in it.)

Everyone has been a child. All can understand through muffled memory how childhood was. But none has been old except those who are that now.   —Bert Kruger Smith (Old age is when you know all the answers but nobody asks you the questions.)

I have discovered the secret formula for a carefree Old Age: ICR = FI—"If You Can't Recall It, Forget It."   —Goodman Ace

A one-time U. S. Ambassador in Europe, astonishing in view of his age, is said to have approached all problems with a closed mind and an open fly.   —John Kenneth Galbraith

Life is a country that the old have seen, and lived in. Those who have to travel through it can only learn from them.
                    —Joseph Joubert (1754–1824)

I am in the prime of senility.   —Joel Chandler Harris

I'll never make the mistake of bein' seventy again!
                                        —Casey Stengel

To grow old is to pass from passion to compassion.
                                        —Albert Camus

Youth is a blunder; manhood a struggle; old age a regret.
                    —Benjamin Disraeli (1804–1881)

Forty is the old age of youth; fifty the youth of old age.
                    —Victor Hugo (1802–1885)

To know how to grow old is the master work of wisdom, and one of the most difficult chapters in the great art of living.
                    —Henri Frédéric Amiel (1821–1881)

Methuselah lived to be 969 years old . . . You boys and girls will see more in the next fifty years than Methuselah saw in his whole lifetime.   —Mark Twain

There are very few humorists who have written first-rate humor after they've become elderly.   —Richard Armour

Whatever poet, orator or sage may say of it, old age is still old age.
                                        —Sinclair Lewis

As soon as a man acquires fairly good sense, it is said that he is an old fogy.   —Ed Howe

Old-fogyism is comfortably closing in.   —Edmund Wilson

The older they get the better they were when they were younger.
                                        —Jim Bouton

Whoever saw old age that did not applaud the past and condemn the present?   —Michel de Montaigne (1533–1592)

*   *

The girl who felt my stare and raised her eyes/Saw I was only an old man, and looked away/As people do when they see something not quite nice.   —T. E. Matthews

How can the moribund old man reason back to himself the romance, the mystery, the imminence of great things with which our old earth tingled for him in the days when he was young and well?
                                                    —William James

*   *

When your friends begin to flatter you on how young you look, it's a sure sign you're getting old.   —Mark Twain

You've heard of the three ages of man: youth, age, and "you're looking wonderful!"   —Francis Joseph, Cardinal Spellman

*   *

About the only good thing you can say about old age is, it's better than being dead!   —Stephen Leacock

Growing old isn't so bad when you consider the alternative.
                                                    —Maurice Chevalier

---

It is this very awareness that one is no longer an attractive object that makes life so unbearable for so many elderly people.
                                                    —Simone de Beauvoir

Age is not all decay; it is the ripening, the swelling, of the fresh life within, that withers and bursts the husk.
                                                    —George Macdonald

*   *

The only time when you really live is from thirty to sixty.
                                                    —Hervey Allen

You've got to be fifty-nine years ole t'believe a feller is at his best at sixty.   —Frank McKinney Hubbard ("Kin Hubbard")

*   *

I pray . . . /That I may seem, though I die old,/A foolish, passionate man.   —William Butler Yeats

Young men want to be faithful and are not; old men want to be faithless and cannot.   —Oscar Wilde (1854–1900) (That gleam in his eye is merely the sun reflected in his bifocals.)

OPINION

It is not best that we should all think alike; it is difference of opinion which makes horse races.   —Mark Twain

No one can have a higher opinion of him than I have—and I think he is a dirty little beast.   —W. S. Gilbert

People are usually more firmly convinced that their opinions are precious than that they are true.   —George Santayana

An adult who ceases after youth to unlearn and relearn his facts and to reconsider his opinions . . . is a menace to a democratic community.   —Edward Thorndike

What plays the mischief with the truth is that men will insist upon the universal application of a temporary feeling or opinion.
                              —Herman Melville (1819–1891)

When I say "everybody says so," I mean *I* say so.   —Ed Howe
(When I want your opinion I'll give it to you.)

Compulsory unification of opinion achieves only the unanimity of the graveyard.   —Justice Robert Jackson

It requires ages to destroy a popular opinion.
              —Voltaire (François Marie Arouet) (1694–1778)

Public opinion in this country is everything.
                              —Abraham Lincoln (1809–1865)

Opinions cannot survive if one has no chance to fight for them.
                              —Thomas Mann

Man tends to treat all his opinions as principles.
                              —Herbert Agar

Public opinion is a compound of folly, weakness, prejudice, wrong feeling, right feeling, obstinacy, and newspaper paragraphs.
                              —Sir Robert Peel (1788–1850)

If all mankind minus one were of one opinion, and only one person were of the contrary opinion, mankind would be no more justified in silencing that one person than he, if he had the power, would be justified in silencing mankind.
                              —John Stuart Mill (1806–1873)

Error of opinion may be tolerated where reason is left free to combat it.   —Thomas Jefferson (1743–1826)

We are all of us, more or less, the slaves of opinion.
—William Hazlitt (1778–1830)

The world is governed by opinion.
—Thomas Hobbes (1588–1679)

Few people are capable of expressing with equanimity opinions which differ from the prejudices of their social environment.
—Albert Einstein

Every new opinion, at its starting, is precisely in a minority of one.
—Thomas Carlyle (1795–1881)

* *

It is clear that thought is not free if the profession of certain opinions makes it impossible to earn a living.   —Bertrand Russell

The oppression of any people for opinion's sake has rarely had any other effect than to fix those opinions deeper, and render them more important.   —Hosea Ballou (1771–1852)

OPIUM FOR UNDERACHIEVERS

In sexual intercourse it's quality not quantity that counts.
—Dr. David Reuben

Why should we be in such desperate haste to succeed, and in such desperate enterprises? If a man does not keep pace with his companions, perhaps it is because he hears a different drummer.
—Henry David Thoreau (1817–1862)

Modesty is the polite concession worth makes to inferiority.
—Comtesse Diane

. . . the race is not to the swift, nor the battle to the strong . . . but time and chance happeneth to them all.
—The Bible (Ecclesiastes 9:11)

What I aspired to be/And was not, comforts me.
—Robert Browning (1812–1889)

Everybody is ignorant, only on different subjects.
—Will Rogers

Remember, no one can make you feel inferior without your consent.
—Eleanor Roosevelt

I have tried to touch the feeling of people who have self-propelled themselves in life and have been successful in attaining something they find they don't really want.   —Elia Kazan

Only mediocrities rise to the top in a system that won't tolerate wavemaking.   —Laurence J. Peter

No man is a failure who is enjoying life.   —William Feather

It is impossible to escape the impression that people commonly use false standards of measurement—that they seek power, success and wealth for themselves and admire them in others, and that they underestimate what is of true value in life.   —Sigmund Freud

The definition of affluence is generally pinned to what comes in, not to the quality of life as it's lived.   —Peter Schrag

The chief value of money lies in the fact that one lives in a world in which it is overestimated.   —H. L. Mencken

Renown is a source of toil and sorrow; obscurity is a source of happiness.   —Johann L. von Mosheim (1694–1755)

The suffering of the rich is among the sweetest pleasures of the poor.
—R. M. Huber

Sometimes the pilgrimage from rags to riches is a journey from rage to wretchedness.   —R. M. Huber

---

Are you not ashamed of heaping up the greatest amount of money and honour and reputation, and caring so little about wisdom and truth and the greatest improvement of the soul?
—Socrates (470?–399 B.C.)

My belief is that to have no wants is divine.   —Socrates

*   *

It is the chiefest point of happiness that a man is willing to be what he is.   —Desiderius Erasmus (1465–1536)

The true perfection of man lies not in what man has, but in what man is.   —Oscar Wilde (1854–1900)

The students would be much better off if they could take a stand against taking a stand.   —David Riesman

Oh blessed a thousand times the peasant who is born, eats and dies without anybody bothering about his affairs.
—Giuseppe Verdi

*   *

Failure has gone to his head.   —Wilson Mizner

True success is overcoming the fear of being unsuccessful.

—Paul Sweeney

OPTIMISM / PESSIMISM

Ah, but a man's reach should exceed his grasp—or what's a heaven for? —Robert Browning (1812–1889)

An optimist is a driver who thinks that empty space at the curb won't have a hydrant beside it. —*Changing Times*

A pessimist is a man who looks both ways before crossing a one-way street. —Laurence J. Peter

The basis of optimism is sheer terror. Oscar Wilde (1854–1900) (An optimist expects his dreams to come true; a pessimist expects his nightmares to.)

Optimism is a kind of heart stimulant—the digitalis of failure.

—Elbert Hubbard

Pessimist: One who, when he has the choice of two evils, chooses both. —Oscar Wilde

Pessimists have already begun to worry about what is going to replace automation. —Laurence J. Peter

There is no sadder sight than a young pessimist.

—Mark Twain

A pessimist is a man who thinks all women are bad. An optimist is one who hopes they are. —Chauncey Depew

An optimist is one who believes marriage is a gamble.

—Laurence J. Peter

An optimist may see a light where there is none, but why must the pessimist always run to blow it out? —Michel de Saint-Pierre (Many an optimist has become rich simply by buying out a pessimist.)

The optimist proclaims that we live in the best of all possible worlds, and the pessimist fears this is true. —James Branch Cabell (An optimist is one who makes the best of it when he gets the worst of it.)

ORATORY

The politicians were talking themselves red, white and blue in the face. —Clare Boothe Luce

My father gave me these hints on speech-making: "Be sincere . . . be brief . . . be seated."   —James Roosevelt

The best audience is one that is intelligent, well-educated—and a little drunk.   —Alben W. Barkley

The man with power but without conscience, could, with an eloquent tongue . . . put this whole country into a flame.

—Woodrow Wilson

Why don't th' feller who says, "I'm not a speechmaker," let it go at that instead o' givin' a demonstration?

—Frank McKinney Hubbard ("Kin Hubbard")

A speech is a solemn responsibility. The man who makes a bad thirty-minute speech to two hundred people wastes only a half hour of his own time. But he wastes one hundred hours of the audience's time—more than four days—which should be a hanging offense.

—Jenkin Lloyd Jones

Spartans, stoics, heroes, saints and gods use a short and positive speech.   —Ralph Waldo Emerson (1803–1882)

The object of oratory is not truth but persuasion.

—Thomas Babington Macaulay (1800–1859)

The finest eloquence is that which gets things done.

—David Lloyd George

*   *

A mighty thing is eloquence . . . nothing so much rules the world.

—Pope Pius II (1405–1464)

All epoch-making revolutionary events have been produced not by the written but by the spoken word.   —Adolf Hitler

*   *

Abraham Lincoln wrote the Gettysburg Address while travelling from Washington to Gettysburg on the back of an envelope.

—Louis Untermeyer

I should be glad if I could flatter myself that I came as near to the central idea of the occasion in two hours as you did in two minutes.

—Edward Everett (1794–1865), to Abraham Lincoln

If you haven't struck oil in your first three minutes, *stop boring!*

—George Jessel

A speech is like a love affair. Any fool can start it, but to end it requires considerable skill.   —Lord Mancroft

*   *

I never failed to convince an audience that the best thing they could do was to go away.
—Thomas Love Peacock (1785–1866)

I sometimes marvel at the extraordinary docility with which Americans submit to speeches.   —Adlai Stevenson

ORIGINALITY

Originality exists in every individual because each of us differs from the others. We are all primary numbers divisible only by ourselves.
—Jean Guitton

Where it [opinion] does not exist, the *status quo* becomes stereotyped, and all originality, even the most necessary, is discouraged.
—Bertrand Russell

People who take time to be alone usually have depth, originality, and quiet reserve.   —John Miller

Originality does not consist in saying what no one has ever said before, but in saying exactly what you think yourself.
—James Stephens

The merit of originality is not novelty; it is sincerity. The believing man is the original man; whatsoever he believes, he believes it for himself, not for another.   —Thomas Carlyle (1795–1881)

Originality is the art of concealing your source.
—Franklin P. Jones

What is originality? Undetected plagiarism.   —Dean William R. Inge (Originality is the fine art of remembering what you hear but forgetting where you heard it.)

*   *

Books serve to show a man that those original thoughts of his aren't very new after all.   —Abraham Lincoln (1809–1865)

He has left off reading altogether to the great improvement of his originality.   —Charles Lamb (1775–1834)

*   *

My guess is that well over 80 percent of the human race goes through life without having a single original thought.
—H. L. Mencken

Everything has been thought of before, but the problem is to think of it again. —Johann W. von Goethe (1749–1832)

* *

Every thought is new when an author expresses it in a manner peculiar to himself. —Marquis de Vauvenargues (1715–1747)

I invent nothing. I rediscover. —Auguste Rodin

About the most originality that any writer can hope to achieve honestly is to steal with good judgment.
—Josh Billings (Henry Wheeler Shaw) (1818–1885)

Many ideas grow better when transplanted into another mind than in the one where they sprang up. —Oliver Wendell Holmes, Jr.

* *

All good things which exist are the fruits of originality.
—John Stuart Mill (1806–1873)

There is nothing new under the sun.
—The Bible (Ecclesiastes 1:9)

* *

Every human being is intended to have a character of his own; to be what no others are, and to do what no other can do.
—William Ellery Channing (1780–1842)

For I fear I have nothing original in me—Excepting Original Sin.
—Thomas Campbell (1777–1844)

OVERPOPULATION

The command *Be fruitful and multiply* [was] promulgated, according to our authorities when the population of the world consisted of two persons. —Dean William R. Inge

When people take leave of their census. —Malcolm K. Jeffrey

We all worry about the population explosion—but we don't worry about it at the right time. —Arthur Hoppe

The mother of the year should be a sterilized woman with two adopted children. —Dr. Paul R. Ehrlich

The idea that population growth guarantees a better life—financially or otherwise—is a myth that only those who sell diapers, baby carriages and the like have any right to believe.

—Fairfield Osborn

The essential cause of environmental pollution is overpopulation.
—Jon Breslaw (Those in favor of birth control have already been born.)

Maximum welfare, not maximum population, is our human objective.
—Arnold Toynbee

Overpopulation is really the root of all evil, and just because there are still a few countries left that can feel deprived because they haven't been subject to progress, it doesn't necessarily mean that we have room for any more people on spaceship earth.

—Konrad Lorenz

We have been God-like in our planned breeding of our domesticated plants and animals, but we have been rabbit-like in our unplanned breeding of ourselves.   —Arnold Toynbee

If the children already born each have only two children themselves . . . in twenty-seven to thirty-five years the population of the world will double.   —Tarzie Vittachi

Five dollars invested in population control is worth one hundred dollars invested in economic growth.   —Lyndon B. Johnson

We have come to a turning point in the human habitation of the earth.   —Barry Commoner

We need to make a world in which fewer children are born, and in which we take better care of them.   —Dr. George Wald

If we are to arrest the growth of U. S. population by the end of the century, the two-child family must voluntarily become the norm.

—Rufus E. Miles, Jr.

PACIFISM

I am an uncompromising pacifist . . . I have no sense of nationalism, only a cosmic consciousness of belonging to the human family.
—Rosika Schwimmer

The absolute pacifist is a bad citizen; times come when force must be used to uphold right, justice and ideals.
—Alfred North Whitehead

PAINTING

This is either a forgery or a damn clever original!
—Frank Sullivan

What sight is sadder than the sight of a lady we admire admiring a nauseating picture?　—Logan Pearsall Smith

I walk in the garden, I look at the flowers and shrubs and trees and discover in them an exquisiteness of contour, a vitality of edge or a vigor of spring as well as an infinite variety of color that no artifact I have seen in the last sixty years can rival . . . Each day, as I look, I wonder where my eyes were yesterday.
—Bernard Berenson

I hope with all my heart there will be painting in heaven.
—Jean Baptiste Camille Corot (1796–1875), on his deathbed

The connoisseur of painting gives only bad advice to the painter. For that reason I have given up trying to judge myself.
—Pablo Picasso

A good painter is to paint two main things, namely men and the working of man's mind.   —Leonardo da Vinci (1452–1519)

I do not paint a portrait to look like the subject, rather does the person grow to look like his portrait.   —Salvador Dali

Painting is easy when you don't know how, but very difficult when you do.   —Edgar Degas

There are three kinds of people in the world: those who can't stand Picasso, those who can't stand Raphael, and those who've never heard of either of them.   —John White

---

Only work which is the product of inner compulsion can have spiritual meaning.   —Walter Gropius

If [the artist] sees nothing within him, then he should also refrain from painting what he sees before him.
—Caspar David Friedrich (1744–1840)

*   *

When one is painting one does not think.
—Raphael (1483–1520)

When an artist reasons, it's because he no longer understands anything.   —André Derain

---

When I am finishing a picture I hold some God-made object up to it—a rock, a flower, the branch of a tree or my hand—as a kind of final test. If the painting stands up beside a thing man cannot make, the painting is authentic. If there's a clash between the two, it is bad art.   —Marc Chagall

For me, painting is a way to forget life. It is a cry in the night, a strangled laugh.   —Georges Rouault

*   *

Most people see by way of their parents, their masters, or the social milieu in which they live.   —Germain Bazin

Solo works of art are meant to be looked at for their own sake.
—Clement Greenberg

PARALLELS

In making even a cursory examination of the quotations in this book, one cannot but be impressed by the number of parallels of thought expressed by many authors. Generally, like temperaments produce like observations. While "everything has been thought of before," as Goethe noted, the problem is to think of it again. Its rethinking, the reader must at times suspect, is sometimes less than original. Said La Rochefoucauld, "We all of us have sufficient fortitude to bear the misfortunes of others." Said Oscar Wilde, "Philosophy teaches us to bear with equanimity the misfortunes of others." (The likeness does not suffer in translation.) The question is, should one who can express an idea with greater felicity or wit refrain from so doing simply because the idea is not original? For example, the central idea in Anatole France's "The average man, who does not know what to do with his life, wants another one which will last forever," is communicated more effectively in Susan Ertz's paraphrase, "Millions long for immortality who do not know what to do with themselves on a rainy Sunday afternoon." *Many ideas grow better when transplanted.* The following parallels provide the reader with material to ponder in answering the question, "Is originality the fine art of remembering what you hear but forgetting where you heard it?"

———————

If you steal from one another it's plagiarism; if you steal from many, it's research.　　—Wilson Mizner

During a discussion, Professor Brander Matthews was explaining to Nicholas Murray Butler the main points of an article he had written on the subject of plagiarism. "In the case of the first man to use an anecdote there is originality; in the case of the second, there is plagiarism; with the third, it is lack of originality, and with the fourth it is drawing from a common stock." "Yes," interjected Butler, "and in the case of the fifth, it is research."

*　　*

Logic is the art of going wrong with confidence.
　　　　　　　　　　　　　　　—Joseph Wood Krutch

Logic is an instrument used for bolstering a prejudice.
　　　　　　　　　　　　　　　　　—Elbert Hubbard

*　　*

You've no idea what a poor opinion I have of myself—and how little I deserve it.　　—W. S. Gilbert

What a rotten opinion I have of myself, and how little I deserve it.
-—Reg Smythe (Andy Capp)

*   *

A gentleman is one who never strikes a woman without provocation.
—H. L. Mencken

A gentleman is any man who wouldn't hit a woman with his hat on.
—Fred Allen

*   *

I would rather have men ask why I have no statue than why I have one.   —Marcus Porcius Cato (234–149 B.C.)

I would rather that the people should wonder why I wasn't President than why I am.   —Salmon P. Chase (1808–1873)

*   *

Every saint has a past and every sinner has a future.
—Oscar Wilde (1854–1900)

Every sinner should be vouchsafed a future, as every saint has had a past.   —Sarvepalli Radhakrishnan

*   *

There is nothing that fails like success.   —G. K. Chesterton

Take it from me, baby, in America nothing fails like success.
—Budd Schulberg

*   *

Reading is sometimes an ingenious device for drugging thought.
—Sir Arthur Helps (1813–1875)

Reading is sometimes an ingenious device for drugging thought.
—Albert Guérard

*   *

Among the calamities of war may be justly numbered the diminution of the love of truth.   —Samuel Johnson (1709–1784)

The first casualty when war comes is truth.   —Hiram Johnson

*   *

I never read a book before reviewing it. It prejudices me so.
—Sydney Smith (1771–1845)

I never read a book before reviewing it. It prejudices me so.
—Hesketh Pearson

It is wrong to read the books one reviews. It creates a prejudice.
—George Croly

* *

In the world there are only two tragedies. One is not getting what one wants and the other is getting it.   —Oscar Wilde

There are two tragedies in life. One is not to get your heart's desire. The other is to get it.   —George Bernard Shaw

* *

Always forgive your enemies—nothing annoys them so much.
—Oscar Wilde

Love your enemy—it will drive him nuts.   —Eleanor Doan

* *

God is not a cosmic bell-boy.   —Harry Emerson Fosdick

The doctrine of the material efficacy of prayer reduces the Creator to a cosmic bellhop, of a not very bright or reliable kind.
—Herbert J. Muller

* *

There is no greater sorrow than to recall, in misery, the time when we were happy.   —Dante Alighieri (1265–1321)

No greater grief than to remember days of gladness when sorrow is at hand.   —Friedrich Schiller (1729–1805)

* *

My God, My God, why hast thou forsaken me?
—The Bible (Psalm 22)

My God, My God, why hast thou forsaken me?
—The Bible (Matthew 27:46; Mark 15:34)

* *

This country will not be a good place for any of us to live in unless we make it a good place for all of us to live in.
—Theodore Roosevelt

This land of ours cannot be a good place for any of us to live in unless we make it a good place for all of us to live in.
—Richard M. Nixon

PARAPSYCHOLOGY / PRECOGNITION / ESP

Clairvoyance is attaining the respectability of a bona fide science. Arthur C. Clarke has verified the fact, based on the prediction of a fortune-teller that her highly skeptical client would be killed by a prehistoric reptile, which event occurred when shortly afterwards her client visited the American Museum of Natural History and the skeleton of a dinosaur fell upon and crushed him. (The same clairvoyant now predicts that Ford will be shot in the Lincoln Theatre.)

Some things have to be believed to be seen.   —Ralph Hodgson

'Tain't what a man don't know that hurts him; it's what he knows that just ain't so!
                —Frank McKinney Hubbard ("Kin Hubbard")

Lightning had killed her mother and father at a Rosewater Lumber Co. picnic. She was sure lightning was going to kill her, too. And because her kidneys hurt all the time, she was sure the lightning would hit her in the kidneys.   —Kurt Vonnegut, Jr.

Heaven from all creatures hides the book of Fate.
                —Alexander Pope (1688–1744)

I've found a perfect description of mysticism—it's the attempt to get rid of mystery.   —Roger Fry

Matrons, who toss the cup, and see/The grounds of fate in the grounds of tea.   —Charles Churchill (1731–1764)

Skepticism is a hedge against vulnerability.
                —Charles Thomas Samuels

The attempt to define all mystical, transcendental and ecstatic experiences which do not fit in with the categories of consensus reality as psychotic is conceptually limiting and comes from a timidity which is not seemly for the honest, open-minded explorer.
                —John Cunningham Lilly

You can only predict things after they've happened.
                —Eugène Ionesco

I always avoid prophesying beforehand, because it is much better policy to prophesy after the event has already taken place.
                —Winston Churchill

*   *

We still say ESP is spinach and stands for Essentially Silly People.
                —Cleveland Amory

[We] have yet to find a single person who can, *without trickery,* receive even the simplest three-letter word under test conditions.
                —Milbourne Christopher

*   *

I wonder that a soothsayer doesn't laugh whenever he sees another soothsayer.   —Marcus Tullius Cicero (106–43 B.C.)

You can make a better living in the world as a soothsayer than as a truthsayer.   —G. C. Lichtenberg (1742–1799)

* *

The difference between hearsay and prophecy is often one of sequence. Hearsay often turns out to have been prophecy.
—Hubert H. Humphrey

Carriages without horses shall go,/And accidents fill the world with woe/Around the world thoughts shall fly/In the twinkling of an eye.
—Mother Shipton (1488?–1561?)

* *

The best of seers is he who guesses well.
—Euripides (484–406 B.C.)

Records of telepathic support in almost every instance depend upon the statement of one person, usually strongly predisposed to believe in the occult.   —C. E. M. Hansel

---

Prophecy, however honest, is generally a poor substitute for experience.   —Justice Benjamin N. Cardozo

It is one of the commonest of mistakes to consider that the limit of our power of perception is also the limit of all there is to perceive.
—C. W. Leadbeater

* *

I never think of the future. It comes soon enough.
—Albert Einstein

The will to disbelieve is the strongest deterrent to wider horizons.
—Hans Holzer

* *

The prophet and the quack are alike admired for a generation, and admired for the wrong reasons.   —G. K. Chesterton

Whenever the question comes up as to what is wrong with ESP experiments . . . the tactic . . . is to point out all the things that are wrong . . . and quietly to ignore the experiments which cannot be explained away.   —R. A. McConnell

* *

In conditions of great uncertainty people tend to predict the events that they want to happen actually will happen.

—Roberta Wohlstetter

My gran'ther's rule was safer'n 'tis to crow:/Don't never prophesy onless ye know. —James Russell Lowell (1819–1891)

PASSION

A correspondence course of passion was, for her, the perfect and ideal relationship with a man. —Aldous Huxley

Unless a woman has an amorous heart, she is a dull companion.

—Samuel Johnson (1709–1784)

The shame of aging is not that Desire should fail (who mourns for something he no longer needs?): it is that someone else must be told. —W. H. Auden

---

How well I remember the aged poet, Sophocles, when in answer to the question, "How does love suit with age—are you still the man you were?" replied, "Peace, most gladly have I escaped the thing of which you speak; I feel as if I had escaped from a mad and furious master!" —Plato (427?–347 B.C.)

O glorious boon of age, if it does indeed free us from youth's most vicious fault. —Marcus Tullius Cicero (106–43 B.C.)

We are n'er like angels till our passion dies.

—Thomas Dekker (1572?–1632)

Passions are vices or virtues in their highest powers.

—Johann W. von Goethe (1749–1832)

PAST / PRESENT / FUTURE

The trouble with our times is that the future is not what it used to be. —Paul Valéry

The past always looks better than it was. It's only pleasant because it isn't here. —Finley Peter Dunne (Mr. Dooley)

The Good Old Days are neither better nor worse than the ones we're living through right now.   —Artie Shaw (These are the good old days the next generation will hear so much about.)

The best thing about the future is that it comes only one day at a time.   —Abraham Lincoln (1809–1865) (May the happiest days of your past be the saddest days of your future.)

The great achievements of the past were the adventures of adventurers of the past. Only the adventurous can understand the greatness of the past.   —Alfred North Whitehead

The wrecks of the past were America's warnings.
                    —George Bancroft (1800–1891)

Let us not go over the old ground, let us rather prepare for what is to come.   —Marcus Tullius Cicero (106–43 B.C.)

The new circumstances under which we are placed call for new words, new phrases, and for the transfer of old words to new objects.   —Thomas Jefferson (1743–1826) (The past is a good place to visit, but I wouldn't want to live there.)

We are tomorrow's past.   —Mary Webb

Life is a series of collisions with the future; it is not a sum of what we have been but what we yearn to be.   —José Ortega y Gasset (The present is the period when the future pauses for a short while before becoming the past.)

Perhaps the greatest impulse to trying to foresee and plan the future comes from the combination of having new tools with which to do it and the growing realization that every technological and social innovation has repercussions which spread like a wave through the complex interlocked sections of society.   —Ward Madden

If a man takes no thought about what is distant, he will find sorrow near at hand.   —Confucius (c. 551–479 B.C.)

The past must no longer be used as an anvil for beating out the present and the future.   —Paul-Emile Borduas

The future influences the present just as much as the past.
                    —Friedrich Nietzsche (1844–1900)

The past is the present, isn't it? It's the future, too. We all tried to lie out of that but life won't let us.   —Eugene O'Neill

Real generosity toward the future consists in giving all to what is present.   —Albert Camus

Children enjoy the present because they have neither a past nor a future.   —Jean de La Bruyère (1645–1696)

Long-range planning does not deal with future decisions, but with the future of present decisions.   —Peter Drucker

The past is gone; the present is full of confusion; and the future scares hell out of me!   —David Lewis Stein (Now is the time for all good men to come to.)

This is the first age that's paid much attention to the future, which is a little ironic since we may not have one.

—Arthur C. Clarke

God has no power over the past except to cover it with oblivion.

—Pliny the Elder (23–79)

Only the past is immortal.   —Delmore Schwartz

Even God cannot change the past.

—Agathon (447?–401 B.C.)

God cannot alter the past but historians can.

—Samuel Butler

*   *

. . . the tender grace of a day that is dead/Will never come back to me.   —Alfred, Lord Tennyson (1809–1892)

The happy highways where I went and cannot come again.

—A. E. Housman

*   *

Nothing can bring back the hour/Of splendour in the grass, of glory in the flower.   —William Wordsworth (1770–1850)

Moments that can never happen again and never lost their wonder.

—Stephen Spender

*   *

And in today already walks tomorrow.

—Samuel Taylor Coleridge (1772–1834)

You cannot plan the future by the past.

—Edmund Burke (1729–1797)

*   *

If you want the present and the future to be different from the past, Spinoza tells us, study the past, find out the causes that made it what it was and bring different causes to bear.

—Will and Ariel Durant

If you want the present to be different from the past, study the past.
—Baruch Spinoza (1632–1677)

* *

I have seen the future and it is very much like the present—only longer.   —Kehlog Albran

I have seen the future and it doesn't work.   —Robert Fulford

---

My interest is in the future because I am going to spend the rest of my life there.   —Charles F. Kettering

If you want a picture of the future, imagine a boot stamping on the human face—forever . . . And remember that it is forever.
—George Orwell

* *

We can only pay our debt to the past by putting the future in debt to ourselves.   —John Buchan, Lord Tweedsmuir

One generation cannot bind another.
—Thomas Jefferson (1743–1826)

* *

It's futile to talk too much about the past—something like trying to make birth control retroactive.   —Charles E. Wilson

The past at least is secure.
—Daniel Webster (1782–1852)

* *

He is blessed over all mortals who loses no moment of the passing life in remembering the past.
—Henry David Thoreau (1817–1862)

The little present must not be allowed wholly to elbow the great past out of view.   —Andrew Lang

PATIENCE

Prayer of the modern American: "Dear God, I pray for patience. And I want it *right now!*"   —Oren Arnold

The key to everything is patience. You get the chicken by hatching the egg—not by smashing it.   —Arnold Glasow (On second thought, patience may be a virtue, but it will never help a rooster lay an egg.)

Patience—a minor form of despair disguised as virtue.   —Ambrose Bierce (If you're too lazy to start anything, you may get a reputation for patience.)

There are two kinds of people in one's life—people whom one keeps waiting—and the people for whom one waits.   —S. N. Behrman

Beware the fury of a patient man.   —John Dryden (1631–1700)

A woman who has never seen her husband fishing doesn't know what a patient man she has married.   —Ed Howe

PATRIOTISM

A real patriot is the fellow who gets a parking ticket and rejoices that the system works.   —Bill Vaughan

My rackets are run on strictly American lines and they're going to stay that way!   —Al Capone

A loyal American is one who gets mad when an alien cusses the institutions he cusses.   —*Huntington Herald*

If I have to lay an egg for my country, I'll do it.   —Bob Hope

There's one beneficial effect of going to Moscow. You come home waving the American flag with all your might!
                                              —Mary Tyler Moore

True patriotism doesn't exclude an understanding of the patriotism of others.   —Queen Elizabeth II

I should like to be able to love my country and to love justice.
                                              —Albert Camus

Do not . . . regard the critics as questionable patriots. What were Washington and Jefferson and Adams but profound critics of the colonial status quo?   —Adlai Stevenson

The Athenian democracy suffered much from that narrowness of patriotism which is the ruin of all nations.   —H. G. Wells

As soon as any man says of the affairs of state, What does it matter to me? the state may be given up as lost.
                                      —Jean Jacques Rousseau (1712–1778)

Patriotism is not enough.   —Edith Cavell

Ask not what you can do for your country, for they are liable to tell you.   —Mark Steinbeck

If I added to their pride of America, I am happy.
                                              —Carl Sandburg

If a man is fortunate he will, before he dies, gather up as much as he can of his civilized heritage and transmit it to his children.

—Will Durant

Naturally the common people don't want war . . . Voice or no voice, the people can always be brought to the bidding of the leaders . . . All you have to do is to tell them they are being attacked and denounce the pacifists for lack of patriotism.   —Hermann Goering (When the flag is unfurled all reason is in the trumpet.)

[These are] the three virtues: duty, loyalty, patriotism.

—Gordon Liddy

When a bishop at the first shot abandons the worship of Christ and rallies his flock round the altar of Mars, he may be acting patriotically . . . but that does not justify him in pretending . . . that Christ is, in effect, Mars.   —George Bernard Shaw

No other factor in history, not even religion, has produced so many wars as has the clash of national egotisms sanctified by the name of patriotism.   —Preserved Smith

If man commits suicide, it will be . . . because they will obey the clichés of state sovereignty and national honor.

—Erich Fromm

Patriotism is as fierce as a fever, pitiless as the grave, blind as a stone, and irrational as a headless hen.   —Ambrose Bierce

Loyalty must arise spontaneously from the hearts of people who love their country and respect their government.

—Justice Hugo L. Black

One of the great attractions of patriotism—it fulfills our worst wishes. In the person of our nation we are able, vicariously, to bully and cheat. Bully and cheat, what's more, with a feeling that we are profoundly virtuous.   —Aldous Huxley

The standardization of mass-production carries with it a tendency to standardize a mass-mind . . . The worst defect of patriotism is its tendency to foster and impose . . . and so to stifle . . . liberty.

—J. A. Hobson

Some day the American people will erect a monument to his [Senator Joseph McCarthy's] memory.   —Eddie Rickenbacker

Many studies have discovered a close link between prejudice and "patriotism" . . . Extreme bigots are almost always super-patriots.   —Gordon W. Allport

. . . schools are out to teach patriotism; newspapers are out to stir up excitement; and politicians are out to get reelected. None of the three, therefore, can do anything whatever toward saving the human race from reciprocal suicide.   —Bertrand Russell

What is good for the country is good for General Motors, and what's good for General Motors is good for the country.
—Charles E. Wilson

*   *

Every man loves and admires his own country because it produced him.   —Edward Bulwer-Lytton (1803–1873)

Patriotism is your conviction that this country is superior to all other countries because you were born in it.
—George Bernard Shaw

*   *

With malice toward none, with charity for all . . . let us finish the work we are in, to bind up the nation's wounds.
—Abraham Lincoln (1809–1865)

Abandon your animosities and make your sons Americans!
—Robert E. Lee (1807–1870)

*   *

Our country . . . when right, to be kept right; when wrong, to be put right.   —Carl Schurz

That pernicious sentiment, "Our country, right or wrong."
—James Russell Lowell (1819–1891)

*   *

And so, my fellow Americans, ask not what your country can do for you; ask what you can do for your country.
—John F. Kennedy

In the great fulfillment we must have a citizenship less concerned about what the government can do for it and more anxious about what it can do for the nation.   —Warren G. Harding

*   *

Patriotism, to be truly American, begins with the human allegiance.
—Norman Cousins

Human sovereignty transcends national sovereignty.
—Lester B. Pearson

*   *

Love for one's country which is not part of one's love for humanity is not love, but idolatrous worship.   —Erich Fromm

Our country is the world—our countrymen are all mankind.
                              —William Lloyd Garrison (1805–1879)

*   *

Patriotism is the last refuge of a scoundrel.
                              —Samuel Johnson (1709–1784)

Patriotism is the virtue of the vicious.
                              —Oscar Wilde (1854–1900)

*   *

For us, patriotism is the same as the love of humanity.
                              —Mohandas Gandhi

To me, it seems a dreadful indignity to have a soul controlled by geography.   —George Santayana

---

Our country! In her intercourse with foreign nations may she always be in the right; but our country, right or wrong.
                              —Stephen Decatur (1779–1820)

My country right or wrong, is a thing no patriot would think of saying except in a desperate case. It is like saying, "My mother, drunk or sober!"   —G. K. Chesterton

*   *

It is the love of country that has lighted and that keeps glowing the holy fire of patriotism.   —J. Horace McFarland

You'll never have a quiet world till you knock the patriotism out of the human race.   —George Bernard Shaw

*   *

Patriotism is a praiseworthy competition with one's ancestors.
                              —Tacitus (55?–130?)

Whoever serves his country well has no need of ancestors.
                              —Voltaire (François Marie Arouet) (1694–1778)

PEOPLE

Too bad that all the people who know how to run the country are busy driving taxicabs and cutting hair.   —George Burns

When the People contend for their liberty, they seldom get anything for their Victory but new Masters.
—Lord Halifax (George Savile) (1633–1695)

This country, with its institutions, belongs to the people who inhibit it.   —Edgar A. Shoaff

There are too many people, and too few human beings.
—Robert Zend

A significant factor in our history has been the effort, on the one hand, of minority groups to prevent the people from ruling, and, on the other hand, of the people to express their will and to have it applied rationally.   —Bernard Smith

It is only after time has been given for cool and deliberate reflection that the real voice of the people can be known.
—George Washington (1732–1799)

When the people applauded him wildly, he [Phocion] turned to one of his friends and said, "Have I said something foolish?"
—Diogenes Laertius (c. 150 B.C.)

If you want to understand democracy, spend less time in the library with Plato, and more time in the buses with people.
—Simeon Strunsky

There are people who can endure personal tragedies and private griefs exacted by the nation only if they feel the nation itself is worthy.   —Bill Moyers

The people of Germany are just as responsible for Hitler as the people of Chicago are for *The Chicago Tribune*.
—Alexander Woollcott

When people suddenly become prosperous, they also become preposterous.   —Laurence J. Peter

People have one thing in common: they are all different.
—Robert Zend

People who bite the hand that feeds them usually lick the boot that kicks them.   —Eric Hoffer

---

The People, though we think of a great entity when we use the word, means nothing more than so many millions of individual men.
—James Bryce

Society in its full sense . . . is never an entity separable from the individuals who compose it.   —Ruth Benedict

*   *

The tumultuous populace of large cities are ever to be dreaded.
—George Washington

The murdering and thieving rabble of the peasants.
—Martin Luther (1483–1546)

———————

Everything depends on what the people are capable of wanting.
—Enrico Malatesta

The aim is not more goods for people to buy, but more opportunities for them to live.   —Lewis Mumford

*   *

God must love the common man, he made so many of them.
—Abraham Lincoln (1809–1865)

God must hate the common man, he made him so common.
—Philip Wylie

*   *

Men of integrity, by their very existence, rekindle the belief that as a people we can live above the level of moral squalor.
—John Gardner

The mobs of the great cities . . . sores on the body politic.
—Thomas Jefferson (1743–1826)

*   *

It is time to realize that of all the valuable capital the world possesses, the most valuable and most decisive is people.
—Joseph Stalin

The people—that great beast!
—Alexander Hamilton (1757–1804)

PERFECTION

The closest to perfection a person ever comes is when he fills out a job application form.   —Stanley J. Randall

Bachelors' wives and old maids' children are always perfect.
—Nicolas Chamfort

There are no perfect men of course, but some are more perfect than others, and we can use all of those we can get.   —Merle Shain
(On the other hand, nobody can be perfect unless he admits his faults, but if he has faults how can he be perfect?)

PERSEVERANCE

By perseverance the snail reached the ark.   —Charles Haddon Spurgeon (1834–1892) (Correction, please: "snails.")

'Tis known by the name of perseverance in a good cause, and obstinacy in a bad one.   —Laurence Sterne (1713–1768)

It is not necessary to hope in order to undertake, nor to succeed in order to persevere.   —Charles the Bold (1433–1477)

I know of no more encouraging fact than the unquestionable ability of man to elevate his life by a conscious endeavor.
                                         —Henry David Thoreau (1817–1862)

PHILOSOPHY / PHILOSOPHERS

Being a philosopher, I have a problem for every solution.
                                                      —Robert Zend

It is good that a philosopher should remind himself, now and then, that he is a particle pontificating on infinity.
                                             —Will and Ariel Durant

Philosophy may be defined as the art of asking the right questions . . . Awareness of the problem outlives all solutions. The answers are questions in disguise, every new answer giving rise to new questions.   —Abraham Joshua Heschel (Philosophy is that which enables the rich to say there is no disgrace in being poor.)

There is only one thing a philosopher can be relied on to do, and that is to contradict other philosophers.   —William James (A philosopher is a person who says he doesn't care which side his bread is buttered on, because he eats both sides anyway.)

Healthy-mindedness is inadequate as a philosophical doctrine, because the evil facts which it refuses positively to account for are a genuine portion of reality; and they may after all be the best key to life's significance.   —William James

Here is the beginning of philosophy: a recognition of the conflicts between men, a search for their cause, a condemnation of mere opinion . . . and the discovery of a standard of judgment.
                                         —Epictetus (c. 1st century A.D.)

Philosophy is systematic reflection upon the common experience of mankind.   —Robert Maynard Hutchins

Science is what you know, philosophy is what you don't know. —Bertrand Russell (A philosopher is a person who never feels badly after he has made an ass of himself.)

The finding of arguments for a conclusion given in advance is not philosophy, but special pleading.   —Bertrand Russell

To teach men how to live without certainty and yet without being paralyzed by hesitation, is perhaps the chief thing philosophy can still do.   —Bertrand Russell

What is philosophy but a continual battle against custom?
—Thomas Carlyle (1795–1881)

Two things fill the mind with ever new and increasing wonder and awe—the starry heavens above me, and the moral law within me.
—Immanuel Kant (1724–1804)

The various opinions of philosophers have scattered through the world as many plagues of the mind as Pandora's box did those of the body, only with this difference, that they have not left hope at the bottom.   —Jonathan Swift (1667–1745) (On second thought, a philosopher is any person who doesn't want what he can't get.)

The philosophy of one century is the common sense of the next.
—Henry Ward Beecher (1813–1887)

Philosophy removes from religion all reason for existing . . . As the science of the spirit, it looks upon religion as a phenomenon, a transitory historical fact, a psychic condition that can be surpassed.
—Benedetto Croce

Philosophy has the task and the opportunity of helping banish the concept that human destiny here and now is of slight importance in comparison with some supernatural destiny.   —John Dewey

*　　*

Metaphysics is a dark ocean without shores or lighthouse, strewn with many a philosophic wreck.   —Immanuel Kant

Metaphysics may be, after all, only the art of being sure of something that is not so, and logic only the art of going wrong with confidence.   —Joseph Wood Krutch

*　　*

Metaphysics is almost always an attempt to prove the incredible by an appeal to the unintelligible.   —H. L. Mencken

When the speaker and he to whom he speaks do not understand, that is metaphysics.
—Voltaire (François Marie Arouet) (1694–1778)

Until philosophers are kings . . . cities will never cease from ill, nor the human race.   —Plato (427?–347? B.C.)

If I wished to punish a province, I would have it governed by philosophers.   —Frederick the Great (1712–1786)

*   *

Metaphysics is the science of proving what we don't understand.
—Josh Billings (Henry Wheeler Shaw) (1818–1885)

Philosophy—the purple bullfinch in the lilac tree.   —T. S. Eliot

*   *

Miracles are so called because they excite wonder. In unphilosophical minds any rare or unexpected thing excites wonder, while in philosophical minds the familiar excites wonder also.
—George Santayana

I believe that in actual fact, philosophy ranks before and above the natural sciences.   —Thomas Mann

*   *

The philosophers have only interpreted the world; the thing, however, is to change it.   —Karl Marx (1818–1883)

Philosophy: unintelligible answers to insoluble problems.
—Henry Adams

PITY

Pity the meek, for they shall inherit the earth.   —Don Marquis

When a man has pity on all living creatures then only is he noble.
—Buddha (563?–483? B.C.)

I never knew whether to pity or congratulate a man on coming to his senses.   —William Makepeace Thackeray (1811–1863)

PLAGIARISM

Adam was the only man who, when he said a good thing, knew that nobody had said it before him.   —Mark Twain

When a thing has been said and well said, have no scruple; take it and copy it. Give references? Why should you? Either your readers know where you have taken the passage and the precaution is needless, or they do not know and you humiliate them.

—Anatole France

It is a mean thief, or a successful author, that plunders the dead.

—Austin O'Malley

Plagiarists are always suspicious of being stolen from.

—Samuel Taylor Coleridge (1772–1834)

About the most originality that any writer can hope to achieve honestly is to steal with good judgment.

—Josh Billings (Henry Wheeler Shaw) (1818–1885)

What is originality? Undetected plagiarism.

—Dean William R. Inge

Taking something from one man and making it worse is plagiarism.
—George Moore (On the other hand, making it better is originality.)

Plagiarists, at least, have the merit of preservation.

—Benjamin Disraeli (1804–1881)

Fine words! I wonder where you stole them.

—Jonathan Swift (1667–1745)

It is the little writer rather than the great writer who seems never to quote, and the reason is that he is never really doing anything else.

—Havelock Ellis

Call them, if you please, bookmakers, not authors; range them rather among second-hand dealers than plagiarists.

—Voltaire (François Marie Arouet) (1694–1778)

The difference between a bad artist and a good one is: The bad artist seems to copy a great deal; the good one really does.

—William Blake (1757–1827)

The immature poet imitates; the mature poet plagiarizes.

—T. S. Eliot

The immature artist imitates. Mature artists steal.

—Lionel Trilling

*   *

Goethe said there would be little left of him if he were to discard what he owed to others.   —Charlotte Cushman

Remember that God made your eyes—so don't shade your eyes—
plagiarize.   —Tom Lehrer

PLANET EARTH

If we want to make something really superb of this planet, there is
nothing whatever that can stop us.   —Shepherd Mead

I doubt if even China can equal our record of soil destruction.

—Henry Wallace

Take what you can use and let the rest go by.   —Ken Kesey

In wilderness is the preservation of the world.

—Henry David Thoreau (1817–1862)

I'd be astounded if this planet is still going by fifty years from now.
I don't think we will reach 2000. It would be miraculous.

—Alistair Cooke

Maybe a person's time would be as well spent raising food as raising
money to buy food.   —Frank A. Clark

We are wide-eyed in contemplating the possibility that life may exist
elsewhere in the universe, but we wear blinders when contemplating
the possibilities of life on earth.   —Norman Cousins

Today the pressure is on, but we have a choice. Mankind can either
lie down and give up, or we can use all of our productive skills and
knowledge to work for a better future.   —Earl Butz

Is civilization progress? The challenge, I think, is clear; and, as
clearly, the final answer will be given not by our amassing of knowledge, or by the discoveries of our science, or by the speed of our
aircraft, but by the effect our civilized activities as a whole have
upon the quality of our planet's life—the life of plants and animals
as well as that of men.   —Charles A. Lindbergh, Jr.

The service we render others is really the rent we pay for our room
on the earth.   —Sir Wilfred Grenfell

We are going to have to find ways of organizing ourselves coopera-
tively, sanely, scientifically, harmonically and in regenerative spontaneity with the rest of humanity around earth . . . We are not
going to be able to operate our spaceship earth successfully nor for
much longer unless we see it as a whole spaceship and our fate as
common. It has to be everybody or nobody.

—Buckminster Fuller

The most important fact about Spaceship Earth: an instruction book didn't come with it. —Buckminster Fuller

The most dreadful thing of all is that millions of people in the poor countries are going to starve to death before our eyes . . . upon our television sets. —C. P. Snow

I knew that there was something in the nature of homesickness called nostalgia, but I found that there is also a homesickness for the earth. I don't know what it should be called but it does exist. There is nothing more splendid . . . than Mother Earth on which one can stand, work and breathe the wind of the steppes.
—Major Gherman Titov

This could be such a beautiful world. —Rosalind Welcher

The magnificence of mountains, the serenity of nature—nothing is safe from the idiot marks of man's passing. —Loudon Wainwright (On second thought, when the meek eventually inherit the earth it will probably be in such a condition that nobody would have it.)

The lunatic asylum of the solar system.
—Samuel Parkes Cadman

The American people think technology waves a wand and the game goes on . . . Within the next decade there are going to be severe world-wide shortages of metals and raw materials.
—Stewart L. Udall

Our lifetime may be the last that will be lived out in a technological society. —Isaac Asimov

The United States need never run out of its prized petroleum products as long as it has abundant coal. —Carl E. Bagge

A citizen of an advanced industrialized nation consumes in six months the energy and raw materials that have to last the citizen of a developing country his entire lifetime. —Maurice F. Strong

"dear boss it wont be long now it wont be long before man is making deserts on the earth so that nothing but ants and centipedes and scorpions can find a living on it . . . it wont be long till the earth is barren as the moon . . . i relay this information without any fear that humanity will take warning and reform signed archy."
—Don Marquis

Man has lost the capacity to foresee and to forestall. He will end by destroying the earth. —Albert Schweitzer

What is the use of a house if you haven't got a tolerable planet to put it on? —Henry David Thoreau (1817–1862)

In the long run, it is the sum total of the actions of millions of individuals that constitute effective group action . . . get involved in political action. Otherwise, we shall all eventually find ourselves stranded in space on a dead Spaceship Earth with no place to go and no way to get there. —Dr. Paul R. Ehrlich

The planet and mankind are in grave danger of irreversible catastrophe . . . wars of mass destruction, overpopulation, pollution, and the depletion of resources. —Richard A. Falk

We see the opening of an era: it is an era of seeking beyond the confines of our atmosphere; may it be also an era of awakening to the countries of our Earth. —Bertrand de Jouvenel

Remember when atmospheric contaminants were romantically called stardust? —Lane Olinghouse

The U. S. consumes more energy for air conditioning than the total energy consumption of the 800 million people in China.
—Robert O. Anderson

There is a sufficiency in the world for man's need but not for man's greed. —Mohandas Gandhi

---

Ever since our love for machines replaced the love we used to have for our fellow man, catastrophes proceed to increase.
—Man Ray

The fault is in us. —Hannah Arendt

* *

Anything we can conceive, we can achieve—the most underdeveloped territory in the world is under our scalps, and I would that we have calluses on our minds but not bunions on our countryside!
—Dorothy M. Carl

I hope to be remembered as someone who made the earth a little more beautiful. —Justice William O. Douglas

---

Is our environment to be handed over to ceaseless, unthinking development by those who think only of what it could yield to them today? . . . There's a planet who needs your help.
—Garrett De Bell

If we follow the advice of these people [those who oppose nuclear power, increased strip-mining, and stepped-up offshore oil exploration], we might as well go back into the cave. —Hans Bethe

* *

The wild places are where we began. When they end, so do we.
—David Brower

If all these nature kooks had their way, America would still be a wilderness from coast to coast. Thank God there are at least a few businessmen who care about the Gross National Product.
—Harley G. Waller

PLANNING

Our plans miscarry because they have no aim. When a man does not know what harbor he is making for, no wind is the right wind.
—Seneca (4 B.C.–A.D. 65)

We must ask where we are and whither we are tending.
—Abraham Lincoln (1809–1865)

Nothing is more terrible than activity without insight.
—Thomas Carlyle (1795–1881)

Quite as important as legislation is vigilant oversight of administration.   —Woodrow Wilson

PLEASURE AND PAIN

The great pleasure in life is doing what people say you cannot do.
—Walter Bagehot (1826–1877)

Pleasure is frail like a dewdrop, while it laughs it dies.
—Rabindranath Tagore

Pleasure is the only thing to live for. Nothing ages like happiness.
—Oscar Wilde (1854–1900)

I do not believe in doing for pleasure things I do not like to do.
—Don Herold

To the person with a toothache, even if the world is tottering, there is nothing more important than a visit to a dentist.
—George Bernard Shaw

There is no such thing as pure pleasure; some anxiety always goes with it.   —Ovid (43? B.C.–A.D. 18)

POETRY

Poetry is the rhythmical creation of beauty in words.
—Edgar Allan Poe (1809–1849)

Poetry is the presentment in musical form to the imagination, of noble grounds for the noble emotions.

—John Ruskin (1819–1900)

Poetry is the synthesis of hyacinths and biscuits.

—Carl Sandburg

Poetry is fact given over to imagery.   —Rod McKuen

Poetry [involves] the mysteries of the irrational perceived through rational words.   —Vladimir Nabokov

Poetry is the art of uniting pleasure with truth.

—Samuel Johnson (1709–1784)

Poetry is the spontaneous overflow of powerful feelings . . . recollected in tranquillity.   —William Wordsworth (1770–1850)

Poetry is trouble dunked in tears.   —Gwyn Thomas

Poetry is a report of some human experience ordered in terms of concepts involving a value judgment.   —Joseph Wood Krutch

Poetry is not an assertion of truth, but the making of that truth more fully real to us.   —T. S. Eliot

Poetry is simply the most beautiful, impressive, and widely effective mode of saying things.   —Matthew Arnold (1822–1888) (Poetry is that which is lost in translation.)

All poetry [is] putting the infinite within the finite.

—Robert Browning (1812–1889)

I've written some poetry I don't understand myself.

—Carl Sandburg

I take as metaphysical poetry that in which what is ordinarily apprehensible only by thought is brought within the grasp of feeling, or that in which what is ordinarily only felt is transformed into thought without ceasing to be feeling.   —T. S. Eliot

I should define a good poem as one that makes complete sense; and says all it has to say memorably and economically, and has been written for no other than poetic reasons.   —Robert Graves

I could no more define poetry than a terrier can define a rat.

—A. E. Housman

Does the poet create, originate, initiate the thing called a poem, or is his behavior merely the product of his genetic and environmental histories?   —B. F. Skinner

The success of the poem is determined not by how much the poet felt in writing it, but by how much the reader feels in reading it.

—John Ciardi

If . . . it makes my whole body so cold no fire can warm me, I know that is poetry.   —Emily Dickinson (1830–1886)

The poet is a liar who always speaks the truth.

—Jean Cocteau

You will not find poetry anywhere unless you bring some of it with you.   —Joseph Joubert (1754–1824)

Inside every man there is a poet who died young.

—Stefan Kanfer

When power leads man towards arrogance, poetry reminds him of his limitations. When power narrows the area of man's concern, poetry reminds him of the richness and diversity of his existence. When power corrupts, poetry cleanses.   —John F. Kennedy

"It's like the question of the authorship of the *Iliad*," said Mr. Cardan. "The author of that poem is either Homer or, if not Homer, somebody else of the same name."   —Aldous Huxley

There are two ways of disliking poetry: one way is to dislike it, the other is to read Pope.   —Oscar Wilde (1854–1900)

Writing free verse is like playing tennis with the net down. —Robert Frost (On second thought, free verse is the triumph of mind over meter.)

Poets are born, not paid.   —Wilson Mizner

Publishing a volume of verse is like dropping a rose petal down the Grand Canyon and waiting for the echo.   —Don Marquis

*   *

He does not write at all whose poems no man reads.
                    —Martial (A.D. 40–102)

To have great poetry there must be great audiences, too.
                    —Walt Whitman (1819–1892)

*   *

I think that one possible definition of our modern culture is that it is one in which nine-tenths of our intellectuals can't read any poetry.   —Randall Jarrell

Indifference to poetry is one of the most conspicuous characteristics of the human race.   —Robert S. Lynd

*   *

A poet dares be just so clear and no clearer . . . He unzips the veil from beauty, but does not remove it. A poet utterly clear is a trifle glaring.   —E. B. White

When you read and understand a poem, comprehending its rich and formal meanings, then you master chaos a little.
                                                          —Stephen Spender

---

A poem begins in delight and ends in wisdom.   —Robert Frost

A poem should not mean/But be.   —Archibald MacLeish

POLLUTION

Pollution is nothing but the resources we are not harvesting. We allow them to disperse because we've been ignorant of their value.
                                                      —Buckminster Fuller

Sanctions against polluters are feeble and out of date, and, in any case, are rarely invoked.   —Ralph Nader

. . . the thoughts of Plato and Machiavelli . . . don't seem quite enough armor for a world beset with splitting the atoms, urban guerrillas, nineteen varieties of psychotherapists, amplified guitars, napalm, computers, astronauts, and an atmosphere polluted simultaneously with auto exhaust and TV commercials.
                                                          —John Fischer

While Chrysler competes with Buick for the getaway, cancer competes with emphysema for the layaway.   —Robert Rienow

There is a definite association between community air pollution and high mortality rates.   —Dr. Leroy E. Burney

The planet and mankind are in grave danger of irreversible catastrophe . . . wars of mass destruction, overpopulation, pollution, and the depletion of resources.   —Richard A. Falk

No witchcraft, no enemy action had silenced the rebirth of new life in this stricken world. The people had done it themselves.
                                                          —Rachel Carson

Only within the moment of time represented by the present century has one species—man—acquired significant power to alter the nature of his world.   —Rachel Carson

The most alarming of all man's assaults upon the environment is the contamination of air, earth, rivers, and sea . . . this pollution is for the most part irrecoverable.   —Rachel Carson

The continued pollution of the earth, if unchecked, will eventually destroy the fitness of this planet as a place for human life . . . Nuclear war . . . would reduce [combatant nations] to chaotic remnants, incapable of supporting an organized effort for recovery . . . world-wide radioactive contamination, epidemics, ecological disasters, and possibly climatic changes would so gravely affect the stability of the biosphere as to threaten human survival everywhere on the earth.   —Barry Commoner

---

To look to private business for solutions to pollution may be futile. Its horizons are deliberately limited to those factors which are considered to be of immediate importance, principally economic, and the hidden costs to the society at large tend to be ignored.

—Frank M. Potter, Jr.

The most important pathological effects of pollution are extremely delayed and indirect.   —René Dubos

*   *

The fouling of the nest which has been typical of man's activity in the past on a local scale now seems to be extending to the whole system.   —Kenneth Boulding

We are locked into a system of "fouling our own nest," so long as we behave only as independent, rational, free-enterprisers.

—Garrett Hardin

POTENTIAL

Treat people as if they were what they ought to be and you help them to become what they are capable of being.

—Johann W. von Goethe (1749–1832)

By virtue of being born to humanity, every human being has a right to the development and fulfillment of his potentialities as a human being.   —Ashley Montagu

There is no meaning to life except the meaning man gives his life by the unfolding of his powers.   —Erich Fromm (On second thought, when asked what he considered to be the potential of a twenty-year-old rookie, Casey Stengel said, "Well, in ten years he has a good chance of becoming thirty.")

Abasement, degradation is simply the manner of life of the man who has refused to be what it is his duty to be.   —José Ortega y Gasset (We have left undone those things which we ought to have done.)

One of the saddest experiences which can come to a human being is to awaken, gray-haired and wrinkled, near the close of an unproductive career, to the fact that all through the years he has been using only a small part of himself.   —V. W. Burrows

Compared to what we ought to be, we are only half awake. We are making use of only a small part of our physical and mental resources. Stating the thing broadly, the human individual thus lives far within his limits. He possesses power of various sorts which he habitually fails to use.   —William James

The deepest personal defeat suffered by human beings is constituted by the difference between what one was capable of becoming and what one has in fact become.   —Ashley Montagu

If you're going to write, don't pretend to write down. It's going to be the best you can do, and it's the fact that it's the best you can do that kills you.   —Dorothy Parker

POVERTY

I've known what it is to be hungry, but I always went right to a restaurant.   —Ring Lardner

Poverty must have many satisfactions, else there would not be so many poor people.   —Don Herold

Very few people can afford to be poor.
                                        —George Bernard Shaw

Poverty is an anomaly to rich people; it is very difficult to make out why people who want dinner do not ring the bell.
                                        —Walter Bagehot (1826–1877)

Poverty . . . has no sharper pang than this, that it makes men ridiculous.   —Juvenal (60?–140)

. . . and place the real disgrace of poverty not in owning to the fact but in declining to struggle against it.
                                        —Thucydides (471?–400? B.C.)

The poor you always have with you.   —Jesus (John 12:8)

War on nations change maps. War on poverty maps change.
                                        —Muhammad Ali

You never find people laboring to convince you that you may live very happily upon a plentiful income.
                                        —Samuel Johnson (1709–1784)

For every talent that poverty has stimulated it has blighted a hundred. —John Gardner

If a free society cannot help the many who are poor, it cannot save the few who are rich. —John F. Kennedy

The law, in its majestic equality, forbids the rich as well as the poor, to sleep under bridges, to beg in the streets and to steal bread.
—Anatole France

The critics were asking that we postpone consideration of the causes of poverty until no one was poor. —John Kenneth Galbraith

The conspicuously wealthy turn up urging the character-building value of privation for the poor. —John Kenneth Galbraith

The leaders of the French Revolution excited the poor against the rich; this made the rich poor, but it never made the poor rich.
—Fisher Ames (1758–1808)

How can you trust people who are poor and own no property? . . . Inequality of property will exist as long as liberty exists.
—Alexander Hamilton (1757–1804)

Those who suffer levels of life well below those that are possible, even though they live better than medieval knights or Asian peasants, are poor. —Michael Harrington

Here is the most familiar version of social blindness: "The poor are that way because they are afraid of work. And anyway they all have big cars. If they were like me they could pay their own way. But they prefer to live on the dole and cheat the taxpayers."
—Michael Harrington

Must the hunger become anger and the anger fury before anything will be done? —John Steinbeck

Modern poverty is not the poverty that was blest in the Sermon on the Mount. —George Bernard Shaw

Every stable government in history has depended on the resignation of the poor to being poor.
—Félicité de Lamennais (1782–1854)

Advertising is designed to create, and does create, dissatisfaction . . . Advertising intended for an audience that can afford what it offers also works . . . on those who cannot afford it; it inflames the desires of the poor without offering them any satisfaction at all. Perhaps the poor are "better off than ever before," as some say, but they can hardly be expected to be satisfied with this after watching television . . . Television might justly be called a *riot box*.
—Charles A. Reich

Not he who has little, but he who wishes more, is poor.
—Seneca (4 B.C.–A.D. 65) (What troubles the poor is the money they can't get, and what troubles the rich is the money they can't keep.)

We have not yet reached the goal but . . . we shall soon, with the help of God, be in sight of the day when poverty shall be banished from this nation.   —Herbert Hoover (How soon is a political *soon*?)

This Administration here and now declares unconditional war on poverty in America.   —Lyndon B. Johnson

*   *

What is the use of being kind to a poor man?
                —Marcus Tullius Cicero (106–43 B.C.)

Why should anybody be interested in some old man who was a failure?   —Ernest Hemingway

*   *

The big majority of Americans, who are comparatively well off, have developed an ability to have enclaves of people living in the greatest misery without almost noticing them.
                —Gunnar Myrdal

America is an enormous frosted cupcake in the middle of millions of starving people.   —Gloria Steinem

---

Give me your tired, your poor,/Your huddled masses yearning to breathe free,/The wretched refuse of your teeming shore./Send these, the homeless, the tempest-tossed to me,/I lift my lamp beside the golden door.   —Emma Lazarus (1849–1887)

The worst country to be poor in is America.
                —Arnold Toynbee

*   *

I have the impression that when we talk so confidently of liberty, we are unaware of the awful servitude . . . of poverty when means are so small that there is literally no choice.   —Barbara Ward

Of all the preposterous assumptions of humanity over humanity, nothing exceeds most of the criticisms made on the habits of the poor by the well-housed, well-warmed, and well-fed.
                —Herman Melville (1819–1891)

* *

Wealth is conspicuous, but poverty hides.   —James Reston

You don't have to look for distress; it is screaming at you!
                                        —Samuel Beckett

POWER

The measure of man is what he does with power.
                              —Pittacus (650?–569? B.C.)

If I were running the world I would have it rain only between 2 and
5 A.M. Anyone who was out then ought to get wet.
                              —William Lyon Phelps

The first and great commandment is, Don't let them scare you.
                              —Elmer Davis

The reputation of power *is* power.
                              —Thomas Hobbes (1588–1679)

Beware the man who rises to power from one suspender.
                              —Edgar Lee Masters

Power always has to be kept in check; power exercised in secret,
especially under the cloak of *national security,* is doubly dangerous.
                              —William Proxmire

Power breeds isolation. Isolation leads to the capricious use of
power. In turn, the capricious use of power breaks down the normal
channels of communication between the leader and the people
whom he leads. This ultimately means the deterioration of power
and with it the capacity to sustain unity in our society. This is the
problem we face today.   —George Reedy

The ideas of economists and political philosophers, both when they
are right and when they are wrong, are more powerful than is commonly understood. Indeed, the world is ruled by little else.
                              —John Maynard Keynes

Power may justly be compared to a great river; while kept within its
bounds it is both beautiful and useful, but when it overflows its
banks, it is then too impetuous to be stemmed; it bears down all
before it, and brings destruction and desolation wherever it comes.
                              —Andrew Hamilton (d. 1741)

Idealism is the noble toga that political gentlemen drape over their
will to power.   —Aldous Huxley (Today we call it *pragma-
tism.*)

Even weak men when united are powerful.
—Friedrich Schiller (1729–1805)

To the meaningless French idealisms, Liberty, Equality, and Fraternity, we oppose the German realities, Infantry, Cavalry, and Artillery.   —Prince Bernhard von Bülow

The wrong sort of people are always in power because they would not be in power if they were not the wrong sort of people.
—Jon Wynne-Tyson

The lesson of all history warns us that we should negotiate only when our military superiority is so convincing that we can achieve our objective at the conference table, and deny the aggressor theirs.
—Richard M. Nixon

While nobody can seriously maintain that the greatest number must have the greatest wisdom, or the greatest virtue, there is no denying that, under modern social conditions, they are likely to have the most power.   —Walter Lippmann

---

Fortunately, there are still those among us who have a healthy irreverence toward power, even as they seek it.   —Weir Reid

I often say of George Washington that he was one of the few in the whole history of the world who was not carried away by power.
—Robert Frost

*   *

Those in power want only to perpetuate it.
—Justice William O. Douglas

No one with absolute power can be trusted to give it up even in part.
—Justice Louis D. Brandeis

*   *

Power never takes a back step—only in the face of more power.
—Malcolm X

Is it altogether a Utopian dream, that once in history a ruling class might be willing to make the great surrender, and permit social change to come about without hatred, turmoil, and waste of human life?   —Upton Sinclair

*   *

I could not stop something I knew was wrong and terrible. I had an awful sense of powerlessness.   —Andrei Sakharov

Power undirected by high purpose spells calamity; and high purpose by itself is utterly useless if the power to put it into effect is lacking.
—Theodore Roosevelt

*   *

Power is what men seek, and any group that gets it will abuse it. It is the same old story.   —Lincoln Steffens *(Plus ça change, plus c'est la même chose.)*

Power intoxicates men. When a man is intoxicated by alcohol, he can recover, but when intoxicated by power, he seldom recovers.
—James F. Byrnes

*   *

No extraordinary power should be lodged in any one individual.
—Thomas Paine (1737–1809)

Power does not corrupt. Fear corrupts, perhaps the fear of a loss of power.   —John Steinbeck

---

As for the men in power, they are so anxious to establish the myth of infallibility that they do their utmost to ignore truth.
—Boris Pasternak

Power does not corrupt men; but fools, if they get into a position of power, corrupt power.   —George Bernard Shaw

*   *

Power dements even more than it corrupts, lowering the guard of foresight and raising the haste of action.
—Will and Ariel Durant

Power corrupts, but lack of power corrupts absolutely.
—Adlai Stevenson

*   *

The only prize much cared for by the powerful is power. The prize of the general is not a bigger tent, but command.
—Oliver Wendell Holmes, Jr.

Power corrupts the few, while weakness corrupts the many.
—Eric Hoffer

*   *

I have never been able to conceive how any rational being could propose happiness to himself from the exercise of power over others.
—Thomas Jefferson (1743–1826)

When asked why he wanted to become President, JFK replied, "Because that's where the power is!"

PRAISE

Modesty is the only sure bait when you angle for praise.
— G. K. Chesterton

The deepest principle of *Human Nature* is the craving to be appreciated. —William James (The reason flattery makes people feel good is because they know they deserve it.)

Vanity is so secure in the heart of man that everyone wants to be admired: even I who write this, and you who read this.
—Blaise Pascal (1623–1662) (You can flatter any man by telling him he's the kind of man who can't be flattered.)

The hunger for applause is the source of all conscious literature and heroism. —Duc de La Rochefoucauld (1613–1680)

He who refuses praise the first time that it is offered does so because he would hear it a second time. —Duc de La Rochefoucauld

I much prefer a compliment, insincere or not, to sincere criticism.
—Plautus (254?–184 B.C.) (Man lives by praise; most of us would rather be hurt by flattery than helped by criticism.)

The trouble with most of us is that we would rather be ruined by praise than saved by criticism. —Norman Vincent Peale

PREJUDICE

I am free of all prejudices. I hate every one equally.
—W. C. Fields

If we were to wake up some morning and find that everyone was the same race, creed and color, we would find some other causes for prejudice by noon. —Senator George Aiken

All looks yellow to a jaundiced eye.
—Alexander Pope (1688–1744)

Sentence first, verdict afterwards.
—Lewis Carroll (Charles Lutwidge Dodgson) (1832–1898)

In Rhodesia a white truck driver passed a group of idle natives and muttered, "They're lazy brutes!" A few hours later he saw natives heaving two-hundred pound sacks of grain onto a truck, singing in rhythm to their work. "Savages!" he grumbled. "What do you expect?" —Gordon W. Allport

Prejudice is an opinion without judgment.
                    —Voltaire (François Marie Arouet) (1694–1778)

Prejudice is the reason of fools.   —Voltaire

Prejudice may be defined as thinking ill of others without sufficient warrant.   —Gordon W. Allport (Or it might be defined as the lazy man's substitute for thinking.)

A prejudice is a vagrant opinion without visible means of support.
                                                —Ambrose Bierce

A "pattern of reaction" is the sum total of the ways we act in response to events, to words and to symbols . . . in their more obvious forms we call them prejudices.   —S. I. Hayakawa (On second thought, the difference between a prejudice and a conviction is that you can explain a conviction without getting mad.)

The mind of the bigot is like the pupil of the eye; the more light you pour upon it, the more it will contract.   —Oliver Wendell Holmes, Jr. (In other words, when a bigot answers your questions, he resents it if you question his answers.)

Nothing is so firmly believed as that which is least known.
—Michel de Montaigne (1533–1592) (On the other hand, prejudice is a great laborsaving device—it enables you to form an opinion without having to dig up the facts.)

Prejudgments become prejudices only if they are not reversible when exposed to new knowledge.   —Gordon W. Allport

The prejudices of ignorance are more easily removed than the prejudices of interest; the first are blindly adopted, the second willfully preferred.   —George Bancroft (1800–1891)

Individuals having no religious affiliation show on the average less prejudice than do church members.   —Gordon W. Allport

It is never too late to give up your prejudices.
                        —Henry David Thoreau (1817–1862)

Most men, when they think they are thinking, are merely rearranging their prejudices.   —Knute Rockne

It is well for people who think to change their minds occasionally in order to keep them clean. For those who do not think, it is best at least to rearrange their prejudices once in a while.
                                                —Luther Burbank

*   *

Prejudice is never easy unless it can pass itself off for reason.
—William Hazlitt (1778–1830)

A prejudiced person will almost certainly claim that he has sufficient warrant for his views.   —Gordon W. Allport

*   *

Opinions founded on prejudice are always sustained with the greatest violence.   —Francis Jeffrey (1773–1850)

If we believe absurdities we shall commit atrocities.
—Voltaire (François Marie Arouet) (1694–1778)

*   *

The multitude, convinced that the Christians were atheists who ate human flesh and thought incest no crime, displayed against them a fury so passionate as to embarrass and alarm their rulers.
—Matthew Arnold (1822–1888)

A man convinced against his will/Is of the same opinion still.
—Samuel Butler (1612–1680)

*   *

There are few liberals . . . who have not a well-furnished compartment of race prejudice, even if it is usually suppressed.
—Gunnar Myrdal

Everyone is a prisoner of his own experiences. No one can eliminate prejudices—just recognize them.   —Edward R. Murrow

*   *

There are only two ways to be quite unprejudiced and impartial. One is to be completely ignorant. The other is to be completely indifferent. Bias and prejudice are attitudes to be kept in hand, not attitudes to be avoided.   —Charles P. Curtis

One may no more live in the world without picking up the moral prejudices of the world than one will be able to go to hell without perspiring.   —H. L. Mencken

*   *

Prejudice not being founded on reason cannot be removed by argument.   —Samuel Johnson (1709–1784)

In the matter of therapy, humanity is in the highest degree irrational, so that there is no prospect of influencing it by reasonable arguments . . . Against prejudice one can do nothing.
—Sigmund Freud

Ignorance is less remote from truth than prejudice.
—Denis Diderot (1713–1784)

The people who are the most bigoted are the people who have no convictions at all. —G. K. Chesterton

* *

It is time to turn from quarrels and to build our White ramparts again. The alliance with foreign races means nothing but death for us. —Charles A. Lindbergh, Jr.

The chief cause of human errors is to be found in the prejudices picked up in childhood. —René Descartes (1596–1650)

* *

Deep-rooted prejudices entertained by the whites; ten thousand recollections by the blacks of the injuries they have sustained . . . will divide us into parties, and . . . will probably never end but in the extermination of the one or the other race.
—Thomas Jefferson (1743–1826)

I am bigoted enough to believe in white supremacy in the South.
—George Deatherage

I deplore the fact that throughout the South today subversive elements are attempting to convince the Negro that he should be placed on social equality with white people. —Martin Dies

Given a thimbleful of facts we rush to make generalizations as large as a tub. —Gordon W. Allport

THE PRESIDENCY / PRESIDENTS

You are apprehensive of monarchy; I, of aristocracy. I would therefore have given more power to the President and less to the Senate. —John Adams (1735–1826), to Thomas Jefferson

I should like to be known as a former President who minded his own business. —Calvin Coolidge

Nothing is easier than spending public money. It does not appear to belong to anybody. The temptation is overwhelming to bestow it on somebody. —Calvin Coolidge

Politics should be the part-time profession of every citizen.
—Dwight D. Eisenhower (The President of today is the postage stamp of tomorrow.)

Once upon a time my political opponents honored me as possessing the fabulous intellectual and economic power by which I created a world-wide depression all by myself.   —Herbert Hoover

The destruction of our State governments or the annihilation of their control over the local concerns of the people would lead directly to revolution and anarchy, and finally to despotism and military domination . . . But of equal, and indeed, of incalculable importance is the union of these States, and the sacred duty of all to contribute to its preservation by a liberal support of the general government in the exercise of its just powers.
                              —Andrew Jackson (1767–1845)

Each generation . . . has a right to choose for itself the form of government it believes most promotive of its own happiness.
                              —Thomas Jefferson (1743–1826)

The care of human life and happiness . . . is the first and only legitimate object of good government.   —Thomas Jefferson

I know of no safe depository of the ultimate powers of the society but the people themselves.   —Thomas Jefferson

No man will ever bring out of the Presidency the reputation which carries him into it.   —Thomas Jefferson

To myself, personally, it brings nothing but increasing drudgery and daily loss of friends.   —Thomas Jefferson

Our safest guide to what we do abroad is always what we do at home.   —Lyndon B. Johnson

When we got into office, the thing that surprised me most was to find that things were just as bad as we'd been saying they were.
                              —John F. Kennedy

Senators who go down to defeat in vain defense of a single principle will not be on hand to fight for that or any other principle in the future.   —John F. Kennedy

This country, with its institutions, belongs to the people who inhabit it. Whenever they shall grow weary of the existing Government, they can exercise their constitutional right of amending it, or their revolutionary right to dismember or overthrow it.
                              —Abraham Lincoln (1809–1865)

The legitimate object of government is to do for a community of people whatever they need to have done, but cannot do at all, in their separate and individual capacities.

—Abraham Lincoln (1809–1865)

We do our best that we know how at the moment, and if it doesn't turn out, we modify it.   —Franklin Delano Roosevelt

The successful politician is he who says what everybody is thinking most often and in the loudest voice.   —Theodore Roosevelt

I sit here all day trying to persuade people to do the things they ought to have sense enough to do without my persuading them. That's all the powers of the President amount to.

—Harry S Truman

The Buck Stops Here.   —Harry S Truman

The basis of our political systems is the right of the people to make and to alter their constitutions of government.

—George Washington (1732–1799)

I know not how better to describe our form of government in a single phrase than by calling it a government by the chairmen of the Standing Committees of Congress.   —Woodrow Wilson

The informing function of Congress should be even preferred to its legislative function.   —Woodrow Wilson

They say Wilson has blundered. Perhaps he has but I notice he usually blunders forward.   —Thomas Alva Edison

I would rather be right than President.

—Henry Clay (1777–1852)

The office of President is such a bastardized thing, half royalty and half democracy, that nobody knows whether to genuflect or spit.

—Jimmy Breslin

When I was a boy I was told that anybody could become President; I'm beginning to believe it.   —Clarence Darrow

The duty of the President to see that the laws be executed is a duty that does not go beyond the laws or require him to achieve more than Congress sees fit to leave within his power.

—Oliver Wendell Holmes, Jr.

It is the President's decision to choose how to impart information to the people.   —John Ehrlichman

---

If you are as happy, my dear sir, on entering this house as I am in leaving it and returning home, you are the happiest man in this country.

—James Buchanan (1791–1868), to Abraham Lincoln

I have been told I was on the road to hell, but I had no idea it was just a mile down the road with a Dome on it.

—Abraham Lincoln

*   *

The necessary and constructive use of government must not lead to a doctrinaire and expedient use of government.

—Dwight D. Eisenhower

No public man can be just a little crooked.   —Herbert Hoover

---

When a man has cast his longing eye on offices, a rottenness begins in his conduct.   —Thomas Jefferson

When a man assumes a public trust, he should consider himself as public property.   —Thomas Jefferson

*   *

I am a man of limited talents from a small town. I don't seem to grasp that I am President.   —Warren G. Harding

Government after all is a very simple thing.

—Warren G. Harding

*   *

In all my years of public life I have never obstructed justice . . . Your President is no crook!   —Richard M. Nixon

In America any boy may become President and I suppose it's just one of the risks he takes.   —Adlai Stevenson

PRIDE

Though pride is not a virtue, it is the parent of many virtues.

—M. C. Collins

Likeness begets Love; yet proud Men hate one another.

—Thomas Fuller (1608–1661)

There is a paradox in pride: it makes some men ridiculous, but prevents others from becoming so.   —Charles Caleb Colton (1780–1832) (Would the boy you were be proud of the man you are?)

A man never feels more important than when he receives a telegram containing more than ten words.   —George Ade

No one in the world except a mortified saint is actually displeased at the fact of becoming rather important.   —R. H. Benson

One of the best temporary cures for pride and affectation is sea-sickness; a man who wants to vomit never puts on airs.
—Josh Billings (Henry Wheeler Shaw) (1818–1885)

Pride has a greater share than goodness of heart in the remonstrances we make to those who are guilty of faults; we reprove not so much with a view to correct them as to persuade them that we are exempt from those faults ourselves.
—Duc de La Rochefoucauld (1613–1680)

PRINCIPLES

Nothing can bring you peace but the triumph of principles.
—Ralph Waldo Emerson (1803–1882)

It is easy to be tolerant of the principles of other people if you have none of your own.   —Sir Herbert Samuel

And suddenly, reaching the last frontiers, when man is already stricken with poverty and nakedness and deprived of everything that seemingly adorns his life—then he finds in himself enough firmness to support himself on the final step and give up his life, but not his principles.   —Alexander I. Solzhenitsyn

One cannot found a religion by putting together principles.
—Erich Fromm

In matters of principle, stand like a rock; in matters of taste, swim with the current.   —Thomas Jefferson (1743–1826)

Our differences are politics. Our agreements, principles.
—William McKinley

Let a man proclaim a new principle. Public sentiment will surely be on the other side.   —Thomas B. Reed

---

I would rather be an opportunist and float than go to the bottom with my principles round my neck.   —Stanley Baldwin (In politics a man must learn to rise above principle.)

You can't learn too soon that the most useful thing about a principle is that it can always be sacrificed to expediency.
—Somerset Maugham

Back of every noble life there are principles that have fashioned it.
—George Horace Lorimer

It is easier to fight for one's principles than to live up to them.
                                                —Alfred Adler

*   *

The trial of principle: without it a man hardly knows whether he
is honest or not.   —Henry Fielding (1707–1754)

It doesn't pay well to fight for what we believe in.   —Lillian
Hellman (On second thought, if you don't believe in principle you
can still collect the interest.)

PROBLEMS

A problem well stated is a problem half solved.
                                —Charles F. Kettering

It isn't that they can't see the solution. It is that they can't see the
problem.   —G. K. Chesterton

To be human is no solution, any more than ceasing to be so.
                                —Emile M. Cioran

We are confronted by a condition, not a theory.
                                —Grover Cleveland

In such a strait the wisest may well be perplexed and the boldest
staggered.   —Edmund Burke (1729–1797)

The only problems money can solve are money problems. Many
of the problems the world faces today are the eventual result of
short-term measures taken last century.   —Jay W. Forrester

The certainties of one age are the problems of the next.
                                —R. H. Tawney

The message from the moon . . . is that no problem need any
longer be considered insoluble.
                                —Norman Cousins

We live in the midst of alarms; anxiety beclouds the future; we
expect some new disaster with each newspaper we read.
                                —Abraham Lincoln (1809–1865)

Probe the earth and see where your main roots run.
                                —Henry David Thoreau (1817–1862)

A good problem statement often includes: (a) what is known, (b)
what is unknown, and (c) what is sought.   —Edward Hodnett

To solve a problem it is necessary to think. It is necessary to think even to decide what facts to collect.

—Robert Maynard Hutchins

PROFIT

To get profit without risk, experience without danger, and reward without work, is as impossible as it is to live without being born.
—A. P. Gouthey

There is no way of keeping profits up but by keeping wages down.
—David Ricardo (1772–1823)

The society of excess profits for some and small returns for others, the society in which a few prey upon the many, the society in which few took advantage and many took great disadvantage, must pass.   —Wendell L. Willkie

In freeing peoples . . . our country's blessing will also come; for profit follows righteousness.   —Senator Albert J. Beveridge

Is it not . . . too true that capitalists have often seemed to regard the men whom they used as mere instruments of profit, whose physical and mental powers it was legitimate to exploit with as slight cost to themselves as possible, either of money or of sympathy?
—Woodrow Wilson

The worst crime against working people is a company which fails to operate at a profit.   —Samuel Gompers

It is a socialist idea that making profits is a vice; I consider the real vice is making losses.   —Winston Churchill

No man profiteth but by the loss of others.
—Michel de Montaigne (1533–1592)

What is a man profited, if he shall gain the whole world, and lose his own soul?   —The Bible (Matthew 16:26)

The man who holds that every human right is secondary to his profit must now give way to the advocate of human welfare.
—Theodore Roosevelt

PROGRESS

What we call "progress" is the exchange of one nuisance for another nuisance.   —Havelock Ellis

To make headway, improve your head.   —B. C. Forbes

Is it progress if a cannibal uses knife and fork?
                                        —Stanislaw J. Lec

Progress is the process whereby the human race is getting rid of whiskers, the vermiform appendix, and God.
                                        —H. L. Mencken

There's always an easy solution to every human problem—neat, plausible and wrong.   —H. L. Mencken

The biggest problem in the world/Could have been solved when it was small.   —Witter Bynner (On second thought, the trouble with being tolerant is that people think you don't understand the problem.)

It is in the realm of uncertainties that progress, if it is ever encountered, must lie.   —Edward Searles

You can't sit on the lid of progress. If you do, you will be blown to pieces.   —Henry J. Kaiser

For most Americans, progress means accepting what is new because it is new, and discarding what is old because it is old.
                                        —Lewis Mumford

Those who speak most of progress measure it by quantity and not by quality.   —George Santayana

Nothing but the victory of laughter over dogma.
                                        —Benjamin Decasseres

The worst superstition of the nineteenth and twentieth centuries is called progress. It is certain there will be no progress until there is an end to that kind of progress.   —George Faludy

In their worship of the machine, many Americans have settled for something less than a full life, something that is hardly even a tenth of life, or a hundredth of a life. They have confused progress with mechanization.   —Lewis Mumford

You've got to be a fool to want to stop the march of time.
                                        —Pierre Auguste Renoir

Planned obsolescence is another word for progress.
                                        —James Jeffrey Roche

Every step of progress means a duty repudiated, and a scripture torn up.   —George Bernard Shaw

The test of our progress is not whether we add more to the abundance of those who have much; it is whether we provide enough for those who have too little.   —Franklin Delano Roosevelt

The reasonable man adapts himself to the world; the unreasonable one persists in trying to adapt the world to himself. Therefore all progress depends on the unreasonable man.

—George Bernard Shaw

In times like these, it helps to recall that there have *always* been times like these.   —Paul Harvey

A hundred years from now, I dare say, some dreamy collector will pay a cool thousand for an old milk bottle, and I wish I had the equivalent for what my hot-water bag will bring in 2034. Why we should be so beguiled by the antique is a riddle that perhaps only the interior decorator can solve.   —Cornelia Otis Skinner

A fashion ten years before its time is indecent. Ten years after its time it is hideous. After a century it becomes romantic.
—James Laver (On second thought, the history of science is the only history which displays cumulative progress of knowledge, hence the progress of science is the only yardstick by which we can measure the progress of mankind.)

PROPERTY

The moment the idea is admitted into society that property is not as sacred as the laws of God . . . anarchy and tyranny commence.
—John Adams (1735–1826)

We stand for the maintenance of private property.

—Adolf Hitler

The rights and interests of the laboring man will be protected and cared for, not by the labor agitators but by the Christian men to whom God in His infinite wisdom has given the control of the property interest of this country.   —George Baer

The power of perpetuating our property in our families is one of the most valuable and interesting circumstances belonging to it, and that which tends the most to the perpetuation of society itself.
—Edmund Burke (1729–1797)

The preservation of the rights of private property was the very keystone of the arch upon which all civilized governments rest.
—Joseph H. Choate

The man who has half a million dollars in property . . . has a much higher interest in the government than the man who has little or no property.   —Noah Webster (1758–1843)

What our generation has forgotten is that the system of private property is the most important guaranty of freedom, not only for those who own property, but scarcely less for those who do not.
—Friedrich Hayek

In every society where property exists there will ever be a struggle between rich and poor. Mixed in one assembly, equal laws can never be expected; they will either be made by the members to plunder the few who are rich, or by the influential to fleece the many who are poor.   —John Adams

But above all, a prince must refrain from taking property, for men forget the death of a father more quickly than the loss of their patrimony.   —Niccolò Machiavelli (1469–1527)

All men are created equally free and independent, and have certain inherent rights . . . among which are the enjoyment of life and liberty, with the means of acquiring and possessing property.
—George Mason (1725–1792)

Property is the fruit of labor: property is desirable; it is a positive good.   —Abraham Lincoln (1809–1865)

The only dependable foundation of personal liberty is the personal economic security of private property.   —Walter Lippmann

The reason why men enter into society is the preservation of their property.   —John Locke (1632–1704)

Democracy . . . began as a system which gave suffrage to those who had proved their worth by acquiring real property and to no other.   —John Kenneth Galbraith

The function of Government must be to favor no small group at the expense of its duty to protect the rights of personal freedom and of private property of all its citizens.
—Franklin Delano Roosevelt

. . . and when some raised the cry for the bombing of the Krupp armament plant, it was pointed out that this, after all, was private property.   —Alexander Kendrick

It's possible to own too much. A man with one watch knows what time it is; a man with two watches is never quite sure.
—Lee Segall

I would suggest the taxation of all property equally whether church or corporation.   —Ulysses S. Grant (1822–1885)

Should the working man think freely about property? Then what will become of us the rich? Should soldiers think freely about war? Then what will become of military discipline? Away with thought! Back into the shades of prejudice, lest property, morals, and war should be endangered.　　—Bertrand Russell

It is the preoccupation with possession, more than anything else, that prevents men from living freely and nobly.

　　　　　　　　　　　　　　　　　—Bertrand Russell

The interests of those who own the property used in industry . . . is that their capital should be dear and human beings cheap.

　　　　　　　　　　　　　　　　　—R. H. Tawney

In most countries, people grow fiercely possessive of their property. It is a bastion of conservatism.　　—Gordon W. Allport

Private property . . . is the creature of society and is subject to the calls of that society even to the last farthing.

　　　　　　　　　　　　　—Benjamin Franklin (1706–1790)

By abolishing private property one deprives the human love of aggression.　　—Sigmund Freud

When Marx spoke of *private property* he was not referring to *personal property*. Private property meant the means of production of the capitalist who hires property-less individuals under conditions the latter is forced to accept.　　—Erich Fromm

PSYCHIATRY

A psychiatrist is a fellow who asks you a lot of expensive questions your wife asks for nothing.　　—Joey Adams (Psychiatry enables us to correct our faults by confessing our parents' shortcomings.)

A neurotic is a man who builds a castle in the air. A psychotic is the man who lives in it. A psychiatrist is the man who collects the rent.　　—Jerome Lawrence

The psychotic says two and two are five and the neurotic knows two and two are four, and hates it.　　—Gordon Gammack

Tell us your phobias and we will tell you what you are afraid of.

　　　　　　　　　　　　　　　　　—Robert Benchley

Anybody who goes to see a psychiatrist ought to have his head examined.　　—Samuel Goldwyn

A psychiatrist is a man who goes to the Folies-Bergère and looks at the audience.　　—Mervyn Stockwood

Psychiatrist—a person who pulls habits out of rats.

　　　　　　　　　　　　　　　　　—Dr. Douglas Bush

Psychiatry is the art of teaching people how to stand on their own feet while reclining on couches.   —Shannon Fife

The Superego is that part of the personality which is soluble in alcohol.   —Professor Harold Lasswell

All of us are constantly being bombarded by particles of misplaced schizophrenia.   —Roger Price

Mental health problems do not affect three or four out of every five persons but one out of one.   —Dr. William Menninger

We're all on the same side—we're out to get me.
                                                              —Bob Schneider

We are all born mad. Some remain so.   —Samuel Beckett

I can't figure out where I leave off and everyone else begins.
                                                              —George McCabee

A psychiatrist is a person who owns a couch and charges you for lying on it.—Edwin Brock (What's more, there's nothing wrong with your sex life that the right psychoanalyst can't exaggerate.)

You learn more about yourself while campaigning for just one week than in six months spent with a psychoanalyst.
                                                              —Adlai Stevenson

The diseases of the mind are more destructive than those of the body.   —Marcus Tullius Cicero (106–43 B.C.)

In most mental illnesses the capacity to relax is as much impaired as the integrity of a bone is destroyed by fracture.
                                                              —Abraham Myerson

The ability to divorce one's mind from one's actions is a symptom of psychological aberration.   —Walter Goodman

Generous people are rarely mentally ill people.
                                                              —Dr. Karl Menninger

PUBLISHING / PUBLISHERS

Literature is like any other trade; you will never sell anything unless you go to the right shop.   —George Bernard Shaw

The talk at the clubs is that Woodrow Wilson's boom as a presidential candidate was started by the Harper publications to sell his books.   —W. A. Swanberg

Posterity—what you write for after being turned down by publishers.   —George Ade

Publishers are demons, there's no doubt about it.
—William James

A publisher lives by what he feels. Authors do too, but authors are blind moles working their solitary way along their individual tunnels; the publisher is like the Pied Piper of Hamelin, piping his way along a path he wants them to follow. —Lovat Dickson

The trouble with the publishing business is that too many people who have half a mind to write a book do so. —William Targ

You will please fix the lowest fee possible.
—Schott Publishers, to Franz Peter Schubert

When the last sheet of Dr. Johnson's lexicography was put into his hands, his printer heaved a sigh and said, "Thank God I have done with him at last!"

A book reviewer is usually a barker before the door of a publisher's circus. —Austin O'Malley

During the final stages of publishing a paper or a book, I always feel strongly repelled by my own writing . . . it appears increasingly hackneyed and banal and less worth publishing. —Konrad Lorenz (On second thought, before publishers' blurbs were invented, authors had to make their reputations by writing.)

It circulated for five years, through the halls of fifteen publishers, and finally ended up with Vanguard Press, which, as you can see, is rather deep into the alphabet. —Patrick Dennis

No author is a man of genius to his publisher.
—Heinrich Heine (1797–1856)

QUESTIONS

Where is everybody?   —Carl Sandburg (replying to the question, "What was it the last man on earth said?")

I keep six honest serving men/They taught me all I knew:/Their names are What and Why and When/And How and Where and Who.   —Rudyard Kipling

He's been that way for years—a born questioner but he hates answers.   —Ring Lardner

There are three great questions which in life we have over and over again to answer: Is it right or wrong? Is it true or false? Is it beautiful or ugly? Our education ought to help us to answer these questions.   —John Lubbock (1803–1865)

I can evade questions without help; what I need is answers.
                                                —John F. Kennedy

Scott Buchanan . . . taught me that the questions that can be answered are not worth asking.   —Milton Mayer

By nature's kindly disposition most questions which it is beyond man's power to answer do not occur to him at all.
                                                —George Santayana

Judge a man by his questions rather than by his answers.
          —Voltaire (François Marie Arouet) (1694–1778)

QUOTATIONS / QUOTING

Hush, little bright line, don't you cry,/You'll be a cliché by and by.
                                                —Fred Allen

The surest way to make a monkey of a man is to quote him.
                                                —Robert Benchley

Quoting: The act of repeating erroneously the words of another.
                                                —Ambrose Bierce

Next to being witty yourself, the best thing is being able to quote
another's wit.   —Christian N. Bovee

A good conversationalist is not one who remembers what was said,
but says what someone wants to remember.
                                                —John Mason Brown

The widsom of the wise and the experience of the ages are perpetuated by quotations.   —Benjamin Disraeli (1804–1881)

The wise make proverbs and fools repeat them.
                                        —Isaac D'Israeli (1766–1848)

It is little service to the reader to print windy, dozen-page letters
of no high quality when a few quoted phrases and a sentence of
summary would have conveyed the nature of most of them.
                                                —John Skow

In the dying world I come from, quotation is a national vice.
                                                —Evelyn Waugh

I often quote myself. It adds spice to my conversation.
                                                —George Bernard Shaw

When you see yourself quoted in print and you're sorry you said it,
it suddenly becomes a misquotation.   —Laurence J. Peter

Some for renown, on scraps of learning dote,/And think they grow
immortal as they quote.   —Edward Young (1683–1765)

You could compile the worst book in the world entirely out of selected passages from the best writers in the world.
                                                —G. K. Chesterton

Most anthologists . . . of quotations are like those who eat cherries
. . . first picking the best ones and winding up by eating everything.   —Nicolas Chamfort

When someone has the wit to coin a useful phrase, it ought to be
acclaimed and broadcast or it will perish.   —Jack Smith

Stay at home in your mind. Don't recite other people's opinions.
I hate quotations. Tell me what you know.
                    —Ralph Waldo Emerson (1803–1882)

I think we must . . . quote whenever we feel that the allusion is
interesting or helpful or amusing.   —Clifton Fadiman

When a thing has been said and well said, have no scruple; take it
and copy it.   —Anatole France

I quote others only the better to express myself.
                    —Michel de Montaigne (1533–1592)

The difference between my quotations and those of the next man
is that I leave out the inverted commas.   —George Moore

To say that anything was a quotation was an excellent method, in
Eleanor's eyes, for withdrawing it from discussion.
                    —H. H. Munro ("Saki")

Many excelled me: I know it./Yet I am quoted as much as they.
                    —Ovid (43? B.C.–A.D. 18), his epitaph

Democracy will not be salvaged by men who talk fluently, debate
forcefully, and quote aptly.   —Lancelot Hogben

It is a good thing for an uneducated man to read books of quotations.   —Winston Churchill

I never did a single wise thing in the whole course of my existence,
although I have written many which have been thought so.
                    —Walter Savage Landor (1775–1864)

Shake was a dramatist of note;/He lived by writing things to quote.
                    —H. C. Bunner

There are two kinds of marriages—where the husband quotes the
wife, or where the wife quotes the husband.   —Clifford Odets

Learning is often spoken of as if we were watching the open pages
of all the books which we have ever read, and then, when occasion
arises, we select the right page to read aloud to the universe.
                    —Alfred North Whitehead

Stronger than an army is a quotation whose time has come.
                    —W. I. E. Gates

To each reader those quotations are agreeable that neither strike
him as hackneyed nor rebuke his ignorance.   —H. W. Fowler

I suppose every old scholar has had the experience of reading something in a book which was significant to him, but which he could
never find again. Sure he is that he read it there, but no one else
ever read it, nor can he find it again, though he buy the book and
ransack every page.   —Ralph Waldo Emerson

SIXTEEN GREAT QUOTATIONS

(1) Power tends to corrupt and absolute power corrupts absolutely.   —Lord Acton

(2) You grow up the day you have the first real laugh—at yourself.   —Ethel Barrymore

(3) When a man has pity on all living creatures then only is he noble.   —Buddha

(4) Nothing in life is to be feared. It is only to be understood.
  —Marie Curie

(5) Anyone who has begun to think places some portion of the world in jeopardy.   —John Dewey

(6) Our concern is not how to worship in the catacombs but how to remain human in the skyscrapers.
  —Abraham Joshua Heschel

(7) Do not take life too seriously. You will never get out of it alive.   —Elbert Hubbard

(8) A great many people think they are thinking when they are merely rearranging their prejudices.   —William James

(9) He that is without sin among you, let him first cast a stone.
  —Jesus

(10) Who shall guard the guardians themselves?   —Juvenal

(11) The more the change, the more it is the same thing.
  —Alphonse Karr

(12) And what doth the Lord require of thee, but to do justly, and to love mercy, and to walk humbly with thy God?
  —The Bible (Micah 6:8)

(13) What is honored in a country will be cultivated there.
  —Plato

(14) Those who cannot remember the past are condemned to repeat it.   —George Santayana

(15) I am a man; nothing human is alien to me.   —Terence

(16) He who hates vices hates mankind.   —Thrasea

R

RACE / RACISM

Racism is the snobbery of the poor.   —Raymond Aron

Well-adjusted people may get caught up in a tangle of social forces that makes them goose-step their way toward such abominations as the calculated execution of six million Jews . . . It may be comforting to believe that the horrors of World War II were the work of a dozen or so insane men, but it is a dangerous belief, one that may give us a false sense of security.   —Molly Harrower

Thwarted lives have the most character-conditioned hate . . . The easiest idea to sell anyone is that he is better than someone else. The appeal of the Ku Klux Klan and racist agitators rests on this type of salesmanship.   —Gordon W. Allport

I am convinced that when the intellectual history of our times comes to be written, the idea of *race,* both the popular and the taxonomic, will be viewed for what it is: a confused and dangerous idea which happened to fit the social requirements of a thoroughly exploitative period in the development of Western man.   —Ashley Montagu

I think that the degree of probability with which racial genetic differences can be stated is not adequate as a basis for policies to deal with racial issues.   —Arthur Jensen (That is, racial superiority is a mere pigment of the imagination.)

There is no evidence that there is any advantage in belonging to a
pure race. The purest races now in existence are the Pygmies, the
Hottentots, and the Australian aborigines . . . The ancient Greeks
. . . who were the most civilized, were also the most mixed.
                                                        —Bertrand Russell

We are the first race in the world, and the more of the world we inherit the better it is for the human race.   —Cecil Rhodes

I am the half-breed question.   —Louis Riel

There is no more evil thing in this world than race prejudice . . .
It justifies and holds together more baseness, cruelty, and abomina-
tion than any other sort of error in the world.   —H. G. Wells

Racism is man's gravest threat to man—the maximum of hatred
for a minimum of reason.   —Abraham Joshua Heschel

*   *

Any projection that does not expect that we will be a racist and
alienated society for a long while is simply unrealistic.
                                                        —Robert L. Heilbroner

Segregation in the South is a way of life. It is a precious and sacred
custom. It is one of our dearest and most treasured possessions. It
is the means whereby we live in social peace, order and security.
                                                        —Judge Thomas P. Brady

---

Nothing is so convincing as the consciousness of the possession of
Race. The man who belongs to a distinct, pure race, never loses the
sense of it.   —Houston Stewart Chamberlain

All who are not of good race in this world are chaff.
                                                        —Adolf Hitler

*   *

Why would we have different races if God meant us to be alike and
associate with each other?   —Lester G. Maddox

We are all descendants of Adam and we are all products of racial
miscegenation.   —Lester B. Pearson

RADICAL

Radical: A person whose left hand does know what his other left
hand is doing.   —Bernard Rosenberg

Since it is now fashionable to laugh at the conservative French Academy, I have remained a rebel by joining it.

—Jean Cocteau

The radical invents the views. When he has worn them out, the conservative adopts them. —Mark Twain

If a man is right he can't be too radical; if he is wrong, he can't be too conservative.

—Josh Billings (Henry Wheeler Shaw) (1818–1885)

The discouragement of radical thought must lead to the closed society and closed mind —Catholicism through its liking for ignorance, Protestantism, through its approval of money making, respectability, and the whole drowned and mitered body of the *status quo*.

—Jacquetta Hawkes

The sterile radical is basically . . . conservative. He is afraid to let go of the ideas and beliefs he picked up in his youth lest his life be seen as empty and wasted. —Eric Hoffer

What this country needs is radicals who will stay that way regardless of the creeping years. —John Fischer

REACTION

I have a feeling that at any time about three million Americans can be had for any militant reaction against law, decency, the Constitution, the Supreme Court, compassion and the rule of reason.

—John Kenneth Galbraith

There's something else I dislike just as much as creeping socialism, and that's galloping reaction. —Adlai Stevenson

The march of the human mind is slow. —Edmund Burke (1729–1797) (A reactionary is a man whose political opinions always manage to keep up with yesterday.)

Riots in the cities are invitations for repressive action to men who have fought every effort to ease conditions of ghetto life.

—Walter Goodman

The more there are riots, the more repressive action will take place, and the more we face the danger of a right-wing take-over and eventually a fascist society. —Martin Luther King, Jr.

The Rightists are conducting their own private battle. They are against Communism without being for freedom. They are against ignorance without being for education. They are against sin without being for God. —J. Edgar Hoover

It is time for them who have joined it . . . to recognize that the John Birch Society is rapidly losing whatever it had in common with patriotism or conservatism—and to do so before their own minds become warped by adherence to its unrolling psychosis of conspiracy.   —William F. Buckley, Jr.

Frightened reactionaries cannot distinguish between heresy and conspiracy, and, in addition, identify communism with any decent thing they wish to destroy. By making reckless charges of conspiracy where there is only honest heresy, they prevent intelligent choice.
—Sidney Hook

No one man can terrorize a whole nation unless we are all his accomplices.
—Edward R. Murrow, of Senator Joseph McCarthy

The last thing a scientist would do is cling to a map because he inherited it from his grandfather, or because it was used by George Washington or Abraham Lincoln.   —S. I. Hayakawa

New opinions are always suspected, and usually opposed, without any other reason but because they are not already common.
—John Locke (1632–1704)

All that was new in them was false and what was true was old.
—Professor Haughton's opinion of Darwin's findings

Loyalty to a petrified opinion never yet broke a chain or freed a human soul.   —Mark Twain

REALITY

You may be sure that when a man begins to call himself a "realist," he is preparing to do something he is secretly ashamed of doing.
—Sydney Harris

In America today there is a marked reluctance to accept reality . . . the indiscriminate commingling in the national mind of man as he is and as one might wish him to be.   —Gordon Liddy

Human kind cannot bear very much reality.   —T. S. Eliot

Talk of revolution is one way of avoiding reality.
—John Kenneth Galbraith

Reality is always more conservative than ideology.
—Raymond Aron

The conservative is the realist, taking over the side of all that is real, abiding, basic, fundamental. — E. Merrill Root

The whole art of politics consists in directing rationally the irrationalities of men. — Reinhold Niebuhr (A realist lets circumstances decide which end of the telescope to look through.)

REASON

Learn to reason forward and backward on both sides of a question. — Thomas Blandi

There's a mighty big difference between good, sound reasons and reasons that sound good. — Burton Hillis

Alas, reason is not effective against faith, or against searches for miracles by the desperate. — Dr. Michael B. Shimkin

Since attaining the full use of my reason no one has ever heard me laugh. — Earl of Chesterfield (1694–1773)

If the work of God could be comprehended by reason, it would be no longer wonderful, and faith would have no merit if reason provided proof.
— Pope Gregory I (Saint Gregory the Great) (540–604)

Most of our so-called reasoning consists in finding arguments for going on believing as we already do.
— James Harvey Robinson

Emotion has taught mankind to reason.
— Marquis de Vauvenargues (1715–1747)

I do not feel obliged to believe that that same God who has endowed us with sense, reason, and intellect has intended us to forego their use. — Galileo Galilei (1564–1642)

He who will not reason, is a bigot; he who cannot is a fool; and he who dares not is a slave.
— Sir William Drummond (1585–1649)

*   *

Question with boldness even the existence of God; because, if there be one, he must more approve of the homage of reason than that of blindfolded fear. — Thomas Jefferson (1743–1826)

My reason is not framed to bend or stoop; my knees are.
— Michel de Montaigne (1533–1592)

Reason—the Devil's harlot.　　—Martin Luther (1483–1546)

The gods plant reason in mankind, of all good gifts the highest.
　　　　　　　—Sophocles (496?–406 B.C.)

*　　　*

I believe in instinct, not in reason. When reason is right, nine times out of ten it is impotent, and when it prevails, nine times out of ten it is wrong.　　—A. C. Benson (On second thought, nine times out of ten the man who listens to reason is thinking of some way to refute it.)

For here we are not afraid to follow truth wherever it may lead, nor to tolerate error so long as reason is free to combat it.
　　　　　　　—Thomas Jefferson

REFORM

A reformer is a guy who rides through a sewer in a glass-bottomed boat.　　—Jimmy Walker (He wants his conscience to be your guide.)

Every reform is only a mask under cover of which a more terrible reform, which dares not yet name itself, advances.
　　　　　　　—Ralph Waldo Emerson (1803–1882)

There are a thousand hacking at the branches of evil to one who is striking at its root.　　—Henry David Thoreau (1817–1862)

The hole and the patch should be commensurate.
　　　　　　　—Thomas Jefferson (1743–1826)

We think we are on the right road to improvement because we are making experiments.　　—Benjamin Franklin (1706–1790)

A reform is a correction of abuses; a revolution is a transfer of power.　　—Edward Bulwer-Lytton (1803–1873)

We must reform if we would conserve.
　　　　　　　—Franklin Delano Roosevelt

He that will not apply new remedies must expect new evils, for time is the greatest innovator.　　—Francis Bacon (1561–1626)

RELIGION

Religion: A daughter of Hope and Fear, explaining to Ignorance the nature of the Unknowable.　　—Ambrose Bierce

My atheism, like that of Spinoza, is true piety towards the universe and denies only gods fashioned by men in their own image to be servants of their human interests.   —George Santayana

Adam, poor man! Punished for nothing.   —Elie Wiesel

With soap baptism is a good thing.
—Robert G. Ingersoll (1833–1899)

If I break wind in Wittenberg they smell it in Rome.
—Martin Luther (1483–1546)

Put God to work for you and maximize your potential in our divinely ordered capitalist system.   —Norman Vincent Peale

It is now quite lawful for a Catholic woman to avoid pregnancy by a resort to mathematics, though she is still forbidden to resort to physics and chemistry.   —H. L. Mencken

Clergyman: A man who undertakes the management of our spiritual affairs as a method of bettering his temporal ones.
—Ambrose Bierce

It often happens that I wake at night and begin to think about a serious problem and decide I must tell the Pope about it. Then I wake up completely and remember that I am the Pope.
—Pope John XXIII

The Roman pontiff can and ought to reconcile himself, and come to terms with progress, liberalism, and modern civilization.
—Pope Pius IX (1792–1878)

The dogma of the infallibility of the Bible is no more self-evident than is that of the infallibility of the popes.
—Thomas Henry Huxley (1825–1895)

Man is great only when he is kneeling.   —Pope Pius XII

Prayer is not asking. It is a longing of the soul.
—Mohandas Gandhi

Theology is an effort to explain the unknowable in terms of the not worth knowing . . . [it] is not only opposed to the scientific spirit; it is opposed to every other form of rational thinking.   —H. L. Mencken (A philosopher is a blind man in a dark room looking for a black cat that isn't there. A theologian is the man who finds it.)

To despise legitimate authority, no matter in whom it is invested, is unlawful; it is rebellion against God's will.   —Pope Leo XIII

Doctrines get inside of a man's own reason and betray him against himself. Civilized men have done their fiercest fighting for doctrines.
—William Graham Sumner

Imagine that you are creating a fabric of human destiny with the object of making men happy in the end . . . but that it was essential and inevitable to torture to death only one tiny creature . . . and to found that edifice on its unavenged tears: would you consent to be the architect on those conditions? *Tell me, and tell the truth!*
—Feodor Dostoevski (1821–1881)

A great deal of intelligence can be invested in ignorance when the need for illusion is deep. —Saul Bellow

Most men's anger about religion is as if two men should quarrel for a lady they neither of them care for.
—Lord Halifax (George Savile) (1633–1695)

It may be that the only type of defensive war the Christian can wage today is on war itself. —Leslie Dewart

Religious awe is the same organic thrill which we feel in a forest at twilight, or in a mountain gorge. —William James

Medical materialism finished up Saint Paul by calling his vision on the road to Damascus "a discharging lesion of the occipital cortex, he being an epileptic." —William James

You have not converted a man because you have silenced him.
—John, Viscount Morley

Doubt isn't the opposite of faith; it is an element of faith.
—Paul Tillich

An atheist is a man who believes himself an accident.
—Francis Thompson

Intellectually, religious emotions are not creative but conservative.
—John Dewey

The people no longer believe in principles, but will probably periodically believe in saviours.
—Jacob Burckhardt (1818–1897)

To claim to be a Christian or Jew who loves God and neighbor and not to take an active part in the formation of just social policies affecting those neighbors would seem to deny complete fulfillment of one's faith. —Reubin Askew

There can be no surer sign of decay in a country than to see the rites of religion held in contempt.
—Niccolò Machiavelli (1469–1527)

I consider myself a Hindu, Christian, Moslem, Jew, Buddhist, and Confucian. —Mohandas Gandhi

The pursuit of happiness belongs to us, but we must climb around or over the church to get it.   —Heywood Broun

When a man is freed of religion, he has a better chance to live a normal and wholesome life.   —Sigmund Freud

*   *

It is the test of a good religion whether you can joke about it.
    —G. K. Chesterton

A converted cannibal is one who, on Friday, eats only fishermen.
    —Emily Lotney

*   *

All religions must be tolerated . . . for . . . every man must get to heaven his own way.
    —Frederick the Great (1712–1786)

We must respect the other fellow's religion, but only in the same sense and to the extent that we respect his theory that his wife is beautiful and his children smart.   —H. L. Mencken

---

. . . this loathsome combination of Church and State.
    —Thomas Jefferson (1743–1826)

. . . the fatal theory of the separation of Church and State.
    —Pope Leo XIII

*   *

So far as religion of the day is concerned, it is a damned fake . . . Religion is all bunk.   —Thomas Alva Edison

Science without religion is lame, religion without science is blind.
    —Albert Einstein

*   *

Religion is excellent stuff for keeping common people quiet.
    —Napoleon Bonaparte (1769–1821)

I want nothing to do with any religion concerned with keeping the masses satisfied to live in hunger, filth and ignorance.
    —Jawaharlal Nehru

*   *

It is conceivable that religion may be morally useful without being intellectually sustainable.   —John Stuart Mill (1806–1873)

The fact that a believer is happier than a skeptic is no more to the point than the fact that a drunken man is happier than a sober one.
—George Bernard Shaw

REPUBLICAN PARTY / REPUBLICANS

The Republican Party either corrupts its liberals or it expels them.
—Harry S Truman

Every Republican candidate for President since 1936 has been nominated by the Chase National Bank.   —Robert A. Taft

The Republican Convention [1928] opened with a prayer. If the Lord can see his way clear to bless the Republican Party the way it's been carrying on, then the rest of us ought to get it without even asking.   —Will Rogers

The Republicans have a habit of having three bad years and one good one, and the good one always happens to be election year.
—Will Rogers

The trouble with the Republican Party is that it has not had a new idea for thirty years.   —Woodrow Wilson

RESPONSIBILITY

The price of greatness is responsibility.   —Winston Churchill

Few things help an individual more than to place responsibility upon him, and to let him know that you trust him.
—Booker T. Washington

Our responsibility: every opportunity, an obligation; every possession, a duty.   —John D. Rockefeller, Jr.

I feel the responsibility of the occasion. Responsibility is proportionate to opportunity.   —Woodrow Wilson

To let oneself be bound by a duty from the moment you see it approaching is part of the integrity that alone justifies responsibility.
—Dag Hammarskjöld

The ability to accept responsibility is the measure of the man.
—Roy L. Smith

Man must cease attributing his problems to his environment, and learn again to exercise his will—his personal responsibility in the realm of faith and morals.   —Albert Schweitzer

REVOLUTION / REBELLION

Contrary to prevalent opinion . . . I indicated that wars and revolutions were not disappearing but would grow in the twentieth century to an absolutely unprecedented height . . . that democracies were declining, giving place to various kinds of despotisms.
—P. A. Sorokin

The path that leads from moral standards to political activity is strewn with our dead selves.   —André Malraux (Revolution is an idea that has found bayonets.)

Civil confusions often spring from trifles but decide great issues.
—Aristotle (384–322 B.C.)

The free souls are in revolt. And you cannot meet a revolution with a referendum.   —Israel Zangwill

Revolution is not a dinner party, nor an essay, nor a painting, nor a piece of embroidery; it cannot be advanced softly, gradually, carefully, considerately, respectfully, politely, plainly and modestly.
—Mao Tse-tung

The export of revolution is nonsense. Every country makes its own revolution if it wants to, and if it does not want to, there will be no revolution.   —Joseph Stalin

In revolutions authority remains with the greatest scoundrels.
—Georges Jacques Danton (1759–1794)

If you feed the people just with revolutionary slogans they will listen today, they will listen tomorrow, they will listen the day after tomorrow, but on the fourth day they will say, "To hell with you!"
—Nikita Khrushchev

God forbid we should ever be twenty years without such a rebellion!
—Thomas Jefferson (1743–1826)

The destruction of our State governments or the annihilation of their control over the local concerns of the people would lead directly to revolution and anarchy, and finally to despotism and military domination.   —Andrew Jackson (1767–1845)

Those who make peaceful revolution impossible will make violent revolution inevitable.   —John F. Kennedy

Remember always that all of us, and you and I especially, are descended from migrants and revolutionists.
—Franklin Delano Roosevelt, to the D.A.R.

Revolutionary movements attract the best and worst elements in a given society.   —George Bernard Shaw

The successful revolutionary is a statesman, the unsuccessful one a criminal.   —Erich Fromm

The purity of a revolution can last a fortnight.
                                                        —Jean Cocteau

Revolutions are ambiguous things. Their success is generally proportionate to their power of adaptation and to be reabsorbed within them of what they rebelled against.
                                                        —George Santayana

Oppressed people are frequently very oppressive when first liberated . . . They know best two positions. Somebody's foot on their neck or their foot on somebody's neck.
                                                        —Florence Kennedy

---

Every successful revolution puts on in time the robes of the tyrant it has deposed.   —Barbara Tuchman

Nothing is clearer in history than the adoption by successful rebels of the methods they were accustomed to condemn in the forces they deposed.   —Will and Ariel Durant

* *

Men who use terrorism as a means to power, rule by terror once they are in power.   —Helen MacInnes

How a minority,/Reaching majority,/Seizing authority,/Hates a minority.   —Leonard H. Robbins

---

Every act of rebelling expresses a nostalgia for innocence.
                                                        —Albert Camus

I have seen gross intolerance shown in support of tolerance.
                                        —Samuel Taylor Coleridge (1772–1834)

RICHES

The rich man and his daughter are soon parted.
                                —Frank McKinney Hubbard ("Kin Hubbard")

To suppose as we all suppose, that we could be rich and not behave as the rich behave, is like supposing that we could drink all day and stay sober.   —Logan Pearsall Smith

Many speak the truth when they say that they despise riches, but they mean the riches possessed by other men.

—Charles Caleb Colton (1780–1832)

Most of us hate to see a poor loser—or a rich winner.

—Harold Coffin

Ignorance is degrading when found in company with riches.

—Arthur Schopenhauer (1788–1860)

Prosperity of the middling and lower orders depends upon the fortunes and light taxes of the rich.   —Andrew Mellon

---

It is the wretchedness of being rich that you have to live with rich people.   —Logan Pearsall Smith

The only thing I like about rich people is their money.

—Lady Astor

*   *

Few rich men own their own property. The property owns them.

—Robert G. Ingersoll (1833–1899)

Banks and riches are chains of gold, but still chains.

—Edmund Ruffin (1794–1865)

My riches consist not in the extent of my possessions but in the fewness of my wants.   —J. Brotherton

I've been rich and I've been poor; rich is better.

—Sophie Tucker

*   *

If I keep my good character, I shall be rich enough.

—Platonicus (c. 1st century B.C.)

It doesn't matter if you're rich or poor, as long as you've got money.

—Joe E. Lewis

SAINTS

The saints are the sinners who keep on going.
—Robert Louis Stevenson (1850–1894)

Saint: A dead sinner revised and edited.   —Ambrose Bierce

The way of the world is to praise dead saints and to persecute living ones.   —Nathaniel Howe

That the saints may enjoy their beatitude and the grace of God more abundantly, they are permitted to see the punishment of the damned in hell.   —Saint Thomas Aquinas (1225–1274)

We do not insist that the more saintly of two surgeons shall operate on us for appendicitis.   —John Erskine

Saints should always be judged guilty until they are proved innocent.   —George Orwell

I don't believe in God, but I do believe in His saints.
—Edith Wharton

Many of the insights of the saint stem from his experience as a sinner.   —Eric Hoffer

Saintship is the exclusive possession of those who have either worn out or never had the capacity to sin.   —Elbert Hubbard

SCIENCE

Aristotle could have avoided the mistake of thinking that women have fewer teeth than men by the simple device of asking Mrs. Aristotle to open her mouth.   —Bertrand Russell

Art is I; science is we.   —Claude Bernard

[Scientists] are Peeping Toms at the keyhole of eternity.
                                                    —Arthur Koestler

Every sentence I utter must be understood not as an affirmation, but as a question.   —Niels Bohr

All science is concerned with the relationship of cause and effect. Each scientific discovery increases man's ability to predict the consequences of his actions and thus his ability to control future events.
                                                    —Laurence J. Peter

A new scientific truth does not triumph by convincing its opponents, but rather because its opponents die, and a new generation grows up that is familiar with it.   —Max Planck

Science is a flickering light in our darkness, it is but the only one we have and woe to him who would put it out.   —Morris Cohen

In science the credit goes to the man who convinces the world, not to the man to whom the idea first occurs.   —Sir William Osler

Science commits suicide when it adopts a creed.
                                        —Thomas Henry Huxley (1825–1895)

No amount of experimentation can ever prove me right; a single experiment can prove me wrong.   —Albert Einstein (When his theory was questioned, Einstein replied, only half in jest, "the facts are wrong.")

The scientist . . . is at the moving edge of what's happening.
                                                    —Dr. Gerald M. Edelman

Science seeks generally only the most useful systems of classification: these it regards for the time being, until more useful classifications are invented as *true*.   —S. I. Hayakawa

Science is nothing but developed perception, integrated intent, common sense rounded out and minutely articulated.
                                                    —George Santayana

Science is facts; just as houses are made of stones, so is science made of facts; but a pile of stones is not a house and a collection of facts is not necessarily science.   —Henri Poincaré

As long as men are free to ask what they must—free to say what they think—free to think what they will—freedom can never be lost and science can never regress.   —J. Robert Oppenheimer

If I have been able to see farther than others, it was because I stood on the shoulders of giants.   —Sir Isaac Newton (1642–1727)

The age of innocent faith in science and technology may be over . . . every major advance in the technological competence of man has enforced revolutionary changes in the economic and political structure of society.   —Barry Commoner

Scientific and humanist approaches are not competitive but supportive, and both are ultimately necessary.   —Robert C. Wood

The social problems raised by science must be faced and solved by the social sciences and the humanities.   —Harold Dodd

We have to live today by what truth we can get today and be ready tomorrow to call it falsehood.
     —William James (Science is a history of superseded theories.)

In formal logic, a contradiction is the signal of defeat: but in the evolution of real knowledge it marks the first step in progress toward a victory.   —Alfred North Whitehead

---

But I have seen the science I worshipped and the aircraft I loved destroying the civilization I expected them to serve.
     —Charles A. Lindbergh, Jr.

We . . . repeatedly enlarge our instrumentalities without improving our purpose.   —Will Durant

*   *

The universe is full of magical things patiently waiting for our wits to grow sharper.   —Eden Phillpots

Weed—a plant whose virtues have not yet been discovered.
     —Ralph Waldo Emerson (1803–1882)

*   *

Science is the refusal to believe on the basis of hope.
     —C. P. Snow

The radical novelty of modern science lies precisely in the rejection of the belief, which is at the heart of all popular religion, that the forces which move the stars and atoms are contingent upon the preferences of the human heart.   —Walter Lippmann

*   *

Truth in science can be defined as the working hypothesis best suited to open the way to the next better one.   —Konrad Lorenz

The demonstrably true statements of the sciences which, especially in recent times, have the uncomfortable inclination never to stay put, although, at any given moment they are, and must be, valid for all.
—Hannah Arendt

And science, we should insist, better than any other discipline, can hold up to its students and followers an ideal of patient devotion to the search for objective truth, with vision unclouded by personal or political motive.   —Sir Henry Hallett Dalt

It is a mistake to believe that a science consists in nothing but conclusively proved propositions, and it is unjust to demand that it should. It is a demand only made by those who feel a craving for authority in some form and a need to replace the religious catechism by something else, even if it be a scientific one.
—Sigmund Freud

SECURITY

We hear of a silent generation, more concerned with security than integrity, with conforming than performing, with imitating than creating.   —Thomas J. Watson

If money is your hope for independence you will never have it. The only real security that a man can have in this world is a reserve of knowledge, experience and ability.   —Henry Ford

The fly that doesn't want to be swatted is most secure when it lights on the fly swatter.   —G. C. Lichtenberg (1742–1799)

It is much more secure to be feared than to be loved.
—Niccolò Machiavelli (1469–1527)

There is nothing more demoralizing than a small but adequate income.   —Edmund Wilson

Too many people are thinking of security instead of opportunity. They seem more afraid of life than death.   —James F. Byrnes

It is remarkable that the security which *endangers* freedom, which suppresses incentive is always the security of workers, of farmers, or of small business men.   —Barrows Dunham

I believe . . . that security declines as security machinery expands.
—E. B. White

The desire for safety stands against every great and noble enterprise.
—Tacitus (55?–130?)

The lust for comfort, that stealthy thing that enters the house as a guest and then becomes a host and then a master.

—Joseph Conrad

Security is mortal's chiefest enemy.   —Ellen Terry

Man's security comes from within himself, and the security of all men is founded upon the security of the individual.   —Manly Hall

Atom bomb stockpiles are no guarantee of security. Until lust and greed and murder are removed from the hearts of men, there is, there can be, no peace or security.   —A. P. Gouthey

SELF-DECEPTION

When a man points a finger at someone else, he should remember that four of his fingers are pointing at himself.   —Louis Nizer (If he has five fingers.)

Life is the art of being well deceived.

—William Hazlitt (1778–1830)

The art of living is the art of knowing how to believe lies.

—Cesare Pavese

All mirrors are magical mirrors; never can we see our faces in them. —Logan Pearsall Smith (If you want to see how you look asleep, stand in front of a mirror with your eyes shut.)

Nothing is more unpleasant than a virtuous person with a mean mind.

—Walter Bagehot (1826–1877)

A Puritan's a person who pours righteous indignation into the wrong things.   —G. K. Chesterton

There is perhaps no phenomenon which contains so much destructive feeling as *moral indignation,* which permits envy or hate to be acted out under the guise of *virtue.*   —Erich Fromm

People like the exposure of wickedness . . . in high places. It gives them a sense of ultimate righteousness of the world . . . the squirming of those who are caught allows people to indulge in a certain legitimate sadism which, otherwise, they would feel obliged to suppress.   —John Kenneth Galbraith

Let me have my own way exactly in everything, and a sunnier and pleasanter creature does not exist.

—Thomas Carlyle (1795–1881)

The same people who can deny others everything are famous for refusing themselves nothing.   —Leigh Hunt (1784–1859)

SERVICE

You have not done enough, you have never done enough, so long as it is still possible that you have something to contribute.

—Dag Hammarskjöld

No one is useless in this world who lightens the burdens of another.

—Charles Dickens (1812–1870)

Every kind of service necessary to the public good becomes honorable by being necessary.   —Nathan Hale (1755–1776)

There is no higher religion than human service. To work for the common good is the greatest creed.   —Albert Schweitzer

SEX

The Sexual Revolution: Conquest of the last frontier, involving the efficient management and manipulation of reproductive organs for the purpose of establishing the New Puritanism.

—Bernard Rosenberg

Whoever named it necking was a poor judge of anatomy.

—Groucho Marx

I'm a practicing heterosexual . . . but bisexuality immediately doubles your chances for a date on Saturday night.

—Woody Allen

It was not the apple on the tree, but the pair on the ground, I believe, that caused the trouble in the garden.   —M. D. O'Connor

If you aren't going all the way, why go at all?   —Joe Namath

He was one of those men who come in a door and make any woman with them look guilty.   —F. Scott Fitzgerald

And here's the happy bounding flea—/You can not tell the he from she./But she can tell and so can he.   —Roland Young

If I told you you have a beautiful body, you wouldn't hold it against me would you?   —David Fisher

One man's remorse is another man's reminiscence.   —Gerald Horton Bath (There's nothing wrong with a person's sex life that the right psychoanalyst can't exaggerate.)

Among the porcupines, rape is unknown.   —Gregory Clark

Freud found sex an outcast in the outhouse, and left it in the living room an honored guest.   —W. Beran Wolfe

The more potent a man becomes in the bedroom, the more potent he is in business.   —Dr. David Reuben

I wish I could change my sex as I change my shirt.

—André Breton

Sexual technology could best be served by orgasms which came on the beat of society's best machines.   —Norman Mailer

Men always fall for frigid women because they put on the best show.

—Fanny Brice

If it is not erotic, it is not interesting.   —Fernando Arrabal

---

Lord give me chastity—but not yet.

—Saint Augustine (354–430)

The trouble with life is that there are so many beautiful women and so little time.   —John Barrymore (It's so hard for an old rake to turn over a new leaf.)

*   *

A little theory makes sex more interesting, more comprehensible, and less scary—too much is a put-down, especially as you're likely to get it out of perspective and become a spectator of your own performance.   —Dr. Alex Comfort

Perspective, I soon realized, was a fine commodity, but utterly useless when I was in the thick of things.   —Ingrid Bengis (And it's the only game that is never called off on account of darkness.)

*   *

There is no known way of increasing male sperm production.

Drs. William Masters and Virginia E. Johnson

Nothing is so pathetic, because it is so ridiculous, as the great and high tragedy of *Faust,* wherein murder, damnation, hell, choirs of angels, God, and the Devil become cosmically involved in a sexual affair between a human male and female.   —Abraham Myerson

*   *

Of all sexual aberrations, chastity is the strangest.

—Anatole France

Chastity is the most unnatural of the sexual perversions.

—Rémy de Gourmont

As to marriage or celibacy, let a man take which course he will, he will be sure to repent. —Socrates (470?–399 B.C.)

Marriage has many pains but celibacy has no pleasures.
—Samuel Johnson (1709–1784)

* *

'Tis the Devil inspires this evanescent ardor, in order to divert the parties from prayer. —Martin Luther (1483–1546)

Sexual pleasure, wisely used and not abused, may prove the stimulus and liberator of our finest and most exalted activities.
—Havelock Ellis

* *

The sexual drive is nothing but the motor memory of previously experienced pleasure. —Wilhelm Reich

When grown-ups do it it's kind of dirty—that's because there's no one to punish them. —Tuesday Weld

SIMILES

His voice was as intimate as the rustle of sheets.
—Dorothy Parker

Like a struggling spiritualist slipping her card into a passing coffin.
—Derek Marlowe

Like trying to convince an eight-year-old that sexual intercourse is more fun than a chocolate ice cream cone. —Howard Gossage

. . . in the position of a virgin washed ashore on a Devil's Island of convicted rapists. —Mario Puzo

Like telling a man going to the electric chair that he has a choice of AC or DC. —Goodman Ace

Facing me sat a stout man with a hard red face like a book of rules.
—Anthony Carson

They made love as though they were an endangered species.
—Peter De Vries

Like challenging a school of piranhas to a game of water polo.
—Thomas H. Middleton

He has the gall of a shoplifter returning an item for a refund.
—W. I. E. Gates

Like using a guillotine to cure dandruff. —Clare Boothe Luce

As futile as a clock in an empty house. —James Thurber

SINCERITY

You can be sincere and still be stupid.   —Charles F. Kettering

A little sincerity is a dangerous thing, and a great deal of it is absolutely fatal.   —Oscar Wilde (1854–1900)

Always be sincere, even when you don't mean it.   —Irene Peter

I am not sincere, not even when I say I am not.   —Jules Renard

When a man says he approves of something in principle, it means he hasn't the slightest intention of putting it into practice.
                    —Prince Otto von Bismarck (1815–1898)

Whenever a fellow tells me he is bipartisan, I know he's going to vote against me.   —Harry S Truman

It is dangerous to be sincere unless you are also stupid.
                    —George Bernard Shaw

SKEPTICISM / SKEPTICS

A skeptic is a person who would ask God for his ID card.
                    —Edgar A. Shoaff

To the naive, skepticism often seems malicious perversity: "Only some secret enemy in the inward degenerate nature of man," said Topsell, "could lead anyone to doubt the existence of the unicorn."
                    —Bergen Evans

The first step toward philosophy is incredulity.
                    —Denis Diderot (1713–1784)

For the sceptic there remains only one consolation: if there should be such a thing as superhuman law, it is administered with subhuman efficiency.   —Eric Ambler

The more fervent opponents of Christian doctrine have often enough shown a temper which, psychologically considered, is indistinguishable from religious zeal.   —William James

What thinking man is there who still requires the hypothesis of a God?   —Friedrich Nietzsche (1844–1900)

Nature confuses the skeptics and reason confutes the dogmatists.
                    —Blaise Pascal (1623–1662)

The farce is finished. I go to seek a vast perhaps.
                    —François Rabelais (1495?–1553)

Skepticism is a hedge against vulnerability.

—Charles Thomas Samuels

Skepticism, like chastity, should not be relinquished too readily.
—George Santayana (If seeing is believing, some skeptics wouldn't look.)

SLEEP

The vigorous are no better than the lazy during one half of life, for all men are alike when asleep.   —Aristotle (384–322 B.C.)

Oh sleep! it is a gentle thing,/Beloved from pole to pole.

—Samuel Taylor Coleridge (1772–1834)

Sleep that knits up the ravell'd sleave of care.

—William Shakespeare (1564–1616)

Up, sluggard, and waste not life; in the grave will be sleeping enough.   —Benjamin Franklin (1706–1790)

He slept the deep sleep of the unjust.

—Sir Herbert Beerbohm Tree

Early to bed and early to rise is a bad rule for anyone who wishes to become acquainted with our most prominent and influential people.   —George Ade

SLOGANS

There's a difference between a philosophy and a bumper sticker.

—Charles M. Schulz

Augustus was sensible that mankind is governed by names; nor was he deceived in his expectation that the senate and people would submit to slavery, provided they were respectfully assured that they still enjoyed their ancient freedom.

—Edward Gibbon (1737–1794)

Man is a creature who lives not upon bread alone, but primarily by catchwords.   —Robert Louis Stevenson (1850–1894)

A good catchword can obscure analysis for fifty years.

—Wendell L. Willkie

Our major obligation is not to mistake slogans for solutions.

—Edward R. Murrow

SMOKING

Smoking is a shocking thing—blowing smoke out of our mouths into other people's mouths, eyes, and noses, and having the same thing done to us.   —Samuel Johnson (1709–1784)

Tobacco, divine, rare, superexcellent tobacco, which goes far beyond all the panaceas, potable gold and philosopher's stones, a sovereign remedy to all diseases.   —Robert Burton (1577–1640)

The only way to stop smoking is to just stop—no ifs, ands or butts.
—Edith Zittler

I'm glad I don't have to explain to a man from Mars why each day I set fire to dozens of little pieces of paper, and then put them in my mouth.   —Mignon McLaughlin

I have made it a rule never to smoke more than one cigar at a time.
—Mark Twain

There's been no top authority saying what marijuana does to you. I really don't know that much about it. I tried it once but it didn't do anything to me.   —John Wayne

Cigarettes dull the faculties, stunt and retard the physical development, unsettle the mind, and rob the persistent user of will power and the ability to concentrate.   —Dick Merriwell

SOCIETY

The mutual and universal dependence of individuals who remain indifferent to one another constitutes the social network that binds them together.   —Karl Marx (1818–1883)

The best things and best people rise out of their separateness; I'm against a homogenized society because I want the cream to rise.
—Robert Frost

The idea that egotism is the basis of the general welfare is the principle on which competitive society has been built.
—Erich Fromm

What is not good for the hive is not good for the bee.
—Marcus Aurelius (121–180)

The mayor is perhaps the most important single social force for good or evil in America today.   —Richard Lee

There are people into whose heads it never enters to conceive of any better state of society than that which now exists.
>—Henry George (1839–1897)

The elimination of war should be the major task of social education. —Konrad Lorenz

Society is always taken by surprise at any new example of common sense. —Ralph Waldo Emerson (1803–1882)

As we ascend the social ladder, viciousness wears a thicker mask. —Erich Fromm (The most useful of all social graces is the ability to yawn with your mouth closed.)

It is impossible in a democratic society to think of a single measure for the improvement of social well-being which is not subject to subversion by ill-conceived minority or even majority pressures.
>—John Kenneth Galbraith

Every man is the creature of the age in which he lives; very few are able to raise themselves above the ideas of the time.
>—Voltaire (François Marie Arouet) (1694–1778)

No society has ever been found without a government . . . No normal human being ever existed who was not the product of his culture, as well as of his genes. —Stuart Chase (A sociologist is a scientist who blames crime on everything and everyone, except the person who commits it.)

*   *

Society is divided into two classes: the shearers and the shorn; we should always be with the former against the latter.
>—Charles de Talleyrand (1754–1838)

A government that robs Peter to pay Paul can always depend upon the support of Paul. —George Bernard Shaw

SOCIOECONOMICS

Undermine the entire structure of society by leaving the pay toilet door ajar so the next person can get in free. —Taylor Mead

Economics is a subject that does not greatly respect one's wishes.
>—Nikita Khrushchev

The cost of living has gone up another dollar a quart.
>—W. C. Fields

Planned Economy: Where everything is included in the plans except economy. —Carey McWilliams

Everything in the world may be endured except continual prosperity.
—Johann W. von Goethe (1749–1832)

So long as a man enjoys prosperity, he cares not whether he is beloved.   —Marcus Annaeus Lucan (39–65)

Having a little inflation is like being a little pregnant—inflation feeds on itself and quickly passes the "little" mark.   —Dian Cohen

Economists think the poor need them to tell them that they are poor.
—Peter Drucker

In all recorded history there has not been one economist who has had to worry about where the next meal would come from.
—Peter Drucker

Don't put the fate of your business in the delusions of economists.
—Peter Drucker

Practical men . . . are usually the slaves of some defunct economist.   —John Maynard Keynes

I absolutely disagree with the theory that you can upgrade the poor by giving them better housing.   —Kevin P. Phillips

An economist is an expert who will know tomorrow why the things he predicted yesterday didn't happen today.
—Laurence J. Peter

The gap in our economy is between what we have and what we think we ought to have—and that is a moral problem, not an economic one.   —Paul Heyne

If our economy of freedom fails to distribute wealth as ably as it has created it, the road to dictatorship will be open to any man who can persuasively promise security to all.   —Will and Ariel Durant

Economy is the art of making the most of life. The love of economy is the root of all virtue.   —George Bernard Shaw

The society of money and exploitation has never been charged . . . with assuring the triumph of freedom and justice.   —Albert Camus (Economics is the art of trying to satisfy infinite needs with limited resources.)

A study of economics usually reveals that the best time to buy anything is last year.   —Marty Allen

One of the soundest rules I try to remember when making forecasts in the field of economics is that whatever is to happen is happening already.   —Sylvia Porter

*   *

If all economists were laid end to end, they would not reach a conclusion.   —George Bernard Shaw

If the nation's economists were laid end to end, they would point in all directions.   —Arthur H. Motley

SOLITUDE

In Genesis it says that it is not good for a man to be alone, but sometimes it's a great relief.   —John Barrymore

Girls who wear zippers shouldn't live alone.
                                    —John W. Van Druten

Anything for a quiet life; as the man said when he took the situation at the lighthouse.   —Charles Dickens (1812–1870)

Solitude: A good place to visit, but a poor place to stay.
          —Josh Billings (Henry Wheeler Shaw) (1818–1885)

I never found the companion that was so companionable as solitude.
                    —Henry David Thoreau (1817–1862)

Oh blessed a thousand times the peasant who is born, eats and dies without anybody bothering about his affairs.   —Giuseppe Verdi

The right to be let alone is the most comprehensive of rights and the right most valued in civilized man.
                              —Justice Louis D. Brandeis

Deep down, Erikson wants profoundly to be respected and admired— and very deep down he wants to be left alone.
                                    —Stanley Hoffmann

The physical union of the sexes . . . only intensifies man's sense of solitude.   —Nicolas Berdyaev

If you are afraid of being lonely, don't try to be right.
                                        —Jules Renard

This great misfortune—to be incapable of solitude.
                    —Jean de La Bruyère (1645–1696)

I will arise and go now, and go to Innisfree,/And a small cabin build there, of clay and wattles made;/Nine bean rows will I have there, a hive for the honey bee,/And live alone in the bee-loud glade.
                              —William Butler Yeats

One of the greatest necessities in America is to discover creative solitude.   —Carl Sandburg

In solitude, be a multitude to thyself.

—Tibullus (54?–18? B.C.)

Get away from the crowd when you can. Keep yourself to yourself, if only for a few hours daily.   —Arthur Brisbane

By all means use sometimes to be alone.

—George Herbert (1593–1633)

*   *

I was never less alone than while by myself.

—Edward Gibbon (1737–1794)

Never less alone than when alone.

—Samuel Rogers (1763–1855)

The best thinking has been done in solitude. The worst has been done in turmoil.   —Thomas Alva Edison

Men fear silence as they fear solitude, because both give them a glimpse of the terror of life's nothingness.   —André Maurois

SPACE

If it were not for space, all matter would be jammed together in one lump and that lump wouldn't take up any room.

—Irene Peter

The message from the moon which we have flashed to the far corners of this planet is that no problem need any longer be considered insoluble.   —Norman Cousins

Put three grains of sand inside a vast cathedral, and the cathedral will be more closely packed with sand than space is with stars.

—Sir James Jeans

Someday I would like to stand on the moon, look down through a quarter of a million miles of space and say, "There certainly is a beautiful earth out tonight."

—Lieutenant Colonel William H. Rankin

The realization that our small planet is only one of many worlds gives mankind the perspective it needs to realize sooner that our own world belongs to all of its creatures, that the moon landing marks the end of our childhood as a race and the beginning of a newer and better civilization.   —Arthur C. Clarke

Solutions to the problem of space flight, if not adopted, will be because something better has turned up.   —Arthur C. Clarke (Since 1968 we have spent 364 billion dollars on war; 27 billion dollars on space; and less than 2 billion dollars on community development and housing.)

Clarke is undoubtedly a firm believer in the Freudian dictum that adult happiness lies in the fulfillment of unfulfilled childhood aspirations.   —Stanley Kubrick

To expect us to feel "humble" in the presence of astronomical dimensions merely because they are big, is a kind of cosmic snobbery . . . what is significant is mind.   —Sir Herbert Samuel

When it is dark enough you can see the stars.
—Ralph Waldo Emerson (1803–1882)

The fault, dear Brutus, is not in our stars/But in ourselves.
—William Shakespeare (1564–1616)

Nothing puzzles me more than time and space, and yet nothing puzzles me less, for I never think about them.
—Charles Lamb (1775–1834)

[Space travel] is an extravagant feat of technological exhibitionism.
—Lewis Mumford

The drive toward complex technical achievement offers a clue to why the U. S. is good at space gadgetry and bad at slum problems.
—John Kenneth Galbraith

*   *

That's one small step for man, one giant leap for mankind.
—Neil A. Armstrong

If only for a brief moment all the people in the world were united.
—John Swigert

*   *

By thought I embrace the universal.
—Blaise Pascal (1623–1662)

The universe is not hostile, nor yet is it friendly. It is simply indifferent.   —John H. Holmes

---

I see nothing in space as promising as the view from a Ferris wheel.
—E. B. White

I would be very ashamed of my civilization if we did not try to find out if there is life in outer space.   —Carl Sagan

*   *

Moon rocks are OK when everyone is eating.

—Goodman Ace

That potential alone [to expand mind and spirit] urges man to
continue his search—not to wait, as some insist, until he can first
set his own world completely in order.   —Mayo Mohs (If
Earthlings cannot cooperate with their fellow inhabitants, what
makes them think they can cooperate with the inhabitants of other
planets?)

*   *

What if Columbus had been told, "Chris, baby, don't go now. Wait
until we've solved our No. 1 Priorities—war and famine; poverty
and crime; pollution and disease; illiteracy and racial hatred—and
Queen Isabella's own brand of 'internal security.'"

—W. I. E. Gates

We never stop investigating. We are never satisfied that we know
enough to get by. Every question we answer leads on to another
question. This has become the greatest survival trick of our species.

—Desmond Morris

SPORTS

As I understand it, sport is hard work for which you do not get
paid.   —Irvin S. Cobb

If the people don't want to come out to the park, nobody's going
to stop 'em.   —Yogi Berra

I want to thank everybody who made this day necessary.

—Yogi Berra

You can't think and hit at the same time.   —Yogi Berra

Rockne wanted nothing but "bad losers." Good losers get into the
habit of losing.   —George E. Allen

You don't save a pitcher for tomorrow. Tomorrow it may rain.

—Leo Durocher

Pro football is like nuclear warfare. There are no winners, only
survivors.   —Frank Gifford

If you watch a game, it's fun. If you play it, it's recreation. If you
work at it, it's golf.   —Bob Hope

I play in the low 80's. If it's any hotter than that, I won't play.

—Joe E. Lewis

Golf is an awkward set of bodily contortions designed to produce a graceful result.　　—Tommy Armour

Golf is like a love affair: if you don't take it seriously, it's no fun; if you do take it seriously, it breaks your heart.　　—Arnold Daly

The only reason I ever played golf in the first place was so I could afford to hunt and fish.　　—Sam Snead

Golf is a good walk spoiled.　　—Mark Twain (It's good sportsmanship to not pick up lost golf balls while they are still rolling.)

Have you ever noticed what golf spells backwards?

　　　　　　—Al Boliska

When I was forty, my doctor advised me that a man in his forties shouldn't play tennis. I heeded his advice carefully and could hardly wait until I reached fifty to start again.　　—Justice Hugo Black

If you see a tennis player who looks as if he is working very hard, then that means he isn't very good.　　—Helen Wills Moody

The only thing on the level is mountain climbing.

　　　　　　—Eddie Quinn

Horses and jockeys mature earlier than people—which is why horses are admitted to race tracks at the age of two, and jockeys before they are old enough to shave.　　—Dick Beddoes

If all the year were playing holidays,/To sport would be as tedious as to work.　　—William Shakespeare (1564–1616)

You gotta be a man to play baseball for a living but you gotta have a lot of little boy in you, too.　　—Roy Campanella

I hate all sports as rabidly as a person who likes sports hates common sense.　　—H. L. Mencken

I had pro offers from the Detroit Lions and Green Bay Packers, who were pretty hard up for linemen in those days. If I had gone into professional football the name Jerry Ford might have been a household word today.　　—Gerald Ford (on February 3, 1974)

STATISTICS

There are three kinds of lies: lies, damned lies, and statistics.

　　　　　　—Benjamin Disraeli (1804–1881)

Statistics are like a bikini. What they reveal is suggestive, but what they conceal is vital.　　—Aaron Levenstein

He uses statistics as a drunken man uses lamp posts—for support rather than for illumination.　　—Andrew Lang

Statistics are for losers.   —Scotty Bowman

Do not put your faith in what statistics say until you have carefully considered what they do not say.   —William W. Watt (Facts are stubborn things, but statistics are more pliable.)

Then there is the man who drowned crossing a stream with an average depth of six inches.   —W. I. E. Gates

I am one of the unpraised, unrewarded millions without whom Statistics would be a bankrupt science. It is we who are born, who marry, who die, in constant ratio.   —Logan Pearsall Smith

Statistics—figures used as arguments.

—Leonard Louis Levinson

Figures won't lie, but liars will figure.   —Charles H. Grosvenor

I always find that statistics are hard to swallow and impossible to digest. The only one I can ever remember is that if all the people who go to sleep in church were laid end to end they would be a lot more comfortable.   —Mrs. Robert A. Taft

STYLE

All the fun's in how you say a thing.   —Robert Frost

Style, in its finest sense, is the last acquirement of the educated mind.   —Alfred North Whitehead

Style is effectiveness of assertion.   —George Bernard Shaw

Every style that is not boring is a good one.
          —Voltaire (François Marie Arouet) (1694–1778)

Style is self-plagiarism.   —Alfred Hitchcock

For every artist with something to say but the inability to say it well, there are two who could say something well if they had something to say.   —Paul C. Mills

One major problem is his [John Dewey's] writing style, which has the monotonous consistency of peanut butter . . . Like many in his generation, Dewey was in revolt against lofty sentiments and fine writing so his style was in part a rebellion against Style.
          —Joseph Featherstone

I am seldom interested in what he [Ezra Pound] is saying, but only in the way he says it.   —T. S. Eliot

Take care of the sense and the sounds will take care of themselves.
          —Lewis Carroll (Charles Lutwidge Dodgson) (1832–1898)

No style is good that is not fit to be spoken or read aloud with effect.   —William Hazlitt (1778–1830)

It is style which complements affirmation with limitation and with humility; it is style which makes it possible to act effectively, but not absolutely; it is style which enables us to find harmony between the pursuit of ends essential to us, and the regard for the views, the sensibilities, the aspirations of others; it is style which is the deference that action pays to uncertainty; it is above all style through which power defers to reason.   —J. Robert Oppenheimer

If any man wishes to write a clear style, let him first be clear in his thoughts.   —Johann W. von Goethe (1749–1832)

Those who write clearly have readers; those who write obscurely have commentators.   —Albert Camus

*   *

No writer long remains incognito.   —E. B. White

Chopin may now publish anything without putting his name to it . . . it is impossible to be for a moment uncertain as to its source.
     —Robert Schumann (1810–1856)

*   *

Style is the man himself.   —Georges de Buffon (1707–1788)

The style is the man. Rather say the style is the way the man takes himself. If it is with outer seriousness, it must be with inner humor. If it is with outer humor, it must be with inner seriousness.
     —Robert Frost

You wouldn't say an ax handle has style to it. It has beauty, and appropriateness of form, and a "this-is-how-it-should-be-ness." But it has no style because it has no mistakes. Style reflects one's idiosyncrasies. Your personality is apt to show more to the degree that you did not solve the problem than to the degree that you did.
     —Charles Eames

Style is the physiognomy of the mind, and a safer index to character than the face.   —Arthur Schopenhauer (1788–1860)

SUCCESS

Success is a journey, not a destination.   —Ben Sweetland

There is only one success—to be able to spend your life in your own way.   —Christopher Morley

You have reached the pinnacle of success as soon as you become uninterested in money, compliments, or publicity.

—Dr. O. A. Battista

Behind every successful man is a woman—with nothing to wear.

—L. Grant Glickman

The toughest thing about success is that you've got to keep on being a success.   —Irving Berlin

Success is like dealing with your kid or teaching your wife to drive. Sooner or later you'll end up in the police station.

—Fred Allen

The exclusive worship of the bitch-goddess *Success* [is] our national disease.   —William James

The essence of success is that it is never necessary to think of a new idea oneself. It is far better to wait until somebody else does it, and then to copy him in every detail, except his mistakes.

—Aubrey Menen

We live in a war of two antagonistic ethical philosophies, the ethical policy taught in the books and schools, and the success policy.

—William Graham Sumner

Success is counted sweetest/By those who ne'er succeed.

—Emily Dickinson (1830–1886)

Why should we be in such desperate haste to succeed, and in such desperate enterprises? If a man does not keep pace with his companions, perhaps it is because he hears a different drummer.

—Henry David Thoreau (1817–1862)

If one advances confidently in the direction of his dreams, and endeavors to live the life which he has imagined, he will meet with a success unexpected in common hours.

—Henry David Thoreau

Success is the one unpardonable sin against one's fellows.

—Ambrose Bierce

Only the brave deserve the fair, but only rich, fat, cowardly merchants can afford same.   —Chinese Proverb

How can they say my life isn't a success? Have I not for more than sixty years got enough to eat and escaped being eaten?

—Logan Pearsall Smith

Success has made failures of many men.   —Cindy Adams

It takes twenty years to make an overnight success.

—Eddie Cantor

Actually, I'm an overnight success. But it took twenty years.

—Monty Hall

There are only two ways of getting on in this world: by one's own industry, or by the weaknesses of others.

—Jean de La Bruyère (1645–1696)

Six essential qualities that are the key to success: Sincerity, personal integrity, humility, courtesy, wisdom, charity.

—Dr. William Menninger

* *

The two leading recipes for success are building a better mousetrap and finding a bigger loophole.   —Edgar A. Shoaff

Success is simply a matter of luck. Ask any failure.

—Earl Wilson

SUFFERING

Man cannot remake himself without suffering. For he is both the marble and the sculptor.   —Alexis Carrel

Out of suffering have emerged the strongest souls; the most massive characters are seared with scars.   —E. H. Chapin

To be willing to suffer in order to create is one thing; to realize that one's creation necessitates one's suffering, that suffering is one of the greatest of God's gifts, is almost to reach a mystical solution of the problem of evil.   —J. W. N. Sullivan

Some people would like him [Albert Schweitzer] a lot better now, if only he had suffered more.   —Kurt Vonnegut, Jr.

Every man on the foundation of his own sufferings and joys, builds for all.   —Albert Camus

When two cultures collide is the only time when true suffering exists.

—Hermann Hesse

It is not true that suffering ennobles the character; happiness does that sometimes, but suffering for the most part, makes men petty and vindictive.   —Somerset Maugham

---

If you suffer, thank God!—it is a sure sign that you are alive.

—Elbert Hubbard

The greatest of all perplexities in theology has been to reconcile the infinite goodness of God with his omnipotence. Nothing puts a greater strain upon the faith of the common man than the existence of utterly irrational suffering in the universe.

—Walter Lippmann

Who will tell whether one happy moment of love, or the joy of breathing or walking on a bright morning and smelling the fresh air, is not worth all the suffering and effort which life implies?

—Erich Fromm

No greater grief than to remember days of gladness when sorrow is at hand.   —Friedrich Schiller (1729–1805)

SUICIDE

There is only one truly philosophical problem, and that is suicide.

—Albert Camus

Suicide was naturally the consistent course dictated by the logical intellect. (Is suicide the ultimate sincerity? There seems to be no way to refute the logic of suicide but by the illogic of instinct.)

—William James

A tendency to self-destruction seems to be inherent in the over-developed human brain.   —A. T. W. Simeons

To contemplate suicide is surely the best exercise of the imagination.

—Phyllis Webb

When a man despairs, he does not write; he commits suicide.

—George Monro Grant

Men just don't seem to jump off the bridge for big reasons; they usually do so for *little* ones.   —W. H. Ferry

Suicide is belated acquiescence in the opinion of one's wife's relatives.   —H. L. Mencken

The thought of suicide is a great consolation; with its help you can get through many a bad night.

—Friedrich Nietzsche (1844–1900)

A high percentage of persons over sixty commit suicide.

—*Newsweek* magazine

I have had just about all I can take of myself.

—S. N. Behrman, at seventy-five

After spending some money in his sleep, Hermon the miser was so hopping mad he hanged himself.   —Lucilius (2nd century B.C.)

Too busy with the crowded hour to fear to live or die.
                    —Ralph Waldo Emerson (1803–1882)

He who has a why to live can bear almost any how.
                                —Friedrich Nietzsche

*   *

I am ignorant and impotent and yet, somehow or other, here I am,
unhappy, no doubt, profoundly dissatisfied . . . In spite of everything I survive.   —Aldous Huxley

If one truly has lost hope, one would not be on hand to say so.
                                    —Eric Bentley

*   *

There must be a hell of a lot of people in the world like me—who
want to die but haven't got the guts.   —Horace McCoy

Often the test of courage is not to die but to live.
                    —Conte Vittorio Alfieri (1749–1803)

SUPERSTITION

A superstition is a premature explanation that overstays its time.
                                    —George Iles

Superstition is a religion of feeble minds.
                        —Edmund Burke (1729–1797)

To become a popular religion, it is only necessary for a superstition
to enslave a philosophy.   —Dean William R. Inge

So urgent on the vulgar is the necessity of believing, that the fall of
any system of mythology will probably be succeeded by the introduction of some other mode of superstition.
                        —Edward Gibbon (1737–1794)

Religions are born and may die, but superstition is immortal. Only
the fortunate can take life without mythology.
                            —Will and Ariel Durant

*   *

You know, Tolstoy, like myself, wasn't taken in by superstitions
like science and medicine.   —George Bernard Shaw

There is a superstition in avoiding superstition.
                        —Francis Bacon (1561–1626)

SURVIVAL

Mere survival is an affliction. What is of interest is life, and the direction of that life.   —Guy Fregault

The human race's prospects of survival were considerably better when we were defenceless against tigers than they are today when we have become defenceless against ourselves.

—Arnold Toynbee

The more we exploit nature, the more our options are reduced, until we have only one: to fight for survival.   —Morris K. Udall

I felt as though my country was stirring deeply within me, like a great gentle thing which didn't need anyone's death to survive.

—Jean Guéhenno

The ultimate value of life depends upon awareness, and the power of contemplation rather than upon mere survival.

—Aristotle (384–322 B.C.)

In the fight for survival, a tie or split decision simply will not do.

—Merle L. Meacham

A nation without the means of reform is without means of survival.

—Edmund Burke (1729–1797)

TACT

In the battle of existence, talent is the punch; tact is the clever footwork.   —Wilson Mizner

Tact is the art of making a point without making an enemy.
                                    —Howard W. Newton

Mention not a halter in the house of him that was hanged.
                                    —George Herbert (1593–1633)

Tact: Tongue in check.   —Sue Dytri

Tact: Ability to tell a man he's open-minded when he has a hole in his head.   —F. G. Kernan

Tact consists in knowing how far to go too far.

                                    —Jean Cocteau

Tact is the ability to describe others as they see themselves. —Abraham Lincoln (1809–1865) (And to convince them they know more than you do.)

TASTE

For those who like this sort of thing, this is the sort of thing they like.   —Max Beerbohm

There is no accounting for tastes, as the woman said when some-body told her her son was wanted by the police.
—Franklin P. Adams

Taste is the literary conscience of the soul.
—Joseph Joubert (1754–1824)

Anybody who doesn't like this book is healthy.   —Groucho Marx (commenting on Oscar Levant's book, *Memoirs of an Amnesiac*)

An ass is beautiful to an ass, and a pig is beautiful to a pig.
—John Ray

I explained to him I had simple tastes and didn't want anything ostentatious, no matter what it cost me.   —Art Buchwald

Good taste and humor are a contradiction in terms, like a chaste whore.   —Malcolm Muggeridge

No one ever went broke underestimating the taste of the American public.   —H. L. Mencken

Do not do unto others as you would that they should do unto you. Their tastes may not be the same.   —George Bernard Shaw

I might go so far as to say that any writer who produced a book of unquestioned good taste has written a tasteless book . . . There is no taste in life or nature. It is simply the way it is . . . There is shocking bad taste in the Old Testament, abominable taste in Homer and execrable taste in Shakespeare.   —John Steinbeck

Taste is only to be educated by contemplation, not of the tolerably good, but of the truly excellent. I therefore show you only the best works; and when you are grounded in these, you will have a standard for the rest, which you will know how to value, without over-rating them.   —Johann W. von Goethe (1749–1832)

Every one to his taste, as the woman said when she kissed her sow.
—François Rabelais (1495?–1553)

TAXES

The only thing that hurts more than paying an income tax is not having to pay an income tax.   —Lord Thomas R. Duwar (Under either of our two forms of government: the short form and the long form.)

We are not the bosses of taxpayers; they are ours.   —T. Coleman Andrews (Director, Internal Revenue Service, 1955)

The income tax has made more liars out of the American people than golf has. Even when you make a tax form out on the level, you don't know when it's through if you are a crook or a martyr.
—Will Rogers

Nothing makes a man and wife feel closer, these days, than a joint tax return. —Gil Stern (Few of us ever test our powers of deduction, except when filling out an income tax form.)

Every child born in America can hope to grow up to enjoy tax loopholes. —TRB (Richard Strout)

Blessed are the young, for they shall inherit the national debt.
—Herbert Hoover

If Patrick Henry thought that taxation without representation was bad, he should see how bad it is with representation.
—The Old Farmer's Almanac

The reward of energy, enterprise and thrift—is taxes.
—William Feather

There is just one thing I can promise you about the outer-space program: Your tax dollar will go farther.
—Wernher von Braun

Why does a slight tax increase cost you two hundred dollars and a substantial tax cut save you thirty cents? —Peg Bracken

Capital punishment: The income tax. —Jeff Hayes

I'm proud to be paying taxes in the United States. The only thing is—I could be just as proud for half the money.
—Arthur Godfrey

I would suggest the taxation of all property equally whether church or corporation. —Ulysses S. Grant (1822–1885)

Collecting more taxes than is absolutely necessary is legalized robbery. —Calvin Coolidge

Governments last as long as the under-taxed can defend themselves against the over-taxed. —Bernard Berenson

*   *

Count the day won when, turning on its axis,/This earth imposes no additional taxes. —Franklin P. Adams (The primary requisite for any new tax law is for it to exempt enough voters to win the next election.)

Taxes are going up so fast that government is likely to price itself right out of the market. —Dan Bennett

Anybody has a right to evade taxes if he can get away with it. No citizen has a moral obligation to assist in maintaining the government.   —J. Pierpont Morgan

Why shouldn't the American people take half my money from me? I took all of it from them.   —Edward A. Filene

*   *

The trouble with being a breadwinner nowadays is that the Government is in for such a big slice.   —Mary McCoy

People want *just* taxes more than they want *lower* taxes. They want to know that every man is paying his proportionate share according to his wealth.   —Will Rogers

TEACHING

She used to be a schoolteacher but she has no class now.
    —Fred Allen

You don't have to think too hard when you talk to a teacher.
    —J. D. Salinger

To teach is to learn.   —Japanese Proverb

I hear and I forget. I see and I remember. I do and I understand.
    —Chinese Proverb

Successful teachers are effective in spite of the psychological theories they suffer under.   —Educational Proverb

The art of teaching is the art of assisting discovery.
    —Mark Van Doren

A teacher affects eternity; no one can tell where his influence stops.
    —Henry Adams

Teaching is not a lost art, but the regard for it is a lost tradition.
    —Jacques Barzun

The mediocre teacher tells. The good teacher explains. The superior teacher demonstrates. The great teacher inspires.
    —William Arthur Ward

Why in the world are salaries higher for administrators when the basic mission is teaching.   —Governor Jerry Brown

Most educators would continue to lecture on navigation while the ship is going down.   —James H. Boren

In teaching it is the method and not the content that is the message . . . the drawing out, not the pumping in.

—Ashley Montagu

For every person wishing to teach there are thirty not wanting to be taught.   —W. C. Sellar and R. J. Yeatman

At this time it is still almost axiomatic that quite a number of pedagogues are inclined to consider the whole world as their classroom and will continue to examine and give homework to any casual strangers that happen to cross their paths.

—Alexander King

Cultural inbreeding is a dominant factor in the selection of teachers; for the most part, children are taught by teachers brought up in the same state.   —Robert S. and Helen M. Lynd

If I had a child who wanted to be a teacher, I would bid him Godspeed as if he were going to a war. For indeed the war against prejudice, greed and ignorance is eternal, and those who dedicate themselves to it give their lives no less because they may live to see some fraction of the battle won.   —James Hilton

I beg of you to stop apologizing for being a member of the most important . . . profession in the world.   —William G. Carr

---

You can teach a student a lesson for a day; but if you can teach him to learn by creating curiosity, he will continue the learning process as long as he lives.   —Clay P. Bedford

The job of a teacher is to excite in the young a boundless sense of curiosity about life, so that the growing child shall come to apprehend it with an excitement tempered by awe and wonder.

—John Garrett

He is either dead or teaching school.

—Zenobius (1st century B.C.)

Those who can, do; those who can't, teach.   —George Bernard Shaw (And those who can't teach, teach the teachers.)

TEMPTATION

What makes resisting temptation difficult, for many people, is that they don't want to discourage it completely.

—Franklin P. Jones

All the things I really like to do are either immoral, illegal or fattening.   —Alexander Woollcott

To cease smoking is the easiest thing I ever did. I ought to know because I've done it a thousand times.　　—Mark Twain

I find I always have to write something on a steamed mirror.
　　　　　　　　　　　　　　　　　—Elaine Dundy

There is not any memory with less satisfaction than the memory of some temptation we resisted.　　—James Branch Cabell (The trouble with resisting temptation is that you may not get another chance.)

The surest protection against temptation is cowardice.
　　　　　　　　　　　　　　　　　—Mark Twain

The only way to get rid of temptation is to yield to it. . . . I can resist everything but temptation.　　—Oscar Wilde (1854–1900)

Don't worry about avoiding temptation—as you grow older, it starts avoiding you.　　—*The Old Farmer's Almanac*

THEATER

You need three things in the theatre—the play, the actors, and the audience, and each must give something.　　—Kenneth Haigh

I got all the schooling any actress needs. That is, I learned to write enough to sign contracts.　　—Hermione Gingold

The art of acting consists in keeping people from coughing.
　　　　　　　　　　　　　　　—Sir Ralph Richardson

I didn't like the play, but then I saw it under adverse conditions—the curtain was up.　　—Groucho Marx

Perfectly Scandalous was one of those plays in which all of the actors, unfortunately, enunciated very clearly.　　—Robert Benchley

Tank-town performance of *Uncle Tom's Cabin*: The dogs were poorly supported by the cast.　　—Don Herold

By increasing the size of the keyhole, today's playwrights are in danger of doing away with the door.　　—Peter Ustinov

An actor is a sculptor who carves in snow.
　　　　　　　　　　　　　　　—Edwin Booth (1833–1893)

Every actor in his heart believes everything bad that's printed about him.　　—Orson Welles

There are two kinds of directors in the theater. Those who think they are God and those who are certain of it.
　　　　　　　　　　　　　　　—Rhetta Hughes

Actors are the only honest hypocrites.   —William Hazlitt
(1778–1830) (The girl who has half a mind to become an actress
doesn't realize that that's what it requires.)

If a farmer fills his barn with grain, he gets mice; if he leaves it
empty, he gets actors.   —Bill Vaughan

I don't see why people want new plays all the time. What would
happen to concerts if people wanted new music all the time?
                                                —Clive Barnes

Acting is not being emotional, but being able to express emotion.
                                                —Kate Reid

Actresses don't have husbands, they have attendants.
                                                —Margaret Anglin

A fan club is a group of people who tell an actor he's not alone in
the way he feels about himself.   —Jack Carson

Father Time is the make-up man responsible for the physical changes
that determine the parts the average actor is to play.
                                                —Fred Allen

When you're a young man, Macbeth is a character part. When
you're older, it's a straight part.   —Sir Laurence Olivier

THOUGHT

We think in generalities, we live in detail.
                                                —Alfred North Whitehead

Every good thought you think is contributing its share to the ultimate
result of your life.   —Grenville Kleiser

Change your thoughts and you change your world.
                                                —Norman Vincent Peale

What right have you to think? Haven't you been in the Police force
long enough to know that?   —J. C. Snaith

He thinks things through very clearly before going off half-cocked.
                                                —General Carl Spaatz

Sixty minutes of thinking of any kind is bound to lead to confusion
and unhappiness.   —James Thurber

The fundamental fact about the Greek was that he had to use his
mind. The ancient priests had said, "Thus far and no farther. We

set the limits of thought." The Greeks said, "All things are to be examined and called into question. There are no limits set on thought."   —Edith Hamilton

A conclusion is the place where you got tired thinking.
                                        —Martin H. Fischer

Thought makes the whole dignity of man; therefore endeavor to think well, that is the only morality.
                                        —Blaise Pascal (1623–1662)

It isn't what people think that is important, but the reason they think what they think.   —Eugène Ionesco

There are two ways to slide easily through life; to believe everything or to doubt everything. Both ways save us from thinking.
                                        —Alfred Korzybski

For my thoughts are not your thoughts, neither are your ways my ways.   —The Bible (Isaiah 55:8)

Remember happiness doesn't depend upon who you are or what you have; it depends solely upon what you think.
                                        —Dale Carnegie

Action and faith enslave thought, both of them in order not to be troubled or inconvenienced by reflection, criticism, and doubt.
                                        —Henri Frédéric Amiel (1821–1881)

All great discoveries are made by men whose feelings run ahead of their thinking.   —C. H. Parkhurst

It is nonsense to say there is not enough time to be fully informed . . . Time given to thought is the greatest time-saver of all.
                                        —Norman Cousins

We cannot unthink unless we are insane.   —Arthur Koestler

The no-mind not-thinks no-thoughts about no-things.
                                        —Buddha (563?–483? B.C.)

Many people have played themselves to death. Many people have eaten and drunk themselves to death. Nobody ever thought himself to death.   —Gilbert Highet

Write down the thoughts of the moment. Those that come unsought for are commonly the most valuable.
                                        —Francis Bacon (1561–1626)

To me the meanest flower that blows can give/Thoughts that do often lie too deep for tears.
                                        —William Wordsworth (1770–1850)

It may be laid down as an axiom that a man who does not live the
life of the mob will not think its thoughts either.
                                        —Lewis Browne

The dissenter is every human being at those moments of his life
when he resigns momentarily from the herd and thinks for himself.
                                        —Archibald MacLeish

                    *   *

Few people think more than two or three times a year. I have made
an international reputation for myself by thinking once or twice a
week.   —George Bernard Shaw

Men can live without air for a few minutes, without water for about
two weeks, without food for about two months—and without a new
thought for years on end.   —Kent Ruth

                    *   *

They talk most who have the least to say.
                                        —Matthew Prior (1664–1721)

The thoughtless are rarely wordless.   —Howard W. Newton

                    *   *

There is no expedient to which a man will not resort to avoid the
real labor of thinking.   —Sir Joshua Reynolds (1723–1792)

There is no expedient to which a man will not go to avoid the real
labor of thinking.   —Thomas Alva Edison

                    *   *

Where all men think alike, no one thinks very much.
                                        —Walter Lippmann

It is not best that we should all think alike; it is difference of opinion which makes horse races.   —Mark Twain

                    *   *

The fatal tendency of mankind to leave off thinking about a thing
when it is no longer doubtful, is the cause of half their errors.
                                        —John Stuart Mill (1806–1873)

Civilization advances by extending the number of important operations which we can perform without thinking.
                                        —Alfred North Whitehead

                    *   *

People should think things out fresh and not just accept conventional terms and the conventional way of doing things.

—Buckminster Fuller

For God's sake don't let us think. If we did there would be an end to society.   —Lucas Cleeve

TIME

I would I could stand on a busy corner, hat in hand, and beg people to throw me all their wasted hours.   —Bernard Berenson

The Present is a Point just passed.   —David Russell

Time is but the stream I go a-fishing in.

—Henry David Thoreau (1817–1862)

Time walks by your side, ma'am, unwilling to pass.

—Christopher Fry

Methinks I see the wanton hours flee,/And as they pass, turn back and laugh at me.

—George Villiers, 2nd Duke of Buckingham (1628–1687)

In reality, killing time/Is only the name for another of the multifarious ways/By which Time kills us.   —Sir Osbert Sitwell

Time wounds all heels.   —Jane Ace

Time goes, you say? Ah no!/Alas, Time stays, we go.

—Austin Dobson

Time is a circus always packing up and moving away.

—Ben Hecht

Living is entirely too time-consuming.   —Irene Peter

Time has no divisions to mark its passing. There is never a thunderstorm to announce the beginning of a new month or year.

—Thomas Mann

Backward, turn backward, O Time, in your flight,/And tell me just one thing I studied last night.   —Hobart Brown

TOLERANCE

Tolerance is the positive and cordial effort to understand another's beliefs, practices, and habits without necessarily sharing or accepting them.   —Joshua Liebman

Wouldn't it be a helluva joke if all this were really burnt cork and you people were being tolerant for nuthin'?   —Dick Gregory

Stevens' mind was so tolerant that he could have attended a lynching every day without becoming critical.   —Thorne Smith

The trouble with being tolerant is that people think you don't understand the problem.   —Merle L. Meacham

Most people would rather defend to the death your right to say it than listen to it.   —Robert Brault

Once lead this people into war and they will forget there ever was such a thing as tolerance.   —Woodrow Wilson

Whereas each man claims his freedom as a matter of right, the freedom he accords to other men is a matter of toleration.   —Walter Lippmann (He magnanimously accords to others the right to be wrong.)

Tolerance is the virtue of the man without convictions.
                                        —G. K. Chesterton

I have seen gross intolerance shown in support of tolerance.
                        —Samuel Taylor Coleridge (1772–1834)

I hate people who are intolerant.   —Laurence J. Peter

Art, if it is to be reckoned as one of the great values of life, must teach men . . . tolerance.   —Somerset Maugham

No man has a right in America to treat any other man tolerantly, for tolerance is the assumption of superiority.
                                        —Wendell Willkie

TOMBS / STATUES / MONUMENTS

The tombstone is about the only thing that can stand upright and lie on its face at the same time.   —Mary Wilson Little (Many a tombstone inscription is a grave error.)

They [the Turkish Sayyids and Afghan Lodis] built their fine domed tombs for their future repose before they died. It was possible that they foresaw that no one would think well enough of them to do so afterward.   —John Kenneth Galbraith

Many people's tombstones should read, "Died at 30. Buried at 60."
                                        —Nicholas Murray Butler

A great life has passed into the tomb/And there awaits the requiem of winter's snows.   —Louis H. Sullivan

The monuments of the nations are all protests against nothingness after death; so are statues and inscriptions; so is history.

—General Lew Wallace

Wrapt in the cold embraces of the tomb.

—Alexander Pope (1688–1744)

E'en from the tomb the voice of nature cries,/E'en in our ashes live their wonted fires.   —Thomas Gray (1716–1771)

TRAVEL

In America there are two classes of travel—first class and with children.   —Robert Benchley

Thanks to the miles of superhighways under construction, America will soon be a wonderful place to drive—if you don't want to stop.

—Fletcher Knebel

A tourist is a fellow who drives thousands of miles so he can be photographed standing in front of his car.   —Emile Ganest (A few reels of your vacation pictures soon put your guests in a traveling mood.)

One of the most common disrupters of marital bliss is the choice of where to spend a vacation. What this country needs is an ocean in the mountains.   —Paul Sweeney

Airline travel is hours of boredom interrupted by moments of stark terror.   —Al Boliska

A good holiday is one spent among people whose notions of time are vaguer than yours.   —J. B. Priestley

There is no place to go, and so we travel! You and I, and what for, just to imagine that we could go somewhere else.

—Edward Dahlberg

Natives who beat drums to drive off evil spirits are objects of scorn to smart Americans who blow horns to break up traffic jams.

—Mary Ellen Kelly

It is not worth while to go around the world to count the cats in Zanzibar.   —Henry David Thoreau (1817–1862)

See one promontory, one mountain, one sea, one river, and see all.

—Socrates (470?–399 B.C.)

Restore human legs as a means of travel. Pedestrians rely on food for fuel and need no special parking facilities.

—Lewis Mumford

TRUTH

Express a mean opinion of yourself occasionally; it will show your friends that you know how to tell the truth. —Ed Howe

Why *shouldn't* truth be stranger than fiction? Fiction, after all, has to make sense. —Mark Twain

The credibility gap is so wide that our suspicions are confirmed by any official denial. —Laurence J. Peter

Tell the truth/But tell it slant.

—Emily Dickinson (1830–1886)

The opposite of a correct statement is a false statement. But the opposite of a profound truth may well be another profound truth.

—Niels Bohr

True genius resides in the capacity for evaluation of uncertain, hazardous, and conflicting information. —Winston Churchill

For of course the true meaning of a term is to be found by observing what a man does with it, not by what he says about it.
   —P. W. Bridgman ("Ask not what we say but what we do!")

The most striking contradiction of our civilization is the fundamental reverence for truth which we profess and the thorough-going disregard for it which we practice. —Vilhjalmur Stefansson

Let us begin by committing ourselves to the truth—to see it like it is, and tell it like it is—to find the truth, to speak the truth, and to live the truth. —Richard M. Nixon (accepting the GOP presidential nomination in 1968)

An intimate truth is also a universal truth. —John Cournos

One unerring mark of the love of truth is not entertaining any proposition with greater assurance than the proofs it is built upon will warrant. —John Locke (1632–1704)

I never give them hell. I just tell the truth and they think it's hell.

—Harry S Truman

The truth is more important than the facts.

—Frank Lloyd Wright

Fraud and falsehood only dread examination. Truth invites it.

—Thomas Cooper (1759–1839)

The victor will never be asked if he told the truth.

—Adolf Hitler

I have come to the conclusion that a person should never accept any statement or even fact as being the absolute truth . . . No statement should be believed merely because it has been made by an authority.   —Hans Reichenbach

To be persuasive, we must be believable,/To be believable, we must be credible,/To be credible, we must be truthful.

—Edward R. Murrow

The truth is so simple that it is regarded as pretentious banality.

—Dag Hammarskjöld

It is not truth that makes man great, but man who makes truth great.   —Confucius (c. 551–479 B.C.)

Poetry is not the assertion of truth, but the making of that truth more fully real to us.   —T. S. Eliot

It is an old maxim of mine that when you have excluded the impossible, whatever remains, however improbable, must be the truth.

—Sir Arthur Conan Doyle

False views . . . do very little harm, for everyone takes a salutary pleasure in proving their falseness; and when this is done, one path towards error is closed and the road to truth is often at the same time opened.   —Charles Darwin (1809–1882)

If error is corrected whenever it is recognized as such, the path of error is the path of truth.   —Hans Reichenbach

*   *

Truth or tact? You have to choose. Most times they are not compatible.   —Eddie Cantor

Whatever is only almost true is quite false, and among the most dangerous of errors, because being so near truth, it is the more likely to lead astray.   —Henry Ward Beecher (1813–1887)

*   *

What plays the mischief with the truth is that men will insist upon the universal application of a temporary feeling or opinion.

—Herman Melville (1819–1891)

Truth—what we think it is at any given moment of time.

—Luigi Pirandello

I have never been sure I am right, but I'm also sure nobody else has this thing called truth.   —Saul Alinsky

No man thoroughly understands a truth until he has contended against it. —Ralph Waldo Emerson (1803–1882)

* *

The best test of truth is the power of the thought to get itself accepted in the competition of the market.
—Oliver Wendell Holmes, Jr.

The dictum that truth always triumphs over persecution is one of those pleasant falsehoods which men repeat after one another till they pass into commonplace, but which all experience refutes.
—John Stuart Mill (1806–1873)

TYRANNY / TYRANTS

The best government is a benevolent tyranny tempered by an occasional assassination.
—Voltaire (François Marie Arouet) (1694–1778)

I have sworn upon the altar of God, eternal hostility against every form of tyranny over the mind of man.
—Thomas Jefferson (1743–1826)

The tyranny of legislators is at present, and will be for many years, our most formidable danger. The tyranny of the executive will arise in its turn, but at a more distant period. —Thomas Jefferson

The only consolation that a democracy suggests . . . is that every member of the state has a chance of arriving at a share in the chief magistracy, and consequently of playing the tyrant in his turn.
—J. B. Priestley

A despot easily forgives his subjects for not loving him, provided they do not love each other.
—Alexis de Tocqueville (1805–1859)

Righteous vengefulness . . . has always made new tyrannies out of aging liberations. —Erik Erickson

Necessity is the argument of tyrants, it is the creed of slaves.
—William Pitt the Younger (1759–1806)

The tyrant is nothing but a slave turned inside out.
—Herbert Spencer

Tyrants have not yet discovered any chains that can fetter the mind.
—Charles Caleb Colton (1780–1832) (What about brainwashing?)

Justice without force is powerless; force without justice is tyrannical. —Blaise Pascal (1623–1662)

U

UN-AMERICAN

They'll [the Un-American Activities Committee] nail anyone who ever scratched his ass during the National Anthem.

—Humphrey Bogart

Un-American is simply something that somebody else does not agree to.　　—Maury Maverick (In the 1950's, Edgar C. Bundy, executive secretary of the Church League of America, led a campaign that declared the Girl Scout Handbook un-American.)

The Supreme Court is the greatest single threat to the Constitution.

—Senator James Eastland

Who would be cleared by their [un-American] Committees? Not Washington, who was a rebel. Not Jefferson, who wrote that all men are created equal and whose motto was *rebellion to tyrants is obedience to God* . . . Not Lincoln, who admonished us to have malice toward none, charity for all; or Wilson, who warned that our flag was *a flag of liberty of opinion as well as of political liberty;* or Justice Holmes, who said that our Constitution is an experiment [and] that *we should be eternally vigilant against attempts to check the expression of opinions that we loathe and believe to be fraught with death.*　　—Henry Steele Commager

UNIVERSE

My theology, briefly, is that the universe was dictated but not signed.   —Christopher Morley

A man said to the universe, "Sir, I exist." "However," replied the universe, "the fact has not created in me a sense of obligation."
                                        —Stephen Crane (1871–1900)

The universe is one of God's thoughts.
                                        —Friedrich Schiller (1729–1805)

Taken as a whole, the universe is absurd.
                                        —Walter Savage Landor (1775–1864)

The universe is but one vast Symbol of God.
                                        —Thomas Carlyle (1795–1881)

URBANIZATION

Man is the animal that intends to shoot himself out into interplanetary space, after having given up on the problem of an efficient way to get himself five miles to work and back each day.
                                        —Bill Vaughan

Our national flower is the concrete cloverleaf.
                                        —Lewis Mumford

If we become two people—the suburban affluent and the urban poor, each filled with mistrust and fear of the other—then we shall effectively cripple each generation to come.
                                        —Lyndon B. Johnson

The increasing tempo of urbanization and growth is already depriving many Americans of the right to live in decent surroundings.
                                        —White House message, 1965

The planner's problem is to find ways of creating, within the urban environment, the sense of belonging.   —Leo Marx

The population-environment movement is absolutely inseparable from the antiwar movement, the drive for urban rehabilitation, prison reform, and—most importantly—the civil rights movement.
                                        —Dr. Paul R. Ehrlich

Yet several common fallacies about urban America continue to persist—despite the lessons of New York City. One is that bigness brings greatness—and the second that the continued urbanization of of our country—no matter how misdirected—is a fatalistic reality that is beyond our control.　　—Charles N. Kimball

Town life nourishes and perfects all the more civilized elements in man—Shakespeare wrote nothing but doggerel lampoon before he came to London.　　—Oscar Wilde (1854–1900)

We do pretty much whatever we want to. Why can't we live in good cities?　　—Philip Johnson

The problem of the cities . . . is the most urgent, the most difficult, and the most frightening American domestic problem . . . since the Civil War.　　—Joe Alsop

Men come together in cities in order to live: they remain together in order to live the good life.　　—Aristotle (384–322 B.C.)

We must have towns that accommodate different educational groups, different economic groups, different ethnic groups, towns where all can live in one place.　　—Margaret Mead

VALUES

Today we are afraid of simple words like *goodness* and *mercy* and *kindness*. We don't believe in the good old words because we don't believe in the good old values anymore. And that's why the world is sick.   —Lin Yutang

I'd rather have roses on my table than diamonds on my neck.
                                              —Emma Goldman

A man who dares to waste one hour of time has not discovered the value of life.   —Charles Darwin (1809–1882)

Man's judgments of value follow directly his wishes for happiness—they are an attempt to support his illusions with arguments.
                                              —Sigmund Freud

We live in a vastly complex society which has been able to provide us with a multitude of material things, and this is good, but people are beginning to suspect that we have paid a high spiritual price for our plenty.   —Euell Gibbons

The adherents of the *status quo* never had it so bad. There has always been a conflict between those who feel their values are eternal and those who feel they are relative.   —R. Kostelanetz

The New Leftists believe in the omnipotence of the deed and the irrelevance of the goal.   —Arthur Schlesinger, Jr.

THE VICE-PRESIDENCY / VICE-PRESIDENTS

The Vice Presidency is sort of like the last cooky on the plate. Everybody insists he won't take it, but somebody always does.
—Bill Vaughan

I don't know anything about being President. I just found out today how to be vice-president.   —Alexander Throttlebottom

My country has contrived for me the most insignificant office that ever the invention of man contrived or his imagination conceived.
—John Adams (1735–1826)

Once there were two brothers: one ran away to sea, the other was elected Vice-President—and nothing was ever heard from either of them again.   —Thomas Marshall

The Vice-Presidency of the United States isn't worth a pitcher of warm spit.   —John Nance Garner

VICTORY AND DEFEAT

Anybody can win, unless there happens to be a second entry.
—George Ade

In the fight between you and the world, back the world.
—Franz Kafka

Without victory there is no survival!   —Winston Churchill

Victory has a hundred fathers but defeat is an orphan.
—Count Galeazzo Ciano

Victory has a hundred memories but defeat has amnesia.
—W. I. E. Gates

Even victors are by victory undone.
—John Dryden (1631–1700)

Winning is overemphasized. The only time it is really important is in surgery and war.   —Al McGuire

The victor belongs to the spoils.   —F. Scott Fitzgerald

Truth is with the victor—who, as you know, also controls the historians.   —Rolf Hochhuth

In war there is no substitute for victory.
—Douglas MacArthur

I do not think that winning is the most important thing. I think winning is the only thing.   —Bill Veeck (discussing his long experience as a baseball executive)

When you win, nothing hurts.   —Joe Namath

To be vanquished and yet not surrender, that is victory.
—Josef Pilsudski

Every man's got to figure to get beat sometime.   —Joe Louis

VIOLENCE

I have definitional problems with the word "violence." I don't know what the word "violence" means.   —William Colby

I am one three-billionth of the world history today.   —Arthur Bremer (who attempted to assassinate Governor George Wallace)

If someone is violent toward those who seek freedom, that's bad. But if those who seek freedom use violence to achieve it, that's good.   —Michelangelo Antonioni

Assassination . . . should be used as the vote should ideally be used, that is, bearing in mind only the public good.
—Edward Hyams

Southern congressmen center their strategy against anti-lynching legislation by claiming that it would be unconstitutional and an infringement upon states' rights.   —Gunnar Myrdal

In some cases non-violence requires more militancy than violence.
—Cesar Chavez

A violently active, dominating, intrepid, brutal youth—that is what I am after.   —Adolf Hitler

You do not destroy an idea by killing people; you replace it with a better one.   —Edward Keating

An assassin is one who takes life easily.   —Laurence J. Peter

Violence is fine against simple folk ten thousand miles away and shocking against injustice in our own land.
—Arthur Schlesinger, Jr.

The state calls its own violence law, but that of the individual crime.
—Max Stirner

There appears to be irrefutable evidence that the mere fact of physical over-crowding induces violence.   —Harvey Wheeler

The tendency to identify manhood with a capacity for physical violence has a long history in America.   —Marshall Fishwick

There is perhaps no phenomenon which contains so much destructive feeling as *moral indignation* which permits envy or hate to be acted out under the guise of *virtue*.   —Erich Fromm

Many of the same people who have no difficulty in finding extenuating circumstances to account for the violence of the hardhats, find it impossible to accept any explanations for the violence of the students.   —Norman Cousins

---

There is an illusion of central position, justifying one's own purposes as right and everybody else's as wrong, and providing a proper degree of paranoia. Righteous ends, thus approved, absolve of guilt the most violent means.   —Robert Ardrey

Violent disorder once set in motion may spawn tyranny, not freedom.   —Charles E. Wyzanski, Jr.

*   *

You know what I think about violence. For me it is profoundly moral, more moral than compromises and transactions.
                                                    —Benito Mussolini

Answer violence with violence!   —Juan Perón

Whatever little we have gained we have gained by agitation, while we have uniformly lost by moderation.
                                  —Daniel O'Connell (1775–1847)

Terror is nothing else than justice, prompt, secure and inflexible!
                      —Maximilien de Robespierre (1758–1794)

*   *

Violence alone, violence committed by the people, violence organized and educated by its leaders, makes it possible for the masses to understand social truths and gives the key to them.
                                                    —Frantz Fanon

Violence is counter-productive and produces changes of a sort you don't want. It is a very dangerous instrument and can destroy those who wield it.   —John Gardner

VIRTUE / VICE

Virtue has always been conceived of as victorious resistance to one's vital desire.   —James Branch Cabell

Virtue has need of limits.
—Baron de Montesquieu (1689–1755)

When we are planning for posterity, we ought to remember that virtue is not hereditary.　—Thomas Paine (1737–1809) (Virtue is learned at mother's knee; vice at other joints.)

Some people with great virtues are disagreeable, while others with great vices are delightful.
—Duc de La Rochefoucauld (1613–1680)

Virtue, perhaps, is nothing more than politeness of soul.
—Honoré de Balzac (1799–1850)

The formula for Utopia on earth remains always the same: to make a necessity of virtue.　—Clifton Fadiman

Woman's virtue is man's greatest invention.
—Cornelia Otis Skinner

There are some jobs in which it is impossible for a man to be virtuous.　—Aristotle (384–322 B.C.)

Any of us can achieve virtue, if by virtue we merely mean the avoidance of the vices that do not attract us.　—Robert S. Lynd

Virtue is insufficient temptation.　—George Bernard Shaw

* *

Virtue does not consist so much in abstaining from vice, as in not having an affection for it.　—W. T. Eldridge

How easy it is to be virtuous when we have no inclination to be otherwise.　—Dolf Wyllarde

---

As to virtue . . . it is an act of the will, a habit which increases the quantity, intensity and quality of life. It builds up, strengthens and vivifies personality.　—Alexis Carrel

Be virtuous and you will be eccentric.　—Mark Twain

* *

Virtue is its own reward.　—John Dryden (1631–1700)

Virtue is its own revenge.　—E. Y. Harburg

VOCATION

Each honest calling, each walk of life, has its own elite, its own aristocracy based upon excellence of performance.
—James Bryant Conant

Nothing splendid has ever been achieved except by those who dared believe that something inside them was superior to circumstances.
—Bruce Barton

We are told that talent creates its own opportunities. But it sometimes seems that intense desire creates not only its own opportunities, but its own talents. —Eric Hoffer

Always take a job that is too big for you. —Harry Emerson Fosdick (It is the surest path to reach your level of incompetency.)

We work not only to produce but to give value to time.
—Eugène Delacroix (1798–1863)

If at first you don't succeed you're running about average.
—M. H. Alderson

There is no future in any job. The future lies in the man who holds the job. —Dr. George Crane

———

Every calling is great when greatly pursued.
—Oliver Wendell Holmes, Jr.

It is well for a man to respect his own vocation whatever it is and to think himself bound to uphold it and to claim for it the respect it deserves. —Charles Dickens (1812–1870)

*   *

There never has been any thirty-hour week for men who had anything to do. —Charles F. Kettering

By working faithfully eight hours a day, you may eventually get to be a boss and work twelve hours a day. —Robert Frost

———

The world is full of willing people; some willing to work, the rest willing to let them. —Robert Frost

If people really liked to work, we'd still be plowing the land with sticks and transporting goods on our backs. —William Feather

WAR AND PEACE

An infallible method of conciliating a tiger is to allow oneself to be devoured.   —Konrad Adenauer

When women have a voice in national and international affairs, war will cease forever.   —Augusta Stowe-Gullen

War hath no fury like a non-combatant.   —C. E. Montague

So far war has been the only force that can discipline a whole community, and until an equivalent discipline is organized, I believe that war must have its way.   —William James

If men recognize no law superior to their desires, then they must fight when their desires collide.   —R. H. Tawney

The day when nobody comes back from a war it will be because the war has at last been properly organized.   —Boris Vian

I will not bathe my hands in the blood of the people of Mexico, nor will I participate in the guilt of those murders which have been and will hereafter be committed by our army there.
          —Joshua R. Giddings (1795–1864)

You furnish the pictures and I'll furnish the war.
          —William Randolph Hearst, to Frederic Remington

They told me it would disrupt my life less if I got killed sooner.
—Joseph Heller

But in modern war . . . you will die like a dog for no good reason.
—Ernest Hemingway

The next dreadful thing to a battle lost is a battle won.
—Arthur Wellesley, Duke of Wellington (1769–1852)

War, like any other racket, pays high dividends to the very few . . . The cost of operations is always transferred to the people who do not profit.   —General Smedley Butler

If we justify war it is because all peoples always justify the traits of which they find themselves possessed.   —Ruth Benedict

War would end if the dead could return.   —Stanley Baldwin

What difference does it make to the dead . . . whether the mad destruction is wrought under the name of totalitarianism or the holy name of liberty or democracy?   —Mohandas Gandhi

Thank heaven for the military-industrial complex. Its ultimate aim is peace in our time.   —Barry Goldwater

The world will never have lasting peace so long as men reserve for war the finest human qualities.   —John Foster Dulles

I think that people want peace so much that one of these days government had better get out of their way and let them have it.
—Dwight D. Eisenhower

Do not needlessly endanger your lives until I give you the signal.
—Dwight D. Eisenhower

We flattened cities in Germany and Japan in World War II. I don't know what's so sacred about Hanoi . . . Let world opinion go fly a kite.   —Mendel Rivers

One of the problems we're going to have to solve is to make the Armed Forces so popular, everyone wants to get in.
—General Lewis B. Hershey

Our chiefs are killed . . . The little children are freezing to death. My people . . . have no blankets, no food . . . My heart is sick and sad . . . I will fight no more forever.   —Chief Joseph

War will exist until that distant day when the conscientious objector enjoys the same reputation and prestige that the warrior does today.   —John F. Kennedy

We have the power to make this the best generation of mankind in the history of the world—or to make it the last.
—John F. Kennedy

Henceforth the adequacy of any military establishment will be tested by its ability to preserve the peace.　　—Henry Kissinger

What we lawyers want to do is to substitute courts for carnage, dockets for rockets, briefs for bombs, warrants for warheads, mandates for missiles.　　—Charles Rhyne

No protracted war can fail to endanger the freedom of a democratic country.　　—Alexis de Tocqueville (1805–1859)

In the future no one wins a war. It is true, there are degrees of loss, but no one wins.　　—Brock Chisholm

War is too important to be left to the generals.
　　　　　　　　　　　　　　　　　—Georges Clemenceau

The possibility of war increases in direct proportion to the effectiveness of the instruments of war.　　—Norman Cousins

Where is the indignation about the fact that the United States and Soviet Union have accumulated thirty thousand pounds of destructive force for every human being in the world?
　　　　　　　　　　　　　　　　　—Norman Cousins

Very little is known about the War of 1812 because the Americans lost it.　　—Eric Nicol

Are bombs the only way of setting fire to the spirit of a people? Is the human will as inert as the past two world-wide wars would indicate?　　—Gregory Clark

Instead of the government taking over industry when the war broke out, industry took over the government.　　—Claire Gillis

The air age fans mankind with a sharp choice between Winged Prose or Winged Death.　　—Billy Bishop

Everyone, when there's a war in the air, learns to live with a new element: falsehood.　　—Jean Giraudoux

Every nation sincerely desires peace; and all nations pursue courses which if persisted in, must make peace impossible.
　　　　　　　　　　　　　　　　　—Sir Norman Angell

There never was a time when, in my opinion, some way could not be found to prevent the drawing of the sword.
　　　　　　　　　　　　—Ulysses S. Grant (1822–1885)

A man who experiences no genuine satisfaction in life does not want peace . . . Men court war to escape meaninglessness and boredom, to be relieved of fear and frustration.
　　　　　　　　　　　　　　　　　—Nels F. S. Ferre

In war, when a commander becomes so bereft of reason and perspective that he fails to understand the dependence of arms on Divine guidance, he no longer deserves victory.

—General Douglas MacArthur

The way to win an atomic war is to make certain it never starts.

—General Omar Bradley

Today the real test of power is not capacity to make war but capacity to prevent it.   —Anne O'Hare McCormick

*   *

Peace is not only better than war, but infinitely more arduous.

—George Bernard Shaw

War is only a cowardly escape from the problems of peace.

—Thomas Mann

*   *

Peace is an armistice in a war that is continuously going on.

—Thucydides (471?–400? B.C.)

Diplomacy has rarely been able to gain at the conference table what cannot be gained or held on the battlefield.

—General Walter Bedell Smith

*   *

Of all armies those which long for war most ardently are the democratic ones, but of all peoples those most deeply attached to peace are the democratic nations.

—Alexis de Tocqueville (1805–1859)

Democracy, with its promise of international peace, has been no better guarantee against war than the old dynastic rule of kings.

—Jan C. Smuts

*   *

There are no warlike peoples—just warlike leaders.

—Ralph Bunche

Better pointed bullets than pointed speeches.

—Prince Otto von Bismarck (1815–1898)

*   *

It would indeed be a tragedy if the history of the human race proved to be nothing more than the story of an ape playing with a box of matches on a petrol dump.   —David Ormsby Gore

I launched the phrase "The war to end war"—and that was not the least of my crimes.   —H. G. Wells

In wartime, truth is so precious that she should always be attended by a bodyguard of lies.   —Winston Churchill

In time of war the first casualty is truth.   —Boake Carter

*   *

We prefer world law in the age of self-determination—we reject world war in the age of mass extermination.

—John F. Kennedy

War can only be abolished through war.   —Mao Tse-tung

*   *

Never think that war, no matter how necessary, nor how justified, is not a crime.   —Ernest Hemingway

Human war has been the most successful of all our cultural traditions.   —Robert Ardrey

WEALTH

It is better to have old secondhand diamonds than none at all.

—Mark Twain

Wealth—any income that is at least one hundred dollars more a year than the income of one's wife's sister's husband.

—H. L. Mencken

Nothing is more admirable than the fortitude with which millionaires tolerate the disadvantages of their wealth.   —Rex Stout

In every well-governed state wealth is a sacred thing; in democracies it is the *only* sacred thing.   —Anatole France

The only thing wealth does for some people is to make them worry about losing it.   —Comte de Rivarol (1753–1801)

We have among us a class of mammon worshippers, whose one test of conservatism or radicalism is the attitude one takes with respect to accumulated wealth. Whatever tends to preserve the wealth of the wealthy is called conservatism, and whatever favors anything else, no matter what, they call socialism.

—Richard T. Ely

. . . the idea, which is popular with rich men, that industrial disputes would disappear if only the output of wealth were doubled, and every one were twice as well off, not only is refuted by all practical experience, but is in its very nature founded upon an illusion. For the question is not one of amounts but of proportions.

—R. H. Tawney

Hereditary wealth is in reality a premium paid to idleness.

—William Godwin

The people came to realize that wealth is not the fruit of labor but the result of organized protected robbery.   —Frantz Fanon

The hopes of the Republic cannot forever tolerate either undeserved poverty or self-serving wealth.   —Franklin Delano Roosevelt (What about undeserved wealth?)

If a rich man is proud of his wealth, he should not be praised until it is known how he employs it.

—Socrates (470?–399 B.C.)

The only question with wealth is what you do with it.

—John D. Rockefeller, Jr.

*   *

We must have a political state powerful enough to deal with corporate wealth, but how are we going to keep that state with its augmenting power from being captured by the force we want it to control?   —Vernon Louis Parrington

We can have democracy in this country or we can have great wealth concentrated in the hands of a few, but we can't have both.

—Justice Louis D. Brandeis

Those who own the country ought to govern it.

—John Jay (1745–1829)

It is to be regretted that the rich and powerful too often bend the acts of government to their selfish purposes.

—Andrew Jackson (1767–1845)

*   *

Wealth may be an excellent thing, for it means power, it means leisure, it means liberty.

—James Russell Lowell (1819–1891)

Those who condemn wealth are those who have none and see no chance of getting it.   —William Penn Patrick

*   *

I have no complex about wealth. I have worked hard for my money, producing things people need. I believe that the abie industrial leader who creates wealth and employment is more worthy of historical notice than politicians or soldiers.   —J. Paul Getty

Wealth is a power usurped by the few to compel the many to labor for their benefit.   —Percy Bysshe Shelley (1792–1822)

WELFARE

The assumption underlying the false beliefs [anent welfare] is that "respectable" people are always happier working than not working and will gladly accept any employment offered them. But if this is so, then the belief that those on welfare inhabit a kind of paradise denied those who must grub out a living cannot be true.
—Tom Burnam

The United States spends less proportionately on social welfare than almost any other industrial country.   —*Time* magazine

We are faced with a choice between the work ethic that built this nation's character—and the new welfare ethic that could cause the American character to weaken.   —Richard M. Nixon

HEW [Health, Education, Welfare] has testified that the incidence of fraud among welfare recipients is about four-tenths of one percent . . . nothing to compare with estimates by the IRS (Internal Revenue Service) that 34 percent of private interest income goes unreported.   —*The New Republic* magazine

It is one of the fundamental changes of the last fifty years that in all Western countries the principle has been adopted that every citizen must have a minimum material security . . . Yet, while this principle has been adopted, there is still, among most businessmen, intense hostility against it, and especially its widening application; they speak contemptuously of the *welfare state* as killing private initiative and the spirit of adventure, and in fighting social security measures they pretend to fight for the freedom and initiative of the worker. That these arguments are sheer rationalizations is evidenced by the fact that the same people have no qualms about praising economic security as one of the chief aims of life.
—Sigmund Freud

WINE

Wine that maketh glad the heart of man.
—The Bible (Psalms 104:15)

From wine what sudden friendship springs!
                              —John Gay (1685–1732)

Wine gives great pleasure, and every pleasure is of itself a good.
                              —Samuel Johnson (1709–1784)

He talked with more claret than clarity.   —Susan Ertz

Claret is the liquor for boys; port for men; but he who aspires to be
a hero must drink brandy.   —Samuel Johnson

One of the disadvantages of wine is that it makes a man mistake
words for thoughts.   —Samuel Johnson

Diogenes was asked what wine he liked best; and he answered as
I would have done when he said: "Somebody else's."
                              —Michel de Montaigne (1533–1592)

The wine of Arpad Haraszthy has a bouquet all its own. It tickles
and titillates the palate. It gurgles as it slips down the alimentary
canal. It warms the cockles of the heart, and it burns the sensitive
lining of the stomach.   —Ambrose Bierce

No poems can live long or please that are written by water-drinkers.
                              —Horace (65–8 B.C.)

It's a naive wine without any breeding, but I think you'll be amused
by its presumption.   —James Thurber

WISDOM

A prudent question is one-half of wisdom.
                              —Francis Bacon (1561–1626)

The beginning of wisdom is the definition of terms.
                              —Socrates (470?–399 B.C.)

A man begins cutting his wisdom teeth the first time he bites off
more than he can chew.   —Herb Caen

From the errors of others a wise man corrects his own.
                              —Publilius Syrus (c. 1st century B.C.)

Common sense in an uncommon degree is what the world calls
wisdom.   —Samuel Taylor Coleridge (1772–1834) (A wise
man who stands firm is a statesman, a foolish man who stands firm
is a catastrophe.)

The best way I know of to win an argument is to start by being in
the right.   —Quentin Hogg, M.P.

After wisdom comes wit.   —Evan Esar

Stoicism is the wisdom of madness and cynicism the madness of wisdom.   —Bergen Evans

A poet begins in delight and ends in wisdom.   —Robert Frost

The art of being wise is the art of knowing what to overlook.
     —William James

There are three sides to every story—yours, mine, and all that lie between.   —Jody Kern

I do not believe in the collective wisdom of individual ignorance.
     —Thomas Carlyle (1795–1881)

It's easier to be original and foolish than original and wise.
     —Gottfried Wilhelm Leibniz (1646–1716)

I see no wisdom in saving up indignation for a rainy day.
—Heywood Broun (If you wish to live wisely, ignore sayings—including this one.)

And here, poor fool, with all my lore/I stand no wiser than before.
     —Johann W. von Goethe (1749–1832)

It's easier to be wise for others than for ourselves.
     —Duc de La Rochefoucauld (1613–1680)

We give advice, but we cannot give the wisdom to profit by it.
—Duc de La Rochefoucauld. (A word to the wise is—unnecessary.)

Perhaps we are wiser, less selfish and more far-seeing than we were two hundred years ago. But we are still imperfectly all these good things, and since the turn of the century it has been remarked that neither wisdom nor virtue have increased as rapidly as the need for both.   —Joseph Wood Krutch

---

Wisdom is meaningless until our own experience has given it meaning . . . and there is wisdom in the selection of wisdom.
     —Bergen Evans

We can be knowledgeable with other men's knowledge, but we cannot be wise with other men's wisdom.
     —Michel de Montaigne (1533–1592)

WIT AND HUMOR

There's no trick to being a humorist when you have the whole government working for you.   —Will Rogers

Most of the time I don't have much fun. The rest of the time I don't have any fun at all.   —Woody Allen

I have a fine sense of the ridiculous, but no sense of humor.
                                        —Edward Albee

Many live by their wits but few by their wit.   —Laurence J. Peter (On the other hand, the witty man merely says what you would have said if you had thought of it.)

It is a great misfortune neither to have enough wit to talk well nor enough judgment to be silent.
                    —Jean de La Bruyère (1645–1696)

Impropriety is the soul of wit.   —Somerset Maugham

Wit is the salt of conversation, not the food.
                    —William Hazlitt (1778–1830)

Wit sometimes enables us to act rudely with impunity.   —Duc de La Rochefoucauld (1613–1680) (In other words, to step on a man's toes without spoiling his shoeshine.)

The man who sees the consistency in things is a wit; the man who sees the inconsistency in things is a humorist.
                                    —G. K. Chesterton

Wit lies in the likeness of things that are different, and in the difference of things that are alike.
                    —Madame de Staël (1766–1817)

The structure of the joke is . . . the juxtaposition of the trivial and the mundane . . . We have to reconcile the paradox of it all. The joke mirrors that paradox.   —Woody Allen (Viz. I'm not afraid to die. I just don't want to be there when it happens.)

Wit is cultured insolence.   —Aristotle (384–322 B.C.)

A satirist is a man who discovers unpleasant things about himself and then says them about other people.   —Peter McArthur

The purpose of satire is to strip off the veneer of comforting illusion and cozy half-truth. And our business, as I see it, is to put it back again.   —Michael Flanders

The job of satire is to frighten and enlighten.
                                    —Richard Condon

A taste for irony has kept more hearts from breaking than a sense of humor, for it takes irony to appreciate the joke which is on oneself.   —Jessamyn West (Irony is when you buy a suit with two pair of pants, and then burn a hole in the coat.)

A sense of humor keen enough to show a man his own absurdities will keep him from the commission of all sins, or nearly all, save those that are worth committing.   —Samuel Butler

The difficulty with humorists is that they will mix what they believe with what they don't; whichever seems likelier to win an effect.
—John Updike

Hanging is too good for a man who makes puns; he should be drawn and quoted.   —Fred Allen (Sarcasm is the sour cream of wit.)

A pun is the lowest form of humor—when you don't think of it first.
—Oscar Levant

A person reveals his character by nothing so clearly as the joke he resents.   —G. C. Lichtenberg (1742–1799)

Levity is the soul of wit.   —Melville D. Landon (Eli Perkins)

My method is to take the utmost trouble to find the right thing to say, and then to say it with the utmost levity.
—George Bernard Shaw

Wit is the rarest quality to be met with among people of education.
—William Hazlitt

Those who cannot miss an opportunity of saying a good thing are not to be trusted with the management of any great question.
—William Hazlitt

What I want to do is to make people laugh so that they'll see things seriously.   —William K. Zinsser

It is the uncensored sense of humor . . . which is the ultimate therapy for man in society.   —Evan Esar

It was one of those parties where you cough twice before you speak, and then decide not to say it after all.   —P. G. Wodehouse

After all, what was *Medea*? Just another child custody case.
—Frank Pierson

If lawyers are disbarred and clergymen defrocked, doesn't it follow that electricians can be delighted; musicians denoted; cowboys deranged; models deposed; tree surgeons debarked and dry cleaners depressed?   —Virginia Ostman

A piano is a piano is a piano is a piano.
—Gertrude Steinway (Jack Freedman)

Humor is an affirmation of dignity, a declaration of man's superiority to all that befalls him.   —Romain Gary

Humor is the sense of the Absurd which is despair refusing to take itself seriously.   —Arland Ussher

*   *

Humor is laughing at what you haven't got when you ought to have it.   —Langston Hughes

Most comics make jokes to defend themselves against what they see as a hostile and inhumane world . . . often a deeply felt rage.
—Samuel S. Janus

*   *

The secret source of humor itself is not joy but sorrow. There is no humor in heaven.   —Mark Twain

Humor is emotional chaos remembered in tranquility.
—James Thurber

Defining and analyzing humor is a pastime of humorless people.
—Robert Benchley

The main obligation is to amuse yourself.   —S. J. Perelman

*   *

Humor may be defined as the kindly contemplation of the incongruities of life, and the artistic expression thereof . . . The essence of humor is human kindliness.   —Stephen Leacock

There's no possibility of being witty without a little ill-nature.
—Richard Brinsley Sheridan (1751–1816)

WOMEN / WOMEN'S LIB

Men seldom make passes at a girl who surpasses.
—Franklin P. Jones

Once made equal to man, woman becomes his superior.
—Socrates (470?–399 B.C.)

I asked a Burmese why women, after centuries of following their men, now walk ahead. He said there were many unexploded land mines since the war.   —Robert Mueller

The male sex still constitutes in many ways the most obstinate vested interest one can find.   —Lord Longford

There are no women composers, never have been and possibly never will be.   —Sir Thomas Beecham

A science career for women is now almost as acceptable as being cheerleader.   —Myra Barker

The real theatre of the sex war is the domestic hearth.
          —Germaine Greer

Most hierarchies were established by men who now monopolize the upper levels, thus depriving women of their rightful share of opportunities to achieve incompetence.   —Laurence J. Peter

When an individual is kept in a situation of inferiority, the fact is that he does become inferior.   —Simone de Beauvoir

You're used. Used by what you are, eat, believe and who you sleep with. You can stop it. If you want equality, it has to start in bed. If he won't give it to you there, rip him off.   —Jane Gallion

Despite my thirty years of research into the feminine soul, I have not yet been able to answer . . . the great question that has never been answered: What does a woman want?   —Sigmund Freud

The only question left to be settled now is, are women persons?
          —Susan B. Anthony

Well, it's hard for a mere man to believe that woman doesn't have equal rights.   —Dwight D. Eisenhower

But if God had wanted us to think with our wombs, why did He give us a brain?   —Clare Boothe Luce

If particular care and attention is not paid to the ladies, we are determined to foment a rebellion and will not hold ourselves bound by any laws in which we have no voice or representation.
          —Abigail Adams (1744–1818)

Social science affirms that a woman's place in society marks the level of civilization.   —Elizabeth Cady Stanton

Resolved, that the women of this nation in 1876, have greater cause for discontent, rebellion and revolution than the men of 1776.   —Susan B. Anthony

I found nothing grand in the history of the Jews nor in the morals inculcated in the Pentateuch. I know of no other books that so fully teach the subjection and degradation of women.
          —Elizabeth Cady Stanton

A woman reading Playboy feels a little like a Jew reading a Nazi manual.   —Gloria Steinem

A woman has to be twice as good as a man to go half as far.
—Fannie Hurst

In practical life, the woman is judged by man's law, as if she were a man, not a woman.   —Henrik Ibsen

No man is as anti-feminist as a really feminine woman.
—Frank O'Connor

I consider that women who are authors, lawyers, and politicians are monsters.   —Pierre Auguste Renoir

The only way women could have equal rights nowadays would be to surrender some.   —Burton Hillis

The modern rule is that every woman must be her own chaperone.
—Amy Vanderbilt

When women kiss it always reminds one of prize fighters shaking hands.   —H. L. Mencken

Women prefer men who have something tender about them—especially the legal kind.   —Kay Ingram

A woman may race to get a man a gift but it always ends in a tie.
—Earl Wilson

There's a difference between beauty and charm. A beautiful woman is one I notice. A charming woman is one who notices me.
—John Erskine

Verily the best of women are those who are content with little.
—Mohammed (570–632)

A Frenchwoman, when doublecrossed, will kill her rival; the Italian woman would rather kill her deceitful lover; the Englishwoman simply breaks off relations—but they all will console themselves with another man.   —Charles Boyer

———

Women get more unhappy the more they try to liberate themselves.
—Brigitte Bardot

I don't mind living in a man's world as long as I can be a woman in it.   —Marilyn Monroe

*   *

To the woman He said, "I will greatly multiply your pain in child bearing; in pain you shall bring forth children yet your desire shall be for your husband, and he shall rule over you."
—The Bible (Genesis 3:16)

Simpson succeeded in proving that there was no harm in giving anaesthetics to men, because God put Adam into a deep sleep when He extracted his rib. But male ecclesiastics remained unconvinced as regards the sufferings of women, at any rate in childbirth.

—Bertrand Russell

* *

A society in which women are taught anything but the management of a family, the care of men, and the creation of the future generation is a society which is on the way out.   —L. Ron Hubbard

A woman is but an animal, and an animal not of the highest order.

—Edmund Burke (1729–1797)

Male domination has had some very unfortunate effects. It has made the most intimate of human relations, that of marriage, one of master and slave, instead of one between equal partners.

—Bertrand Russell

Whether women are better than men I cannot say—but I can say they are certainly no worse.   —Golda Meir

* *

Men and women must receive equal pay for equal work in production. Genuine equality between the sexes can only be realized in the process of the socialist transformation of society as a whole.

—Mao Tse-tung

Women should remain at home, sit still, keep house, and bear and bring up children.   —Martin Luther (1483–1546)

* *

The loveliest and purest of God's creatures, the nearest thing to an angelic being that treads this terrestrial ball, is a well-bred, cultured, Southern white woman, or her blue-eyed, golden-haired little girl.

—Judge Thomas P. Brady

Give a woman a job and she grows balls.   —Jack Gelber

WONDER

Wonders will never cease.   —Sir Henry Bate Dudley

It is man's destiny to ponder on the riddle of existence and, as a by-product of his wonderment, to create a new life on the earth.

—Charles F. Kettering

Religion has for centuries been trying to make men exult in the *wonders* of creation, but it has forgotten that a thing cannot be completely wonderful so long as it remains sensible.

—G. K. Chesterton

Men love to wonder, and that is the seed of science.

—Ralph Waldo Emerson (1803–1882)

Wonder rather than doubt is the root of knowledge.

—Abraham Joshua Heschel

Wonder is the feeling of a philosopher, and philosophy begins in wonder.   —Socrates (470?–399 B.C.)

The process of scientific discovery is, in effect, a continual flight from wonder.   —Albert Einstein

The larger the island of knowledge, the longer the shoreline of wonder.   —Ralph W. Sockman

WORDS

Syllables govern the world.   —John Selden

Man does not live by words alone, despite the fact that sometimes he has to eat them.   —Adlai Stevenson

I never write *metropolis* for seven cents because I can get the same price for *city*. I never write *policeman* because I can get the same money for *cop*.   —Mark Twain

When I use a word, it means just what I choose it to mean—neither more nor less.   —Lewis Carroll (Charles Lutwidge Dodgson) (1832–1898) (Words use us as much as we use words.)

The most valuable of all talents is that of never using two words when one will do.   —Thomas Jefferson (1743–1826) (And four words—*The rest is silence*—when three—*It is finished*—will do?)

He is as good as his word—and his word is no good.

—Seumas MacManus

Lexicographer: A writer of dictionaries, a harmless drudge.
—Samuel Johnson (1709–1784) (A synonym is the word you use when you can't spell the right one and therefore can't find it in the dictionary.)

Why shouldn't we quarrel about a word? What is the good of words if they aren't important enough to quarrel over? Why do we choose one word more than another if there isn't any difference between them?   —G. K. Chesterton

Oaths are but words, and words are but wind.
                         —Samuel Butler (1612–1680)

When an idea is wanting a word can always be found to take its place.   —Johann W. von Goethe (1749–1832)

In two words: im possible.   —Samuel Goldwyn

I wish he would explain his explanation.
                    —George Gordon, Lord Byron (1788–1824)

Similes are like songs of love:/They much describe; they nothing prove.   —Matthew Prior (1664–1721)

Words are, of course, the most powerful drug used by mankind.
                         —Rudyard Kipling

We have too many high sounding words, and too few actions that correspond with them.   —Abigail Adams (1744–1818)

Words fascinate me. They always have. For me, browsing in a dictionary is like being turned loose in a bank.   —Eddie Cantor

Words are one of our chief means of adjusting to all the situations of life. The better control we have over words, the more successful our adjustment is likely to be.   —Bergen Evans

They believed their words. Everybody shows a respectful deference to certain sounds that he and his fellows can make. But about feelings people really know nothing. We talk with indignation or en- thusiasm; we talk about oppression, cruelty, crime, devotion, self- sacrifice, virtue, and we know nothing real beyond the words.
—Joseph Conrad (Too tired for words means to listen to any.)

He can compress the most words into the smallest idea of any man I ever met.   —Abraham Lincoln (1809–1865)

The thoughtless are rarely wordless.   —Howard W. Newton

*   *

Colors fade, temples crumble, empires fall, but wise words endure.
                         —Edward Thorndike

The paper burns, but the words fly away.
                    —Ben Joseph Akiba (c. 50–132)

*   *

We should have a great many fewer disputes in the world if words were taken for what they are, the signs of our ideas only, and not for things themselves.   —John Locke (1632–1704)

These Macedonians are a rude and clownish people; they call a spade a spade.   —Plutarch (46?–120?)

Clothe an idea in words and it loses its freedom of movement.
—Egon Friedell

A word is not a crystal, transparent and unchanged; it is the skin of a living thought and may vary greatly in color and content according to the circumstances and time in which it is used.
—Oliver Wendell Holmes, Jr.

*   *

I would say that music is the easiest means in which to express . . . but since words are my talent, I must try to express clumsily in words what the pure music would have done better.
—William Faulkner

Words are the best medium of exchange of thoughts and ideas between people.   —William Ross

*   *

At the beginning there was the Word—at the end just the Cliché.
—Stanislaw J. Lec

I had always assumed that cliché was a suburb of Paris, until I discovered it to be a street in Oxford.   —Philip Guedalla

WORK

All work and no play makes Jack a dull boy—and Jill a wealthy widow.   —Evan Esar

I go on working for the same reason that a hen goes on laying eggs.
—H. L. Mencken

One of the greatest labor-saving inventions of today is tomorrow.
—Vincent T. Foss (Many people quit looking for work when they find a job.)

A great many people have . . . asked how I manage to get so much work done and still keep looking so dissipated.
—Robert Benchley

What's not worth doing is not worth doing well.   —Don Hebb

We work to become, not to acquire.   —Elbert Hubbard

When a man tells you that he got rich through hard work, ask him *whose*?   —Don Marquis (Millions are idle—even if they have jobs. Some carve great careers while others simply chisel.)

If we are dreamers who laud the self-indulgent life, we suspect that we really wish we could buckle down to work. Should we begin to work, however, we must anticipate that we will soon bemoan the lazy life we left behind.   —Harvey Mindess

If one defines the term "dropout" to mean a person who has given up serious effort to meet his responsibilities, then every business office, government agency, golf club and university faculty would yield its quota.   —John Gardner

A society that gives to one class all the opportunities for leisure, and to another all the burdens of work, dooms both classes to spiritual sterility.   —Lewis Mumford

Work is the refuge of people who have nothing better to do.
                                    —Oscar Wilde (1854–1900)

Like every man of sense and good feeling, I abominate work.
                                    —Aldous Huxley

Work expands so as to fill the time available for its completion.
                              —Northcote Parkinson (Parkinson's "Law.")

There are certain natures to whom the work is nothing, the act of working, everything.   —Arthur Symons

My father taught me to work, but not to love it. I never did like to work, and I don't deny it. I'd rather read, tell stories, crack jokes, talk, laugh—anything but work.
                              —Abraham Lincoln (1809–1865)

I'm a great believer in luck, and I find the harder I work the more I have of it.   —Thomas Jefferson (1743–1826)

Working with people is difficult, but not impossible.
                                    —Peter Drucker

When people are serving, life is no longer meaningless.
                                    —John Gardner

No other technique for the conduct of life attaches the individual so firmly to reality as laying emphasis on work; for his work at least gives him a secure place in a portion of reality, in the human community.   —Sigmund Freud (Two can live as cheaply as one—if they both have good jobs.)

A man's work is his dilemma: his job is his bondage, but it also gives him a fair share of his identity and keeps him from being a bystander in somebody else's world.   —Melvin Maddocks

A Darwinian nation of economic fitness abhors idleness, dependence, non-productivity.   —Simone de Beauvoir

This new attitude towards effort and work as an aim in itself may be assumed to be the most important psychological change which has happened to man since the end of the Middle Ages . . . the development of a frantic activity and a striving to do something.

—Erich Fromm

Italians come to ruin most generally in three ways—women, gambling, and farming. My family chose the slowest one.

—Pope John XXIII

A farm is a hunk of land on which, if you get up early enough mornings and work late enough nights, you'll make a fortune—if you strike oil on it.   —"Fibber" McGee (Jim Jordan)

*   *

Nothing is really work unless you would rather be doing something else.   —James M. Barrie

Anyone can do any amount of work provided it isn't the work he is supposed to be doing at that moment.   —Robert Benchley

*   *

An *unemployed* existence is a worse negation of life than death itself. Because to live means to have something definite to do—a mission to fulfill—and in the measure in which we avoid setting our life to something, we make it empty . . . Human life, by its very nature, has to be dedicated to something.

—José Ortega y Gasset

Without work all life goes rotten.   —Albert Camus

*   *

A considerable number of persons are able to protect themselves against the outbreak of serious neurotic phenomena only through intense work.   —Karl Abraham

They intoxicate themselves with work so they won't see how they really are.   —Aldous Huxley

*   *

More and more university students are convinced that work in American society is morally empty, aesthetically ugly, and, under conditions of automation, economically unnecessary.

—Michael Harrington

The students react to my praise of toil with great applause and loud demands for a holiday from work.

—John Kenneth Galbraith

* *

Work is what you do so that some time you won't have to do it any more. —Alfred Polgar

If you don't want to work you have to work to earn enough money so that you won't have to work. —Ogden Nash

---

I've met a few people in my time who were enthusiastic about hard work. And it was just my luck that all of them happened to be men I was working for at the time. —Bill Gold

Most people like hard work. Particularly when they are paying for it. —Franklin P. Jones

* *

It is not enough to be busy . . . the question is: what are we busy about? —Henry David Thoreau (1817–1862)

You know what happens in the beehive? They kill those drones.

—Congressman William Poage

WORLD / WORLD GOVERNMENT

If the human race wishes to have a prolonged and indefinite period of material prosperity, they have only got to behave in a peaceful and helpful way toward one another, and science will do for them all they wish and more than they can dream.

—Winston Churchill

Political internationalism without economic internationalism is a house built upon sand. For no nation can reach its fullest development alone. —Wendell L. Willkie (All the world's a stage, and most of us are stagehands.)

This organization [the United Nations] is created to prevent you from going to hell. It isn't created to take you to heaven.

—Henry Cabot Lodge

* *

The only security for the American people today, or for any people, is to be found through the control of force rather than the pursuit of force.   —Norman Cousins

The League of Nations is a declaration of love without the promise of marriage.   —Admiral Alfred von Tirpitz

The thought that we're in competition with Russians or with Chinese is all a mistake, and trivial. We are one species, with a world to win . . . It is only such a world that now can offer us life and the chance to go on.   —Dr. George Wald

Foreign Aid—taxing poor people in rich countries for the benefit of rich people in poor countries.   —Bernard Rosenberg

To write off the United Nations' achievements in keeping the peace because of its inability to be effective in Czechoslovakia or Vietnam, would be like writing off medical science because it has not yet found a cure for cancer.   —George Bush (The only thing the member states of the UN have in common is their ability to see one another's faults.)

The first condition is the abolishment of the war threat . . . This must lead eventually to some form of economic, international cooperation, and planning, to forms of world government and to complete disarmament.   —Erich Fromm

The journey of a thousand leagues begins with a single step. So we must never neglect any work of peace within our reach, however small.   —Adlai Stevenson

We are all apt to believe what the world believes about us.
    —George Eliot (Mary Ann Evans) (1819–1880)

The realization that our small planet is only one of many worlds gives mankind the perspective it needs to realize sooner that our own world belongs to all of its creatures, that the moon landing marks the end of our childhood as a race and the beginning of a newer and better civilization . . . it is not easy to see how the more extreme forms of nationalism can long survive when men have seen the Earth in its true perspective as a single small globe against the stars.   —Arthur C. Clarke

We are citizens of the world; and the tragedy of our times is that we do not know this.   —Woodrow Wilson

People who develop the habit of thinking of themselves as world citizens are fulfilling the first requirement of sanity in our time.

—Norman Cousins

* *

My country is the world. My countrymen are all mankind.

—William Lloyd Garrison (1805–1879)

All wars are civil wars, because all men are brothers . . . Each one owes infinitely more to the human race than to the particular country in which he was born.

—François Fénelon (1651–1715)

* *

The United States has the power to destroy the world, but not the power to save it alone.   —Margaret Mead

If mankind recognizes that war is impossible . . . that all national rivalries are foolish . . . if they get together any kind of an extension of detente . . . then we may pull out of it all the better for it.   —Isaac Asimov

———————

There must be, not a balance of power, but a community of power; not organized rivalries, but an organized common peace.

—Woodrow Wilson

While we are sleeping two-thirds of the world is plotting to do us in.

—Dean Rusk

* *

Traditional nationalism cannot survive the fissioning of the atom. One world or none.   —Stuart Chase

I consider world government absolutely impossible to attain.

—Walter Lippmann

* *

Scientists can collaborate in achieving the goal of international security if they take a stand in the face of public opinion for the establishment of an international body with both a permanent personnel and a permanent military force.   —Albert Einstein

Coexistence—what the farmer does with the turkey—until Thanksgiving.   —Mike Connolly

* *

What shall we do to be saved? In politics, establish a constitutional cooperative society of world government. In economics, find working compromises between free enterprise and socialism.

—Arnold Toynbee

The world organization debates disarmament in one room and, in the next room, moves the knights and pawns that make national arms imperative. —E. B. White

WORRY

If the grass is greener in the other fellow's yard—let him worry about cutting it. —Fred Allen

Archie doesn't know how to worry without getting upset.

—Edith Bunker

A person must try to worry about things that aren't important so he won't worry too much about things that are. —Jack Smith

If I knew what I was so anxious about, I wouldn't be so anxious.

—Mignon McLaughlin

When I look back on all these worries I remember the story of the old man who said on his deathbed that he had had a lot of trouble in his life, most of which never happened.

—Winston Churchill

WRITING / WRITERS

Someday I hope to write a book where the royalties will pay for the copies I give away. —Clarence Darrow

I wrote a short story because I wanted to see something of mine in print other than my fingers. —Wilson Mizner

I love being a writer. What I can't stand is the paperwork.

—Peter De Vries

Nature not content with denying him the ability to think, has endowed him with the ability to write. —A. E. Housman

Masterpieces are no more than the shipwrecked flotsam of great minds. —Marcel Proust

Sir, no man but a blockhead ever wrote except for money.

—Samuel Johnson (1709–1784)

A sequel is an admission that you've been reduced to imitating yourself. —Don Marquis

The man who writes about himself and his own time is the only man who writes about all people and about all time.

—George Bernard Shaw

If I had to give young writers advice, I'd say don't listen to writers talking about writing. —Lillian Hellman

Nothing you write, if you hope to be good, will ever come out as you first hoped. —Lillian Hellman

The root of all bad writing is to compose what you have not worked out for yourself. Unless words come into the writer's mind as fresh coinages for what the writer himself knows that he knows, knows to be true, it is impossible for him to give back in words that direct quality of experience which is the essence of literature.

—Alfred Kazin

Writing is the only profession where no one considers you ridiculous if you earn no money. —Jules Renard

Writing is the hardest way of earning a living, with the possible exception of wrestling alligators. —Olin Miller

If you want to get rich from writing, write the sort of thing that's read by persons who move their lips when they're reading to themselves. —Don Marquis

What no wife of a writer can ever understand is that a writer is working when he's staring out of the window.

—Burton Rascoe

You write a hit play the same way you write a flop.

—William Saroyan

Sometimes I think it sounds like I walked out of the room and left the typewriter running. —Gene Fowler

When audiences come to see us authors lecture, it is largely in the hope that we'll be funnier to look at than to read.

—Sinclair Lewis

If you have one strong idea, you can't help repeating it and embroidering it. Sometimes I think that authors should write one book and then be put in a gas chamber. —John P. Marquand

A writer's problem does not change. He himself changes and the world he lives in changes but his problem remains the same. It is always how to write truly and having found what is true, to project it in such a way that it becomes a part of the experience of the person who reads it. —Ernest Hemingway

Failure is very difficult for a writer to bear, but very few can manage the shock of early success. —Maurice Valency

First you're an unknown, then you write one book and you move up to obscurity.   —Martin Myers

There is only one trait that marks the writer. He is always watching. It's a kind of trick of mind and he is born with it.
—Morley Callaghan

A writer's mind seems to be situated partly in the solar plexus and partly in the head.   —Ethel Wilson

I think the whole glory of writing lies in the fact that it forces us out of ourselves and into the lives of others.
—Sherwood Anderson

It took me fifteen years to discover I had no talent for writing, but I couldn't give it up because by that time I was too famous.
—Robert Benchley

Your manuscript is both good and original; but the part that is good is not original, and the part that is original is not good.
—Samuel Johnson

He was one of those men who think that the world can be saved by writing a pamphlet.   —Benjamin Disraeli (1804–1881)

Writing a book is an adventure. To begin with, it is a toy and an amusement. Then it becomes a mistress, then it becomes a master, then it becomes a tyrant. The last phase is that just as you are about to be reconciled to your servitude, you kill the monster, and fling him to the public.   —Winston Churchill

There is no need for the writer to eat a whole sheep to be able to tell what mutton tastes like. It is enough if he eats a cutlet.
—Somerset Maugham

Literature is an occupation in which you have to keep proving your talent to people who have none.   —Jules Renard

I put a piece of paper under my pillow, and when I could not sleep I wrote in the dark.   —Henry David Thoreau (1817–1862)

If writers were good businessmen, they'd have too much sense to be writers.   —Irvin S. Cobb

The tools I need for my trade are paper, tobacco, food, and a little whiskey.   —William Faulkner

I write at high speed because boredom is bad for my health. It upsets my stomach more than anything else. I also avoid green vegetables. They're grossly overrated.   —Noel Coward

An essayist is a lucky person who has found a way to discourse without being interrupted.   —Charles Poore

Whenever I apply myself to writing, literature comes between us.
—Jules Renard

Just how difficult it is to write biography can be reckoned by anybody who sits down and considers just how many people know the real truth about his or her love affairs.   —Rebecca West

The best time for planning a book is while you're doing the dishes.
—Agatha Christie

An author ought to write for the youth of his own generation, the critics of the next, and the schoolmasters of ever afterwards.
—F. Scott Fitzgerald

No passion in the world is equal to the passion to alter someone else's draft.   —H. G. Wells

If you're going to write, don't pretend to write down. It's going to be the best you can do, and it's the fact that it's the best you can do that kills you!   —Dorothy Parker

Talent is like a faucet; while it is open, one must write. Inspiration is a farce that poets have invented to give themselves importance.
—Jean Anouilh

Good writing is a kind of skating which carries off the performer where he would not go.
—Ralph Waldo Emerson (1803–1882)

How can you write if you can't cry?   —Ring Lardner

Unprovided with original learning, unformed in the habits of thinking, unskilled in the arts of composition, I resolved to write a book.
—Edward Gibbon (1737–1794)

The profession of book-writing makes horse racing seem like a solid, stable business.   —John Steinbeck

*   *

Read over your compositions and, when you meet a passage which you think is particularly fine, strike it out.   —Samuel Johnson

In composing, as a general rule, run your pen through every other word you have written; you have no idea what vigor it will give your style.   —Sydney Smith (1771–1845)

*   *

Whenever you feel an impulse to perpetrate a piece of exceptionally fine writing, obey it . . . and delete it before sending your manuscript to the press.   —Sir Arthur Quiller-Couch

The most essential gift for a good writer is a built-in, shock-proof shit detector.   —Ernest Hemingway

*   *

I've always believed in writing without a collaborator, because where two people are writing the same book, each believes he gets all the worries and only half the royalties.   —Agatha Christie

I never can understand how two men can write a book together; to me that's like three people getting together to have a baby.
—Evelyn Waugh

No one can write decently who is distrustful of the reader's intelligence, or whose attitude is patronizing.   —E. B. White

I'm a lousy writer; a helluva lot of people have got lousy taste.
—Grace Metalious, author of *Peyton Place*

*   *

I never desire to converse with a man who has written more than he has read.   —Samuel Johnson

I would never read a book if it were possible for me to talk half an hour with the man who wrote it.   —Woodrow Wilson

*   *

The only sensible ends of literature are, first, the pleasurable toil of writing; second, the gratification of one's family and friends; and lastly, the solid cash.   —Nathaniel Hawthorne (1804–1864) (And not necessarily in that order.)

The two most beautiful words in the English language are: "Check enclosed."   —Dorothy Parker

*   *

My purpose is to entertain myself first and other people secondly.
—John D. MacDonald

Anything that is written to please the author is worthless.
—Blaise Pascal (1623–1662)

XEROX

Xerox: A trademark for a photocopying device that can make rapid reproductions of human error, perfectly.
—Merle L. Meacham

The Rockettes are so perfect you'd think they were Xeroxed.
—Irene Peter

She has as much originality as a Xerox machine.
—Laurence J. Peter

X-RATED

Nobody, including the Supreme Court, knows what obscenity is.
—Norman Dorsen

I never trust a man unless I've got his pecker in my pocket.
—Lyndon B. Johnson

Let him turn and twist slowly in the wind.   —John Ehrlichman

Yippies, hippies, yahoos, Black Panthers, lions and tigers alike—I would swap the whole damn zoo for the kind of young Americans I saw in Vietnam.   —Spiro Agnew

How much do you think I'll get for my autobiography?
—Arthur Bremer (After his arrest for attempting to assassinate Governor George C. Wallace.)

There are also a lot of nice buildings in Haiphong. What their contributions are to the war effort I don't know, but the desire to bomb a virgin building is terrific. —Commander Henry Urban, Jr.

The doves in this country and some of the media are the cause of fifty-some-odd-thousand Americans being killed and all that money being spent, and all that inflation. —George C. Wallace

If any demonstrator ever lays down in front of my car, it'll be the last car he'll ever lay down in front of. —George C. Wallace

If Satan himself, with all the superhuman genius and diabolical ingenuity at his command had tried to create a permanent element of disintegration and force for destruction of the nations, he could have done no better than to invent the Jews. —Willis Carto

I think Hitler was too moderate. —J. B. Stoner

If people demonstrate in a manner to interfere with others, they should be rounded up and put in a detention camp.
—Richard G. Kleindienst

Better murder an infant in its cradle than nurse an unacted desire.
—William Blake (1757–1827)

Another improvement . . . was that we built our gas chambers to accommodate two thousand people at one time.
—Rudolf Hess

In my own firm opinion, the Communists have one of their own actually in the Presidency. For this third man, Eisenhower, there is only one possible word to describe his purpose and his actions. The word is *treason!*
—Robert Welch

Nothing would please the Kremlin more than to have the people of this country choose a second-rate President.
—Richard M. Nixon

I have asked you for a moral and spiritual restoration in the land and give thanks that in Thy sovereignty Thou hast permitted Richard M. Nixon to lead us at this momentous hour of our history.
—Billy Graham

The White House has had no involvement whatever in this particular incident [the Watergate break-in]. —Richard M. Nixon

The tragic lesson of guilty men walking free in this country has not been lost on the criminal community. —Richard M. Nixon

American policy has been to scrupulously respect the neutrality of the Cambodian people.   —Richard M. Nixon

The Italians . . . you can't find one who is honest.
                                                                    —Richard M. Nixon

Give the investigators an *hors d'oeuvre* and maybe they won't come back for the main course.   —Richard M. Nixon

I don't give a shit what happens. I want you all to stonewall it. Let them plead the Fifth Amendment, cover up, or anything else if it'll save the plan.   —Richard M. Nixon

In all my years of public life I have never obstructed justice.
                                                                    —Richard M. Nixon

Stop the world . . . Nixon wants to get back on!
                                                                    —David Fisher

YESTERDAY / TODAY / TOMORROW

Procrastination—the art of keeping up with yesterday.
                                        —Don Marquis

Forever and a Day. High up in the North in the land called Svith-jod, there stands a rock. It is one hundred miles high and one hundred miles wide. Once every thousand years a little bird comes to this rock to sharpen its beak. When the rock has thus been worn away, then a single day of eternity will have gone by.
                              —Hendrik Willem van Loon

Often do the spirits of great events stride on before the events/ And in today already walks to-morrow.
                    —Samuel Taylor Coleridge (1772–1834)

I am not afraid of tomorrow, for I have seen yesterday and I love today.   —William Allen White

The farther backward you can look, the farther forward you are likely to see.   —Winston Churchill

Every age is modern to those who are living in it.
                              —Justice Benjamin N. Cardozo

We have to live today by what truth we can get today and be ready tomorrow to call it falsehood.   —William James

Yesterday is a cancelled check; tomorrow is a promissory note; today is the only cash you have—so spend it wisely.

—Kay Lyons

There are so many things that we wish we had done yesterday, so few that we feel like doing today. —Mignon McLaughlin

We are tomorrow's past. —Mary Webb

The pace of events is moving so fast that unless we can find some way to keep our sights on tomorrow, we cannot expect to be in touch with today. —Dean Rusk

Never put off till tomorrow what you can do the day after to-morrow. —Mark Twain

---

Each morning puts a man on trial and each evening passes judgment. —Roy L. Smith

Tomorrow is the most important thing in life. Comes into us at midnight very clean. It's perfect when it arrives and it puts itself in our hands. It hopes we've learned something from yesterday.

—John Wayne

YOUTH

It's hard for the modern generation to understand Thoreau, who lived beside a pond but didn't own water skis or a snorkel.

—Bill Vaughan

The closest you can get to your youth is to start repeatin' your follies. —Reg Smythe (Andy Capp)

Only the young die good. —Oliver Herford

Youthquake: An eruption followed by a twitch, a tic, and much sullen or ashen silence. —Bernard Rosenberg

. . . undergraduates . . . were always in revolt. They were never static. The only way they could form their minds was by opposing accepted opinion. —Helen MacInness

Like its politicians and its wars, society has the teenagers it deserves. —J. B. Priestley (There's nothing wrong with teenagers that telling them won't aggravate.)

Between twenty-five and thirty-five you're too young to do anything well; after thirty-five you're too old. —Fritz Kreisler

Oh, to be only half as wonderful as my child thought I was when he was small, and only half as stupid as my teen-ager now thinks I am. —Rebecca Richards

Youth is the trustee of posterity.

—Benjamin Disraeli (1804–1881)

It is youth that has discovered love as a weapon.

—Peter Ustinov

If youth is a defect, it is one that we outgrow too soon.

—Robert Lowell

The young have aspirations that never come to pass, the old have reminiscences of what never happened.

—H. H. Munro ("Saki")

The joy of the young is to disobey—but the trouble is, there are no longer any orders.   —Jean Cocteau (The modern class of youngsters are alike in many disrespects.)

In case you're worried about what's going to become of the younger generation, it's going to grow up and start worrying about the younger generation.   —Roger Allen

A boy's will is the wind's will,/And the thoughts of youth are long, long thoughts.   —Henry Wadsworth Longfellow (1807–1882)

That age is best which is the first/When youth and blood are warmer.   —Robert Herrick (1591–1674)

Yet, Ah, that Spring should vanish with the Rose!/That Youth's sweet-scented manuscript should close!

—Edward Fitzgerald (1809–1883)

I only know that summer sang in me/A little while, that in me sings no more.   —Edna St. Vincent Millay

---

Our moral mentors told us it was an age of unprecedented license and corruption, and that we boys and girls who had just cracked our shells were a brood of vipers from the pit.   —Elmer Davis

The denunciation of the young is a necessary part of the hygiene of older people.   —Logan Pearsall Smith

*   *

Young men have a passion for regarding their elders as senile.

—Henry Adams

. . . and another lot of young people will appear, and consider us completely outdated, and they will write ballads to express their loathing of us, and there is no reason why this should ever end.

—Alfred Jarry

*   *

I am not young enough to know everything.
                                        —James M. Barrie

We are none of us infallible—not even the youngest of us.
                                        —W. H. Thompson

———————

I must say that the intolerance of the young people appeals to me.
It's a good sign when a youngster is temperamentally in revolt
against the world in general. All those amongst my pupils who
have gone far were natural rebels, born, as my teacher Renan puts
it, "with an imprecation on their lips."
                                        —Roger Martin du Gard

Nobody can be so amusingly arrogant as a young man who has
just discovered an old idea and thinks it is his own.
                                        —Sydney Harris

*   *

The real lost souls don't wear their hair long and play guitars.
They have crew cuts, trained minds, sign on for research in biological warfare, and don't give their parents a moment's worry.
                                        —J. B. Priestley

What is more enchanting than the voices of young people when
you can't hear what they say?   —Logan Pearsall Smith

Z

ZEAL

Passions are fashions. —Clifton Fadiman

Through zeal, knowledge is gotten, through lack of zeal, knowledge is lost; let a man who knows this double path of gain and loss thus place himself that knowledge may grow.
—Buddha (563?–483? B.C.)

I do not love a man who is zealous for nothing.
—Oliver Goldsmith (1728–1774)

His zeal was hollow; his sermons were like students' songs imperfectly recalled by a senile don. —John Rae

ZIPPERS

A dress that zips up the back will bring a husband and wife together. —James H. Boren

ZOOS

All they [zoos] actually offer to the public in return for the taxes spent upon them is a form of idle and witless amusement, compared to which a visit to a penitentiary, or even to a State Legislature in session, is informing, stimulating and ennobling.

—H. L. Mencken

Zoo: An excellent place to study the habits of human beings.

—Evan Esar

The quizzical expression of the monkey at the zoo comes from his wondering whether he is his brother's keeper or his keeper's brother.   —Evan Esar

Clearly, then, the city is not a concrete jungle, it is a human zoo.

—Desmond Morris

When I was a kid I said to my father one afternoon, "Daddy, will you take me to the zoo?" He answered, "If the zoo wants you let them come and get you."   —Jerry Lewis

INDEX OF NAMES AND AUTHORS

528